TWENTIETH-CENTURY
STYLE &
DESIGN

TWENTIETH-CENTURY
STYLE &
DESIGN

STEPHEN BAYLEY
PHILIPPE GARNER
·DEYAN SUDJIC·

VNR VAN NOSTRAND REINHOLD COMPANY

NEW YORK   CINCINNATI   TORONTO   LONDON   MELBOURNE

Published by Van Nostrand Reinhold Company Inc.
135 West 50th Street
New York, New York 10020

Macmillan of Canada
Division of Gage Publishing Limited
164 Commander Boulevard
Agincourt, Ontario M1S 3C7, Canada

Library of Congress Catalog Card Number 84-3706
ISBN 0-442-23008-7

Library of Congress Cataloging in Publication Data

Garner, Philippe.
  Twentieth-century style and design.

  1. Architecture, Modern—20th century. 2. Decorative arts—
History—20th century. 3. Design, Industrial—History—20th
century. I. Title.
NA680.G36 1986   745.4'442   84-3706
ISBN 0-442-23008-7

16 15 14 13 12 11 9 8 7 6 5 4 3 2 1

Conceived, designed and produced by Robert Adkinson Limited,
London

Editorial Director: Clare Howell
Editor: Lucy Trench
Art Director: Christine Simmonds
Designer: Laurence Bradbury
Design Assistant: Sarah Collins
Picture Researcher: Anne-Marie Ehrlich

Phototypesetting by
Tradespools, Frome, Somerset

Colour and black-and-white origination by
New Interlitho, Milan

Printed and bound in Italy by
New Interlitho, Milan

Consultant Editor: Philippe Garner

Architecture and Urban Design: Deyan Sudjic
Decorative Arts: Philippe Garner
Industrial Design: Stephen Bayley

Robert Adkinson Limited would like to thank Jonathan Woodham of
Brighton Polytechnic for his assistance in the Industrial Design
chapters.

Frontispiece **Studios for
TVAM, London, by Terry
Farrell, 1983.**

CONTENTS

Introduction by Philippe Garner   6

**1 PIONEERS OF TWENTIETH-CENTURY
   DESIGN 1900–1915**   8
Architecture and Urban Design   10
Decorative Arts   38
Industrial Design   68

2 THE TWENTIES AND THIRTIES   80
Architecture and Urban Design   82
Decorative Arts   106
Industrial Design   128

3 THE FORTIES AND FIFTIES   150
Architecture and Urban Design   152
Decorative Arts   168
Industrial Design   188

4 THE SIXTIES TO THE PRESENT   212
Architecture and Urban Design   214
Decorative Arts   246
Industrial Design   278

Select Biographies   298
Select Bibliography   306
Index   308
Acknowledgments   320

INTRODUCTION

It was Nikolaus Pevsner in *Pioneers of the Modern Movement* (1936) who first attempted to trace a linear evolution towards the Holy Grail of a concept of 'Modern Design'. This would truly reflect the needs and circumstances of the twentieth century and transform the lives of every modern man. According to Modernist theory decorative, populist, decadent or bourgeois aberrations would disappear and the Architect would take on supreme powers to resolve the dilemma of modern urban man, alienated in a world dominated by the machine. The Bauhaus, with interdisciplinary teaching revolving around the unifying role of the architect, was hailed as the template for all schools of 'pure' design.

Hindsight, however, has enabled us to reassess the soaring vision of the Modern Movement. Critics, so long in awe of its ideology, surely the most forceful trend in design in this century, have come to recognize that the supposed purism of the Modernists was as much overlaid with symbol as any other design mode. Modernist semiology was cryptic and self-centred to a point that only the initiated could interpret, and the masses were never truly welcome in this élitist ivory tower. It has become apparent that although not overtly decorative Modernist design is as much the result of a preoccupation with style and appearances as the creations of the most commercial product-design studio.

Indeed, if the twentieth century has been consistent in anything, it has been in its pattern of contrasts and contradictions. In 1900 the asymmetrical exuberance of Art Nouveau was paralleled by the disciplined rectilinear geometry of Charles Rennie Mackintosh and Josef Hoffmann; a decade later, while Peter Behrens was applying a functionalist creed to the German manufacturing company AEG, Paul Poiret and others were bringing a sumptuous exoticism to the Paris stage, to fashion and to other aspects of decorative design; at the 1925 Paris exhibition the luxurious pavilion of Jacques-Emile Ruhlmann expressed decorative extremes which could hardly be further from the stark, intellectual, utopian vision expressed in Le Corbusier's Pavillon de l'Esprit Nouveau. Even the Bauhaus was not immune to Expressionist influences, and in the thirties the development of Modernism into the International Style co-existed with surrealist, neo-romantic and other decorative trends. At the same time the rapid expansion of mass-production techniques and the need to counter the effects of the Depression brought about the birth of industrial design studios.

After the Second World War the yearning for fantasy and frivolity found form in Parisian couture, the Festival of Britain and the stylish products of Italy's *Ricostruzione*. On the other hand, the Hochschule für Gestaltung in Germany sought to revive the ideals of the Bauhaus, and the design studios of the United States were developing highly commercial styling and visual, if not technical, obsolescence. In the fifties and sixties, too, Modernism performed an intellectual volteface and cast aside its apostolic role to become the prestige style of corporate capitalism, the International Style of steel-and-glass office blocks. But it soon came under attack for the poverty of its expression and the disastrous results of its attempts at social engineering.

Recognizing the need for what Robert Venturi described as 'complexity and contradiction', designers can now treat Modernism merely as another style to be enjoyed by a self-conscious, fashionable élite. Post-Modernism and Radical Design have challenged dogma and promoted a return to visual wealth and variety, in which popular, vernacular and historical sources are all exploited for their ironical or subliminal potential. Design, though inextricably related to the manipulation of consumer markets, seems more concerned with human needs; the manipulators and the manipulated co-exist and fluidly exchange roles and ideas.

Now the wisest orthodoxy is one which is cautious of dogma and wary of isolating the seemingly typical or absolute when reviewing the past. It is increasingly evident that what design history has hailed as representative is all too often the view of the avant-garde minority; today's absolutes rapidly become period pieces. Instead, it is better to appreciate the products of the twentieth century in their very diversity, for the character of any artifact, from a major architectural project to an ephemeral magazine layout, derives its impact not only from its intrinsic qualities but also from its relationship with the other artifacts with which it jostles and competes for our attention.

Since design is so integral to our lives there is a need to survey the entire scope of its activities since the beginning of the century, from fashion to housing, from consumer durables to advertising. But just as it is convenient to categorize design in terms of styles and movements, it is also usual to divide it into spheres of activity. For the sake of convenience this book follows this practice and discusses separately Architecture and Urban Design, Decorative Arts and Industrial Design. No one category, however, can be fully understood in isolation from the others, for inter-disciplinary synthesis has been a marked feature of the century and many of the most important designers have worked across these arbitrary barriers.

The aesthetic historian is constantly tempted to bring order to the complex, frequently contradictory, facts, events and movements which have influenced design and its expression. Every artifact must have its pigeonhole, its stylistic label; every stylistic expression its precursors, its supporting theory and its destiny. Academic viewpoints can tailor the record of events and achievements to justify a hypothesis, and they often give greater credit to those movements in design which have boasted the most glamorous or persuasive theories. Indeed, the conflict between theory and idealism on one hand and material realities on the other has been a dominant theme in the design history of this century. The designer's cherished vision of a level of taste to which he can educate his audience has often conflicted with the real needs and desires of the public at large.

The very terms style and design convey much of the variety and conflict with which this survey is concerned. 'Style' in this context may be seen as expressing the outward appearance of things, whereas 'design' may be defined as a concern with function and rational form, of which 'style' is the changing face. Though such distinctions and definitions have rarely been totally satisfactory, the present survey does attempt to evaluate the application of design in the twentieth century and to describe those variant styles which have, from decade to decade, been the expression of that application.

As the century progresses and the scope of mass production widens, it becomes more and more difficult to distinguish between decorative arts and industrial design. Generally speaking, this book describes as 'decorative' those objects which serve a purely decorative, non-functional purpose. Also included in this section are those objects, such as chairs and lights, which are certainly functional, but were either hand-made or were produced in small quantities for a limited market, and therefore enjoyed a certain status and prestige. For more than one hundred years design theorists have demanded greater recognition for the role of mass production. Finally their demands have been met, and the most stylish, luxurious and sophisticated products of our age are now being manufactured by machines rather than craftsmen.

Philippe Garner

Poster designed by Peter
Behrens for AEG, around 1907,
incorporating a light fitting
also by Behrens.

1/PIONEERS OF TWENTIETH-CENTURY DESIGN

Circa 1900 to circa 1915

At the beginning of the century designers were forced to acknowledge the power of technology and the demands of a rapidly changing society. Peter Behrens' work for the German electrical goods manufacturer AEG was a landmark in the development of a modern spirit. In his commitment to total design he applied himself to every aspect of AEG's activities—the posters and graphics, the products themselves and even the factory buildings—endowing them with a style that was entirely practical and contemporary, yet also mindful of the past. At the same time he created a role model for the industrial designer, who has come to occupy a more and more influential position in our lives. Other designers, too, particularly Charles Rennie Mackintosh in Scotland, Henry van de Velde in Belgium, and the members of the Sezession in Vienna, were also developing a style for the new century, and the decorative, curvilinear forms of French Art Nouveau, despite the good intentions behind them, seemed less appropriate to the modern world than the more geometrical and rectilinear approach.

ARCHITECTURE AND URBAN DESIGN

Was there really a watershed at the end of the nineteenth century, cutting off the architecture of our own times from all that had gone before? Were the 1890s, as Henry-Russell Hitchcock claimed, a major historical frontier, dividing the historicism of the past from the Modernism that, despite its many detractors, has been the dominant mode of architectural expression in the twentieth century?

For a couple of decades, perhaps between 1940 and 1960, this appeared to many people to be a self-evident fact: Louis Sullivan's department store for Carson, Pirie, Scott in Chicago, Frank Lloyd Wright's Winslow House, and Charles Voysey's own house outside London did represent something that was entirely different from the suave classicism of Sir Charles Barry, say, or the patrician charms of McKim, Mead & White, or even the pomp and circumstance of Garnier's Paris Opera

House. Even though Voysey might disavow Modernism, he and the others in the first group could all be presented as working within the framework of an architecture that was responding to social and technological changes. All, to a greater or lesser extent, were self-consciously attempting to create a new kind of architecture, if not always from first principles then at least in a spirit of reform. But the latter group seemed, to some critics, to be merely continuing the academic reworking of defunct architectural traditions. That many of them were able to muster remarkable talents was not in doubt, but to those who did see twentienth-century architecture as a complete break with the past, the refusal of such architects to participate in that break condemned them to a historical blind alley. Thus, by the 1960s, Sir Edwin Lutyens could be written off as a talent

Below Frank Lloyd Wright's house for W. H. Winslow in River Forest, Illinois, designed in 1893. The facade, despite its classical symmetry, shows a new awareness of the plasticity of space.

'clean out of his time' by at least one reputable critic. Now Lutyens has been rehabilitated, seized upon by those who seek to show that Modernism was but a temporary aberration. He is presented as proof of a continuing link between the traditional mode of architectural expression of the past and the would-be Post-Modernism of the present.

At the same time, the reputations of many of the modern masters have themselves come under attack. Few, even among those sympathetic to Modernism, would now claim that the significance of a figure such as Walter Gropius extends much further than a few of his early buildings and his influence as an educator.

This is an inevitable process. Time has always had a way of telescoping changes and shifting the relative importance of events and individuals. Seen from too close even a stylistic molehill can look like a mountain of a movement. Reputations, of both critics and architects, are commonly established by demolishing those of their predecessors. Prevailing orthodoxies are overturned, only to be replaced by succeeding prevailing orthodoxies. But to push this process too far, as have some of the architectural revisionists of this century, is to take just as narrow a view as those who would have cast Lutyens out into the darkness of obscurity.

Something worthwhile and exciting *did* happen to architecture around the turn of this century. It might not have been quite such a revolutionary, or so iconoclastic, a movement as it was once depicted to be; but exaggeration and sloganeering are understandable parts of any campaign to win acceptance for a new school. Behind the slogans

Above **Charles Voysey always disassociated himself from the Modern Movement, and his house in Chorleywood, Hertfordshire, of 1899, with its evocation of the English vernacular, demonstrates his attachment to the Arts and Crafts.**

was enough creative power to change the shape of architecture for the rest of the century. Eight decades later, the majority of new architecture still acknowledges at least a grudging debt to the heroic period of Modernism. Some of the oversimplifications and slogans of that period have, of course, come back to haunt Modernism, notably the claim that form should follow function. This, proposed by Louis Sullivan and many others, is an inadequate even solecistic view. Yet it was by no means a new one, and it carries echoes of other architectural writers all the way from Vitruvius to Viollet-le-Duc and Morris.

Also architects had long talked of the need to design buildings that were true to their method of construction and made good use of technological innovation. Modernism presented itself as being primarily concerned with these issues. But in fact there have been many architects working in quite different traditions who had been equally conscious of them.

Indeed, the mastery of technology and construction was not always a strong point among the moderns, despite their rhetoric about the need to create an architecture for an industrial, machine-dominated age. In fact the means adopted by them to do this were often more symbolic than real, and when the pioneers of the 1920s opted for precise geometric forms they fabricated them with laborious craft techniques that belied their mechanical inspirations.

The recognition of these apparent inconsistencies, however, does not seriously undermine the power and appeal of Modernism. What has made it such a long-lasting and vigorous school is its ability to create memorable imagery and a vocabulary of form and detail that are, to a greater or lesser extent, appropriate to the present. Given the individualistic and questioning traditions of western culture it is inevitable that such a form of expression should have been sought ever since the close of the eighteenth century. Along the way there have been many short-lived attempts at discovering it; most, despite brief bursts of popularity, have withered. Modernism by contrast has not. For all its shortcomings, and for all the sometimes barbarous ends to which it has been put, the Modern Movement has lasted long enough to become a permanent part of the vocabulary of architecture.

Leading Modernists contended that architecture was not simply a question of superficial style. Le Corbusier wrote in *Vers une Architecture*, 'The styles of Louis XIV, XV, XVI or Gothic, are to architecture what a feather is on a woman's head; it is sometimes pretty, though not always, and never

anything more.' He and others like him wanted to rescue architecture from this feeble eclecticism and return to the deeper values that lie behind superficial facadism, the values, according to Le Corbusier, of mass, surface and plan.

The precursors

The most fundamental question for artists and architects working in the nineteenth century was that of how to come to terms with the reshaping of society by industrialization. The coming of factory production meant new materials, new working methods, new economies of scale and even new building types. It also severed the links between artist, architect and craftsman—perhaps terminally—and architecture itself became an organized profession for the first time. It signalled the end of a living, vernacular building tradition as cheap, industrially produced materials could be shipped through newly constructed canals and railways to take the place of local stones, brick or timber. And, of course, it triggered off a population explosion in the cities which vastly increased the sheer volume of building. For many, given the sprawling, cholera-wracked monsters that cities were becoming, the reaction to this was a violent rejection of industry and all things industrial.

In England in particular, the earliest country to go through the industrial revolution, this was especially true. From Pugin to Morris, the English developed a strongly utopian streak that was against the machine, against the city, and which looked instead to the simple artless virtues of the craft-based rural past.

William Morris was an ambiguous figure, combining passionate socialist beliefs with a private income derived from mining shares and an interior decorating business that could only survive on the patronage of the rich. Despite an apprenticeship in George Edmund Street's office he never actually built anything, but this did not prevent him from becoming a major influence on architecture both in England and the rest of Europe.

Build me a house, 'very medieval in spirit', Morris asked his friend from Street's office, Philip Webb, in 1859, after he himself had finally decided to give up architecture in favour of the decorative arts. But the house which Webb built, with Morris's collaboration and with adornments to the interior from many of the other members of the Pre-Raphaelite Brotherhood, is a far cry from the formalist exercises in facadism of its day. Webb himself was later to deprecate the Red House—so-called from the colour of its bricks rather than any political message—saying that no architect should

be allowed to design a house until past forty. Its free plan is inspired by Street and Butterfield, both committed Gothicists, but the house is anything but archaeological in its approach. Instead, the dramatic massing, the austere exterior and the restrained decoration can be seen as precursors of the back-to-first-principles architecture of the early moderns.

Morris and Webb, with their somewhat puritanical socialism and, in Morris's case, elaborate programmes for millennial reform, also set the scene for the high moral tone and utopian promises of the moderns—themes which were sustained until the 1960s and later. Morris, initially more under the spell of Ruskin than of Marx, argued for a healing of the breach between designers and makers that had been opened up by the factory. Only then, he believed, could a new and organic architecture once more flourish. These arguments were given some force by the curious spectacle of the competition to design the new Foreign Office in London, a struggle which epitomized the vapid battle of styles between classicism and Gothic. (This was finally resolved in 1861 when Gilbert Scott elected to swallow his principles and build the classical design selected by Lord Palmerston.)

In translation, the writing of Ruskin and Morris, along with pictures from the catalogues of Morris & Co., the enterprise that Morris established to manufacture goods according to his principles, began to have a strong influence on the Continent and on America's Eastern seaboard. Indeed,

Above **The Red House, Bexley Heath, designed by Philip Webb in 1859 for his friend William Morris, is essentially an exercise in medievalizing romanticism. Yet it is furnished with a radical freedom and vigour.**

Walter Gropius's 1919 manifesto for the Bauhaus called, in terms that could have been Morris's, for the rescue of all the arts from the isolation in which each then found itself. The Bauhaus was to train the craftsmen, painters and sculptors of the future and to embark on cooperative projects in which all their skills would be combined. Beneath Lyonel Feininger's woodcut cover illustration of a cathedral, Gropius proclaimed, 'There is no essential

Below **Lyonel Feininger's Expressionist woodcut executed for Walter Gropius's manifesto for the founding of the Bauhaus in 1919. Gropius himself spoke of Morris as an inspiration.**

difference between the artist and the craftsman. Let us then create a new guild of craftsmen without the class distinctions that raise an arrogant barrier between craftsman and artist.' Writing in 1924, he went on to spell out the Bauhaus debt to 'Ruskin and Morris in England ... and others who consciously sought and found the first ways to the reunification of the world of work with the creative artists'.

Although Webb's Red House was firmly part of High Victorian Gothic, it was also among the first built realizations of the Arts and Crafts movement. Taking Ruskin's high moral tone and Morris's passion for medievalism, the Arts and Crafts architects attempted to tame the brutishness of industrialization, not with another fashionable historicist style but with a fresh, undogmatic approach that, initially at least, attempted to use the process of building and making as the starting point of architectural design. At one end of the movement were Morris and Webb, at the other was Charles Voysey who went further than Webb ever did in ridding his buildings of any historic stylistic references.

With his characteristic use of stark white rough-cast finishes, forming a taut skin over plain, unadorned facades, Voysey produced buildings which came close to the work of Charles Rennie Mackintosh and the Viennese school. Indeed Voysey and other members of the Arts and Crafts movement became enormously influential in Europe. At the end of his long career Voysey went out of his way to condemn Modernism, but nevertheless his work did include such extraordinary free designs as his factory for the Sanderson Company of 1902 in west London. Stripped of any historical references, it resembles nothing so much as one of Voysey's own furniture designs. A similar independence of spirit can be seen in all Voysey's houses, from Orchards, his own home in Chorleywood, to the finest of his designs, the group of houses he built in the Lake District. Though obviously inspired by elements of the English vernacular tradition, with gables, leaded wide porches, strapwork doors and half-timbering, Voysey abstracted these elements into a highly personal formula.

Inspired as much by commercial rivalry as a spirit of artistic inquiry, other European powers, particularly Germany, were eager to learn the lessons of the English school as represented by Voysey. Hermann Muthesius was dispatched to the Kaiser's embassy in London in 1896 to report on architecture and design. The result was the influential book *Das Englische Haus*, published in

Berlin in 1904, which did much to spread Voysey's fame on the Continent.

England and its Arts and Crafts movement made a number of contributions to the European mainstream. In addition to Voysey's polished and sophisticated evocation of the vernacular, and the richer currents of work represented by Norman Shaw or Lutyens, there was the English view of urbanism. The squalor of the nineteenth-century city, in sharp contrast to the post-industrial paradise depicted in his prophetic novel *News from Nowhere*, implanted in Morris a distaste for the city that was part and parcel of his hatred of industrialization in general. This view become a persistent strand in English thinking that eventually influenced the formulation of Ebenezer Howard's Garden City movement.

Taking as his model the garden suburb of Bedford Park, laid out in 1880 to the west of London's then boundaries by Norman Shaw,

Howard advocated the best of both worlds' utopianism. He proposed the building of small, self-contained new towns of up to 30,000 people, in which the local industries and small farms could cater for all the needs of the inhabitants, providing an escape from both rural poverty and urban squalor. Though not himself an architect—Howard worked as a House of Commons clerk—his book *Tomorrow: A Peaceful Path to Reform*, published in 1898, was to lead to the building of Hampstead Garden Suburb and at least two garden cities near London, Letchworth, started in 1903, and Welwyn, begun in 1919. However popular and financially successful these have been, they are still far from Howard's vision of a self-sufficient and balanced community. Rather they are desirable locations for upper-middle-class families with jobs in the nearby metropolis.

The principles behind these developments shaped the face of British town-planning and have

Above Laid out in 1880 to Norman Shaw's plan, with individual buildings designed by a variety of architects, Bedford Park, London, was the first realized product of the Garden City movement.

proved enormously influential elsewhere as well. Unfortunately, though, the architectural expression given to the early garden cities by Sir Raymond Unwin and his partner, Barry Parker, hardly lived up to the promise of Howard's plans, since they worked in a pared-down rustic-cottage style not very far removed from that of Webb but with far less scope for expression. At Hampstead the involvement of Lutyens did lead to the creation of a more distinguished architecture, but nevertheless

the cottage style became the model for such developments all around the world.

Howard, and others like him, believed that low density was the key to the success of the garden city developments. But the fundamentally anti-urban, green-field planning of their approach can be seen as sowing the seeds for the more radical and destructive attempts at urban restructuring later in the century. Similarly, the moral tone that Howard adopted, his belief in the uplifting power of

Below Hampstead Garden Suburb, London, was planned by Raymond Unwin and Barry Parker in the years after 1905. It is distinguished by Sir Edwin Lutyens' treatment of the central square and two churches.

planning and architecture and its capacity to transform the lives of ordinary people for the better, heralded another of the preoccupations of the Modernists, that of social engineering. Despite Morris's own fire and brimstone rhetoric and the fact that he founded his own political party, his Arts and Crafts followers were essentially unrevolutionary. They believed in tradition, even though they might have been unhappy with certain aspects of their society. Nevertheless, they laid the ground for a series of much more far-reaching departures.

The engineers' contribution

'Naval architects and mechanical engineers do not, when building a steamship, or a locomotive, seek to recall the forms of sailing ships, or harnessed stagecoaches of the Louis XIV period. They obey, unquestioningly, the new principles which are given them, and produce their own character and styles.' So argued Viollet-le-Duc. But although his view was to be highly influential and has been much repeated in various forms, it was in fact inaccurate. When the first motor cars were designed they did look exactly like horseless carriages, and this affectation has returned to inspire the Detroit styling studios at regular intervals.

Equally, the prefabricated cast-iron buildings, produced both in England and America for shipping around the world or for erection nearer home, used moulds to recreate the forms of stone and the style of classicism. James Bogardus for example, the famous New York iron-master, even went so far as to install the newly invented Otis passenger lift in one of his buildings, but he retained an architect to reproduce the classical facades in iron.

Those nineteenth-century innovations, steel skeleton construction, passenger lifts and reinforced concrete, certainly did reshape the face of the world's cities. Yet they brought no single identifiable architectural style with them. Technique did stimulate innovative architects and designers but it was never the whole explanation for the stylistic changes that took place. Other factors—the purpose for which the materials are used and the organization and methods of the people who use them—are also involved, so the problem of the appropriateness of materials to a particular style only really becomes pressing when they are pushed to their limits. Then they are deployed in buildings of a scale far beyond that for which the stylistic mode was originally developed, and innovation becomes essential.

Opposite above **Built to Paxton's designs, the Crystal Palace for the 1851 Great Exhibition was a masterpiece of prefabrication that was to inspire architects long after its removal to south London.**

Opposite below **There was no historical precedents for a building such as the Crystal Palace, with its use of cast iron, timber and glass, so stylistic references were at a minimum.**

Left **The cast-iron conservatories of the Victorian botanical gardens, such as the Palm House of 1844 at Kew, showed that the Crystal Palace was not entirely an isolated case.**

To modern eyes the Crystal Palace building for the Great Exhibition of 1851 in London appears to encapsulate almost all of the preoccupations of that strand of modern architecture known as 'High Tech'. It was a lightweight structure, built up of modular, factory-made components, brought together on site and assembled with a minimum of traditional building skills in the interests of speed, economy and quality of finish. Built at the behest of Prince Albert and with the advice of Henry Cole, the Great Exhibition was intended to house the whole range of modern production in one giant hall. To find a suitable design, a competition had been held, with the architect Charles Barry among the judges as well as the engineers Stephenson and Brunel. In the event, despite a large response, none of the entries was judged suitable and the judges themselves prepared a design that was equally poorly regarded.

Finally, Joseph Paxton, once gardener to the Duke of Devonshire and a man with no formal training either as an engineer or an architect, came to the rescue with a design sketched initially on the back of a telegram form. Unlike the heavy brick buildings proposed by others, his scheme was for a lightweight, glassy structure that would cause the minimum of visual disturbance to the much cherished surroundings of Hyde Park. The glass—Paxton's design called for 900,000 square feet of it, one-third of Britain's total annual production of glass in 1840—also helped to overcome the problem of illuminating such a cavernous interior in the days before artificial light.

The Crystal Palace was built with remarkable speed. The three-storey-high structure, 1848 feet long and 408 feet wide, was completed in just nine months, thanks to the use of an unprecedented degree of prefabrication.

There was no model for a building type such as the Crystal Palace, and thus no question of the recreation of some historical precedent. It did, however, have some forerunners in the shape of contemporary greenhouses, particularly those of Decimus Burton and Richard Taylor at Kew, and Paxton's own work at Chatsworth. Pioneering though it was, the Crystal Palace was not quite such

a forward-looking building as is sometimes supposed. Though much of its structure was indeed cast iron, it also depended on a great deal of laminated timber to support its sweeping vaulted roof. Unfortunately it was this timber that helped the building's final destruction when it caught fire on the south London site where it had been re-erected after the Great Exhibition ended.

The Crystal Palace inspired no obvious imitators in the short term, and was seen at the time more as a piece of engineering than architecture. In fact, it served to underline the growing divergence of engineers and architects of the day. Such well-known contrasts as the soaring engineering structure of Barlow and Ordish's train-shed for St Pancras Station and Scott's flamboyant Gothic hotel, that fronts the cast-iron structure but entirely fails to come to terms with it, provide a stark commentary on the mismatch between structural potential and stylistic treatment.

Above The Midland Railway Company was looking for an ostentatious building for St Pancras Station to challenge its competitors at Euston and Kings Cross in London. Sir Gilbert Scott was happy to oblige with his astonishing Gothic hotel of 1865.

Right Behind the picturesque facade of St Pancras, Barlow and Ordish's cast-iron train-shed was equally spectacular, and by no means the cultural clash with the hotel that has sometimes been claimed.

Britain's engineers led the way up to the middle years of the nineteenth century, possibly because theirs was the first country in the world to develop a railway system, and it was the railways which provided the cutting edge for technological development in the nineteenth century, just as aerospace has in the twentieth. By the 1870s Britain's railway infrastructure was all but complete, but on the Continent lines were still being constructed, to the benefit of engineers such as Gustave Eiffel.

Eiffel's career came to fruition at about the same time that steel began to become available as an economic building material. He put it to work on such impressive engineering projects as the Douro Bridge in Portugal and the famous Eiffel Tower in Paris, in its day the tallest structure in the world.

Above Gustav Eiffel's Douro Bridge of 1876-7 in Portugal anticipates the clarity and invention of the Eiffel Tower.

21

Above Attacked as a blot on the landscape and now a universal symbol of Paris, the Eiffel Tower is a powerful celebration of the potential of pure engineering as an aesthetic expression.

All of these depended on the lattice beam, a structural principle developed by Eiffel himself which produced structures of the maximum rigidity with the minimum weight by exploiting the way in which girders can be used to brace each other in three dimensions. This principle has recently been developed further to produce the 'space frame' and even the 'geodesic dome'.

Work started on the building of the Eiffel Tower in 1887, to a less than universally enthusiastic response. In particular, a group of French painters and writers petitioned vigorously for the project, perceived as a blot on the landscape, to be stopped. Regrettably this affair has been cited almost ever since to justify each brash and unsightly new intrusion on the Parisian skyline.

In fact, neither the Crystal Palace nor the Eiffel Tower offered direct architectural models, other than an unfortunate precedent for Modernists to treat their buildings as objects in a landscape, rather than accepting the context of the city around them. These two famous landmarks did show, however, that it was entirely possible to express dignity and monumentality without recourse to any historical references.

Technologically speaking, France's other significant contribution to the new architecture was the development of reinforced concrete, turning it into an economical and highly adaptable structural material. Concrete had, of course, been used by the Romans but it was only rediscovered at the start of the nineteenth century, and then used only for such humble products as flower-pots. A number of different builders and engineers then began to experiment with the material, but found that although concrete is very strong in compression, it has very little tensile strength. Rather than use massively oversized beams, the solution opted for by the nineteenth-century inventors was to incorporate first iron and later steel reinforcing rods in those parts of a concrete member which were liable to tensile stress.

In 1892 François Hennebique patented a reinforced concrete frame system which was to be the forerunner of all multi-storey structures in Europe. The restrictions that monolithic structures imposed on internal planning were removed: instead of cellular interiors, concrete-framed structures could be opened out. Equally, their exteriors could be treated as two distinct elements—a concrete load-bearing frame and a lightweight infill cladding panel for climatic control and decorative effect. At about the same time, parallel developments were taking place in the use of structural steel in Chicago.

Hennebique's achievement was capitalized on by Auguste Perret, whose architectural education had been steeped in the classical traditions of the Paris Ecole des Beaux-Arts—an influence incidentally which critics such as Reyner Banham have suggested is largely responsible for the underlying sense of classical order of many of the early

Above Perret's apartment block in Rue Franklin in Paris capitalized on Hennebique's inventions and developed an aesthetic vocabulary based on an expressed structural frame with decorative infill panels.

Left François Hennebique's patent reinforced concrete frame system, as demonstrated by the Villa Hennebique of 1904 at Sceaux, allowed an unparalleled degree of freedom from the tyranny of the massive masonry wall.

Opposite above Tony Garnier's visionary project, the Cité Industrielle, provided a much more urban view of the new city than the English Garden City experiments. It also attempted to come to terms with the aesthetic of new materials and techniques.

Opposite below Chicago's boom-town conditions at the turn of the century allowed for the creation of an entirely new form of architectural language, demonstrated by Carson, Pirie, Scott's department store by Louis Sullivan.

Right Built from 1915 onwards, the engineer Matté Trucco's Lingotto car factory for Fiat in Turin attracted the admiration of Le Corbusier for the sheer scale of its conception and the clarity of its execution.

Above The Lingotto's roof-top testing track was an image of the modern world that appealed to the intoxicated imagination of the Futurists.

Critics from Ruskin onwards had complained that the architecture of the nineteenth century was for the most part a matter of self-conscious stylistic revivals and facadism, a tendency they contrasted with the fresh, original work of the master masons and architects of the past. In one sense at least Perret could be seen as their equal, creating a new means of expression with the principles of what had gone before to help him rather than detailed stylistic solutions. Though not an architect, Matté Trucco's remarkable Lingotto factory for Fiat in Turin, built in the years after 1915, represented the apotheosis of the new concrete approach, producing a building much admired by Le Corbusier.

At the same time that Perret was applying the discipline and order of classicism to unadorned concrete, another ex-student of the Paris Ecole des Beaux-Arts, and a former Rome scholar, was applying it to town-planning. Tony Garnier, a life-long socialist, spent the years at the turn of the century in Rome working on a beautifully presented plan for the Cité Industrielle, an ideal

moderns. Perret consciously set out to create a suitable architectural style for concrete, and with such buildings as his apartment block in the Rue Franklin in Paris of 1902, went a long way towards achieving it. Using a reinforced concrete frame he eliminated stylistic frills but addressed himself instead to those questions of mass, form and surface later postulated by Le Corbusier.

community based very much on the conditions of his native Lyons. The architectural expression is seductive, with heroic civic buildings designed in reinforced concrete. Even more prophetic is the physical division of the city's plan into separate quarters for each major function. Residential areas were planned around local schools, with distinct zones for each of the city's functions, administration, industry and commerce—a model that has inspired town-planners ever since, not always with desirable results.

The conditions of turn-of-the-century Chicago, America's fastest growing boom town, were very different from those of Paris, but they proved even more fruitful for a rapid wave of architectural development. It was here that the Chicago school, led by Sullivan, established itself and from it was to emerge Frank Lloyd Wright. A catastrophic fire in 1870 all but wiped out Chicago, and the rush to rebuild the city created unique opportunities for the group of architects who moved in to take advantage of the situation.

Chicago was the birthplace of the skyscraper, that quintessential image of modernity for much of the twentieth century. New York, it is true, had seen buildings rising up to ten storeys as early as the 1870s and these were called skyscrapers, but they still depended on traditional constructional techniques that were incapable of reaching any great height. In Chicago, however, a city then devoid of any architectural tradition, William Le Baron Jenney invented in 1883 the construction technique that made the modern skyscraper possible, leading to ever taller buildings that quickly eclipsed their New York rivals. He built the Home Life Insurance building in which external masonry walls were not load-bearing, but were supported instead on cantilevered brackets riveted to the internal metal frame. Though it was technically the most advanced building of its time, Jenney's design was outwardly conventional enough. It was left to Louis Sullivan, an East–Coast trained architect who had started his career in the office of Frank Furness, the most flamboyantly eclectic of all America's Gothic-inspired designers, to come up with a true skyscraper style.

The greatest of Sullivan's designs, the Carson, Pirie, Scott department store of 1899–1904 and the Guaranty building of 1894 in Buffalo, along with work by other members of the Chicago school, such as John Root and Daniel Burnham, created a distinctive, streamlined and powerful style. This, while it had none of the ideological content of the European moderns, was as vigorous as anything that came in the next thirty years.

Opposite above Edwin Lutyens, although decried by the Modernists in the 1950s for his traditional approach, did in fact experiment with technology, as in his outwardly medievalizing Castle Drogo of 1910–30 in Devon.

Opposite below The most spectacular of Lutyens' projects was his master plan for New Delhi, carried out between 1912 and 1927, a fusion of classical western and Indian motifs.

Below Gunnar Apslund's Stockholm City Library is a sophisticated example of his neo-classical style, which was to be highly influential in Britain in the years before the Second World War.

Sullivan's work was enriched by highly personal decorative detail which he designed himself. Free of historical or literal references, yet organic in inspiration, Sullivan used it to set off the clarity and simplicity of the frankly expressed structural frames of his buildings.

It was Sullivan who in 1896 coined the famous slogan 'Form follows function', a much misunderstood phrase, often mistakenly taken as an article of faith of Modernism. In fact, Sullivan's own work was always much richer than that of other, more doctrinaire, functionalists, and he himself always valued the symbolic aspects of architecture.

The traditionalists

A sharp reaction to Modernism arose, particularly in Britain and America, during the 1970s when it was roundly condemned by many architects, and even more by non-architectural opinion formers, for its lack of expression. This led to a re-examination of those architects who continued to practise well into the twentieth century in a variety of styles that could all be characterized as in some way traditional. As a description of so diverse a group this is not perhaps entirely satisfactory, for few of them were reluctant to make full use of the new materials and many of them produced work which actually represented quite a radical departure from the styles of the nineteenth century. However, they were united at least by a commitment to the representational qualities of architecture, that is to the motifs of architecture built up over centuries and thus invested with implicit meaning for society. It was a commitment that stood in sharp contrast to the geometric abstractions of the Modernists, and by its very nature was likely to enjoy a much more widespread appeal than the refined and somewhat élitist approach of the Modernists.

While critics and historians such as Sigfried Giedion, writing in *Space, Time and Architecture*, and Nikolaus Pevsner (*Pioneers of Modern Design, Outline of European Architecture* and much else) held sway, the traditionalists received little critical attention. Now, however, a new generation is engaged in a reassessment of the traditionalists and their contribution to the architecture of the twentieth century.

Traditionalism had many faces, from the work of such Scandinavians as Gunnar Apslund, whose Stockholm City Library of 1920–8 makes references to neo-classicism that are almost subliminal, to the full-blown grand manner of Edwin Lutyens. The latter was able to move from the discreet charms of his Art and Crafts based country houses to the grandiloquence of his baroque planning New Delhi just at the time that the Modernists were assuming control of the mainstream.

Traditionalism may be an adequate word to describe the suave *belle époque* work of Mewès and Davis, who built the Ritz Hotel (1904–6) in London using the very latest American invention, the structural steel frame, but clad it in what appears to be solid loadbearing masonry. But it is

Right For a brief period the tallest building in the world, Cass Gilbert's 1913 skyscraper for Woolworths in New York is an attempt to treat the high rise as a conventional architectural composition.

Below Hood and Howell's Gothic skyscraper for the *Chicago Tribune* was built in 1922. The design was selected in competition against entries from many of the European avant-garde.

more difficult to justify it in connection with Cass Gilbert, a Beaux-Arts trained architect who began his career in the offices of McKim, Mead & White and then went on to design the sixty-storey Woolworth office building in New York in 1913, richly ornamented with French Gothic embellishments. For many years this, and various other historically inspired skyscrapers such as Hood and Howell's competition-winning Chicago Tribune Tower of 1922, were treated as bizarre and misconceived aberrations. But to the American architects of the 1980s, searching for a style to recapture the identity and glamour of the first wave of New York high rises, the precedents set by Gilbert and others proved highly apposite.

The revolutionaries

The speed with which the style now universally known as Art Nouveau, but also labelled 'Modern', 'Jugendstil', 'Sezessionism', and 'Liberty', spread throughout Europe at the turn of the century would seem to prove that the world was ready and waiting for a radical change in architecture. The climate was right in the declining years of the nineteenth century for a style that represented a complete break with the past, which was self-consciously new, modern and forward-looking. Art Nouveau did look very different from anything that had gone before and proved remarkably seductive to both designers and architects.

It is certainly possible to see in Art Nouveau parallels with the Arts and Crafts ideals of Morris, particularly in the way it drew on natural forms for inspiration and in the emphasis placed on workmanship; the writings of Viollet-le-Duc were equally influential. But when all is said and done, Victor Horta's own house in Brussels, built in 1898 and the very first manifestation of Art Nouveau, *was* an astonishing departure. The plan and facade were distinctive, if not to contemporary eyes extreme, but even more remarkable was the interior. This, with its frank, flamboyant use of metal structure for decoration and its lush, sensuous lines inspired by graphic design and painting, quite clearly had no precedents in architecture.

Technically, it was engineers such as Eiffel who made possible Horta's brand of Art Nouveau, with its emphasis on lightness and transparency. But the speed with which it was taken up reflected a widespread feeling among the cultural avant-garde that it was time for a complete break with the past. By 1900 Art Nouveau was flourishing in Germany, Austria, Italy, France and Belgium; closely related developments were to be seen in England, Scotland, Spain and even Sullivan's Chicago. It had many manifestations. In the brasseries of Paris and the shops of Brussels and Berlin it was a hugely popular commercial style; it could be readily applied as a fashionable camouflage, its main characteristics were easily copied and it could be executed in relatively cheap materials. But in Barcelona Art Nouveau, as interpreted by Antonio Gaudí, had a distinctiveness and wilful individuality that seemed appropriate to the newly discovered sense of Catalan national identity.

Gaudí never used the term himself, but his work at Park Güell, from 1900, and his slightly later apartment blocks, the Casa Batlló and Casa Milá, can be interpreted as Art Nouveau, with their sinuous eroded curves and their use of free, naturally inspired ornament. On the other hand,

the remarkable, unfinished and unresolved Sagrada Familia church seems more a deliberate attempt to establish a locally inspired monument in Barcelona—one which, given Spain's Moorish and somewhat bizarre Gothic heritage, is perhaps not quite so freakish there as it would be in most European cities.

Gaudí's strange aesthetic sense sometimes produced buildings that were more sculpture than architecture, but though much of his imagery was personal and esoteric he was also able to work within the rigours of highly advanced engineering techniques. For all that, his work seems introverted and backward-looking when set beside, say, Horta's Maison du Peuple in Brussels of 1896

Below left Gaudí's Casa Batlló in Barcelona is an extraordinary fusion of Art Nouveau with freakish imagery, bone-like structure and applied ornament.

Below right A wilful, personal vision, Gaudí's Sagrada Familia, his unfinished monument in Barcelona, demonstrates the power of architecture to embody nationalist aspirations.

Right The staircase of Victor Horta's own house in Brussels, an important example of Art Nouveau's potential for using structure as ornament and organic forms as inspiration.

Near right and far right The newly installed Paris Métro with its twisted metal shapes epitomized the avant-garde Art Nouveau style pioneered by Hector Guimard. The prefabricated metalwork established a striking identity for the system and turned utility into an ornament for the urban setting.

or Hector Guimard's prefabricated Parisian Métro stations. These two suggest the possibility of Modernism working hand in hand with industrial production methods that contradicts the widely held view that Art Nouveau is merely a flat, two-dimensional style for interior decorators.

Gaudí is often compared with his younger contemporary Charles Rennie Mackintosh, both being presented as maverick geniuses confined to the periphery of mainstream events. It is true that there are parallels. Mackintosh's home city of Glasgow was, like Barcelona, undergoing an industrial boom at the end of the nineteenth century at a time when both the Scots and Catalans were beginning to reassert their endangered cultural identity.

Mackintosh's work, like Gaudí's earlier build-ings, also displays elements of a national tradition. His masterpiece, the Glasgow School of Art, contains details which can be traced to the sixteenth-century fortified towers of the Scottish borders. This Scots baronial theme is given further expression in his country houses, the most notable being Hill House at Helensburgh designed in 1902. In its roughcast white walls, Hill House suggests the manner of Voysey. Its details are self-consciously forceful and crude, the antithesis of Mackintosh's refined decoration in the Art School library or the tea-rooms in Glasgow designed for Miss Cranston.

Like Gaudí, Mackintosh is represented, particu-larly in Britain, as an isolated figure with too personal a vision to provide the inspiration for more than a tiny band of followers. It is true that his

Above The Glasgow School of Art, an award-winning design from 1898, remains Mackintosh's masterpiece. Combining the hard texture of sandstone with much decorative ironwork, he created a style that was to have repercussions throughout Europe.

Opposite left Joseph Olbrich's building for the Sezession, in Vienna, is clearly influenced by Mackintosh and openly proclaims its avant-garde principles.

The summit of Mackintosh's achievements, however, went beyond Art Nouveau. At the Art School in Glasgow, built in two stages after an architectural competition in 1898, he developed an entirely new mode of spatial planning, in which he devised a floor plan to allow different volumes to flow into each other, in contrast to the cellular facadism of the past.

Art Nouveau was a movement that burnt itself out soon, evaporating by 1910 almost as quickly as it had appeared. Its very success, with an almost universal application in every fashionable city in the world, seems to have rapidly consumed its fragile imagery and it quickly became a bore. But its radical reassessment of how architecture could look and its clean break with the past were an inspiration for a whole group of architects attempting to establish themselves in these years.

In Vienna the impulse that grew out of Art Nouveau went further than anywhere else in Europe. But it was also the city which, in the shape of Adolf Loos, produced the most violent reaction to it, not from the traditionalists but from another variety of Modernists.

The Austrian avant-garde emerged in 1896 as a body of architects and painters in revolt against academic establishments. This group, eventually forming a Viennese version of the Salon des Refusés, included members of the Vienna Society of Visual Artists, the architect Otto Wagner, and an enthusiastic nucleus of his students and colleagues, including Josef Hoffmann, Joseph Olbrich, Koloman Moser and Gustav Klimt. The Vereinigung Bildender Künstler Osterreichs, or Association of Austrian Visual Artists, was formally established in April 1897. The group became known as the Sezession and this name, which so well conveys its revolutionary character, has become the most accepted label for the movement. Their work was initially inspired by Art Nouveau, but after Mackintosh's visit it became more rectilinear.

The principal architectural members of the Sezession were Wagner, Olbrich and Hoffmann, who scandalized conservative Viennese opinion with the Sezession building itself. This, the first major achievement of the Sezession, was erected in 1898 to a design by Olbrich based on a sketch by Klimt. They then succeeded in attracting the attention of avant-garde patrons elsewhere in Europe, most notably Grand Duke Ernst, the anglophile ruler of Darmstadt, and the wealthy Stoclet family in Brussels.

Wagner, the elder statesman of the group, Hoffmann's professor and Olbrich's one-time

career was sadly truncated. He left Glasgow in despair and moved to London for the second half of his life, where he built next to nothing and confined himself to furniture, interiors and water-colours. He was shunned by the English Arts and Crafts establishment, who derisively called his followers the 'Spook School'.

Despite his difficulties, the results of his own temperament as much as anything else, Mackintosh proved to be highly influential in Europe. In 1895, aged only twenty-five, he took part in the opening exhibition of Samuel Bing's Maison de l'Art Nouveau in Paris, and five years later he had pride of place at the 1900 Annual Exhibition of the Vienna Sezession. Mackintosh's work was to be seen from Darmstadt to Turin, influencing both the young Peter Behrens and, most particularly, Josef Hoffmann, who was to found the Wiener Werkstätte on the basis of English Art and Crafts principles but with a Mackintosh aesthetic.

Left Olbrich left Austria to work for the Grand Duke of Darmstadt in his artists' colony. The Ernst Ludwig House dates from 1901.

employer, remained rooted in the classical tradition of the Schinkel school, yet was heavily influenced by those who sought to create a modern sensibility. His remarkable Post Office Savings Bank in Vienna of 1904 embraces a host of new materials: aluminium, steel and concrete are mixed with white marble and glass bricks. The result is disciplined and immaculately crafted, but clearly unhistorical in expression.

Olbrich moved to Darmstadt in 1899 to join the artists' colony established by the Grand Duke, and here he met Peter Behrens, the painter turned architect who was to become the leading progenitor of the Modern Movement. Olbrich completed two major buildings in Darmstadt: the Ernst Ludwig House, a monumental structure which restates the themes of the Sezession building in its use of the human figure as a decorative element in combination with abstract but vaguely organic detail; and the Wedding Tower of 1908, a bigger departure carried out in a highly individualistic expressionist mode, which provided Darmstadt with a landmark almost as prominent as a skyscraper.

Hoffmann's work in Vienna, with the conspicuous exception of the Purkersdorf sanatorium, was limited for the most part to private villas and small, perfectly detailed shops, cafés and auditoria. His major work was out of Austria altogether. The

Below In Vienna, Otto Wagner's Post Office Savings Bank demonstrates a remarkable willingness to make use of advanced materials and fresh decorative modes.

Above The Palais Stoclet in Brussels was a showcase of Sezessionist work. Built by Josef Hoffman, it combined architecture of the most uncompromising kind with a wealth of specially commissioned art and furniture for the interiors.

Palais Stoclet in Brussels (1905–11), an austere and dignified structure faced in marble outlined in black granite, was designed as a self-consciously avant-garde showcase, adorned with specially commissioned furniture, murals and artifacts produced by other members of the Sezession. Yet such perfection of craftsmanship, and the hermetic quality of the workmanship, made the Palais Stoclet and the rest of Hoffmann's output a target for the sardonic polemics of Adolf Loos.

This individual, distinguished both as an architect and a critic, was determined to produce what he saw as genuinely modern architecture. Like his adversaries in the Sezession, Loos was an anglophile and saw England at that time as the most progressive force in Europe, politically, aesthetically and industrially. But while Hoffmann admired the English Arts and Crafts school, Loos preferred Britain's discreet aristocratic taste. His essay *Ornament and Crime* had a huge initial

impact, by shock value alone, and its message has reverberated down the years. Popularly regarded as an archetypal Modernist text, but much misunderstood, it was principally an attack on the Sezessionists, along with Henry van de Velde and the Wiener Werkstätte.

Years after the building of the Palais Stoclet, at a public lecture in Paris, Loos delivered a particularly vituperative attack on the Werkstätte and all that it stood for:

'The modern spirit is a social spirit and modern objects exist not just for the benefit of the upper crust, but for everybody. To bring us first-rate work, no architects are needed, no arts and crafts students, and no painting, embroidering, potting, precious-material-wasting daughters of senior civil servants, or other Fräuleins, who regard handicrafts as something whereby one may earn pin-money, or while away one's spare time until one can walk up the aisle.'

Loos's objections were not to ornament in architecture or design *per se*. He was an unashamed élitist and held that those educated enough to appreciate the rarefied sensibilities of Modernism had a duty to live them to the full: 'We go to Beethoven or *Tristan* after the cares of the day. My shoemaker can't. I must not take away his joy [in the ornamentation of the bespoke footwear that he laboriously produced for Loos]. But whoever goes to the Ninth Symphony and then sits down to design a wallpaper is either a rogue or a degenerate.' Even today, Loos's buildings in Vienna, Prague and Paris are stark and shocking exercises in pure form and the sensuous use of unadorned materials.

In the years around the turn of the century, architects from all over Europe, and from America too, began to explore a variety of anti-historical approaches. Inspiration for this was provided by emerging technology and new modes of expression in the visual arts, particularly painting, as well as by an increasing desire in certain young nations to develop a means of national self-expression.

Henry van de Velde, the subject of Loos's scorn, was a Belgian and therefore had worked in a

climate much influenced by the Art Nouveau boom, but he attempted to impose his own personal stamp on this sinuous aesthetic. Like Behrens he turned to architecture having worked as a painter, and he aimed to create a total work of art, controlling not just the building but also its contents. It was this attitude that was criticized by Loos. Van de Velde's most significant architectural work was the Werkbund Exhibition Theatre in Cologne of 1914. Here he banished the graphic lines· of Art Nouveau and worked in a more powerful, three-dimensional manner.

Elsewhere in Europe there was Eliel Saarinen in Finland, who after building Helsinki's main railway station between 1905 and 1914 moved to America on the strength of winning second place in

Above The Goldmann & Salatsch store in Vienna of 1910 shows Adolf Loos at his most suave and polished, suggesting that even though ornament was a crime, bad manners were unforgivable.

Left Eliel Saarinen's railway station for Helsinki employs simplified forms and a powerful composition to create a sense of identity.

Right Berlage's Stock Exchange in Amsterdam, despite its historicist exterior, earned Mies's admiration.

the Chicago Tribune Tower competition. In Holland there was Hendrikus Petrus Berlage, whose Amsterdam Stock Exchange of 1897–1903 was admired by Mies van der Rohe for its austere use of Romanesque vocabulary. Then, in America, there was Frank Lloyd Wright, who began working for Sullivan in Chicago in 1880 and had set up on his own by 1893. His early houses were influential in Europe and undoubtedly had a strong impact on Gropius and Behrens.

Peter Behrens is central to the history of the Modern Movement. He pioneered and integrated into architecture such essentially twentieth-century concepts as industrial design and corporate identity, and his office attracted no less than three of the major European protagonists of the movement: Mies, Gropius and Le Corbusier.

Born in 1868, he spent the early part of his career as a painter, only becoming a self-taught architect in the years after 1901 when he built his own Art

Nouveau influenced house in Darmstadt. His industrial buildings and his influence on Gropius have, not surprisingly, given him a reputation as a proto-functionalist. But even his most famous building, the AEG turbine hall in Berlin of 1909, an iconic image in all early histories of the Modern Movement, is in essence a classical temple, and that classicizing tendency becomes quite clear in such designs as his St Petersburg embassy of 1911. Rather than undermining Behrens' position as a pioneering Modernist, these works in fact underline the strength of the classical tradition in the German wing of the Modern Movement, and in particular in Mies van der Rohe.

Behrens himself described architecture as the art of building. 'It comprises in its name two ideas, the mastery of the practical and the art of the beautiful. There is something exhilarating in being able to combine in one word two ideas—that of practical utility, and that of abstract beauty—which unfortunately have too often been opposed to each other.'

Above The AEG building in Berlin of 1909, the most celebrated of Behrens' buildings because of its seminal role in the emergence of modern architecture, demonstrates his fundamental classicism.

Left Peter Behrens' espousal of the whole spectrum of design, from architecture to product design and graphics, reshaped the role of the architect. But his own house at Darmstadt is entirely comfortable with the surburban villas of its day.

DECORATIVE ARTS

In the development of the applied arts William Morris is as vital a figure as he is in architecture. As a socialist Morris preached good design for every man, but he shunned the only means of achieving this in the age of the machine—that is, through a healthy alliance between the artist and industrialist—in favour of romantic attempts to revive the medieval system of community craft. His ideas were hopelessly impractical but this did not prevent them from becoming very influential both at home and abroad. In Great Britain, they were paralleled by the British love of the gentleman amateur and mistrust of the motivated professional—curious weaknesses in the national temperament which have dogged the story of the applied arts in Britain in the twentieth century—and as such they formed the cornerstone of the Arts and Crafts movement.

The critic Holbrook Jackson, writing in 1913, pinpointed the flaws in the Arts and Crafts dream: 'Morris and his group . . . demonstrated . . . that it was possible to produce useful articles of fine quality and good taste even in an age of debased industry . . . but their demonstration proved also that unless something like a revolution happened among wage-earners none but those of ample worldly means could hope to become possessed of the results of such craftsmanship. The Arts and Crafts movement was thus checked in its most highly organized and enthusiastic period by the habit and necessity of cheapness. It was found possible to educate taste . . . but as quickly as taste was improved by exhibitions of modern craftsmanship, commerce stepped in supplying those who could not afford the necessarily expensive results with cheap imitations. The ogre of shoddiness stood across the path of quality, and many who were set upon the high trail of excellence by the Arts and Crafts movement ended as devotees of fumed oak furniture, and what began as a great movement was in danger of ending as an empty fashion with the word "artistic" for shibboleth.'

The Arts and Crafts movement had important international repercussions, for it served as a model for craft guilds and design schools both in Europe and the United States. At home it undoubtedly encouraged a revival of craft. Carol Hogben, in his perceptive introductory essay to the Victoria & Albert Museum catalogue *English Art and Design 1900–1960* published in 1983, defines the lasting achievements of the movement. After Morris, he wrote, '. . . there was a clearer determination to look for more ordinary, truly national roots, at least closer (if not close) to common man, and it was quite prepared to leave off ornament altogether and

just show plain, virtuous, well-made simple form. One would be thinking, for example, of Mackintosh's light fittings based on squares; of the robust "country" solid wood furniture and blacksmiths' iron of Barnsley and Waals, inherited from tithe-barns and ship-building; of the quill pen uncials of Edward Johnston, or the clean page of Cobden-Sanderson's Doves Press.'

To such a list he might well have added the domestic architecture and furniture of Charles Annesley Voysey and Mackay Hugh Baillie Scott, both showing a fondness for native oak, simple lines, handsome proportions and restrained decoration; or the silver designed by C. R. Ashbee, produced by his Guild of Handicraft workshops, simple, uncluttered vessels, their hammered surfaces deliberately betraying the signs of handwork, their plainness offset by cabochons of semiprecious stones, sometimes by areas of enamel. Nor should one overlook the powerful graphic work of the 'Beggarstaff Brothers', William Nicholson and James Pryde, the marvellous 'transmutation' glazes of William Howson-Taylor's high-fired Ruskin earthenware, the metalwork of

Below 'Liberty & Co. Dress and Decoration'. This plate from a promotional folio of around 1905 demonstrates the wide range of products in fashionable styles sold by Liberty's.

W. A. S. Benson, the revival of fine printing in which the Doves Press shared credit with Charles Ricketts' Vale Press and, of course, Morris's own Kelmscott Press.

The prevalent pattern was of idealistic craftsmen working in isolation from the mainstream of manufacture and distribution, but two important exceptions were the enlightened retailers Arthur Lazenby Liberty and Ambrose Heal. Both played significant roles in commercializing the new styles. Liberty, founder in 1875 of the Regent Street store, had been an early importer of Japanese artifacts and a central figure in the Aesthetic movement, before turning his attention to the Arts and Crafts movement. As a commissioning retailer with a keen eye for the essence rather than merely the surface of fashionable trends, he brought together a group of designers who created the 'Liberty' style. This was a hybrid which combined the rustic 'honesty' of Arts and Crafts with elegant linear designs derived from continental Art Nouveau and, more locally, Celtic traceries. Liberty's great successes were sturdy oak furniture, the stylish silverware designed by Archibald Knox and others under the trademark 'Cymric' and charming fabrics designed by Voysey and the Silver Studio.

Ambrose Heal had joined the family firm in 1893. In 1898 he issued his first *Catalogue of Plain Oak Furniture*, a commercial application of Arts and Crafts principles and an early exercise in functionalist design. Heal deplored the gulf that existed between designers and manufacturers and was foremost among the group which, in 1915, founded the Design and Industries Association. This was modelled on the Deutsche Werkbund, an organization established in Munich in 1907 to promote high standards of industrial design.

The work of Ambrose Heal, like that of Gordon Russell in a similar vein, deserves credit for its worthy crusading spirit, though the results, functional, plain, spartan, seem to overlook the need of the spirit to be uplifted, even amused and flattered, by the things which create an environment. What a telling contrast with the work of Charles Rennie Mackintosh, creator of what Julius Meier-Graefe described as '*chambres garnies pour belles âmes*' (rooms decorated for noble spirits). Mackintosh is an elusive figure. While the details of his career have been well researched, his buildings, furniture, metalwork, graphics well catalogued, the details of his influence on the Vienna Sezessionists fully chronicled, it has still proved difficult to express the particular character of his genius. Nikolaus Pevsner, in his *Pioneers of Modern Design*, quotes Ahlers-Hesterman's fine evocation of the qualities which so thrilled the artists of Vienna: 'Here was indeed the oddest mixture of puritanically severe forms designed for use, with a truly lyrical evaporation of all interest in usefulness. These rooms were like dreams, narrow panels, grey silk, very very slender wooden shafts—verticals everywhere. Little cupboards of rectangular shape and with far-projecting top cornices,

PARADISE LOST
THE AUTHOR
JOHN MILTON

OF MANS FIRST DISOBEDIENCE,
AND THE FRUIT
OF THAT FORBIDDEN TREE,
WHOSE MORTAL TAST
BROUGHT DEATH INTO THE
WORLD, AND ALL OUR WOE,
With loss of Eden, till one greater Man
Restore us, and regain the blissful Seat,
Sing Heav'nly Muse, that on the secret top
Of Oreb, or of Sinai, didst inspire
That Shepherd, who first taught the chosen Seed,
In the Beginning how the Heav'ns and Earth
Rose out of Chaos: Or if Sion Hill
Delight thee more, and Siloa's Brook that flow'd
Fast by the Oracle of God; I thence
Invoke thy aid to my adventrous Song,
That with no middle flight intends to soar
Above th' Aonian Mount, while it pursues
Things unattempted yet in Prose or Rhime.
And chiefly Thou O Spirit, that dost prefer
Before all Temples th' upright heart and pure,
16

Far left Opening page of John Milton's *Paradise Lost*, the edition of 1902-5 published by T. J. Cobden-Sanderson's Doves Press. Clarity and elegance characterize the typography and layouts of this press.

Near left Detail from a design for a frieze by Frances Macdonald, around 1900-05. This is typical of the more Symbolist work of the Glasgow Four.

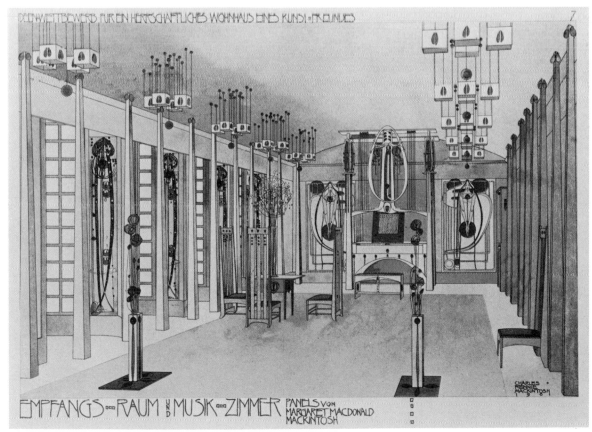

Left Design by Charles Rennie Mackintosh for a Music Room for the House of an Art Lover, 1901. The figurative panels are the work of his wife, Margaret Macdonald Mackintosh. From a series of designs by Mackintosh published in 1902 by Alexander Koch, Darmstadt, in the portfolio Haus Eines Kunst Freundes.

smooth, not of visible frame-and-panel construction; straight, white, and serious-looking, as if they were young girls ready to go to their first Holy Communion—and yet not really; for somewhere there was a piece of decoration like a gem, never interfering with the contour, lines of hesitant elegance, like a faint distant echo of van de Velde. The fascination of these proportions, the aristocratically effortless certainty with which an ornament of enamel, coloured glass, semi-precious

stone, beaten metal was placed, fascinated the artists of Vienna who were already a little bored with the eternal solid goodness of English interiors. Here was mysticism and asceticism, though by no means in a Christian sense, but with much of a scent of heliotrope, with well-manicured hands and a delicate sensuousness. . . . As against the former overcrowding, there was hardly anything in these rooms, except that, say, two straight chairs, with backs as tall as a man, stood on a white carpet and looked silently and spectrally at each other across a little table. . . .'

Decorative Art Nouveau

Leafing through the illustrations in decorative arts journals from around the time of the Paris Exposition Universelle of 1900, we see the elements of a most extraordinary style, now best known as Art Nouveau. The sumptuous furnishings and objects have in common a sense of organic, asymmetric growth; their design is a sophisticated stylization of natural forms, including delicate stem, leaf and flower motifs and languid, long-haired maidens.

These are the dominant characteristics of the expressive, often extravagant, yet short-lived style that pervaded architecture and the applied arts and flourished especially in France. It was, however, first seen in England in 1883 in Arthur H. Mackmurdo's title page for a book on Wren's city churches. Mackmurdo took his inspiration from nature, while a decade later Aubrey Beardsley, the illustrator, was much affected by the strong graphic forms of Japanese prints. Similar influences were astir on the Continent and it was there that the Art Nouveau style reached maturity, with its creative centre in France, particularly in Paris and the provincial town of Nancy. This style, with a strong local character, also enjoyed contemporaneous success in Brussels and individual designers elsewhere, both in Europe and the United States, interpreted it in their own way.

The Art Nouveau style took its name from the Paris shop of Samuel Bing, art critic, connoisseur and entrepreneur, who had been instrumental in promoting the appreciation of Japanese art. Bing was largely responsible for the passion in avant-garde artistic circles for Japanese artifacts, which were a major influence in the revitalization of the decorative arts in France in the 1890s. On 26 December 1895 he inaugurated his Galeries de l'Art Nouveau as a showcase for the best in modern art and design.

Bing cast his net internationally, drawing together the work of those artists who shared his desire to reject historicism and lay the foundations of a new style. As a commissioning retailer he gave

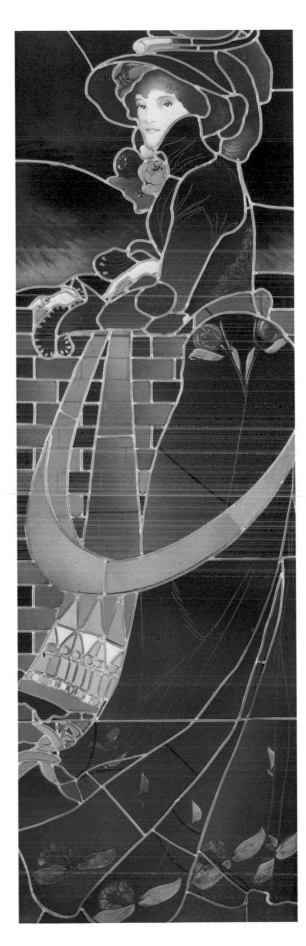

Opposite Display cabinet of white-painted wood decorated with glass mosaic and silver leaf, designed by Charles Rennie Mackintosh, 1904. This is perhaps Mackintosh's most refined achievement in the design of cabinet furniture.

Left Leaded stained-glass panel designed by Georges de Feure, around 1900. De Feure was the most versatile of the trio of artists closely associated with Bing's shop, L'Art Nouveau. His work is distinguished from that of Gaillard or Colonna by an element of Symbolist mystery.

43

Right Plate from *Documents de Bijouterie et Orfèvrerie Modernes*, a folio of designs by Paul Follot published around 1900-5. Follot showed considerable graphic sophistication in his work for La Maison Moderne.

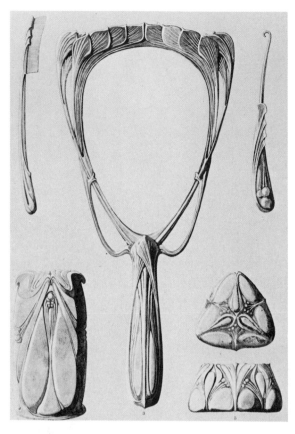

Right The dining-room displayed by Samuel Bing in his Pavillon de l'Art Nouveau at the Exposition Universelle of 1900 in Paris. The furniture and lower frieze were designed by Eugène Gaillard and the murals painted by José Maria Sert.

direction to the work of a group of highly gifted designers, notably Edouard Colonna, Eugène Gaillard and Georges de Feure. An artist of exceptional refinement, de Feure designed in many media and his furniture, fabrics, graphics, stained glass, ceramics and other objects demonstrate his mastery of elegant line, proportion and colour. His tautly delineated women are characteristic of Parisian Art Nouveau at its most sophisticated, combining an exquisite graphic refinement with a decadent, oppressive symbolism.

The high point of Bing's contribution to Art Nouveau was his pavilion at the 1900 Exposition Universelle, a series of richly decorated rooms by Gaillard, Colonna and de Feure, photographs of which survive as a perfect evocation of Art Nouveau in Paris. But by 1905, the year of Bing's death, the style which he had been so instrumental in promoting already seemed outmoded, the victim to some extent of its own curvilinear excesses.

Bing was the most significant though not the only commercial patron of the new style. A rival establishment, La Maison Moderne run by Julius Meier-Graefe, brought together the work of both French and foreign designers. The premises, opened in 1898, were designed by a Belgian, Henry

van de Velde, in a dynamic, abstract, linear mode. Paul Follot and Maurice Dufrène were the most distinguished Frenchmen in Meier-Graefe's team of designers.

Art Nouveau was an all-embracing style, finding expression on every scale from architecture to jewellery. Its characteristics, and the achievements of its leading exponents, were disseminated and popularized in the pages of the illustrated journals which had come into being in the 1890s, notably *Art et Décoration* and *L'Art Décoratif*. By 1900 the aesthetic ideals which had heralded the movement were being translated into a superficial and seductive commercial mode appropriate to ephemeral graphics, decorative bibelots and restaurant interiors, of which no finer example survives than the interior of Maxim's in Paris.

The most prolific and talented popularizer of Art Nouveau was the Paris-based Czech graphic artist Alphonse Mucha. His posters and decorative lithographs, on the eternal themes of women and flowers, combined brilliant draughtsmanship, bold stylizations and emphatic outlines with a hothouse voluptuousness. Perhaps the most individualistic Art Nouveau designer in Paris was Hector Guimard, the designer of the Métro

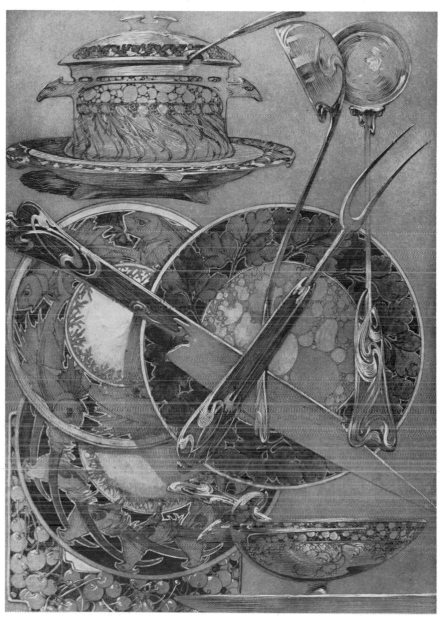

stations, whose architectural schemes, furniture, interiors, graphics and other designs transformed the idea of organic form into a truly sculptural exercise.

In the years around 1900 a variety of objects were produced in Paris which brought together the fluid graphic stylishness of Art Nouveau and the finest traditions of French craftsmanship. Inspired by the new style, the crafts were at a high point. These were years of experiment and achievement in the *arts du feu*, the crafts of glass and ceramics. Emile Gallé from Nancy set new standards of creativity and became an internationally celebrated figure. Less well-known artists followed their own paths of experiment: at Sèvres, Albert-Louis Dammouse fired vessels of the utmost fragility in a brittle,

Above Design for tableware by Alphonse Mucha from the folio *Documents Décoratifs* published in 1902. Mucha's graphics enjoyed great popularity in Paris around 1900.

Left Design for wallpaper by Hector Guimard for the Castel Béranger, a project started in 1895 and completed in 1898.

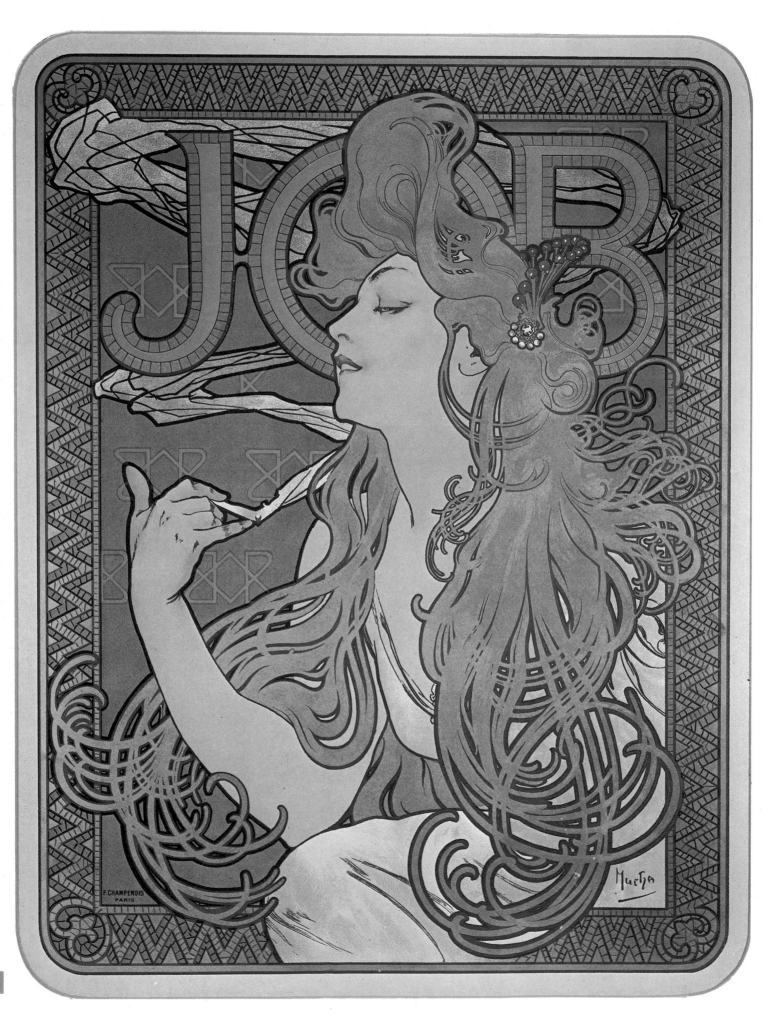

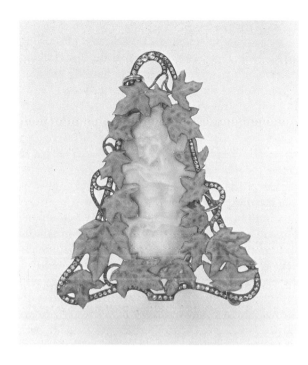

wafer-thin *pâte d'émail*; other fine Sèvres porcelain was decorated in delicate pastels to the designs of de Feure and Colonna.

There was also a fashion for sculptural objects, lamps, *videpoches*, paper-knives, lock-plates or clock-cases, featuring languid Art Nouveau maidens with flowing hair and clinging draperies, amid tendrils and flowers. Maurice Bouval, Raoul Larche, Alexandre Charpentier and Leo Laporte-Blairsy created pieces of considerable merit.

The most dazzling combinations of design and craftsmanship, however, are to be found in the work of the leading jewellers and enamellers of the day, Georges Fouquet, Eugène Feuillâtre, the brothers Henri and Paul Vever and, most especially, René Lalique. The hallmark of Lalique's approach was his bold combination of precious and non-precious materials, gold with carved horn, silver with opalescent glass, precious with semi precious stones or baroque pearls. Materials were employed for their contrasts of colour and texture, the effects enhanced with the superb enamels for which he became justly renowned. Lalique's jewels, often large in scale, show a supremely sophisticated sense of line and design and were conceived as endless variations on the fashionable themes of stylized flowers, insects, animal and human figures. He was an artist–craftsman in the great tradition of the virtuoso goldsmiths of the Renaissance. His versatility was evident in the decoration of his new premises in 1902 in the Cours la Reine, where stucco friezes, carved wood bannisters and wrought-iron balconies demonstrate his unique

ability to bring grace, refinement and imagination to every aspect of decorative design.

Georges Fouquet, a gifted designer of jewellery in his own right, became head of the family business in 1895. His most notable contribution to Art Nouveau was the fruit of his collaboration with Alphonse Mucha, who created the decorations and facade for Fouquet's Rue Royale shop in 1901 and designed a series of spectacular jewels to be executed by Fouquet.

The intellectual origins of French Art Nouveau were to some extent eclipsed by the pursuit of style and luxury for their own sake. High ideals for the revitalization of the applied arts belied the reality of exquisite creations, finely crafted for a privileged few, and a still prevalent mediocrity in mass production. Art Nouveau became a decadent style,

Above right Hair comb by René Lalique, around 1900; carved horn, mother-of-pearl and enamel on gold. This is a typical Lalique combination of precious and non-precious materials.

Above left Pendant by René Lalique, around 1900; gold, enamel and diamonds.

Opposite Poster by Alphonse Mucha for the cigarette-paper manufacturer Job, 1896. This lithograph, with its rich gold details, has the quality of a secular icon. Mucha's work shows endless varitions on the themes of women and flowers.

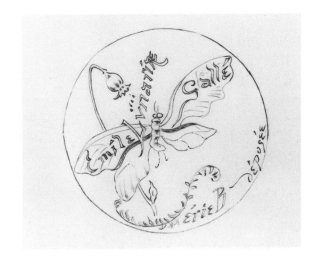

Right Designs for signatures by Emile Gallé, late 1890s, for use on the glassware produced in his workshops.

Right Silver vase, richly decorated in enamels, by Eugène Feuillâtre, around 1900. Feuillâtre, who learned his skills under René Lalique, was one of the leading exponents of enamelling, a craft which enjoyed a revival and was taken to new heights of technical virtuosity in the Art Nouveau period.

a cult of the precious, paralleling the Beardsley era in Britain in its pursuit of artifice. The leading artists were supported by wealthy and refined patrons, none more remarkable than the aesthete Count Robert de Montesquiou, whose portrait by Boldini typifies the *fin-de-siècle* dandy with highly developed sensibilities. Lalique found the ideal patron in Calouste Gulbenkian, who offered an open commission for whatever Lalique could create for him. As a result, the Gulbenkian Foundation in Lisbon now houses a collection of over one hundred examples of Lalique's work.

Feminine beauty and symbolic notions of the Eternal Feminine were favourite preoccupations of Art Nouveau artists, and a number of contemporary celebrities, including the actress Sarah Bernhardt and the dancer Loïe Fuller, assumed the role of Muses. Bernhardt was the inspiration for jewellery by Fouquet and a memorable series of posters by Mucha. Loïe Fuller performed a dance with swirling, diaphanous veils which, in the play of electric light, transformed her into the very embodiment of Art Nouveau. Many sought to capture the ephemeral magic of this performance, among them the graphic artists Jules Chéret, Toulouse-Lautrec and Manuel Orazi, and the sculptors Raoul Larche and Théodore Rivière. The dancer Cléo de Mérode, like Loïe Fuller, performed at the Exposition Universelle and had her own admirers, who attempted to express her enigmatic beauty in various media. Edith la Sylphe wrapped herself in a fabric decorated with fashionable peacock feathers to pose for the camera, her slender body contorted into Art Nouveau curves.

The town of Nancy in Lorraine, through the genius of Emile Gallé, became a centre of activity to rival Paris in the applied and decorative arts. Gallé had taken over the running of a family faience and glass factory, and by 1900, having added furniture to the range of his production, had earned a reputation as one of the most gifted contemporary figures in the area of the applied arts in France.

Gallé was a poet—learned, passionate, sensitive—and a ceaseless experimenter, pushing the medium of glass to previously unknown limits of technical complexity in his efforts to explore its expressive potential. At the very basis of his art was a love of nature. His collected writings, published posthumously in 1908 as *Ecrits pour l'Art*, demonstrate his tenderness and humanity as an advocate of richly symbolic naturalism, as well as his expertise as a chemist and horticulturalist. His motto, carved into the factory doors, was 'Ma racine est au fond des bois' (my roots are in the depths of the woods).

Left Design for a mask by L. Weldon Hawkins, around 1900. Hawkins, an English artist working in Paris, designed a series of masks based on the features of the leading actresses and beauties of the day.

Count Montesquiou was a great admirer of Gallé, introducing him into the exclusive precincts of Parisian salon society and, in his 1897 essay *Orfèvre et Verrier*, praising his work along with that of Lalique. Other clients and patrons of Gallé included Marcel Proust, Princesse Bibesco, Comtesse Greffulhe and the French government, which bought major pieces directly for its own museums and commissioned others as gifts of state.

Gallé deplored the frenzied excesses of Art Nouveau, which he witnessed at the 1900 Exposition Universelle, but his work of this period still reflects the influence of the fashionable style. His own display at the exhibition represents a peak in his career, but unfortunately he died shortly afterwards in 1904.

He inspired numerous local artists and in 1901 formed an association, L'Ecole de Nancy, to

promote shared ideals. Among his contemporaries, the work of the Daum brothers deserves mention; the decorative qualities of their glass were achieved by technical feats that would never have been attempted but for Gallé's example. Another, Louis Majorelle, proved himself an outstanding furniture designer. Taking his cue from Gallé's advocacy of a return to nature as a source of inspiration, he created full, fluid forms, treating wood as a plastic material. His salon, bureau and bedroom suites with gilt-bronze mounts from the first years of the century rank alongside the finest furniture of any period in the vigour of their forms and the luxury of their materials.

Other, more individualistic, variations on Art Nouveau were explored by Antonio Gaudí in Spain, and Carlo Bugatti, first in Milan then in Paris. Gaudí, though primarily an architect, also designed furniture and metalwork, usually for his own buildings. In these he developed his own version of Art Nouveau, eccentric, baroque and highly plastic. Bugatti is known for extravagant, vellum-covered, inlaid wood furniture, strongly Middle Eastern in appearance. For the Turin International Exhibition of 1902 he created furniture entirely covered in decorated vellum. His triumph was the Snail Room in which the continuous seating followed a sinuous course around the room and formed a giant snail-shell in the centre. Bugatti's most refined creations were the silver vessels conceived in the period following his move to Paris in about 1904. Finely executed by Hébrard, they incorporated a bizarre menagerie of stylized insects and beasts, real and imagined.

In Italy Art Nouveau was called the 'stile Liberty' after the well-known shop in London. Its leading exponent was Eugenio Quarti with his restrained use of formalized floral inlays and curvilinear structure.

Art Nouveau and progressive design movements

Art Nouveau in France tended to be primarily decorative, espousing costly materials and dependent on fine craftsmanship; but in Belgium, Vienna and Germany various progressive design movements went beyond this somewhat superficial style and made serious attempts to solve the problems of design in an industrial age.

At the turn of the century Belgium enjoyed considerable prosperity, drawing on the wealth created by the natural resources of its colonies. In the political sphere an influential liberal voice, taking up the cause of the Parti Ouvrier Belge, found a cultural rallying point in Art Nouveau. These middle-class intellectuals saw in the ideals

Opposite Gilt-bronze lamp by Raoul Larche, around 1900. One of the countless works created around 1895-1900 on the theme of Loïe Fuller, whose performances would seem, on the evidence of surviving graphics, photographs and sculpture, to have been the living embodiment of the flowing forms of Art Nouveau.

Left Glass vase conceived by Emile Gallé and made in his Nancy glassworks, around 1902-4. The vessel incorporated a stylized landscape in the difficult *marqueterie sur verre* technique, seen through high-relief, applied glass tree-trunks.

Above The Snail Room designed by Carlo Bugatti for the Turin International Exhibition of 1902. The furnishings in this eccentric manifestation of Art Nouveau are entirely covered in painted vellum.

which lay behind Art Nouveau the foundations of a democratic, rational approach to design, which could be applied to both the decorative arts and industrial production.

Other principles of Art Nouveau—the study of nature and the notion of truth to materials—were applied with conviction in the work of Belgium's two pre-eminent designers, Victor Horta and Henry van de Velde, both of whom also worked as architects. The Parti Ouvrier Belge commissioned Horta to design their Maison du Peuple, built between 1896 and 1899. He and van de Velde aimed to create a total environment, concerning themselves with every detail of applied design, van de Velde even designing the clothes to be worn in his interiors. Their work was a sincere attempt to apply the teachings of Viollet-le-Duc and William Morris to a fashionable mode, and although the necessarily costly end-products fell short of this democratic ideal, they demonstrated nonetheless a considered approach to the relationships of form and function, structure and decoration.

These two designers evolved a vigorous version of Art Nouveau, with a predilection for a more rhythmic, abstracted use of line than their French contemporaries. The linear strength in Belgian Art Nouveau was a feature of distinguished graphics in the posters of Privat-Livemont, Henri Meunier, Fernand Toussaint and others. A further influence on decorative artists was the Belgian Symbolist movement. Symbolist themes appeared in the multi-media pieces of the master jeweller Philippe Wolfers and in many decorative objects incorporating carved ivory, then imported from the Congo and highly fashionable.

In Vienna there emerged the dynamic group of artists and designers whose collective efforts created an important design movement, the Sezession, with far-reaching influence. In its purist mode the Vienna style suggested a course for twentieth-century functionalist design; in its richer, more decorative mode it confirmed Vienna as an internationally significant centre for the applied arts.

The Sezessionists aimed to revitalize the applied arts, as well as architecture, developing new

decorative themes and a true harmony between designers and manufacturers. The director of the Vienna School of Applied Arts, Felician Freiherr von Myrback, was sympathetic to their ideals and, by appointing Sezessionists to teaching posts, instilled the ideals of the movement in a whole generation of students.

The Vienna Sezessionists created a visual vocabulary for the applied arts with clear national characteristics. Their ambitions, however, shared common roots with other progressive design movements in Great Britain, Germany and the United States, as well as with van de Velde's intellectual, pared-down version of Art Nouveau in Belgium. The Viennese were just one part of an international revolutionary movement in the applied arts, of which John Ruskin and William Morris were revered ideological precursors. In its early stages the Vienna style combined richness of detail with vigour of line, but as the ideological fervour waned and commercial exigencies dictated a more decorative style, the movement lost its taut strength and its work became whimsical.

In 1900 Hoffmann had invited Charles Rennie Mackintosh to exhibit alongside the Sezessionists. The influence on the Viennese group was dramatic and Mackintosh's rectilinear approach was adopted immediately as the basis for the new Sezessionist style. Mackintosh and Hoffmann were brought together again in 1902, commissioned by the wealthy banker and art patron Fritz Warndorfer to design, respectively, a music-room and dining-room for his home.

In 1903 Hoffmann and Koloman Moser, with the financial backing of Fritz Warndorfer, founded the Wiener Werkstätte, a craft cooperative on the model of Ashbee's Guild of Handicraft. The Werkstätte, however, proved more versatile and achieved greater commercial success than its British counterpart.

Initially the Werkstätte produced furniture and metalwork of great sophistication in the geometric style inspired by Mackintosh, even the more opulent creations being characterized by carefully disciplined form and decoration. Both Hoffmann and Moser designed dramatic silverware in this

Above **The interior of the Havana Cigar Store, Berlin, designed by Henry van de Velde in 1900. The rhythmic play of taut, abstract line, characteristic of van de Velde's work, is used to fine effect in this commercial interior scheme.**

Below The interior of the Hôtel van Eetvelde, designed by Victor Horta in 1895. This view, through stained-glass doors to a vaulted glass canopy, demonstrates Horta's sensitive handling of light and space.

period, often on strict geometric grids of horizontal and vertical lines. Both displayed versatility in furniture design, creating, when occasion allowed, richly detailed furniture in exotic woods, yet were equally successful in applying their design skills to the problems of inexpensive series production by the firms of Thonet and J. & J. Kohn.

In 1906 Moser left the Werkstätte. This was the turning point, the beginning of a move away from the purist style promoted by Moser and Hoffmann towards the more decorative style that became associated with the Werkstätte after the arrival of Dagobert Peche in 1915. The Palais Stoclet was the

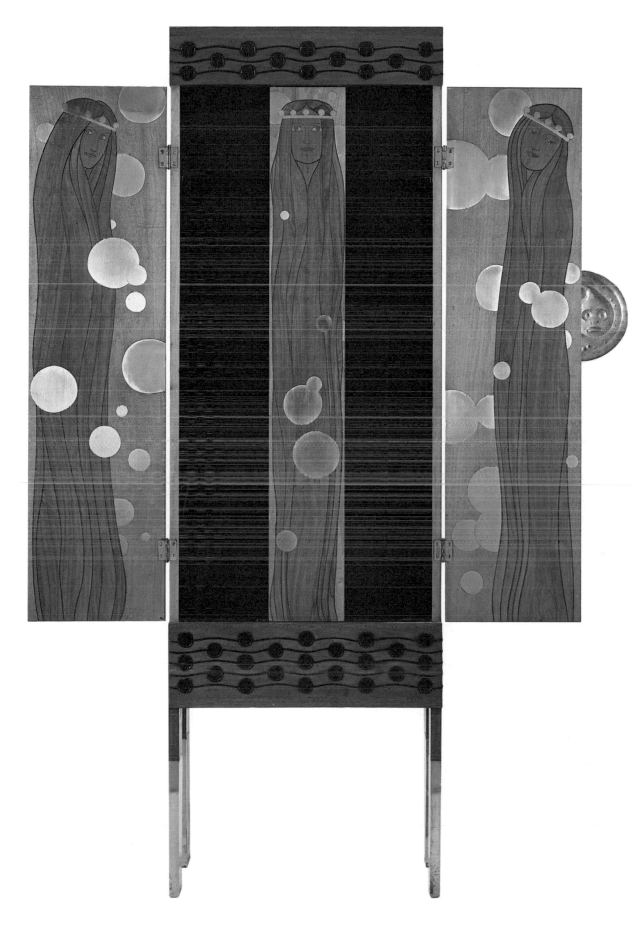

Opposite above right Corner detail and chair in the Hôtel van Eetvelde, designed by Victor Horta in 1895.

Opposite below right Letterbox in the door of the Brussels house which Horta designed in 1898 for his own use. The house is now preserved as the Musée Horta

Left Cabinet designed by Koloman Moser, 1900. A three-legged, corner version of this cabinet was presented by Moser in the eighth exhibition of the Vienna Sezession. The cabinet's decoration is characteristic of Moser's Art Nouveau phase; its form anticipates the trend towards rectilinearity in the years from 1900 to 1906.

Right The hall and staircase of the Palais Stoclet in Brussels. Designed by Josef Hoffmann, the work was executed by the craftsmen of the Wiener Werkstätte between 1905 and 1911.

Below A photograph of Mathilde Flöge around 1905 in a costume designed by herself, probably in collaboration with Gustav Klimt. She is wearing jewellery by Hoffman and is standing before a cabinet by Moser.

supreme achievement of the Werkstätte, a collective project in whose sumptuous interiors could be seen the talents of the Viennese avant-garde at the peak of its creativity.

Art Nouveau enjoyed a brief but exotic flowering in Germany around 1900; a distinctive style evolved which, while exploring the curvilinear elements and the formalized natural motifs of French and Belgian Art Nouveau, remained essentially graphic and two-dimensional rather than sculptural. It became known as Jugendstil, a label taken from the title of a new art journal *Jugend*. This publication, founded in Munich in 1896, and a rival journal *Pan*, founded the previous year in Berlin by Julius Meier-Graefe, were influential in disseminating the fashionable new decorative style throughout Europe.

Munich was the leading artistic centre, and the group of artists based there included Hermann Obrist, August Endell, Richard Riemerschmid, Otto Eckmann and Peter Behrens. Obrist's 'whiplash' cyclamen-embroidered wall-hanging of 1895 and Endell's decorative facades for the Elvira Photographic Studio of 1897 are often cited as masterpieces of the early, organic Art Nouveau phase of Jugendstil. Behrens and Eckmann created sensual graphics of considerable delicacy.

This phase was short-lived and was soon superseded by a less florid and literary mode. The somewhat shadowy figure of Julius Meier-Graefe evidently played an important role in the development of Jugendstil and his intellectual approach encouraged a move away from the decorative elements of Art Nouveau, which had at first found favour, towards a more dynamic, abstract style. He was instrumental in encouraging van de Velde's democratic ideals and belief in functional form and decoration, theories which were to have a considerable impact in Germany in the period up to 1914.

Van de Velde was much influenced by the English Arts and Crafts movement and, in 1901, was invited by Grand Duke Wilhelm of Sachsen-Weimar to set up an arts and crafts school. Here, designers and craftsmen would develop not individually made luxury items but well-designed ob-

jects for series production. This Weimar school was to re-emerge after the First World War under the direction of Walter Gropius as the Bauhaus.

Achievements in the decorative and applied arts in Germany and Austria were disseminated through the various new art journals then popular in culturally aware circles. The Austrian *Ver Sacrum*, first published in 1898, presented the early, Art Nouveau-influenced phase of Vienna Sezessionist work, distinctly similar to that illustrated in *Pan* and *Jugend*. The progress of the applied arts was documented in *Kunst und Handwerk* and *Dekorative Kunst*, both published in Munich, the latter by Meier-Graefe.

In Darmstadt, the influential publisher Alexander Koch published *Deutsche Kunst und Dekoration*. The artists' colony at Darmstadt, in Mathildenhöhe, as well as providing Olbrich and Behrens with architectural work also stimulated experiments in the decorative arts. Behrens started to design and decorate his own house in 1901 and applied himself to the treatment of every detail from the structure to the crockery. The Darmstadt colony flourished until 1914, fostering a group of imaginative designers whose work covered a wide range of fashionable styles, from the most fluid, organic Art Nouveau to the most rigid geometry. A strong unifying thread can be traced through the

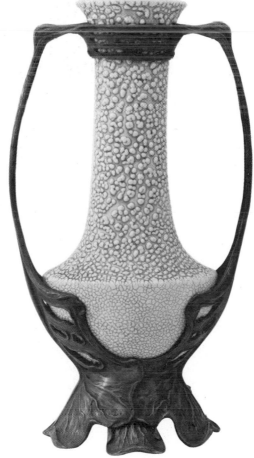

Left Ceramic vase in a bronze mount, designed by Otto Eckmann, around 1900. Eckmann was one of a group of designers who worked in the Art Nouveau style in Munich at this period.

work of Olbrich, Behrens and their colleagues, of whom perhaps the most talented was Hans Christiansen. The Darmstadt style at its most characteristic is a sophisticated development of Jugendstil, relying on the dynamic, rhythmic interplay of abstract form and line.

Progressive design in the United States

The progressive design movements in Europe which marked the period around 1900 had their counterparts in the United States in the work of a small number of designers who embraced a fluid, decorative, Art Nouveau style and others who took their lead from Great Britain from the teachings of Ruskin and Morris and from the model of the Arts and Crafts movement. Their contribution to modern design deserves attention, for in their ranks were artists of merit such as Louis Comfort Tiffany, Will Bradley, Gustav Stickley, the Greene brothers and, of course, Frank Lloyd Wright. Their radical ideas were not popular, however, in turn-of-the-century America, where new fortunes sought the prestige of traditional styles, and the intellectual satisfaction of promoting the avant-garde seemed less attractive to most potential patrons than a display of historicist opulence.

Above Clock designed by Joseph Olbrich, around 1902; cherrywood inlaid with fruitwood and ivory. Olbrich, who had been instrumental in founding the Vienna Sezession, moved to Darmstadt and exerted a strong influence on the Darmstadt version of Art Nouveau.

Near right Decorative lithograph designed by Hans Christiansen, around 1900. Christiansen was among the most versatile and talented of the Darmstadt artists.

Far right: The Chap-Book, a poster designed by Will Bradley, 1895. Bradley was one of the leading exponents of Art Nouveau in American graphics in the 1890s and his style owes much to Aubrey Beardsley.

American Art Nouveau was best expressed in the graphic arts and in the decorative glass and lamps created by Louis Comfort Tiffany. The most influential figure in the graphic arts, especially in the design of posters, was George Frederick Scotson-Clark, who arrived in 1891 from England where he had been a contemporary of Aubrey Beardsley at Brighton Grammar School. The Beardsley influence on his work was very strong and Beardsley's dramatic stylizations, swirling lines and Japanese-influenced flat areas of tone were the single greatest influence on the American school of poster artists. This new school, which flourished from 1894, had no finer exponent than Will Bradley, whose work was marked by an evident self-confidence of line and a distinctive character despite the obvious debt to Beardsley.

Through the nineties and the early 1900s, Bradley was kept busy with commissions for posters and book and magazine covers, and with his work as an art editor of several magazines. Edward Penfield and Louis Rhead, among the most able of Bradley's contemporaries, worked in similar vein, while Maxfield Parrish developed a more personal style, bringing a lyrical charm to his posters, decorative prints and book illustrations.

Louis Comfort Tiffany acquired his own glass furnaces in 1892. With a team of craftsmen, he developed remarkable skills in working hot glass, evolving rich iridescent effects in gold and peacock hues, devising dazzling techniques of internal decoration. His glass vessels and leaded glass and bronze lamps, marketed from the mid-nineties and popular up to the time of his retirement in 1919, were the embodiment of Art Nouveau. Here was a perfect synthesis of form and decoration in designs which firmly rejected historicism, taking instead nature as their source of inspiration.

The American Arts and Crafts movement was promoted by cultural exchanges with Britain, by exhibitions, by the visits of American designers to meet their British mentors and the return visits of various British designers. Ideas also spread through various new journals on the model of the British *The Studio*. Two leading lights of the movement in America, Gustav Stickley and Gilbert Hubbard, had both found inspiration from their travels in Britain and elsewhere in Europe.

Stickley founded his Craftsman Workshops in Syracuse in 1900 and started publishing a journal, *The Craftsman*, in 1901. He translated his ideals into sturdy, well-proportioned, puritanically severe furniture, yet failed to manufacture his designs at a price which was accessible to the wide market he wished to reach. In 1915 he was declared

Left Armchair of oak and leather, designed by Gustav Stickley and made in his workshops, around 1910. Puritanically austere forms, though not without a certain elegance, characterize the American Arts and Crafts furniture of Gustav Stickley.

Below Detail of the richly coloured, leaded glass of a lampshade manufactured in the studios of Louis Comfort Tiffany around 1900.

Opposite **The Winter Garden of the Ritz Hotel in London, designed by Mewès & Davies in 1904. This displays opulence in the grand tradition with neo-classical columns and furniture and typically Edwardian trellis friezes and palms.**

Right **Detail of a leaded glass panel from the lobby of the Francis Little house, Wayzata, designed by Frank Lloyd Wright in 1913.**

bankrupt. Hubbard founded a craft community at East Aurora in 1895, establishing first a fine press, the Roycroft Press, on the model of Kelmscott, and subsequently extending its scope to include other crafts. On the West Coast, the brothers Charles and Henry Greene showed imagination as domestic architects, creating total environments in a refined blend of Japanese and quasi-rustic elements.

Rising above the ebb and flow of fashion was the isolated genius of Frank Lloyd Wright. An architect and designer of great vision, Wright avoided any current style, while still appreciating the need for decoration, and he pursued a personal ideal of harmonious, low-key interiors which satisfied both functional and spiritual requirements. Wright's career spanned more than half a century; his work, transcending fashion, has attracted considerable acclaim yet has defied imitation.

Traditional influences; folk art revivals

The progressive movements which made the applied arts so exciting and innovative at the turn of the century laid the foundations of the international Modern Movement; but they represented only one facet of the decorative arts. The utopian craftsmen who endeavoured to implement the teachings of Ruskin and Morris were a vociferous minority; while the exponents of the more decorative Art Nouveau style attracted much attention but were greatly outnumbered by their traditionalist contemporaries. John Betjeman, discussing the two poles of thought in British design, neatly contrasted 'the tweedy . . . followers of William Morris and the Art Workers' Guild . . .', whose Bible was *The Studio*, with the 'silk-hatted . . . associated with the Royal Academy, *Country Life* and the *Architectural Review*'.

A survey of civic architecture in Edwardian Britain, as elsewhere in Europe or in the United States, confirms the entrenched conservatism of official taste. Wagner's Vienna Post Office, Mackintosh's Glasgow School of Art and Gaudí's Sagrada Familia church were notable exceptions to the current Establishment preference for a familiar hotch-potch of revivalist styles.

Wealth and socialistic ideals were rarely compatible. The homes of America's new industrial barons and Europe's aristocracy and *nouveaux riches*, as well as the interiors of the luxury liners, hotels, clubs and theatres which catered to the wealthy on both sides of the Atlantic, were all characterized by a love of opulence, often in a neo-baroque vein.

In Paris and in French resorts the Beaux-Arts style flourished. Similarly in London, Arthur J. Davis and Charles Mewès, as architects and decorators, used traditionalist grandeur with considerable flair in such interiors as those of the Ritz Hotel and the Royal Automobile Club (1908-11). In the United States many new-found fortunes became associated with extreme opulence; numerous private residences, from Fifth Avenue to Newport, Rhode Island, were built and decorated in a showy hybrid manner, borrowing haphazardly from Europe's stylistic heritage and achieving an overbearing mix of luxury and vulgarity. Even Louis Comfort Tiffany succumbed to the lures of eclecticism in the elaborate decoration which he devised for his own home, Laurelton Hall. The demand for antique furniture in seventeenth- and eighteenth-century styles far outstripped supply and had to be satisfied by countless reproductions and reinterpretations. In Britain, for example, neo-Sheraton furniture enjoyed a vogue, while in France the

Below Detail of the painted decoration on a Rozenburg eggshell earthenware vase designed by J. Schellinck, 1902. These refined, delicate graphics combine Art Nouveau and Javanese batik motifs.

Paris-based cabinet-maker François Linke made virtuoso pieces in the historicist mode.

Revivalist styles were also favoured in court circles in Russia and found their most meticulously wrought, if artistically sterile, expression in the *objets de vertu* of Carl Fabergé. Meanwhile, in Russia as in Scandinavia and certain Central European states, folk art revivals provided scope for compromise by artists who shared the ideals of the Arts and Crafts movement yet were also anxious to express their national heritage. Princess Maria Tenicheva ran the most important of the Russian craftsmen's colonies at Talashkino and financed the journal *Mir Iskusstva*, published with the editorial collaboration of Serge Diaghilev. The arts of the theatre figured prominently in the Talashkino curriculum and were vigorously pro-

moted by Diaghilev. Drawing together a group of talented artists and performers, led by the designers Léon Bakst and Alexandre Benois and the dancer Vaslav Nijinsky, Diaghilev was destined to revolutionize the arts of ballet and to assume an influential role in the emergence of Art Deco.

In the Netherlands, the decorative arts were influenced by the folk art of certain Dutch colonies. The linear, decorative style associated with batik, one of the traditional arts of Java, became the basis for a distinctive Dutch version of Art Nouveau, evident in the graphics of Jan Toorop. It is also seen in the exquisite painted decorations by Juriaan Kok, J. Schellink and others on the delicate eggshell earthenware manufactured by the Rozenburg factory.

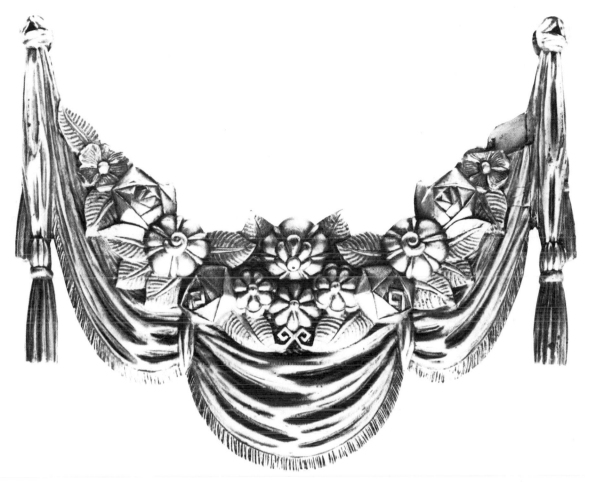

The roots of Art Deco

Art Deco has become a much abused label, all too often used as a catch-all phrase to describe the wide variety of styles to be found in the applied arts of the twenties and thirties. Interest in this period began in the late 1960s and was encouraged by a number of publications. Certain still prevalent misconceptions have their origins in the conflicting use of terms by different authors, not least the varied applications of the label Art Deco.

The most rational use of the term is that proposed by Martin Battersby in his book *The Decorative Twenties*, published in 1969. He defines Art Deco as a specifically French manifestation in the applied arts '. . . which lasted from approximately 1910 until 1925, the year of the important exhibition of the decorative arts in Paris which at once gave the style its name, demonstrated the culmination of the style and, in the same way that the 1900 Exhibition had sounded the knell for Art Nouveau, saw its passing'. Battersby's intimate knowledge of Art Nouveau and its contemporary styles enabled him to analyze Art Deco and to examine its complex roots in such varied influences as the Wiener Werkstätte, the Munich Werkbund, the Ballets Russes and the revival of interest in French eighteenth-century design after the anti-historicist pose of Art Nouveau.

These ideas have also been explored at source by Yvonne Brunhammer of the Musée des Arts Décoratifs, Paris. Her catalogue to the Museum's 1976 'Exposition Cinquantenaire de l'Exposition de 1925' provides a clear analysis of the pre-war emergence of Art Deco, its delayed apotheosis in 1925, the varied influences which shaped the style and which gradually enlarged its vernacular, and its eventual eclipse in favour of the Modernist style.

By about 1905 Art Nouveau had lost its fashionable appeal and the applied arts in France were on the wane, but the emergence of Art Deco reasserted French supremacy. The foundation of the Société des Artistes Décorateurs in 1901 marked the very first stage of this evolution and the society, through its regular autumn exhibitions or *Salons* provided an increasingly important showcase for contemporary designers and craftsmen. Prominent among these were Paul Follot and Maurice Dufrène, both of whom, in the period around 1905, were rejecting the curvilinear excesses of Art Nouveau and looking back to the late eighteenth century for inspiration, so laying the foundations for Art Deco.

Below 'Jewish dancer', a design by Léon Bakst for *Cléopatre*, 1910. Bakst was one of the most brilliant of the designers who collaborated with Diaghilev in the staging of the Ballets Russes, which took Paris by storm in 1910.

The complexity of sources which shaped Art Deco and the idiosyncracies of individual designers make it difficult to define the style; yet certain characteristic motifs emerged which well express its nature. The extravagant, asymmetrical curves of Art Nouveau were replaced by more restrained lines, and a variety of neo-classical symbols, swags, garlands, reeded columns, formalized flowers, bouquets and scrolls became popular. The work of the artist Paul Iribe in the years before the First World War epitomize this new style.

One particular motif, the formalized rose, was first used by Mackintosh and then by the artists of Vienna and *Die Kunst*, before being adopted by Iribe and his contemporaries. This illustrates well the eclectic sources of Art Deco, and by the outbreak of war in 1914, these diverse influences had rapidly become unified into a style which already had a well-defined national character.

The first Paris productions staged by Diaghilev's Ballets Russes were a powerful culture shock. The most spectacular of all was *Schéhérazade* of 1910, a tale of passion in an exotic orientalist setting for which Léon Bakst created costumes and sets dazzling with vibrant colours and exotic flourishes. The impact in fashionable circles was dramatic and the repercussions in many aspects of the applied arts considerable, in fashion design and illustration, interior design and graphics. The Ballets Russes provided an exhilarating new palette of vibrant colours and inspired a taste for the exotic. Among the first to respond to this influence was the couturier Paul Poiret, whose name is central to the story of Art Deco. Poiret had founded his own *maison de couture* in 1903 after working for Jacques Doucet. He favoured a fluid, unrestricted line, liberating the body from tight corsetry. In 1908 he published *Les Robes de Paul Poiret racontées par Paul Iribe*, a book of his fashion designs drawn by a talented young artist and designer who was also to be a significant figure in the story of Art Deco.

In 1911 Poiret published a second volume *Les Choses de Paul Poiret vues par Georges Lepape*. Here, drawn with the utmost grace by the gifted Lepape, was a fashionable adaptation of the Ballets Russes featuring harem costumes, turbans and aigrettes in the clashing oranges and other lively colours associated with Bakst. Another influential project was his founding of the Atelier Martine in 1912 as a design studio and craft workshop involved with all aspects of decorative design. Poiret had travelled in Germany and Austria in 1909 and, inspired by the example of the Wiener Werkstätte, was determined to set up his own workshops along similar lines. The Atelier Martine promoted a taste for bold, stylized floral motifs, Fauve colours and exotic interiors evocative of mythical harems.

Poiret was not alone in being impressed by the sense of purpose and teamwork in German and Austrian designers. In 1910 the Munich Werkbund mounted an exhibition in Paris. Although not necessarily to French taste the exhibits nonetheless presented a unified character, reflecting a successful attempt to train designers in the methods of industrial production. The following year

proposals were put before the French Senate for a major international exhibition which would encourage a similar approach to design and manufacture in France. In 1912 plans were finalized for an exhibition to take place in 1915, but the outbreak of war resulted in an inevitable postponement. Meanwhile, however, the full idiom of Art Deco was taking form. In 1912 the couturier Jacques Doucet sold his collection of paintings and antique furniture, having decided instead to patronize contemporary artists and designers and to decorate his home as the most avant-garde embodiment of modern design. Paul Iribe was invited to supervise the installation of rooms with furniture by Pierre Legrain, Eileen Gray and others, all fresh talents who found in Doucet their first major patron. The 1910 Salon des Artistes Décorateurs was the first occasion on which Jacques-Emile Ruhlmann presented his furniture. The cabinet exhibited at the 1916 salon, with its spectacular bouquet of formalized flowers inlaid in ivory and ebony, is a perfect expression of Art Deco.

Right Corner cabinet designed by Jacques-Emile Ruhlmann, 1916; burr amboyna inlaid with ebony and ivory. The central motif in this cabinet, an early masterpiece in Ruhlmann's career, is the distillation of Art Deco.

Left **Painted screen by Vanessa Bell, 1913. Dating from the first year of the Omega Workshops, the bold, angular abstractions of this study of figures in a landscape anticipate the geometric styles which were to be popular fifteen years later.**

If one is to look for pre-war parallels with French Art Deco elsewhere in Europe, the most obvious comparisons are with the work of the artists of the Wiener Werkstätte evolving from their early austerity towards a more decorative vein. An interesting parallel can also be drawn between the Atelier Martine and the Omega Workshops in Britain. Omega, founded in the summer of 1913, was a group of artists who tried to synthesize the fine and applied arts, drawing together Arts and Crafts ideas with the painterly influences of Post-Impressionism. Duncan Grant, Vanessa Bell, Roger Fry and their colleagues created furniture and furnishings, fabrics, decorative panels and screens, pottery and other objects, all boldly painted with bright formalized flowers, Matisse-like nudes and abstract motifs reflecting a knowledge of Cubist art. Omega products show a wilfully primitive charm but tend to be shoddy. The venture came to an end in 1919.

Wyndham Lewis was a rebel within the Omega group, isolated by his fervent futuristic ideas. These took form through the Vorticist group, in which he played a central role, and in the two issues of his manifesto magazine *Blast*, published in 1914 and 1915. His dynamic, geometrical abstractions bypassed the decorative concerns of Omega and Art Deco, anticipating the cult of the machine in the applied arts. While Art Deco was in full bloom, parallel movements, Vorticism in Britain, De Stijl in the Netherlands, Suprematism in Russia, Futurism in Italy, and the activities of the Weimar school were already heralding the end of this fertile period in the decorative arts in France.

INDUSTRIAL DESIGN

Before the industrial revolution there had been craftsmen and artisans and artists. Each had more or less total control over whatever they created: from the original conception to the execution, an object or a work of art was the product of one individual's imagination and skills. But mass production brought about the division of labour, and manufacturing processes became so complicated and sophisticated that a single individual could no longer expect to be in charge of the creation of an artifact. This structural change introduced a new approach to design.

Although the word has been used since at least the fifteenth century, when Italian writers spoke of 'disegno' in describing the quality of line possessed by an image or artifact, in all essentials 'design' is an industrial or post-industrial concept. With the introduction of mass-production, the people who invented ideas for objects became separated from the people who made them who, again, were separated from the people who sold them. The industrial revolution also created the concept of the market. Personal need, or the whims of a patron, were replaced by a more abstract demand: the tastes of a large, amorphous body of consumers.

The modern designer came into being as an intermediary between industry and the consumer. His role was to adapt the products of industry to the mass market, to make them more useful and durable, perhaps, but to make them more appealing and commercially successful, certainly. Commercial success is the touchstone of achievement in design, although designers in different cultures have often taken different views as to how the achievement is measured or the success validated.

At the beginning of this century there was a reappraisal of the relationship between 'design' and industry as a number of new theories and attitudes emerged. According to Nikolaus Pevsner (*Pioneers of Modern Design*, 1936), William Morris and the Arts and Crafts reformers, Art Nouveau with its rejection of historicism and traditional values, and the functionalism of nineteenth-century engineering were the major influences that led Gropius and others to a new set of values; the twentieth-century reformers believed that applied ornamentation, so prevalent in the former century, was inappropriate to modern industrial design, and that good design and architecture should respect modern materials and technology.

There were, of course, other factors that accounted for these changes. Germany was growing in economic and industrial importance through the development of her new steel, chemical and electrical industries, along with an active and effective state technical education programme. In Britain, far-reaching reforms in art school education had been taking place since the mid-nineteenth century. And everywhere machines were winning increasing admiration and respect, to be confirmed by their efficacy in the First World War. This, the first mechanized war, influenced design in ways both trivial and apocalyptic. At one level, the disappearance among German gunners of the clumsy fob watch introduced the wrist watch (hitherto considered effeminate); on a grander scale, the war showed that aeroplanes (hitherto considered irrelevant to warfare) were valuable tools, and this stimulated many significant developments in aerospace, which span off into mass culture and communications.

Britain: applied art and industry

Looking at the three major industrial nations at the end of the last century—Britain, Germany and the United States—it is apparent that very different attitudes to industry existed. Because the revolution in manufacturing had started first in Britain, in the later eighteenth century, it was inevitable that here disenchantment with industry would set in first. The increase in production entailed an increase in consumption, but neither event brought about an improvement in public taste. In Britain, enlightened critics believed there were moral certainties in matters of taste, and the story of design and art in the second half of Victoria's reign is one of reform and education.

Official bodies—the Department of Science and Art, for instance—set up exhibitions, museums and schools (forming the basis for the Victoria and Albert Museum and the entire art school system). These were intended to provide exemplars for young designers and for industry, and also to act as a stimulant to public taste. Such reforms in art education evolved from the idealistic approach to

Below Electroplated metal tea service designed by Christopher Dresser, 1880, manufactured by James Dixon & Sons. Dresser's unadorned, geometric forms anticipated by half a century the functionalist designs of the Bauhaus.

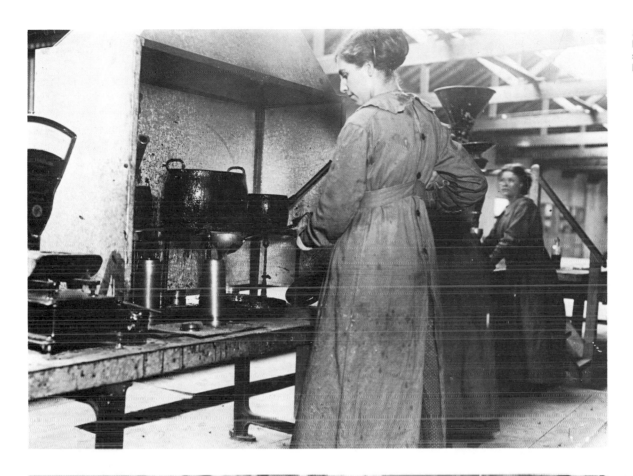

Left Shell workers at Vickers Ltd pouring resin into shrapnel shells to set the bullets, July 1915.

Left Woman munition worker during the First World War. The active role of women during the war contributed to their emancipation in the post-war years.

Right Page from Morris & Co. catalogue around 1910, showing the range of 'Sussex' rush-seated chairs. Such designs were a compromise between Morris's ideal of rustic craft and the need to produce furniture in large series to satisfy a wide market.

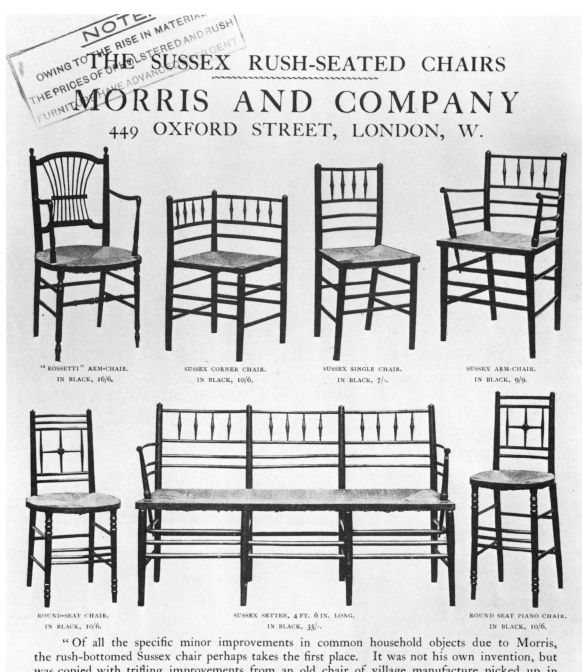

NOTE! OWING TO THE RISE IN MATERIAL THE PRICES OF UPHOLSTERED AND RUSH FURNITURE HAVE ADVANCED 10 PER CENT.

THE SUSSEX RUSH-SEATED CHAIRS
MORRIS AND COMPANY
449 OXFORD STREET, LONDON, W.

"ROSSETTI" ARM-CHAIR. IN BLACK, 16/6.

SUSSEX CORNER CHAIR. IN BLACK, 10/6.

SUSSEX SINGLE CHAIR. IN BLACK, 7/-.

SUSSEX ARM-CHAIR. IN BLACK, 9/9.

ROUND-SEAT CHAIR. IN BLACK, 10/6.

SUSSEX SETTER, 4 FT. 6 IN. LONG. IN BLACK, 35/-.

ROUND SEAT PIANO CHAIR. IN BLACK, 10/6.

"Of all the specific minor improvements in common household objects due to Morris, the rush-bottomed Sussex chair perhaps takes the first place. It was not his own invention, but was copied with trifling improvements from an old chair of village manufacture picked up in Sussex. With or without modification it has been taken up by all the modern furniture manufacturers, and is in almost universal use. But the Morris pattern of the later type (there were two) still excels all others in simplicity and elegance of proportion."

"Life of William Morris" : By Prof. *J. W. Mackail.*

63

craft and design which had been promoted by William Morris (discussed above). Morris's emphasis on 'right making' and his confused, if worthy, insistence that design and morality were all part of a larger framework of humane values influenced the creation of the Central School of Art and Design in London in 1896. This, in turn, established an objective standard for art education that was admired all over the industrialized world. But, in a pattern that was to repeat itself in different fields throughout the twentieth century, these initiatives which originated in Britain were brought to fruition abroad.

Later, in 1915, the Design and Industries Association was founded in London. Intending to stimulate high standards of design in industry, it was very much based on the Deutsche Werkbund. In the early years, however, many of its members were associated with the Arts and Crafts movement and it was less dictatorial than the stern German Werkbund. Until the late 1920s it deliberately rejected Modernism, referred to by one member as 'this modern movement in design', and concentrated instead on 'fitness for purpose'. A typical pronouncement was that of Arthur Clutton Brock, art critic of *The Times* and an enthusiastic DIA member, in his paper 'A Modern Creed of Work' (1916): 'To design a chair well is to fit it to its purpose as a thing to sit upon; and where there is not good design there cannot be art.'

William Morris who, with his followers, rejected industry and all that it represented, was largely responsible for the various prejudices that were to dog the development of an industrial culture in Britain. Morris, believing passionately that only medieval working methods could create beautiful objects and a happy, moral society, freely admitted to despising the achievements of the nineteenth century. He once remarked to a miner, 'I should be glad if we could do without coal.'

He was not alone, however, and when in the 1970s a director of the London School of Economics pointed out that Britain's industrial problems required a cultural solution, he was referring not only to Morris but also to William Arnold, author of *Culture and Anarchy*, whose values were popular with the British establishment. Arnold wrote of railways: 'Your middle-class man thinks it is the highest pitch of development and civilization when his letters are carried twelve times a day from Islington to Camberwell, and from Camberwell to Islington, and if railway trains run to and fro between them every quarter of an hour. He thinks it is nothing that the trains only carry him from an illiberal, dismal life at Islington to an illiberal, dismal life at Camberwell; and the letters only tell him that such is the life there.'

In Britain, the world's first industrial nation, the leaders of society, who often owed their wealth to industry and the mass market, were the first to abjure the city, the source of the riches they enjoyed. Rather as William Morris had boated up the Thames to Kelmscott, they escaped to the spurious gentility of the countryside. The demands of the empire were also to blame because, for generation after generation, some of the most able British students were trained not for the creation of wealth through industry, but for the administration of the colonies.

The consequences of this were to become fully apparent in the twentieth century, when the story of British industry is too often a story of failure and missed opportunities. For example, when Wilbur and Orville Wright travelled to England to sell the idea of their flying machine, they were rebuffed by the Admiralty, who saw no possible military application for the aeroplane. Similarly, the explosive growth of the major electrical companies in Germany was not matched in Britain where, until the 1920s, the major electrical engineering undertakings were foreign-owned.

Left William Morris, from a photograph by Elliot & Fry taken in 1877. Morris was a fearless propagandist for social and artistic reform, but his inspiration lay in the medieval past rather than in the industrialized, urban future.

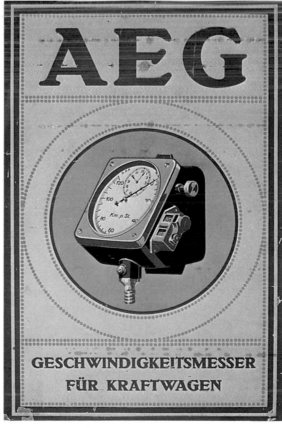

Left Poster designed by Peter Behrens for AEG in 1912. Behrens had a wide-ranging creative influence on this giant German electrical concern, for he designed not only its buildings but also its graphics and products.

C23227

Above **Gottlieb Daimler and his son Adolf in the Benz Patent Motor Car of 1886. The installation of the internal combustion engine, designed by Daimler and Wilhelm Maybach, into a 'horseless carriage' marks the birth of the automobile.**

Germany: reform in industry and education

In contrast to the backward-looking developments in Britain, Germany was undergoing structural changes that were to make it one of the leading industrial nations of this century. The great industrial enterprises of AEG and Daimler were all taking shape in the 1880s and were incorporated within a few years of each other. Perhaps the more significant of these was AEG.

AEG was founded soon after the cosmopolitan intellectual Emil Rathenau had seen Thomas Edison's incandescent light bulbs at the 1881 Exposition Internationale d'Electricité in Paris. Rathenau realized that, as a result of Edison's invention, electricity would at last replace gas as a source of lighting in the home; he also realized that it gave him an opportunity to compete with the established electrical giants, such as Walter Siemens who had perfected the dynamo. The company was first registered in 1883 and it became the Allgemeine Elektrizitäts Gesellschaft (AEG) in 1887. This is more than a footnote to German business history: it is a significant moment in the

history of design. To Rathenau electricity was a fundamental part of the new culture and was going to change the world: steam power, being mechanical, was subject to obvious restrictions in terms of how and where it could be transmitted—only so far as rods, pistons, gears and chains could reach— but electricity was fluid, flexible and virtually infinite in its range and possibilities.

It was Rathenau's AEG which showed Europe how art could best be integrated into modern industry. In July 1907 the Berlin newspapers announced that Professor Peter Behrens, the director of the School of Applied Art in Düsseldorf, had been appointed artistic adviser to AEG. In August of the same year, Behrens wrote an article called 'Kunst und Technik' in which he described his plans for AEG.

Behrens had taught at art schools both at Düsseldorf and Karlsruhe, he was an acquaintance of the artistic radicals of his day, and had become celebrated for his work as an architect and applied artist, particularly in Darmstadt. For his own house in Darmstadt, Behrens had designed every single component, from the cutlery through to the glassware and furniture; Rathenau gave him an opportunity to create an even more ambitious ensemble by inviting him to take charge of the entire appearance of his massive combine. Starting modestly enough with the design of AEG's publications, Behrens soon moved on to both consumer and capital electrical goods. According to his biographer, Tilmann Buddensieg, Behrens 'saw the applied arts as a public utility for the use of society at large'.

Rather like the Victorian reformers in Britain, Behrens hoped that the popular example of his work for AEG, with artistic control of every element of the company's character and production, would raise the level of public taste. He adapted a Venetian renaissance typeface, by Aldus Manutius, for AEG's logotype, and in his consumer goods for AEG, his lamps, kettles, fans and radiators, he eschewed both historicism and modishness, making them absolutely simple and clear. He aimed to create 'those forms that derive directly from . . . machine production'.

It was Behrens' desire to make the fruits of industry widely available, with no compromise. He did not seek style or status for his designs, only a universally acceptable level of quality. But although critics saw this as a threat to individualism, Behrens' interest in design was not without its

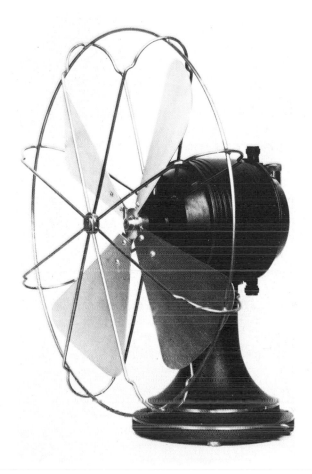

Left Electric fan designed by Behrens for AEG, 1908. Though based on an existing form, this design is uncompromisingly industrial in character; it appears to be dictated simply by function, with no concern for decorative styling.

ELEKTRISCHE TEE- UND WASSERKESSEL
NACH ENTWÜRFEN VON PROF. PETER BEHRENS

Messing vernickelt, streifenartig gehämmert runde Form				Kupfer streifenartig gehämmert runde Form				Messing streifenartig gehämmert runde Form			
PL Nr	Inhalt ca. l	Gewicht ca. kg	Preis Mk.	PL Nr	Inhalt ca. l	Gewicht ca. kg	Preis Mk.	PL Nr	Inhalt ca. l	Gewicht ca. kg	Preis Mk.
3581	0,75	0,75	19,—	3584	0,75	0,75	20,—	3582	0,75	0,75	19,—
3591	1,25	1,0	22,—	3594	1,25	1,0	24,—	3592	1,25	1,0	24,—
3601	1,75	1,1	24,—	3604	1,75	1,1	26,—	3602	1,75	1,1	25,—

ALLGEMEINE ELEKTRICITÄTS-GESELLSCHAFT
ABT. HEIZAPPARATE

Left Kettles designed by Behrens for AEG, around 1919. A small range of standard elements could be assembled in different combinations and materials at different prices.

whimsical, romantic and evocative elements. He once cautioned his readers to remember that 'a motor car should be like a birthday present'.

The ambitions about raising public taste which Peter Behrens held out at AEG were reflected on a national level throughout Germany by the formation in 1907 of the Deutsche Werkbund, which eventually became the most influential and stimulating body in the world of design. The sense of reform in the Werkbund was inherited from the English example of the century before, but, as befits the character of the people, in Germany it took a more practical form. Behrens was a founder member and passionate contributor to the Werkbund's journal *Die Form*, in which he wrote in 1922: 'We have no choice but to make our lives more simple, more practical, more organized and wide-ranging. Only through industry have we any hope of fulfilling our aims.'

The Deutsche Werkbund was founded in Munich and its aim was 'the improvement of industrial products through the combined efforts of artists, industrialists and craftworkers'. Created for education and propaganda, it intended to unite business and industry with the arts and crafts, the better to promote German exports. So although distantly imitative of the English Arts and Crafts guilds and workshops of the later nineteenth century, its purposes were altogether more modern.

By 1914 the Werkbund was ready to have its first major exhibition; this became the occasion of a fierce public debate, creating a schism which has ever since divided design. On the one hand, Hermann Muthesius, author of *Das Englische Haus* and an admirer of Prussian military discipline, supported the concept of *Typisierung*, saying that the Werkbund should encourage the design and production of standardized goods. On the other hand, Henry van de Velde promoted the idea of independent, free, creative artistic expression as the most important influence on design. In fact, the events of the First World War stimulated the standardization of industrial products and technical components far more effectively than any learned debate, and in 1916 the Deutsche Normen Ausschuss (German Standards Commission) was established.

Sweden: the Gustavsberg example

On a smaller scale, experiments in mass-produced taste similar to those at AEG were taking place in the small town of Gustavsberg just outside Stockholm. Founded in 1825, the Gustavsberg ceramic factory had been producing work in the 'National Romantic' style, with overbearing, mannered decoration inspired by Nordic folklore. But in 1896 Gunnar Wennerberg was called in to improve the quality of its production and was appointed artistic director. His influence can be seen in the refined designs that the company exhibited at the 1897 Art and Industry exhibition in Stockholm. Wennerberg's motifs were wild flowers, freshly observed as if in a painting, and in effect he was able to offer Gustavsberg's mass market a version of European Art Nouveau.

Right Publicity material for the Praktika range designed by Wilhelm Kåge for Gustavsberg, 1933. This practical stacking range was a commercial failure.

Left Gustavsberg's 'KG' service of 1917–40 by Wilhelm Kåge was conceived as a 'working man's service', but it remained traditional in form and decoration.

The appointment of Wennerberg was no less significant than that of Peter Behrens, although the effect was different. He extended the influence of art across the company's whole product line and his position as artist-in-residence created a precedent not just for Gustavsberg, but for Scandinavian industry as a whole.

Wilhelm Kåge, a painter and poster designer, joined the company in 1917. Among his first projects was the design of a 'working man's' service (known as KG in the catalogue), almost as if in direct response to Professor Gregor Paulsson's influential essay, *Vackrare Vardagsvara (More Beautiful Things for Everyday Life)*, 1919. Kåge believed that 'from the old, provincial handicrafts to the modern industrial worker's taste there are no pathways'. During his forty-three years at Gustavsberg he was responsible for many formal and functional innovations in ceramic design, which made significant contributions to the standards of living of Gustavsberg's customers, particularly through oven-to-table ware and stacking china; and he proved that quality in design is not necessarily related to cost. There is, however, an essential irony in Kåge's achievement. In 1933 he produced the functionalist, modular dinner service

Praktika, stackable and with dishes that could double as lids, with no hidden recesses to cause cleaning problems; but it proved a commercial failure, unlike the less radical, more decorative service called Pyro. In their different ways, both Behrens at AEG and Kåge at Gustavsberg pointed the way for future developments in German and Swedish industrial design.

Above and opposite right Pyro designed by Wilhelm Kåge for Gustavsberg, 1930. A graceful design that was more successful than the innovative Praktika.

75

Above The Gustavsberg factory around 1890. This company was one of the first modern industries to employ artists in its factories.

The United States: modern methods and management

In the United States the invention and perfection of mail-order marketing by Richard Sears (who founded Sears Roebuck in 1886), the refinement of mass production by Henry Ford, and the creation by Alfred P. Sloan of General Motors out of a rag-bag of refrigerator, car and agricultural equipment companies, laid the basis across the Atlantic for the vigour, vitality and popular appeal of American industrial production.

One of the most significant contributions made by America to the role of industry in twentieth-century culture was that of management science. This theory was based on Marx's examination of the production process and was developed by American work-study engineers, in a pattern of transference that reflected the geographical shift of economic power from Europe to the United States at the end of the nineteenth century.

To Karl Marx, factories and machines were 'means of producing surplus value' and of sub-jugating the work force. But he admired and was impressed by machinery and noted: 'Nature builds no machines, no locomotives, railways, electric telegraphs, self-acting mules. . . . These are products of human industry; natural material transformed into organs of the human will over nature, or of human participation in nature. They are the organs of the human brain, created by the human hand: the power of knowledge objectified.' Marx proposed an analysis of how machinery de-skills men and condemns them to conditions which approximate to slavery, because under the capitalist system workers' wages can never be the equivalent of the wealth they produce.

The most important work-study engineer was an American, Frederick Winslow Taylor, who between 1880 and 1900 originated the 'time and motion study'. In his study of how factories worked, Taylor emphasized the importance of supervision and documentation of the production process: he was scrupulously scientific in his recording of experimental results and he also insisted on handing workers *written* instructions. Taylorism, as it became known, demanded a mental revolution in which management and the work force would cease disputing and 'take their eyes off the division of the surplus . . . towards the size of the surplus'.

Yet while the doctrinaire and authoritarian character of Taylorism alienated many workers, it found a supporter in Walter Rathenau, son of the founder of AEG and later Chancellor of the Weimar Republic before his assassination in 1923. The legacy of Bismarck predisposed Rathenau to accept Taylorism, although he was careful not to mention it by name. Instead, he always referred to Taylor's most famous disciple: Henry Ford.

Henry Ford was first an employee and then a friend of Thomas Edison, whose incandescent light bulb had so attracted Emil Rathenau at the Paris exhibition. Ford was born in remote rural Michigan and the isolation of his childhood was a profound influence on his career. It is by no means untrue to assert that Ford's development of the mass-produced automobile was intended to alleviate the desolate misery of rural America.

Ford resigned his position as chief engineer of the Edison Illuminating Company in 1899 to establish his own motor company in Detroit in 1903. His aim was to produce the 'universal car', but his first eight models, the A, B, C, F, N, R, S, and K were only moderately successful. Then in 1908 came the Model T, the most simple car Ford had yet designed, and with it Ford's epochal

Below, left and right **Mass production and mass consumption characterize twentieth-century civilization. Sears Roebuck's mail order catalogue first appeared in 1896, and offered a wide range of goods to those in even the most remote rural areas.**

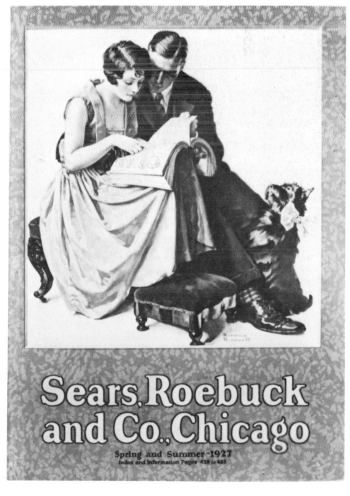

Above Henry Ford and his family in a Model T Ford of 1909-10. The Model T was his first successful design, a 'universal car' that revolutionized motoring.

Right The Citroën Type A of 1919 was Europe's first mass-produced car.

announcement: 'Any customer can have a car painted any colour that he wants so long as it is black.'

This famous statement was, however, only one aspect of a product-design programme that depended on simplicity for its success. The Model T had only four basic units—engine, chassis, front axle, rear axle—and each component was designed for 'absolute reliability . . . and simplicity in operation—because the masses are not mechanics'. The parts were made so cheaply that it was less expensive to buy new ones than have the old ones repaired. Also, these parts were to be sold in hardware stores, like nails, nuts and bolts. Ford said, 'I thought that it was up to me as the designer to make the car so completely simple that no one could fail to understand it.'

From 1914 the Model T was manufactured on production lines which were a demonstration of Frederick Taylor's principles. Taylor had said that work should be organized as an analogue of the machine process. Ford went further and replaced the human imitation of machines with machines themselves. He did not acknowledge his debt to

Taylor and later claimed, in a characteristically memorable image, that his moving production line had been inspired by the overhead trolleys used by Chicago meat-packers for dressing beef.

Ford's twenty-four-hour assembly lines were not so much a dramatic invention of his own as the culmination of a tradition of industrial experiments in America. Like Frederick Taylor, Ford gave his name to a system of values. 'Fordism' revolutionized the working process and, in turn, the way industrial products were conceived, designed and manufactured. In the course of its life final assembly time for the Model T was reduced from twelve to one and a half hours, an achievement that made a significant contribution to Ford's ambition of making the automobile available to everyone. For Ford, efficiency and high volume was everything: 'I have striven toward manufacturing with a minimum of waste, both of materials and human effort, and then toward distribution at a minimum of profit, depending for total profit upon the volume of distribution.'

Ford translated the methods and ideals of standardization into the manufacture of consumer products. The Model T was the paradigm of the mass-produced industrial product: cheap, efficient, readily available and phenomenally successful. By the time production ceased in 1927 more than sixteen million had been produced, and it was in response to this achievement that Alfred P. Sloan hired Harley Earl to give *style* to General Motors' cars, so that they might be differentiated from Ford's more utilitarian products in the market place. This was a critical moment in the history of twentieth-century style and design: the moment when one challenged the other.

Below Model T Fords in production in Trafford Park, Manchester. Ford's application of the principles of 'scientific management' to industrial activity transformed mass production. The Model T was produced all over the world.

The German pavilion
designed by Ludwig Mies van
der Rohe at the International
Exhibition, Barcelona, 1929.

2/THE TWENTIES AND THIRTIES

Ornament versus pure form

The pavilion by Mies van der Rohe for the Barcelona exhibition of 1929 is often seen as the temple of Modernism, and the chairs of hand-buffed steel its thrones. It is, perhaps, the most perfect statement of the Bauhaus belief in total design, in which no detail is too peripheral or mundane for the attention of the designer. However, it also encapsulates much of the irony of Modernism for the materials were rare, costly and hand crafted and, despite the Modernists' avowed commitment to socialistic ideals, it was a far remove from popular taste or pocket. A more pragmatic response to the modern world could be seen in the work of the industrial design studios in America. Harley Earl and others were deliberately using design as a tool to promote sales and were exploiting the imagery of science in the styling of consumer products. Meanwhile the need for decoration, luxury and fantasy was satisfied by Art Deco, to be seen at its most exuberant in the 1925 Paris exhibition, and by subsequent neo-romantic, neo-baroque and surrealist tendencies.

ARCHITECTURE AND URBAN DESIGN

There can be no doubt that the cataclysmic events of the First World War played a large part in paving the way for a radical change in cultural values. But it is misleading to present the war as a complete hiatus, a clean break between the historicism of the past and the new approach of the post-war years. To do so was a convenient device for those who sought to present the war as the climatic event of a decadent world order, opening the path to revolutionary Modernism. The facts, however, are not nearly so clear-cut. Walter Gropius had already established his own architec-

Right Sant 'Elia died before he was able to realize a building, but his evocative drawings of Futurist cities were highly influential and represent an early attempt to come to terms with the machine aesthetic of the modern world.

Below Walter Gropius and Adolf Meyer's Fagus factory of 1910 in Alfeld is often described as the first pure expression of modern architecture.

tural office in Berlin as early as 1910, after three years with Behrens. His Fagus shoe factory at Alfeld, designed in the following year with Adolf Meyer, is often cited as the first expression of the pure Modern mode, with its clearly expressed structural steel frame displayed as a distinct element, differentiated from the non-loadbearing glass curtain–wall.

In fact the Deutsche Werkbund's Cologne exhibition of 1914, with its series of structures by such architects as Hoffmann, van de Velde and Bruno Taut, clearly demonstrated that some kind of modern movement already existed. Furthermore, this could already be characterized as a school containing several different strands. The conflict between the various different factions within Modernism continued unabated during the war years, and in the revolutionary post-war period too. It was not until the Bauhaus was a year or two into its stride, in the early twenties, that an unchallenged orthodox Modernism began to emerge.

At Cologne, Gropius and Meyer's design for a model factory, with its symmetry and intersecting brick planes, shows the influence of Frank Lloyd Wright's mature style. From as early as 1904, Wright's buildings, in particular the Larkin building in Buffalo, the Unity Temple in Oak Park and the Prairie houses, exhibit an architectural approach which, in its planning and handling of space, can only be called Modern. To their use of Wrightian motifs at Cologne, Gropius and Meyer added a pair of glass capsule stair-towers which demonstrated the beginnings of the glass-and-steel purist modernity of the inter-war years.

The factions

Before Filippo Tommaso Marinetti published the Futurist manifesto in February 1909, the medievalizing, anti-machine theories of Ruskin and Morris had received no coherent challenge. Though it did prove possible for some Arts and Crafts inspired architects like Behrens, and even Walter Gropius, to find common ground with those German industrialists within the Deutscher Werkbund, the philosophy which inspired them was, nevertheless, implacably opposed to the spirit of technological change. Futurism, naive, innocent and even sinister as it may seem in the wake of two world wars, was still a real attempt by artists and intellectuals to embrace the tumultuous technological and social changes that were taking place, and not to shrink primly away from them.

'We will sing of great crowds excited by work, by pleasure and by riot; we will sing of the multicoloured polyphonic tides of revolution in the

Left Gropius's model factory, to be seen at the right of the photograph, for the Deutsche Werkbund's Cologne exhibition of 1914. The glass stair-towers contrast with the classical symmetry of the elevation.

Below Frank Lloyd Wright's Unity Temple of 1905-6 in Oak Park was more advanced spatially than any of its European contemporaries.

Right and below Bruno Taut's glass pavilion of 1914 for the Deutsche Werkbund's exhibition in Cologne was an early example of the use of trade fairs as a platform for avant-garde display. It employs modern materials—glass and metal—in a highly Expressionist manner.

modern capitals; we will sing of the vibrant nightly fervour of the arsenals and shipyards, blazing with violent electric moons; greedy railway stations that devour smoke-plumed serpents; factories hung from clouds by the crooked lines of their smoke, bridges that stride the rivers like giant gymnasts, flashing in the sun with the glitter of knives; adventurous steamers that sniff the horizon; deep-chested locomotives whose wheels paw the tracks like the hooves of enormous steel horses, bridled by tubing; and the sleek flight of planes whose propellers chatter in the wind like banners and seem to cheer like an enthusiastic crowd.'

With a programme like this, it is small wonder that the Futurists had nothing but contempt for the handicrafts, and even more for the sentimental myths of the Garden City movements—a contradiction in terms, as they saw it. There was, of course, a considerable degree of overstatement, a deliberate striving to shock in many of their pronouncements, but the manifestos of the Futurists struck a chord in many of the Modern Movement architects who were to follow in their footsteps.

Marinetti went on to spell out his antipathy to Ruskin. In a speech, given in London in 1910, he attacked those 'criss-crossing Italy only to meticulously sniff out the traces of our oppressive past [particularly the cities of Venice, Florence and Rome], the running sores on the face of the peninsula. . . . When, oh when,' he asked, 'will you rid yourselves of the lymphatic ideology of your deplorable Ruskin, with his morbid dreams of primitive rustic life, with his nostalgia for Homeric cheeses and legendary spinning wheels, with his hatred of the machine, of steam, and electricity. This mania for antique simplicity is like a man who in full maturity wants to sleep in his cot again and feed again at the breast of a decrepit old nurse in order to regain the thoughtless state of infancy.'

Apart from this pungent commentary, the Futurists extended their line of attack into every field of life—from food to sculpture. In the realm of architecture, it is impossible to point to any realized Futurist projects, but the visionary schemes of Antonio Sant'Elia and Mario Chiattone provided a rich fund of imagery for those architects who were to succeed them.

Sant'Elia was killed in action during the First World War, before he could realize the promise shown in his extraordinarily powerful drawings, which demonstrated, not for the first time, the fact that paper architecture can be just as important as the built variety.

Left Designed by Hans Poelzig before the First World War, the Luban chemical factory (then in Germany, now in Poland) combines industrial buildings with workers' housing.

With Chiattone, Sant'Elia formed the Nuove Tendenze, and at its first exhibition in 1914 put on show his drawings for the Futurist Città Nuova. 'The problem of modern architecture', he wrote, 'is not a problem of rearranging its lines, not a question of finding new mouldings, new architraves for doors and windows; nor of replacing columns, pilasters and corbels with caryatids, hornets and frogs, but to raise the new-built structure on a sane plane, gleaning every benefit of science and technology, establishing new forms and new lines, new reasons for existence solely out of the special conditions of modern living and its projection as aesthetic value in our sensibilities.' Sant'Elia's drawings, in particular for his station and airport of 1913, clearly foreshadow the planning studies of Le Corbusier. The buildings are smooth-skinned, powerful forms, suggesting both the force and spirit of the new technology.

Like Futurism, Expressionism in architecture was born out of an art movement. But unlike Futurism, it never had a programmatic manifesto. Rather it was a current which affected the thinking and work of many architects, although often only for brief moments in their careers.

The poet Paul Scheerbart and the painter Wassily Kandinsky pointed the way towards Expressionism in architecture—a movement that was largely confined to Germany, or Germany's possessions. Other architects, the rationalist classicizers of the Deutscher Werkbund, looked for standardized 'type' solutions to every building problem, building up a stock vocabulary of architectural approaches. The Expressionists, however, sought to liberate from within their materials and buildings the essence, or the expression of that material

or purpose. Thus, many of their realized works have a wilful, visionary, even bizarre quality. There was a strong streak of mysticism in the work of Bruno Taut for example, architect of the glass pavilion at the 1914 Cologne exhibition.

Hans Poelzig is notable for his industrial buildings at Luban before the First World War, and even more for his truly fantastic design for the Grosse Schauspielhaus theatre in Berlin of 1919. In these he demonstrated that Expressionist architecture could work on a large scale, presenting a real alternative to the stripped rationalism of the more orthodox Modernists.

Left In Poelzig's Schauspielhaus in Berlin of 1919 Expressionist ornament is used to powerful effect.

In the years immediately after the First World War, Expressionism came to be closely associated with revolutionary politics and dissent. It strongly affected Mies van der Rohe in his glass skyscraper designs of 1919, and led to a series of striking works from Erich Mendelsohn, particularly his Einstein Tower and his hat factory at Luckenwalde, as well as the farm complex built by Hugo Haring near Lubeck in 1924. In the person of Hans Scharoun, Expressionism survived into the years after the Second World War, but the supposedly organic nature of its forms and its wilful individualism ran out of steam.

In Holland, Dutch neutrality in the war that raged all around in the years between 1914 and 1918 helped to make it a major architectural force during that period. Hendrikus Petrus Berlage was the architectural elder statesman of the time and proved the catalyst for two completely different schools. As Reyner Banham has observed, De Stijl was one of two movements in Holland whose architecture was derived from Berlage. The other, the Amsterdam School with its wilful, luxuriantly craft-orientated approach, stems only from the *look* of Berlage's buildings, notably the Amsterdam Stock Exchange of 1903.

Berlage, however, also believed in the 'primacy of space, the importance of walls as creators of form, and the need for systematic proportion'. Very much with these ideas in mind, the painter Theo van Doesburg (this name being only one of the several by which he went) launched the De Stijl movement, based on a magazine of that name

Right Erich Mendelsohn's tower of 1921 for Einstein's astronomical laboratory in Potsdam was the realization of a series of sketches. Beneath the stucco, the building is a conventional enough structure.

Right A house by Hans Scharoun at the Deutsche Werkbund's 1927 exhibition. For Scharoun Expressionism was no passing phase and he continued to build in a similar style right up to the 1960s, by which time it had become fashionable again.

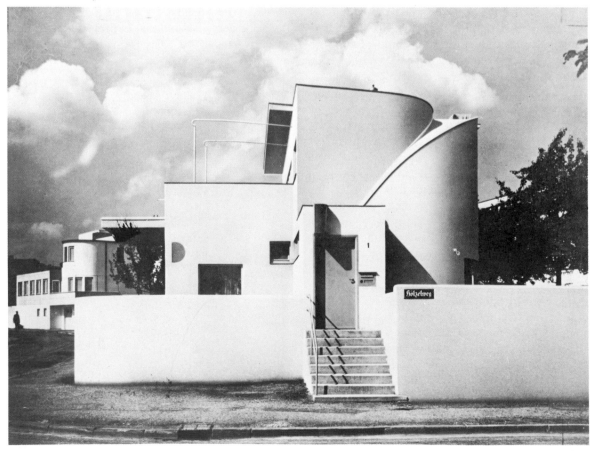

that was first circulated towards the end of 1917. The De Stijl group was made up of an ever-changing cast of painters, sculptors, cabinet makers and architects, of whom van Doesburg was the only constant factor. Initially the Dutch predominated, but eventually De Stijl became a much more international group, serving as a focus for the collection and dissemination of new ideas from Europe, Russia and America.

De Stijl's 1918 manifesto called on 'all those who believe in the reform of art and culture to destroy those things which prevent further development, just as in the new plastic art, by removing the restriction of natural forms, they have eliminated what stands in the way of the expression of pure art.'

Berlage himself had been much taken with the work of Wright, and Robert van't Hoff, an early De Stijl member, had built an accomplished villa in Utrecht in the manner of Wright as early 1916. But under the influence of Piet Mondrian, whose painting had been moving decisively towards complete abstraction since 1910 and his involvement with the Cubists, De Stijl's primary architectural contribution was to create a fully non-representational approach to design. In this, form was reduced to its purest geometric essentials and colour was confined to red, yellow and blue; the primary consideration became the free flow of space within and beyond the building itself. Van Doesburg's manifesto of 1923, *16 Points of a Plastic Architecture*, described the new De Stijl architecture as '*anti-cubic*, that is to say, it does not try to freeze the different functional space cells in one closed cube. Rather it throws the functional space cells, as well as the overhanging planes (balcony volumes), centrifugally from the core of the cube. And through this means, height, width, depth and time (i.e. an imaginary four-dimensional entity) it approaches a totally new plastic expression in open spaces. In this way architecture acquires a more or less floating aspect that, so to speak, works against the gravitational forces of nature.'

Van Doesburg himself was not trained as an architect, though he was to work on several architectural projects of which his interiors for the Café l'Aubette in Strasburg of 1928 were the most notable. In the early days of De Stijl, it was up to other members, practising architects, to put theory into practice. Initially, De Stijl's leading architectural figure was Jacobus Johannes Oud, but he did not stay long with the group. In 1918 he became City Architect for Rotterdam at the early age of twenty-eight, and apart from the Café Unie in Rotterdam and a couple of other projects, his work

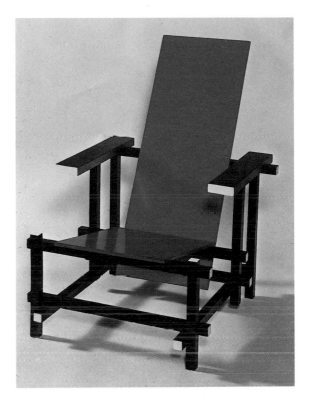

Left Rietveld's red-blue chair represents a summation of the philosophy of the De Stijl group. Intended as a blueprint for a chair that could be reproduced easily, it has in fact now been given the status of a rarefied fine art object.

Below Rietveld's architectural works were few. The most successful was the Schröder house in Utrecht of 1924, structurally traditional but spatially adventurous.

Right Theo van Doesburg, the leading figure in the De Stijl group, was primarily an artist. His most successful building was the Café de l'Aubette in Strasburg, which had murals by Jean Arp.

Opposite above Melnikov's Rusakov workers' club, built in Moscow in 1928, was to be a significant influence on later architects, for instance James Stirling who used its frank exposure of different functional elements in his Leicester building (see page 215).

Opposite below The Soviet pavilion at the Paris exhibition of 1925 conveyed the message of Constructivism to a receptive audience in the West.

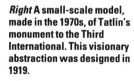

Right A small-scale model, made in the 1970s, of Tatlin's monument to the Third International. This visionary abstraction was designed in 1919.

became much closer to the functionalism of the Germans than to the abstraction of Mondrian and van Doesburg.

Oud's place was taken first by Gerrit Rietveld, a cabinet-maker who went on to design a series of buildings of varying quality. His red-blue chair of 1917 is, in fact, a summation of the De Stijl approach to design. It was also the basis for his Schröder house in Utrecht of 1924, a structure which embodies the De Stijl approach to architecture. Here, despite its orthodox use of load-bearing brick materials, Rietveld's upper–floor plan is arranged in such a way as to allow every space to flow into one unified whole.

In its later years De Stijl's character changed. Van Doesburg recruited, among others, the Russian architect El Lissitsky and the German film-maker Hans Richter—a move which was later to bring van Doesburg into contact with the Bauhaus with violent results.

It would be misleading to equate the Soviet contribution to the architectural and artistic avant-garde of the early decades of the twentieth century too closely with the ideology of political revolution. Of course, it is true that many of the protagonists of the Russian artistic ferment of the period around 1917 did participate actively in the revolution. But not all did, and a large number, including some of those who were involved, found it necessary to leave the Soviet Union in the increasingly hostile and intolerant climate after 1925.

From the beginning, the Bolshevik leadership had little sympathy even for the work of the revolutionary artists who supported their cause. Vladimir Tatlin's monument to the Third International of 1919 was a proposal for a skyscraper. This

would have been almost as high as the twin towers of the World Trade Centre in Manhattan and was inspired in its spiralling exposed steel structure by the Eiffel Tower. It was immediately attacked, both indirectly by Lenin, and directly by Trotsky. As Charles Jencks has pointed out, the former simply declared, 'I cannot value the works of expressionism, futurism, cubism, and other isms as the highest expression of artistic genius. I don't understand them, they give me no pleasure.' Trotsky was even blunter in his hostility. Seizing on Tatlin's idea that the structure should have four rotating meeting-rooms, contained in the

three platonic ideal forms of sphere, cylinder and cube, Trotsky said, 'Meetings surely need not take place in a cylinder, and that cylinder surely need not rotate.' In fact, Tatlin's interest in pure geometry reflected a preoccupation of many self-conscious revolutionary artists that can be traced back at least as far as Boullée.

Even within the avant-garde, there was too much dissension for any one coherent programme to emerge. Naum Gabo, the sculptor, who with his brother Antoine Pevsner is usually credited with founding the Constructivist movement, called the Tatlin tower a confusion between pure art and functionalism.

Lenin personally preferred neo-classicism in architecture, and Stalin insisted upon its use as being the only architectural language to which the masses could respond. But despite this conservatism, the cataclysmic events of the revolution did undoubtedly provide a brief opening for Soviet artists and architects, enabling them to make a much more complete break with tradition, and with architectural history, than was possible elsewhere in Europe. Though the orthodox early histories of the Modern Movement tended to neglect this vanguard role, there is no doubt that during the 1920s Soviet work had a strong influence in France, Germany and the Netherlands. Nikolaus Pevsner, for example, attempted to render Modernism palatable to an English audience by stressing its connections with Ruskin and Morris and ignoring the Constructivists and the Futurists. Yet El Lissitsky, Melnikov and others from the Soviet Union executed a number of projects in the West, mainly in the shape of small-scale temporary pavilions at international exhibitions and these had a powerful impact on their contemporaries. Tatlin, too, was well known abroad, and there was direct communication between the Constructivists and the De Stijl group, as well as with the Bauhaus.

Within the Soviet Union, the break with the old order in the years after 1917 involved a search both for new modes of architectural expression and for entirely new types of building. Communal apartment buildings, workers' clubs and institutes were consciously treated as the proletarian equivalent of the palaces and churches that once formed the landmarks of the city. Soviet Constructivist architects developed an enthusiasm for technology as a scientific and therefore progressive force. Their buildings, or more commonly their projects for buildings, displayed an inordinate passion for structural gymnastics, adopting dynamic, restless forms. And, in a manner that echoed the militant

urbanism of the Italian Futurists, their imagery celebrated the glamour of the modern metropolis and its popular artifacts: electricity, advertising, steam engines, aircraft.

Alexander and Vladimir Vesnin's project for *Pravda's* newspaper offices in Leningrad of 1923 exhibit all these tendencies, in a manner that ironically appears to foreshadow the late-modern skyscrapers of North American cities of the 1970s. Electric lifts are slung on the outside of the buildings, their cages climbing up and down the walls in full view of passers-by. Large-scale adver-

Right Architecture could be used in political propaganda, as in El Lissitsky's cantilivered Lenin tribune project of 1924.

Below In the Vesnins' Palace of Labour project of 1923 the aerials are an energetic expression of modernity.

tising signs are used to adorn the exterior, and a huge digital clock stands as a classically authoritarian gesture on the roof. The Vesnin design is a truly radical attempt to create a new spirit in architecture, while in comparison its German or French contemporaries often seem closer to the older, classical tradition.

The other element that was explored by both artists and architects—and very often these two groups fused in the persons of individuals such as El Lissitsky—was that of the fundamental nature of pure space. This preoccupation inevitably blurred the distinctions between art, architecture and sculpture, synthesizing them in the manner also proposed by De Stijl.

The shattered state of the Soviet economy in post-war years is often blamed for the scarcity of realized examples of work by the Constructivists. But in the later twenties, as the New Economic Policies of the government began to be put into effect, a number of large-scale projects, mainly in housing, were built. Many of these involved the participation of western architects, such as Le Corbusier, Mart Stam and Hannes Meyer.

Perhaps the most characteristic of the Constructivist architects was Lazar Lissitsky, known as El Lissitsky. In his teens he studied briefly in Darmstadt and he later came under the influence of Chagall, before moving to Moscow to become head of the architecture department of the newly established Vkhutemas school of design. It was here that he encountered Tatlin and moved decisively towards Constructivism, developing his Proun projects—graphic representations of spatial explorations that were on the edges of both architecture and sculpture.

Lissitsky designed the Soviet pavilion at the Berlin exhibition of 1922, and spent the following two years in Switzerland, receiving treatment at a TB clinic. It was during these years outside the USSR that Lissitsky encountered van Doesburg, Schwitters and Arp. He began to take a leading role in the development of the European scene as a whole, rather than simply working in the Russian context. But beyond a few highly evocative drawings for schemes such as his 'cloud props' skyscrapers, designed with Mart Stam in 1924 with the aim of providing Moscow with an appropriately modern and revolutionary gateway, Lissitsky left little in the way of realized architecture.

In the years after 1930 the climate in the Soviet Union, like that in Germany, hardened against Modernism in all its forms: with few realized projects of any substance, Russian Constructivism became one of the great might-have-beens of architectural history.

The Bauhaus

Despite its pivotal role in the history of the Modern Movement, and in particular of architecture, the Bauhaus, Walter Gropius's school of art and design, founded in Weimar in 1919, had no architecture department at all in the first eight years of its existence. The theory was that students could be prepared for all branches of design, including the ultimate synthesis of architecture, by getting a thorough training in craft workshops. Certainly it was a good enough grounding to produce individual talents of the order of Marcel Breuer—who was himself to become a master at the Bauhaus after completing his education there.

The Bauhaus has become synonymous with an ordered, German approach to architecture—of the rationalist, reductionist, white-cube variety—but the school itself went through at least two, and perhaps three, radically different incarnations. In its early days, the Bauhaus stood for a brand of semi-mystical Expressionism, in which the main emphasis was on the cooperation between the artist and maker. The students were organized as craft apprentices tied to the local guild system. In fact, this medievalism represents a regression on Gropius's own pre-war position, when he had already begun to investigate the possibility of industrializing the building process. Some commentators have tried to associate this backward step with Gropius's experiences during the slaughter of the First World War, in which the machine's potential for destruction was so starkly revealed. But it also reflected the economic realities of life in Weimar, a small city in which handicrafts and crafts-based industries were vital. Gropius was able to stress the value of the school in the regeneration of the local economy.

The school's prevailing ideology, however, was also a product of those teachers, or 'masters', with whom Gropius chose to surround himself. Of these, by far the most influential in the early years was the painter Johannes Itten. It was Itten who developed the Vorkurs, the foundation course common to all Bauhaus students which is still the basis of design education throughout the world. He was a messianic figure, a devotee of various exotic cults, who affected monkish garments of his own design and a macrobiotic diet. Throughout this period, despite Gropius's oft-proclaimed commitment to architecture as the summation of all the arts, architectural education was largely confined to informal lectures from Gropius's partner, Adolf Meyer.

Despite having two of the most distinguished and advanced buildings of the pre-war period to their credit, the Gropius-Meyer partnership's own work at this time was also heavily influenced by Expressionism. Gropius's Weimar memorial to the victims of the 1921 March Rising is far removed from the Purism that was developing in Holland and, with Le Corbusier, in France.

In 1923 Itten was replaced at the Bauhaus by the young Hungarian painter Lazlo Moholy-Nagy and the new appointment, which came shortly after Theo van Doesburg's brief but explosive visit to Weimar in 1922, heralded a significant shift in direction at the Bauhaus. Van Doesburg's deliberately inflammatory lectures there had divided the school into opposing factions, but henceforth it was to become firmly identified with militant Modernism of the rationalist persuasion. Lingering traces of medievalism and mysticism were expunged, to be replaced by a commitment to functionalism, exemplified by Herbert Bayer's design for the new Bauhaus sanserif alphabet. This eschewed capital letters altogether, on the grounds that it would

Right A reminder of Gropius's Expressionist tendencies, his memorial to the victims of right-wing violence after the First World War was built in Weimar in 1922 and later destroyed by the Nazis.

require the wasteful provision of two alphabets where one would do perfectly well.

In the post-war German setting Gropius's greatest contribution to the Bauhaus was to keep it running at all. Despite rampant inflation, political and military turmoil, and a rising Nazi movement, Gropius kept the school functioning, and as far as possible free from damaging political taints.

Eventually, however, Weimar proved too unsympathetic a climate. The state authority, which had also continued to finance the art academy which the Bauhaus had originally been intended to replace, changed its political complexion, and the Bauhaus's days in Weimar were numbered. Gropius turned what might have been a terminal crisis to the school's advantage. He persuaded the staunchly Social Democratic administration in Dessau to establish a new Bauhaus there, and to underwrite the cost of a brand-new building to be designed by Gropius.

Two years after the move, in 1927, Gropius finally established a proper architecture department within the school. Mart Stam turned down the job of running it, so the position went to Hannes Meyer, an uncompromising Marxist who saw architecture as a revolutionary weapon. He adopted an utterly deterministic and materialist view of culture, opposed to art but dedicated to function. Though it was a view which attracted scorn from others at the Bauhaus, including Mies van der Rohe, Gropius made Meyer his successor when, exhausted by the continual compromises demanded of him he left the school in 1928.

Meyer's plans, which put aesthetics a long way behind sociology, turned the school against itself, with established figures like Klee, Schwitters and Kandinsky all leaving, or threatening to leave. In fact Meyer's policy of subordinating all the departments within the school to building and industrial design was exactly the basis on which the Bauhaus had been founded in the first place. In the end, after a series of intrigues, Meyer was forced to resign in 1930, a political donation from school funds being the ostensible cause.

At this point Mies van der Rohe, who had turned down the directorship in 1928, was prevailed upon to accept it, charged with pulling the school back from the brink of disaster. Against the background of the Nazi seizure of power, this proved an increasingly hopeless struggle. The local Nazis forced the closure of the Dessau Bauhaus and in 1932 it moved yet again, this time to Berlin where Mies rented an old factory building as premises. The Berlin school, too, was closed down for good

after Hitler took absolute power. Given the Nazis' hatred of any form of cultural avant-gardism, it was not an unexpected move, for as early as the 1920s they had been circulating propaganda which denounced modern International Style architecture as suitable only for racial inferiors. But Mies's own position was an ambiguous one: he remained in Germany and attempted an accommodation with the Nazi regime, until travelling to Chicago in 1938 to take up an offer of a teaching post there.

Although it was under the control of architects throughout its existence, the Bauhaus's role in the development of Modern Movement architecture is a complex one. It was, according to its founder Walter Gropius, dedicated to turning out designers free of the stylistic baggage of convention and history. Yet architecturally its major roles were symbolic and its importance lay in its propaganda and proselytizing. The Bauhaus building, however, represented a landmark in the application of Modernist motifs to large-scale buildings, with its curtain walls and rambling floor plan.

During his time at the Bauhaus Gropius maintained a busy private practice, often collaborating with students from the school. He submitted a highly sophisticated entry for the Chicago Tribune Tower competition in 1922, with elements of Constructivism and of De Stijl; and while at Dessau he also built a labour exchange, where for once the stucco surface favoured by Modernists for its smooth, but spurious, machine-like perfection was omitted in favour of brick.

He created above all a platform for Modernism, one which attracted huge public attention. This,

after 1918, he began to explore a quite different means of architectural expression. His glass towers for Berlin of 1919 are often described as Expressionist, as is his heavily sculptured memorial to the assassinated Spartacists Rosa Luxembourg and Karl Liebknecht. Certainly the towers explore the potential of glass, both technically and aesthetically, in a way that suggests the Expressionists.

Another influence was Frank Lloyd Wright, especially in Mies's plan for a brick country house, drawn in 1923. At first sight the plan looks like an abstraction of the De Stijl group, but its flowing sequence of spaces owes a stronger debt to Wright, a debt which Mies was to acknowledge when he reached America. Of Wright, Mies wrote, 'The work of this great master presented an architectural world of unexpected force, clarity of language, and richness of form. Here, finally, was a master builder drawing upon the veritable fountainhead of architecture, who with true originality lifted his creations into the light.'

Until Mies left for America he built little, but what he did build was of the highest quality and crucial to the Germanic variety of Modernism, transforming its halting, experimental vocabulary into a mature means of aesthetic expression.

although it eventually provoked the Nazis into closing down the school, did help to reduce the élitist image of Modernism and turn it into a widespread popular concern.

Like Gropius, Ludwig Mies van der Rohe worked for a period in the office of Peter Behrens, and also like Gropius he began building in a solemn classical style. In his projects before the First World War Mies's work used a traditional mode, inspired partly by the work of Karl Friedrich Schinkel. But

Like most of the first generation of Modernists in Germany, Mies was much involved with the radical activists of the years immediately after the First World War. He became a leading member of the Novembergruppe, the Modernist faction named after the month of Germany's republican

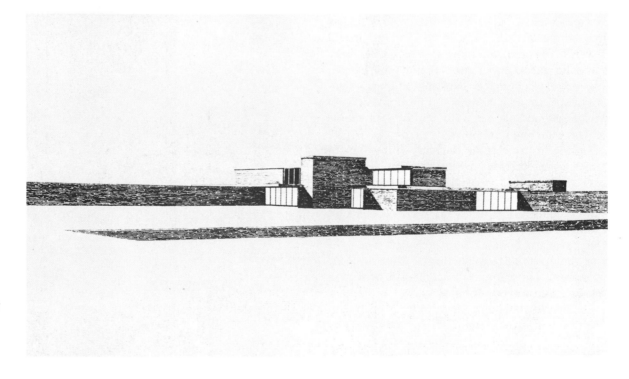

revolution of 1918 and dedicated to the promotion of Modernism in every form.

The series of imaginative projects with which Mies first made his name in the new movement were all shown at Novembergruppe exhibitions. The skyscrapers with crystalline plans, the brick and concrete houses, all treated the new materials in a fresh way, shorn of traditional mannerisms. But while these paper projects brought Mies to the attention of his fellow architects it was not until 1927 that he began to outstrip his peers, for in that year he was appointed director of the highly influential Stuttgart Werkbund exhibition, which included a whole new suburb with buildings by leading international architects of the day.

Mies's work at Stuttgart was cast in the plain white geometry of the period. But a couple of years later he produced his pre-war masterpiece, the German pavilion at the 1929 Barcelona exhibition, in a much richer mode. Here, for the first time, Mies attempted to synthesize Modernism with the timeless, classical basis of architecture. Though designed, like all exhibition buildings, for only a limited lifespan, the Barcelona pavilion was built of the most costly materials, marble, chromed steel and rare onyx. It had little function other than for ceremony, and became instead a perfectly propor-

tioned, immaculately detailed temple to Modernism. For this project, as for many of his other pre-war buildings, Mies and his collaborator Lilly Reich designed a special range of furniture, a move that was entirely in keeping with the Bauhaus commitment towards synthesizing all the arts.

In the Tugendhadt house outside Brno in Czechoslovakia, Mies combined the same ele-

Below **Mies van der Rohe used the Werkbund's Stuttgart exhibition of 1927 to demonstrate the achievements of the first-generation Modernists.**

ments, purpose-designed furniture and sumptuous materials. It was a combination which firmly established Modernism, despite its revolutionary beginnings, as an élite, patrician style. Simplicity and costly materials only worked when carried out with a sufficient budget, and the cut-price imitations of Miesian Modernism were doomed from the start; their constant repetition in debased form did much to undermine Modernism in the 1960s.

Le Corbusier

For all their differences Gropius and Mies had more in common, in their early years at least, with each other than with the other leading protagonists of European Modernism. They both stood, in varying degrees, for the Germanic tradition of simplicity and lack of adornment that stemmed from classicism. But Modernism had other, equally powerful, strands of expression of which Charles Edouard Jeanneret, better known as Le Corbusier, was the most important representative.

Born in 1887 in the Swiss watch-making town of La Chaux-de-Fonds, Le Corbusier eventually established himself in Paris in 1917. His apprenticeship had been long and largely self-taught, and during the course of it he had come into contact with two of the strongest currents of the period, spending two years working for Perret and a shorter period in Behrens' office. Corbusier's own

early buildings reveal a debt to the severity of Behrens, but also display something of the spirit of Josef Hoffmann. Another significant figure was Tony Garnier, Perret's contemporary, who inspired the large-scale plan-making that was to obsess Le Corbusier throughout his career.

If the Germanic strand of Modernism associated with Mies van der Rohe can be linked to a diminution of the significance of the individual—a statement which Mies himself made—then Le Corbusier is its reverse. Le Corbusier is the single hero-figure of Modernism's great period of the 1920s, a period when the currents and manifestos of the pre-war years began to take shape in a recognizable movement.

Throughout his career, Le Corbusier's output was prolific: he worked as an architect, a journalist, a writer, a furniture designer, a painter and a town-planner. Shortly after setting up in Paris he began to experiment with mass-produced low-cost housing, a theme that preoccupied many of the early Modernists as, intoxicated by the birth of production-line car factories, they attempted, always without success, to reap the same benefits of cost effectiveness and speed for the building industry. Gropius worked on a modular mass-produced housing system, and a few years later the American maverick Buckminster Fuller, not an architect but a self-taught designer who had trained as an engineer, got as far as building a prototype with his

Right Le Corbusier's Villa Stein at Garches, outside Paris, is a handsome vision of the world to come. Its Purist aesthetics became a formula for the International Style.

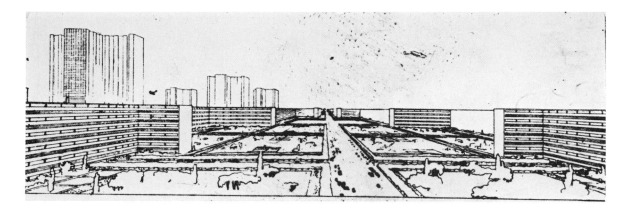

Left Le Corbusier's city for three million people, conceived in 1922. With huge blocks set in regular grids in open parkland, it proved to be all too seductive to future town-planners.

Dymaxion house. But Le Corbusier elevated the idea of mass production to its most poetic form. It was he who coined the slogan for the new house as a *machine for living*—a phrase incidentally which has been much misunderstood, for as Le Corbusier himself always said, architecture must go beyond utilitarianism. What Le Corbusier was doing was to embrace a necessity and give it form and meaning, rather than to let the inevitable process of mechanization take place without any intervention from the designer.

At the same time that Le Corbusier was struggling to establish a building company to market the reinforced-concrete *Dom-ino* system he had designed in 1914, he was also launching a magazine with the painter Amédée Ozenfant, dedicated to the promotion of all things modern. Ozenfant was the author of a post-Cubist movement in painting which he called Purism.

Purism's architectural expression was expounded by Le Corbusier in the magazine and in a series of books that he published, as well as in his projects, which tended at this period to exist only in theory. *Vers une architecture*, first published in 1923 and reprinted all around the world, was the most influential and accessible statement of the new school, not tied to the manifesto of any particular artistic sect, but in a generalized way putting across the message of the new spirit of the age. 'The styles are a lie,' he wrote. 'Architecture is stifled by custom.' Le Corbusier took up the Germanic concept of *Zeitgeist*, that ineluctable force whose unseen hand creates aesthetic responses appropriate to the spirit of the age. 'Style', he wrote, 'is a unity of principle animating all the work of an epoch, the result of a state of mind which has its own special character. Our own epoch is discovering day by day its own style. Our eyes unhappily are as yet unable to discern it.'

Le Corbusier was in no doubt that 'a great epoch' had begun. 'There exists a mass of work conceived in the new spirit, it is to be met particularly in industrial production.' Hence Le Corbusier's continuing preoccupation with industrial design. *Vers une architecture* is full of pictures of steamships, aircraft, motor cars and engineering structures, shockingly juxtaposed with pictures of the Parthe-

non and one of the temples of Paestum. In fact, Le Corbusier was attempting to show how industrial design had proceeded very rapidly, from attempting to echo the horseless carriage in motor cars, for example, to rational, logical pieces of engineering design. This lesson, he believed, had many implications for architecture.

Below The apartments designed by Robert Mallet-Stevens in the Paris street that bears his name show Modernist and Cubist aesthetics transformed into a decorative style.

Right Pierre Chareau designed the Maison de Verre in Paris with Bernard Bijvoet. Carved out of an existing apartment block, it used industrial materials and was a poetic expression of the machine age.

To Le Corbusier, true to his Purist principles, architecture was a matter of light and shade, mass and volume, surface and plan. Above all of plan, for 'the plan is the generator. Without a plan you have lack of order and wilfulness. The plan proceeds from within to without; the exterior is the result of the interior.' But while Le Corbusier proselytized for the acceptance of the machine, he was equally aware of the role of architectural history. The planning of the Purist villas that he built in the 1920s exhibits certain affinities with the villas of Palladio in their planning and the harmonies of their facades. The Villa Stein, of 1927, and the Villa Savoye illustrate Le Corbusier's masterly ability to dignify pure form and to invent new elements of architectural expression. The Villa Savoye, for example, demonstrates Le Corbusier's invention of the piloti, his recurring motif

of raising part of the ground floor upon stilts to allow the house to float within the landscape.

Le Corbusier had an intense feeling for the Mediterranean vernacular, for simple, peasant materials and strong, rough finishes. This was to emerge more fully later in his career, though it informed his planning and use of space even at this period. But architecture was never an end in itself for Le Corbusier. He always saw it as an instrument for changing people's lives, for reorganizing their patterns of living for the better. This was true both in individual buildings and in town-planning.

It was to planning that Le Corbusier devoted a huge part of his professional effort. Unbidden, unpaid and very often without the remotest chance even of thanks, still less of executing his schemes, he poured out a constant stream of plans for cities around the world.

Left Richard Neutra was one of the first European Modernists to reach America, and he quickly established a tradition in California of purist white houses such as the Lovell house of 1929.

Hardly any of these urban schemes were realized. There is a communal apartment building that he planned for Moscow, which was built but put to a very different purpose from that imagined by its designer. And a small group of houses was completed in the Pessac suburb of Bordeaux in accordance with Le Corbusier's theories of prefabrication. But his unrealized vision of the Ville Contemporaine, a planned city for three million inhabitants, has continued to haunt the world. His seductive drawings showed sixty-storey-high glass office buildings set in greenery and surrounded by workers' suburbs, close to their factories. The images of towers in parkland seduced planners and architects everywhere and did indeed provide a model for an automobile-dominated environment, with whose brutal results the cities of the world have yet to come to terms.

While Le Corbusier remains the dominant figure in the French architectural scene of the 1930s, other currents existed also, and by their very presence strengthened the position of Modernists of all complexions.

France proved a much more sympathetic climate for the acceptance of the Modernist aesthetic than, for example, England. It became the fashionably accepted style for a class of metropolitan sophisticates, thanks to the efforts of, among others, Robert Mallet Stevens. This architect was skilled at tailoring the Cubist aesthetic to the tastes of the fashionable, a talent which is exemplified in the apartment block, built in 1927, on the street that bears his name in Paris. Mallet-Stevens collaborated at the Exposition Internationale des Arts Décoratifs et Industriels Modernes, held in Paris in 1925, with another of the seminal figures of the inter-war years, Pierre Chareau. Like Chareau, Mallet-Stevens was to design furniture, but he remained primarily an architect.

Chareau on the other hand was very much an interior designer. Yet, between 1928 and 1932, in collaboration with the Dutchman Bernard Bijvoet, he was to design the Maison de Verre in Paris, an architectural landmark which has inspired a certain breed of architect ever since. The Maison de Verre—consisting of a new flat and a consulting room for a Parisian doctor within an old courtyard—was one of the most powerful celebrations of the poetry of the machine ever realized. With its frankly expressed steel structure, studded rubber flooring and tautly wrought, specially designed furniture, the Maison de Verre was a unique synthesis between architecture and interior design.

Eileen Gray, born in Ireland, but a life long resident of France, approached architecture from a

Below The entrance hall of Le Corbusier's Villa Savoye of 1931 outside Paris employs piloti, a recurring motif of his later years, to great effect. These piloti go under and support the whole house.

Right Berthold Lubetkin's influence on the younger generation of British architects in the inter-war years was profound. He founded the Tecton group and built such accomplished landmarks as the Highpoint flats in Highgate, London, the first phase of which was completed in 1935.

Left In the Penguin Pool of 1943 at the London Zoo, Lubetkin demonstrated that Modernist architecture could be popular with the public. He turned to Ove Arup for advice on the engineering.

similar direction. After training as a painter in London, she moved to Paris in the early part of the century, establishing herself there as a decorator specializing in exotic lacquer work, sumptuous interiors and rich materials. In the later part of the 1920s, however, her preoccupations shifted in a very different direction. She worked on a pair of experimental houses in the South of France, which combined a Chareau-like delight in exposing the mechanics of furniture with a confidence in form and space that won the admiration of Le Corbusier and De Stijl, among others.

The success and failure of the Modernists in the 1920s can be judged by the fact that it was Le Corbusier's design which won the competition for the League of Nations building in Geneva, but it was dropped in favour of an academic, classical scheme. For all that, Modernists throughout Europe felt confident enough of their position by the end of the 1920s to come together in the Congrès Internationaux d'Architecture Moderne, funded by a wealthy Swiss heiress and convened at her family castle. The scheme was to take stock of the tumultuous decade and set the course for the future with a charter, most of whose content was the work of Le Corbusier.

Migration—East and West

The late 1920s and early 1930s represented a period of rapid expansion for Modernism, beyond its European origins. In America, Frank Lloyd Wright occupied an ambiguous position: as heir of Sullivan he represented a Modernist approach, yet he was strongly opposed to the work of many of the Europeans who professed an admiration for his buildings. Soon émigré architects began to establish themselves in America, bringing with them the purism of the Europeans.

Richard Neutra moved to California from his native Austria in 1925. He was one of the first of the wave of European architects to arrive in America in the inter-war years, and one of the few of any consequence to settle on the West Coast. Neutra was a former student of Adolf Loos and a one-time member of Erich Mendelsohn's studio, collaborating on the *Berliner Tageblatt* building of 1921-3. He transported the European concept of Modernism to the West Coast, adapting it in the post-war years to the vernacular of southern California with his free plans and over-flung roofs, which betray a debt as much to Frank Lloyd Wright as to the European masters. The most notable of these buildings is the 1927 Lovell house.

The same process took place in Europe, with architects of the avant-garde taking part in a rapid cultural diaspora which did not go unnoticed by their nationalistic critics. One of the first to reach England was Berthold Lubetkin, originally a Russian, who had studied in Paris. Lubetkin's High Point apartments in London and his establishment of the Tecton group did much to make Britain of the 1930s a receptive home for the stream of Modernist refugees who were to follow.

The most distinguished Europeans to reach England were Gropius, Breuer and Mendelsohn, the latter being the most significant in terms of his work. In partnership with Serge Chermayeff, a Russian who had already established himself in Britain, Mendelsohn, designed the De La Warr Pavilion at Bexhill, a sophisticated example of European Modernism. Unfortunately, though, it had the effect of identifying Modernism in the minds of at least one generation in England with a certain kind of seaside jauntiness later associated with the Festival of Britain school.

The same partnership also built a house in Kensington Church Street in London, next door to the one designed by Gropius and Maxwell Fry. Fry was, in fact, one of the very few indigenous British Modernists of real talent in the pre-war years. After the war he was to collaborate directly with Le Corbusier, and in the 1930s he brought the utopian spirit of social housing to London with his development of low-budget flats for the gas company at Kensal Green. The latter, now sadly neglected, combined geometric sophistication with a high degree of social content.

Below Britain benefited in the 1930s from a steady stream of refugees from totalitarian regimes in Europe, most of whom eventually moved on to America. A distinguished scheme of the period was the De La Warr Pavilion at Bexhill (1935-6) by Serge Chermayeff and Erich Mendelsohn.

Not all the émigrés working in London in the 1930s were of European origin. Also of importance were young architects from the colonies, such as Wells Coates, a Canadian born in Tokyo, who arrived in London in his late twenties. Coates founded the Modern Architecture Research Group (MARS) in 1933 and his talents as an architect are evident in the Isokon flats in Hampstead, but his best work lay in the field of industrial design. Lucas, Connell, Ward was a partnership made up of two New Zealanders and one Englishman, who, particularly with their house at Frognal in Hampstead, demonstrated a talent for adapting the Corbusian model to the English street.

The architects who later were to dominate the post-war era served their apprenticeship in a climate in which European ideas were paramount. This influence is manifest not just in Sir Denys Lasdun's buildings from the 1930s but also in Sir Frederick Gibberd's major pre-war building, Pulman Court in Streatham. However, more typical of the period is the monumentalism of Grey Wornum's classically inspired headquarters for the Royal Institute of British Architects of 1934.

It was the cosmopolitanism of Modernism that justified its claim to be called the International Style. But it also focused the hostility of those who sought to check its spread. In England, Sir Reginald Blomfield, the Edwardian classicist and highly successful commercial architect, dubbed

Below Le Corbusier's Maison Suisse for the University of Paris, completed in 1932, is the summation of his approach, with its glazed curtain walls, main block raised on stilts, and roof terrace.

the Modernists 'modernismus' and considered
them to be a Germanic menace. In Germany itself,
of course, the triumph of the Nazis led to the
departure of all those who wished to build in the
Modern manner, leaving Hitler to create a nationalist style of stripped monumental classicism,
mixed with so-called vernacular architecture.

Yet the vocabulary of Modernism could serve to
express the national integrity of such fiercely
independent and progressive nations as Finland
and Czechoslovakia. In the latter, there were the
Rondo-Cubists such as Gočar who, after the end of
the First World War and the collapse of the Austro-
Hungarian empire, gave their young nation a
distinctive style of its own. In Finland, Alvar Aalto
adapted the work of the Nordic romantic classi-
cists such as Apslund to create a national style that
deployed local technology to make the most of
natural resources, particularly in the use of plywood. After his early experiments in classicism
Aalto's work assumed a lyrical flavour that was
lacking in other interpretations of Modernism.

By the late 1930s Modernism was established in
many parts of the world. Despite the Fascists it was
adopted in Italy by Terragni; in South America, Le
Corbusier's influence had spawned the school
around Oscar Niemeyer in Brazil.

Through a combination of migration and proselytizing, Modernism was now a force in most parts
of the world, apart from those countries such as
Germany and the Soviet Union in which it was
officially regarded with disfavour. It was making
headway in France, where Le Corbusier was
beginning to build large-scale projects such as the
Maison Suisse for the University of Paris and his
Salvation Army Hostel; in England, there were
both the home-grown disciples and new arrivals.

The traditionalists, though, were still the
favoured architects for those projects, sponsored
by the state, that required a monumental content.
Lutyens was given the project of designing an
imperial seat for New Delhi in a classical form that
is echoed in Speer's Berlin. Only in Italy was the
Modernism of Terragni able to coexist with the
demands of officialdom: his Casa del Fascio of 1936
in Como is a model of timeless purity.

DECORATIVE ARTS

Right Commemorative
medallion by P. Turin for the
1925 Exposition
Internationale des Arts
Décoratifs et Industriels
Modernes. This artist created
a series of medallions on the
theme of neo-classical
draped or naked figures and
formalized flowers.

Initially Art Deco had been an exclusive, avant-garde style but in the 1920s it developed a broad, popular mode. In this, the floral and feminine manner of the pre-war period, with its roots in the late eighteenth century, developed and diversified into a second phase, a multi-character commercial repertoire. Floral and neo-classical motifs competed with the increasingly fashionable geometric styles, derived from Cubism and other progressive art movements; and even greater variety was created by the numerous personal interpretations of fashionable themes and motifs, which characterized the work of individual designers.

Art Deco remained, however, a unifying thread within the work of many of France's decorative artists. It was the style associated with the leading commercial design studios, promoted by the major department stores, used in the decoration of luxury liners and consecrated in the 1925 Exposition Internationale. Art Deco's influence extended beyond France, and in the 1920s encouraged the evolution of closely related decorative styles elsewhere, notably in the United States and Vienna.

Meanwhile, a number of France's more exciting designers worked in styles which had little in common with Art Deco, and a new avant-garde emerged which drew directly on the influences of primitive art, Cubism and the aesthetic of the

machine. The work of this group, which included Pierre Legrain, Marcel Coard, Eileen Gray and Gustav Myklos, made Art Deco seem increasingly traditionalist and bourgeois. Pure geometry, allied in a typically French manner with the finest materials and craftsmanship, marked a complete reaction to Art Deco in the work of this avant-garde group and many of their contemporaries.

Parallel with the final flowering of Art Deco and the evolution of a new French avant-garde, both still tied to the rarefied world of luxury goods, was the increasing force of Modernism. This, by the late twenties, had acquired an international momentum and around 1930 assumed the predominant role in the applied arts.

The Paris Exposition and the triumph of Deco

It is ironic that the 1925 Paris Exposition Internationale des Arts Décoratifs et Industriels Modernes had, according to its regulations published in 1922, the intention of admitting only those artifacts which were truly modern in concept; in fact, the exhibition was a celebration of the traditional values of fine craftsmanship, in a style developed a decade earlier. The only significant concession to the Modern Movement was Le Corbusier's Pavillon de l'Esprit Nouveau.

The exhibition consisted of a series of pavilions and shops spread over a large area of central Paris, from the Place de la Concorde to the Invalides. There was a Porte d'Honneur designed by the master-ironworker Edgar Brandt between the Grand Palais and the Petit Palais, and rows of small shops representing various luxury trades lined the Pont Alexandre III, which linked the two areas on either side of the Seine. The monumental architec-

Right Gilt-bronze decorative
plaque designed by Léon
Jallot around 1920. This
incorporates the ubiquitous
Art Deco motif of a vase
brimming with formalized
flowers.

ture of many of the pavilions belied their temporary nature, for they were constructed in wood and plaster. Although the exhibition was international in scope, the United States did not participate, Germany was specifically excluded and the foreign exhibits were greatly overshadowed by the achievements of the French.

The various French pavilions, showing both collaborative and individual work, confirmed the supremacy of French craftsmanship and the extent to which the French were masters of every aspect of luxury-goods production—from furniture and furnishings to ceramics and glass, metalwork and lacquer, fabrics and fashion, decorative sculpture and book design. These displays were mounted by the leading department stores, the major manufacturers (such as Sèvres and the silk industries of Lyons), and the foremost designers and craftsmen. Their impact on the thousands of visitors who flocked through the gates must have been overwhelming. Notions of practicality, functionalism and logic, which were fundamental to the emerging Modernist movement, were absent. Instead, the displays seemed largely concerned with bravura and virtuosity in decoration and manufacture.

Outstanding among the French pavilions was the Pavillon d'un Ambassadeur, which included rooms by Jacques–Emile Ruhlmann, Jean Dunand and André Groult. Earlier Groult had espoused the revival of late-eighteenth-century styles and he was therefore a key figure in the development of Art Deco. His 'Lady's Bedroom' for this pavilion was, however, without precedent, its furniture conceived in sensual, swollen forms and curves, entirely covered in cream sharkskin detailed in ivory.

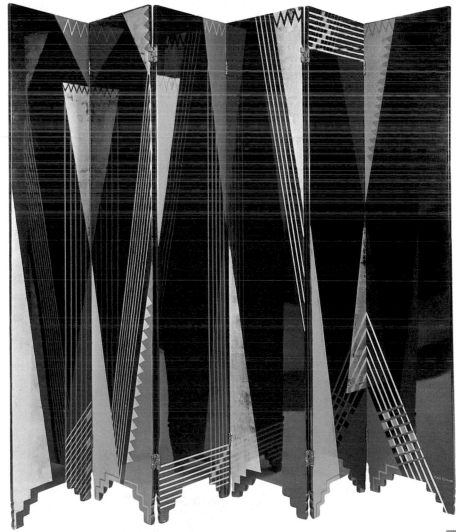

Pride in national achievement in France in the twenties encouraged the vogue for illustrated folios on all aspects of the applied arts. Charles Moreau was the most prolific and perhaps the most discerning of the publishers and his countless tie-bound folios of gravure plates provide full documentation of the products of the decade. The outstanding designers and craftsmen were fêted by their contemporaries and enjoyed the critical appreciation and patronage which enabled them to develop their skills to the full. Interior decoration and cabinet-making were central to the triumph of French craft, and no single figure better represents this triumph than Jacques–Emile Ruhlmann.

Ruhlmann might justly be said to have taken up the mantle of the great cabinet-makers of the eighteenth century. He has often been compared to Riesener in his perfectionism, his concern for faultless finish—irrespective of cost in terms of man-hours or materials—and in the essentially neo-classical quality of his forms. He first attracted attention at the Salon des Artistes Décorateurs before the First World War. In 1910 he opened his decorating firm, and in the period till his death in 1933 earned a reputation as decorator and creator of luxury furniture and furnishings. He favoured exotic woods, notably dark, veined, macassar ebony, rich palisanders and burr amboyna; and he showed judicious restraint in the use of ivory and bronze details or areas of sharkskin and tortoise-shell. Ruhlmann's designs ranged from monumental cabinet pieces to delicate chairs and tables. He would raise massive forms on the most slender of legs, yet his sure eye avoided eccentricity.

At the 1925 Exposition Internationale, Ruhlmann's Pavillon d'un Collectionneur was perhaps the most remarkable of all the exhibits. Designed in an imposing monolithic style by the architect Pierre Patout, this remarkable pavilion was furnished and decorated in Ruhlmann's most grandiose manner. The salon, with its monumental ironwork gates by Edgar Brandt, was a lofty circular room, lit by a grand chandelier and *appliques* of cascading glass beads. It was lined with a rich fabric incorporating the typical formalized flowers and swags of Art Deco, and was decorated with paintings by Jean Dupas and sculptures and other objects by various contemporary artists. Ruhlmann's furniture employed the finest woods,

detailed with ivory and bronze and upholstered in damask and tapestry. It demonstrated his restraint in form and decoration, his incomparable mastery in execution and his meticulous finish.

The art of dinanderie (work in non-precious metals) and lacquer was brilliantly exploited by Jean Dunand, a modest Swiss-born craftsman, who first attracted attention in the early years of the century for his metal vases beaten and wrought into organic forms. Around 1912 he started to use lacquers to enhance the patina of these vases. Fascinated by this demanding medium, he developed, after the interruption of the war years, a mastery of lacquer techniques. For a period of about twenty years Dunand and his team produced a variety of objects, richly decorated with gleaming natural oriental lacquers. The production ranged from jewellery and vases to furniture, screens and vast murals. For the 1925 exhibition Dunand created a black, red and silver lacquered smoking-room within the Pavillon d'un Ambassadeur. His technical virtuosity was matched by his stylistic versatility: he made a speciality of inlaying large areas of lacquer with minute particles of crushed eggshell, and he worked in a variety of styles, ranging from the most dramatic geometry to delicate figurative subjects.

Left Josephine Baker, photographed by d'Ora, Paris, around 1925. The American dancer is shown wearing lacquered metal bracelets by Jean Dunand.

The decorating firm La Compagnie des Arts Français was founded in 1919 by Louis Süe et André Mare and became known as Süe et Mare. They created a distinctive version of Art Deco, their furniture characterized by ample curvaceous forms and adorned with the archetypal Deco themes of swags and formalized bouquets.

There was a widespread fashion for wrought-iron work in the twenties owing much to the talent of Edgar Brandt and his collaborator, the architect-designer Louis Favier. Brandt set up his business in 1919 and incorporated the already-established repertoire of Art Deco motifs, notably the formalized flowers and scalloped spiral scrolls, into decorative panels, screens, consoles, radiator grills, gates, standard lamps and countless other items of furniture or architectural details. He had learned his craft from Emile Robert before the war and, in turn, encouraged other craftsmen.

Glass was a popular medium and two of the leading exponents were François Décorchemont, who produced handsome vessels in *pâte de cristal*, and Maurice Marinot. Another, René Lalique, had abandoned his career as a jeweller in the early years of the century and now produced lamps, car radiator mascots and other decorative glass-ware, which enjoyed great commercial success.

Left Lacquer panel by Jean Dunand, around 1925. Dunand's lacquer work encompasses a wide range of styles, his own designs and those of collaborators.

Right Detail of decorative inlay on a cabinet created by Süe et Mare for Jane Renouardt, 1927; ebony inlaid with mother-of-pearl, abalone and silver.

Near right Art Deco neo-classicism in an illustration by George Barbier, around 1920.

Far right Binding by Pierre Legrain of the 1924 edition of Paul Morand's *Ouvert la Nuit*, executed in 1930 for M. H. de Montbrison.

fine workmanship with dramatic, faultlessly proportioned, undecorated geometric forms.

In the twenties the arts of the book—illustration, the publication of *éditions-de-luxe* and book-binding—all flourished. George Barbier, Paul Jouve and François Louis Schmied were the leading illustrators. Pierre Legrain designed innovative luxury buildings, creating bold geometric designs which spread across front and back covers, and incorporating materials such as sharkskin to contrast with traditional leathers. This idea was developed by Jean Dunand who used lacquered panels in bindings. Other notable binders were Rose Adler, René Kieffer, Georges Cretté and Louis Creuzevault.

The design studios founded by leading department stores played an important role in popularizing Art Deco. These studios were able to produce a wide range of goods and to create complete interior schemes in a unified style. The designs were conceived for series manufacture and could therefore be marketed at prices which allowed a wide diffusion. At the same time, the studios also produced exclusive special commissions and elaborate schemes such as those for the 1925 exhibition.

The first such studio was the Atelier Primavera founded by the Magasin du Printemps in 1913. This was followed after the war by two important studios founded by designers who had already played a key role in the evolution of Art Deco; now, as heads of design studios, they were to make a

The Manufacture Nationale de Sèvres produced Art Deco porcelain vases to the designs of various artists. Individual potters of note included René Buthaud, who decorated his vases with stylish Deco figures, and Emile Decœur, a purist who produced finely proportioned vessels with rich, milky glazes which were greatly admired.

Jean Puiforcat first became known as a silversmith in 1923 and rapidly established himself as the most influential figure in this medium, combining

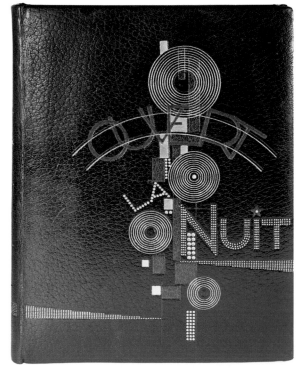

Left The grand dining-room of the luxury transatlantic liner *Normandie*, launched in 1932 as a floating showcase for the work of France's leading designers and craftsmen.

Left The salon of Jacques Doucet's villa at Neuilly, in a photograph published in *L'Illustration*, May 1930, as a posthumous homage to this remarkable patron. Amid sculptures and paintings by Rousseau, Modigliani and Czaky are furnishings by Coard, Legrain, Gray, Groult and Lalique.

considerable impact on the applied arts associated with domestic design. In about 1922 Maurice Dufrène assumed responsibility for the new La Maîtrise studio of the Galeries Lafayette, and Paul Follot became director of the Atelier Pomone of the Bon Marché. The Studium-Louvre was founded in 1923. Follot and Dufrène distinguished themselves with their Art Deco interior schemes at the salons of the Société des Artistes Décorateurs, and with their contributions to the 1925 exhibition. Each was invited to design a room within the Pavillon d'un Ambassadeur. The department store studios provided work for numerous designers, among them Louis Sognot and Jean Burkhalter, for Primavera, Pierre-Paul Montagnac, Eric Bagge and Fernand Nathan for La Maîtrise, René Prou for Pomone, and André Frechet and Maurice Matet for Studium-Louvre.

The great luxury liners of the early twentieth century had, as a rule, been decorated in a lavish yet highly traditional style. A dramatic break with tradition, however, came with the launching in 1927 of the *Ile de France*. This vessel was a floating showcase for the work of some of France's most eminent designers, a promotion for French artistry, skill and contemporary design. The main salon was decorated by Süe et Mare; a large Salon de Thé was decorated by Ruhlmann; a magnificent main staircase with wrought-iron decoration was created by Raymond Subes; and other rooms were conceived by a host of designers including Pierre Patout, René Lalique and Poiret's Atelier Martine.

Yet the *Ile de France* was soon to be superseded, both in physical scale and in the scope of its decor, by the most celebrated and remarkable liner of its era, the *Normandie*, put into service in 1935.

The superb decoration of this ill-fated vessel, gutted by fire in 1942, is well documented. It is easy to list such splendours as the tapestry and gilt-wood salon seating by Goudissart, the neo-classical figures, cornucopias, flowers and galleons of Jean Dupas' etched and painted glass panels, Jean Dunand's large lacquer panels, Lalique's shimmering dining-room. It is less easy to define the stylistic character of these schemes. They combine a late homage to Art Deco, an alternative to Modernist austerity and a reaction against the concept of an official Art Deco style in favour of greater eclecticism and individualism.

Couture patronage and the avant-garde

Charles Frederick Worth, in the late nineteenth century, had transformed the social role of the couturier. Once regarded as tradesmen, designers of high fashion became accepted as social equals by their clients. In the twentieth century couturiers have come to be regarded as arbiters of taste and, from Jacques Doucet to Karl Lagerfeld, have played an influential role as patrons of the avant-garde. Leading figures from the world of fashion have usurped the royal and aristocratic patrons of the past, shaping the style of the applied arts associated with personal and domestic adornment.

Jacques Doucet was the first, and arguably the greatest, couturier patron of contemporary art and design. In the years just before the First World War and through the twenties he fostered the careers of several exceptionally talented designers. Doucet evidently had a canny eye for nascent artistic talent and encouraged young designers, broadening their horizons and introducing them to the primitive and avant-garde contemporary art which he collected. In 1913 he provided the shy young Eileen Gray with her first important commission—a lacquer screen, *Le Destin*, which was to be the first of several pieces she created for him. Others, including Iribe, Pierre Chareau and Pierre Legrain, were enlisted to decorate his Paris home. Legrain owed much to Doucet, his major client through the twenties, and made highly inventive furniture in exotic woods and other materials. Unrestricted by commercial exigencies, he was free to create furniture which reflected his fascination with the motifs of Central African art and the dynamism of contemporary abstract art.

Doucet's last project was the installation of his art collection and modern furniture in a villa at Neuilly, a project supervised by Legrain which brought together a number of gifted and highly individual designers, among them Marcel Coard, Rose Adler, Gustav Myklos, André Groult, Clément Rousseau, Etienne Cournault, Paul Iribe, Josef Czaky and Louis Marcoussis. Doucet and Legrain both died in 1929. In May 1930 the journal *L'Illustration* published a series of colour photographs of the interior schemes in homage to this remarkable couturier.

Doucet's former employee, Paul Poiret, played a major role in the applied arts, equal in importance

Right Fashion plate by Benito, from a portfolio *La Dernière Lettre Persane*, published by Les Fourrures Max, 1920.

to that of Doucet and perhaps wider in its influence. For, while Doucet pursued the esoteric in his collecting and commissioning, Poiret sought a close correlation between dress and decor, and his ideas were widely adopted in fashionable circles. Poiret was a great host, an extravagant entertainer whose ideas were expressed in every aspect of his highly gregarious life style: to launch his orientalist fashions he threw costumed parties on oriental themes, decorated his Paris barge in the style of an imaginary harem and invited Georges Lepape to illustrate these fashionable fantasies.

An important by-product of high fashion, which reflected and emphasized the new status of the industry, was the art of illustration. This attained exceptional heights from about 1910 until, in the late twenties, the camera eventually eclipsed the pen, brush or pencil in recording fashion's ever-changing image. Poiret's own publications of 1908 and 1911, illustrated respectively by Iribe and Lepape, set a high standard of graphic sophistication. A brilliant generation of illustrators emerged under the aegis of enlightened patrons and publishers such as Poiret and Lucien Vogel; their work was widely disseminated through the new fashion magazines, notably *Vogue* and *Harper's Bazaar*. Vogel was responsible for two journals, printed to a very high standard with stencilled colour plates, which employed the most talented illustrators of the day. His *Gazette du Bon Ton*, published between 1912 and 1925, was devoted to fashion; his *Feuillets d'Art* covered both fashion and topical art subjects. Georges Lepape and Edouard Garcia Benito were foremost among this highly talented generation, Lepape a clever colourist and master of

elegant line, Benito a brilliant stylist, reducing his subjects to dramatic, almost abstract lines and forms. The Russian émigré Erté developed a refined, meticulous style of fashion illustration and polished this tight technique through a long career as illustrator and designer for the stage.

Among the numerous examples of couturiers patronizing distinguished designers, certain projects are outstanding. In the very early twenties, Eileen Gray was invited to redecorate an apartment for Mme Mathieu Lévy, known professionally as Suzanne Talbot. The result, featuring lacquer furnishings of great originality, is often illustrated as a remarkable blend of high luxury and proto-Modernist ideas. Another designer, Armand Rateau, created interiors and furnishings for Jeanne Lanvin, in a style which mixed Art Deco with Graeco-Roman and other influences from antiquity. Jean Dunand created lacquer furniture for Madeleine Vionnet and lacquer trimmings for Agnès, the hat designer.

Vienna, the United States and Great Britain

In the continuing activities of the Wiener Werkstätte, Vienna could boast of a group of designers whose work had many parallels with Art Deco. But it also had a national character and found considerable success both at home and abroad. The Werkstätte had evolved from its purist, Mackintosh-inspired beginnings to become, after Moser's departure in 1906, more concerned with decoration. This tendency was increased with the arrival of Dagobert Peche in 1915. Peche was a highly talented decorative designer who was to shape the Werkstätte style of the twenties, just as

Near right Vionnet dress photographed by Cecil Beaton in the New York apartment of Condé Nast, 1929.

Far right Gilt-bronze and glass chandelier designed by Dagobert Peche, 1918. Peche's designs are more delicate and decorative than the austere, geometric work of Moser and Hoffmann of the early years of the Wiener Werkstätte.

Right: The Savoy Cocktail Book published in 1930 with 'decorations by Gilbert Rumbold'. This typifies the fashion for angularity in decoration.

Moser and Hoffmann had been the dominant influences at its inception. Peche's style was characterized by exceptional delicacy, a lightness of touch and even whimsy. His forte was fabric and graphic design, but he also produced charming silverware of considerable invention.

The Werkstätte flourished in the twenties, its expanding activities embracing a wide range of products. By 1928, the year in which the group celebrated a quarter-century of success, Werkstätte designers had proved their abilities in silver and metalwork design, in fashion design and the related arts of jewellery, illustration, lace-making, beadwork and leatherwork. They had produced expressive and decorative work in ceramic and glass, stylish graphics, fabrics, wallpapers and inventive though sometimes disarmingly eccentric furniture. The group members respected the notion of a house style but the work of certain individuals deserves particular attention—E.J. Wimmer's fashion work, Michael Powolny's ceramics, Otto Prutscher's furniture and Carl Otto Czeschka's metalwork. This remarkable design, manufacture and marketing venture came to an end in 1932.

In 1922 Josef Urban had opened a New York retail outlet but despite this, and the material prosperity of the United States before the crash of 1929, there was little interest in the applied arts in

Left Elevator doors for the Chrysler building, New York, designed by William Van Alen, 1928-30.

the early twenties. Also in 1922 Charles Richards published an account, *Art and Industry*, of contemporary art education in America. He wrote, 'This country finds itself . . . today the richest country in the world . . . [yet] in many fields we are sadly unprepared for such world ascendancy and in none is this more true than in the field of art.' The impetus of the American Arts and Crafts movement had come to a halt.

The development of a new American vision in progressive design owed much to the constructive patronage of George C. Booth. In the early and

Opposite above '1919' chair designed by Gerrit Rietveld, a successor to his celebrated red-blue chair and an equally rigorous application of the Constructivist principles of the De Stijl group.

Opposite below Photographic study of locomotive wheels by the American painter and photographer Charles Scheeler, 1939. The cult of the machine was central to the Modernist aesthetic.

mid-twenties, he started to implement his dream of creating a forward-looking educational community for the arts. Enlisting the support of the Finnish architect and designer Eliel Saarinen, he built, in 1926, the Cranbrook Academy, which represented an updating of the Arts and Crafts tradition. It gave a new sense of purpose to American design and Cranbrook's teachers and students were to make a contribution of international importance to the applied arts, notably in the forties and fifties through the work of Charles Eames, Eero Saarinen, Harry Bertoia and Florence Knoll.

In the late twenties, meanwhile, there was a burst of high style in the dramatic decorations conceived to adorn and glorify the new skyscrapers then transforming Manhattan's skyline. Thunderbolts, cascades, stylized animals, ziggurats and purely abstract geometric motifs in polished bronze provided impressive counterpoints to the marble of the foyers. The finest examples were the decorative details, such as the lift-doors designed by Jacques Delamarre for the Chanin building of 1929, and by William Van Alen for the Chrysler building of 1930.

Such stylistic indulgences also enjoyed a vogue in Britain in the years around 1930. Highly formalized figure, plant or animal subjects, or purely abstract geometric motifs, were incorporated in decorative designs on every scale, from the cover of *The Savoy Cocktail Book* of 1930 to the bronze panels for hotels or department stores such as Derry & Toms.

Modernism—sources and characteristics

A complex pattern of influences came together in the mid to late twenties to form the basis of a new international movement. Dubbed 'modernism' by contemporary commentators, it has been elevated to Modernism or the Modern Movement by historians eager to fit design into categories defined by tidy epithets. Perhaps the most dramatic impact and the most lasting influence of Modernism have been in the sphere of architecture. The Modernist spirit, nonetheless, made a considerable impact in all areas of design, from industrial mass production to élitist high fashion, and has remained a major shaping force to the present day.

Modernism is best considered as a conceptual approach rather than as a style. For, despite certain stylistic features common to all Modernist designers, the basic philosophy was interpreted in a variety of ways ranging from the truly ascetic to the self-consciously stylish. Utopian idealists claimed that Modernism was a manifestation of social conscience; yet for those who developed the

elimination of ornament into a chic design trend it was merely a swing of the fashion pendulum. The reality for many designers was a conflict between democratic idealistic concerns and the élitist pursuit of perfect finish and purist form.

The sources from which Modernism developed included progressive design schools, design and craft studios and cooperatives, and avant-garde art movements. From these bases, artists and theorists attacked accepted academic values and suggested a dramatic, dynamic new vernacular of design.

The influence of the Deutsche Werkbund was crucial and its success was such that it inspired the formation of comparable bodies in other countries: in England, the Design and Industries Association founded in 1915; in Sweden, the Svenska Slöjdforeningen, restyled by Gregor Paulsson taking his cue from Germany. Such groups, encouraged by the search for rationalism in the processes of design and manufacture, prepared the way for the clean-lined functionalism of Modernist design. It was their influence that developed industry's awareness of the problems of designing for mass-production, encouraged the elimination of decoration for its own sake and promoted a pursuit of forms which exploited and explained, rather than concealed, the manufacturing process.

The Bauhaus school under the directorship of Walter Gropius played a crucial role as the crucible of Modernist theory. The Bauhaus influence in the applied arts was, however, neither clear-cut nor widespread in its own day, although certain products, notably tubular steel furniture, were widely copied. The artists and designers brought together by the Bauhaus had widely divergent approaches, ranging from Expressionism to formal purism. The approach of Moholy-Nagy, Lyonel Feininger and Oskar Schlemmer was of a quite different order from that of a rationalist such as Marcel Breuer or a purist such as Mies van der Rohe. The lasting achievement of the Bauhaus lies in the work of its outstanding architects, particularly Mies van der Rohe, and in its formulation of the still valid concept of 'pure' design. It aimed to synthesize the disciplines of fine art, architecture and applied art; and it initiated an open-ended debate on the concept of pure form—a Platonic ideal—versus expressive, symbolic form, colour and decoration.

The Dutch group De Stijl made an important contribution to the repertoire of Modernism. Gerrit Rietveld's red-blue chair of 1917 (see page 87) stands as a seminal prototype of Modernist theory put into practice. Self-consciously 'constructed' from machined elements, the chair is a translation of Piet Mondrian's depersonalized canvases into object design. The De Stijl artists provided an influential model for rationalists within the Bauhaus and elsewhere; in Paris, Eileen Gray's change of direction from creator of luxury lacquer-work to designer of functionalist prototypes owed much to her exchanges with the Dutch avant-garde.

The dynamic geometry of various fine art movements also contributed to the language of Modernist design; France's Cubist painters, Russia's Suprematists led by Malevich, Britain's Vorticists and the Dutch Constructivists suggested a radical new vernacular which could be refined into purist forms or reduced to merely decorative conceits. The Italian Futurists, led by Marinetti, extolled, both in their 1910 manifesto and in their creations, the virtues of the machine, glorifying speed, movement and industrialized urban life.

The basic ingredients of Modernist design, culled from these varied sources, were geometric forms, unadorned surfaces and exposed structure. Favourite materials were glass and metal, the latter often nickel-plated or chromium-plated steel. Non-tangible elements—light and space—were exploited with the same fervour with which other eras had used opulent textiles or carved wood. Colour was used with great restraint, white, neutral cream or beige, black, grey and the cold glint of white metal being considered sufficient. In its more expressve vein Modernism used highly stylized motifs derived from machinery, symbols of speed and energy, or crisp geometric abstractions which emphasized its depersonalized character.

Modernism flourished on the idea that man could strive towards an ideal state of harmony with his created environment; on the dream of a perfect relationship between man, machine and product in which form would be determined simply by function and material. Modernism was seen as a celebration of the machine age; the emancipation of the designer from the shackles of style. It often became a cult of the machine and of mechanical production. In their escape from ornament and decorative detail, designers fled traditional stylistic concerns yet developed their own strict canons of taste. Often, in spite of themselves, they became the most sophisticated exponents of style in the elegance of their minimalist perfectionism and their love of flawless detail and proportions.

Modernist emancipation from traditional values was paralleled by the gradual emancipation of women after the First World War and by the cult of physical well-being. In the twenties the first stages in women's hard-won liberation were reflected by fashion. This freedom was expressed by raised

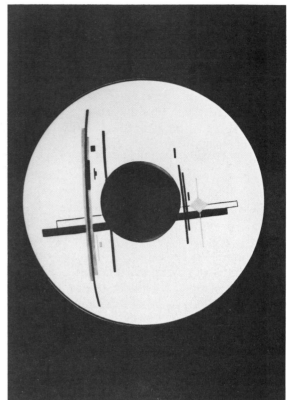

Above left Aluminium chaise longue designed by Marcel Breuer, 1935. Style seems to have been as much a dictating factor as function in this elegant post-Bauhaus design.

Above right Porcelain plate with Suprematist decoration by Chasnik, for the State porcelain factory, 1923. The dynamic geometric motifs of a graphic work by Malevitch have been applied to a standard plate.

Right Modernist carpet designed by Eileen Gray, late 1920s. Miss Gray produced many designs for carpets in the Modernist idiom, often showing the influence of the De Stijl group.

hemlines, unrestricted, straight, boyish silhouettes and by the new short-cropped hair-styles. Modernism attracted the first generation of women designers to excel in a traditionally male preserve. These included Eileen Gray, Charlotte Perriand, Evelyn Wyld and Charlotte Alix in Paris, Marianne Brandt and Lilly Reich at the Bauhaus and Marion Dorn in England.

In the Modernist era a complex phenomenon within the fashionable psyche interwove the cults of speed, the machine and mechanical energy with the new emphasis on female emancipation, sport, vitality and physical energy. The young couturier Gabrielle 'Coco' Chanel caught the mood of the moment with her easy day-wear and sporty, casual, resort wear; she led the fashion for the sun-tanned body as the outward symbol of physical well-being. The 1924 Diaghilev ballet *Le Train Bleu* set its swim-suited dancers, costumed by Chanel, in a stylized resort to which they had travelled on the legendary express train—the theme was as timely as the exotic fantasy of *Schéhérazade* had been fifteen years before. The machine was feared as much as it was revered and in 1926, two years after the success of *Le Train Bleu*, the film-maker Fritz Lang presented in *Metropolis* a vision of the city of the future in which the machine had become an ominous man-eater, the destroyer rather than the saviour of the masses. The cult of the body could be interpreted as a defiance of the supremacy of the machine, but Modernist designers sought a truce between man and machine. The detractors of Modernism would argue, however, that the search for rationalism and order often became a wilful

pursuit of the impersonal, a dehumanizing process which left a spiritual vacuum and was a denial of man's need for variety, fantasy and stimuli.

Modernism—achievements

Modernism became highly fashionable in the late twenties and the thirties, adopted by a host of designers whose work ranged from industrial design to prestige luxury commissions. At the forefront were the designers of the Dutch and German schools which had shaped the movement: the De Stijl designer Gerrit Rietveld designed furniture and light fittings in his 'constructed' style; Mart Stam developed tubular steel furniture and experimented with the steel cantilever chair.

Left Scene from the Diaghilev ballet *Le Train Bleu*, 1924. The dancers, wearing swim-suits designed by 'Coco' Chanel, perform before fashionably angular sets.

Left Scene from *Metropolis*, the 1926 vision of the future presented by the film-maker Fritz Lang.

Right Tubular steel cantilever armchair designed by Mies van der Rohe, 1927, for the Wiessenhof housing project, Stuttgart, and presented in the Werkbund exhibition of 1927.

Opposite left above Cover designed by Herbert Bayer for the 1923 review of the activities of the Bauhaus at Weimar since 1919. Bayer abandoned the use together of upper and lower case letters.

Opposite left below Advertising photograph by John Havinden for ICI's Sesqui soda, January 1933. Havinden skilfully adapted the graphic vernacular of Modernism to advertising photography.

At the Bauhaus Marcel Breuer and Mies van der Rohe took the laurels for furniture design. Breuer designed wooden furniture which acknowledged the debt to the De Stijl group in its self-consciously constructed look; and he subsequently developed simple, logical, elegant forms for chairs and tables in tubular steel and aluminium, which have now become part of the international currency of rational design. Mies was a purist whose statements that 'less is more' and 'God is in the details' proclaimed his meticulous minimalism and perfectionism. His deceptively simple chair and stool for the Barcelona exhibition of 1929 encapsulate his philosophy. This twentieth-century throne chair in hand-buffed steel and hide betrays no signs of handcraft; it assumes its regal role—austere, serene, a harmony of flawless lines and proportions.

Marianne Brandt and Wilhelm Wagenfeld achieved distinction with their metalwork designs composed of rigidly geometric forms. Typography and graphic design achieved notable order and clarity under the influence of Moholy-Nagy, Josef Albers and Herbert Bayer. Here the Bauhaus style was characterized by rationalized sanserif type-faces, the banishing of upper and lower case in combination, and the use of mathematically precise layouts designed on strict grids, sometimes incorporating intersecting diagonals. Moholy-Nagy was also an influential innovator in photography and explored abstract image-making, collage and the use of unexpected vantage points. Bauhaus ideologies also found expression in decorative and functional glass, ceramics, textile design, theatre design, silverware and lighting.

The closure of the Bauhaus and subsequent emigration of many of its members were as important to the decorative arts as to architecture. In England, Breuer designed elegant Modernist furniture in plywood for the firm of Isokon from 1935 to 1937, when he moved to the United States. His ideas for tubular steel furniture, and those of various contemporaries including Wells Coates and Serge Chermayeff, were put into large-scale production by the firm of PEL. Denham MacLaren designed a limited range of stylish glass, chromium-plated metal and marble furniture in a chic version of Modernism around 1930. Hand-woven rugs with bold, painterly, geometric motifs enjoyed a vogue and the most distinguished designers of these fashionable domestic accessories were Francis Bacon, Marion Dorn and Edward McKnight Kauffer; the latter was also a highly skilled poster designer. Ashley Havinden was an able exponent of Modernist typography and graphic design, a master of the eye-catching layout and uncluttered, highly legible script. His brother, John Havinden, explored the virtually uncharted territory of advertising photography in an original Modernist style.

In Scandinavia designers were laying the foundations for the major international role they were to

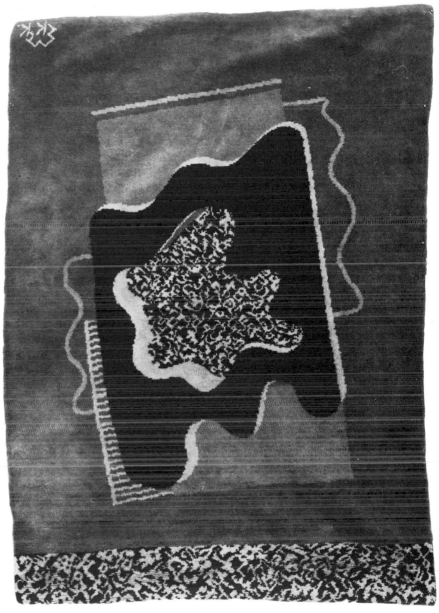

assume after the Second World War. The Scandinavian approach involved the development of rational new forms within the traditional context of a respect for craft and a preference for natural materials, textures and colours. The furniture designers Bruno Mathsson in Sweden and Kaare Klint in Denmark discovered a pleasing balance between innovation and tradition; a Danish designer Poul Henningsen espoused a more radical Modernism; and the Finnish designer and architect Alvar Aalto evolved simple, practical new furniture forms in ply and laminated woods. Aalto's first designs from around 1930 were conceived for the furnishing of the Paimio sanatorium and he set up his own manufacturing firm, Artek,

Above Rug designed by Edward McKnight Kauffer, early 1930s. The abstract motifs are strikingly similar to the fashionable graphics of the early 1980s (see page 275).

Above Armchair designed by Alvar Aalto for the Paimio sanatorium, 1931-2; ply and laminated wood. It is characteristic of the Scandinavian preference for warm, natural materials that Modernist designers should use wood rather than tubular steel.

Right Le Corbusier, photographic portrait by Man Ray, around 1930. The architect is wearing the circular-frame, straight sided spectacles which have since been caricatured as part of the uniform of the 'heroic' architect.

were responsive to the cold chic of steel, glass and crisp geometry.

Le Corbusier had led the way with his Pavillon de l'Esprit Nouveau at the 1925 exhibition, which inspired a whole generation of designers. The series of chairs, notably the chaise-longue, which he designed with Charlotte Perriand between 1928 and 1929, have become hallowed icons of Modernism. Other notable French figures included the architect Pierre Chareau, who used iron and wood in an inventive series of functionalist yet stylish furniture designs. Eileen Gray combined clever practicality and an unwavering sense of style in furniture and lighting design, but some of her work was only to reach production in the 1970s.

The jewellery designs of Fouquet, Sandoz, Templier and Paul Brandt were stunning examples of the application of geometric forms to luxury objects of the utmost refinement. Their work underlined the dichotomy between the democratic principles of the U.A.M. and the French love of fine finish and high style.

The Decorative Thirties

The thirties have been aptly described as the 'Indecisive Decade', a period delineated by two traumatic events, the Wall Street Crash of 1929 and the outbreak of the Second World War just ten years later. The early thirties were overshadowed by the effects of the Depression, the closing years of

in 1935. The Swedish Orrefors glass factory, meanwhile, was pioneering the simple, well-proportioned, functionalist glass which was to become a major Scandinavian contribution to design in the forties and fifties.

Modernist designers in France formed the Union des Artistes Modernes in 1930 as an exhibition society under the direction of René Herbst. The group included the architect-designers Le Corbusier, Charlotte Perriand, Eileen Gray, Robert Mallet-Stevens and Pierre Chareau; the graphic artists Paul Colin and A.M. Cassandre; the sculptors Josef Czaky, Gustav Myklos and Jan and Joël Martel; the jewellery and silverware designers Jean Fouquet, Gérard Sandoz, Raymond Templier and Jean Puiforcat; and the furniture and lighting designers Louis Sognot, Charlotte Alix, Jean Burkhalter, Jean Prouvé and Jacques Le Chevallier.

The U.A.M. manifesto, published in 1934, proclaimed that 'Modern Art is a truly socially aware art—a pure art accessible to all . . .', and quoted Tolstoy, 'Art for an élite is sterile art'. In practice, however, the U.A.M. membership seemed largely preoccupied with creating stylish designs for a sophisticated minority—those who were aware of the intellectual subtleties which dictated the fashionable pared-down forms and

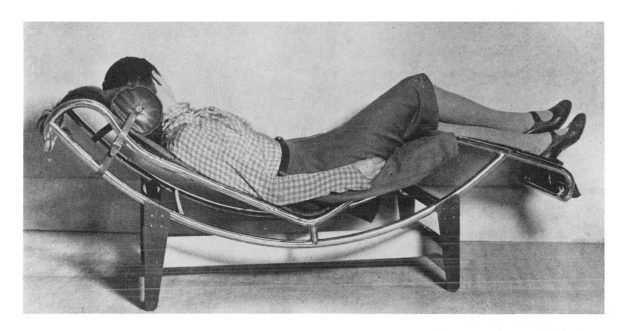

Left Charlotte Perriand reclining on the chaise-longue which she designed in collaboration with Le Corbusier, 1928-9. The photograph illustrated an article by Perriand, 'Wood or Metal?', published in *The Studio* in 1930.

Below Modernist geometry interpreted with considerable chic in a cigarette case decorated with lacquer and crushed eggshell, attributed to Paul Brandt, around 1928-30.

the decade by increasing international unrest. In the applied arts these were years of contrasts, from austere rationalism to extravagant escapism, and the story of design was closely related to social and political pressures.

The very wealthy continued to enjoy their sheltered world of privilege and, through their patronage, helped to keep alive the traditions of fine craft. Designers with more democratic concerns, or with a shrewd eye for the market, evolved modern styles appropriate to series production. These covered both the traditional areas of furniture and furnishings and the more novel categories of consumer goods, including kitchen equipment and electrical goods, for which the thirties saw a considerable increase in demand. A large and increasingly design-conscious middle-class market was emerging despite the Depression, greatly aided by the implementation of credit purchase facilities. This group was to shift the emphasis in consumer-oriented design from the demands of the wealthy few to the needs of a larger though less affluent social stratum, a trend evident in the thirties and destined to dominate post-war design.

At the same time, the demand for furniture and furnishings in traditional styles continued unabated, though with certain new emphases. In this decade emerged a new and influential breed of high-powered interior decorators, several of whom promoted the taste for antiques and antique styles, used in self-conscious, highly theatrical, often witty ways. The thirties witnessed a fashion for elaborate, baroque interiors, the revival of Regency and eighteenth-century styles, and styles inspired by antiquity.

Such fads were symptomatic of the need for escapism which so marked the decade, a need which manifested itself in the enormous success of the Hollywood film industry, which was geared up in the thirties to be a veritable dream-machine creating fantasy and idols for a mass market. A more subtle escapism was the exploration of the subconscious inspired by the Surrealist artists, whose influence on the applied arts, while largely restricted to avant-garde circles, was nonetheless significant in a variety of media including fashion, furniture and graphics.

Another group of decorative artists, known as the Neo-Romantics by virtue of the seductive charm and romantically imaginative qualities

Below **Cecil Beaton, photographic portrait by Paul Tanqueray, 1930s. This image typifies the playful, baroque interpretation of Surrealist themes in fashionable circles in the thirties.**

of their work, made a considerable impact on fashion illustration, the theatre and decorative painting. The group included the highly talented Christian 'Bébé' Berard, a catalystic figure in fashionable Parisian circles, the inventive *trompe-l'œil* artist Eugène Berman and the painter Pavel Tchelitchev. Their work combined *trompe-l'œil* tricks and the imagery of Surrealism with elements of wistful naivety rendered in pastel shades. They found success on both sides of the Channel and across the Atlantic, attracting such patrons and acolytes as the art-dealer Julien Levy and the young photographer and diarist Cecil Beaton. As Modernism became more conventional and entered the mainstream of design, so the fashionable turned to these decorative idioms. Modernism co-existed with decorative fantasies in a decade of seemingly contradictory tendencies.

Decorative design in the thirties drew eclectically on historical references. Borrowings from antiquity can be traced in such diverse manifestations as the furniture and decorative schemes of J. Robsjohn-Gibbings in the United States; the bronze furniture and lamps created in Paris by Alberto Giacometti for the decorator Jean-Michel Frank; the dresses of the couturier Alix, specialist in draperies and tight pleats reminiscent of Greek tunics; and in the fashion photography of George Hoyningen-Huené who was to publish, in 1943, a homage to the beauties of ancient Greek ruins. Historicism was back in vogue and embraced such talents as the whimsical British muralist and illustrator Rex Whistler and the work of interior decorators in both Europe and the United States. Meanwhile, a new generation of French designers and craftsmen was evolving a fresh stylistic repertoire, often drawing on historical references, though they continued to employ the luxurious materials and techniques common to Art Deco. Prominent among them were the decorators and furniture designers, Eugène Printz, André Arbus and Jacques Adnet.

The most exciting decorators included Lady Mendl, an American, born Elsie de Wolfe, who created stylish baroque interiors; Syrie Maugham, who became known in London around 1930 for her restrained monochrome schemes but later favoured a more elaborate theatrical style; and the Frenchman Jean-Michel Frank, a master of understatement in meticulously finished interiors which exploited the subtle contrasts of natural materials and tints. Louis Süe, of Süe et Mare, created extravagant interiors for Helena Rubinstein in the late thirties, and Lady Colefax and Hermann Schriver were prime exponents of the fashion for

Left Interior created for Mme Helena Rubinstein in the late 1930s by Louis Süe, formerly of the decorating firm of Süe et Mare. Baroque furnishings are juxtaposed with Surrealist canvases.

mixing old and new, now something of a cliché. The co–existence of Modernism and romanticism is well illustrated by the baroque fantasies concocted by Charles de Bestegui within the austere volumes of a Paris apartment by Le Corbusier.

A wealthy British art patron, Edward James, like de Bestegui in Paris, carried the taste for the unexpected to almost absurd limits. James became an adventurous patron of Surrealist fantasy in furniture and furnishings as well as on canvas, and it was for James that Salvador Dali designed his anthropomorphic fireplace. Surrealism also brought an element of wit into fashion, to be seen in the work of the couturier Elsa Schiaparelli whose conceits included a hat in the form of a shoe, designed with Dali, coats embroidered with drawings by Jean Cocteau, fabrics printed with *trompe-l'œil* rips, and pockets in the form of lips. She became the most newsworthy figure in Paris fashion.

Right Mural decoration by
Rex Whistler for the dining-
room at Plas Newydd, 1936-7.
Whistler was a master of
these baroque fantasies, a
historicist taste that ran
completely counter to
Modernism.

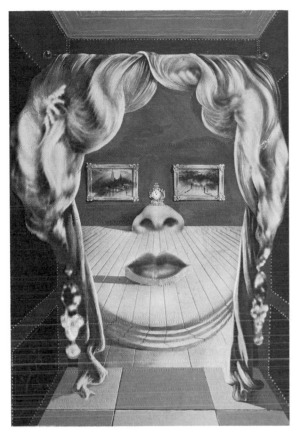

Far left 'Mae West' Surrealist decor by Salvador Dali, conceived in the 1930s for Edward James, an eccentric patron of Surrealism.

Near left 'Shoe' hat and a suit with pockets in the shape of lips (inspired by Dali) by Elsa Schiaparelli. These are typical of the witty conceits by this couturier which brought her a fame tinged with notoriety in the thirties.

High fashion reflected trends in other areas of design. The sleek silhouettes of the early thirties had been in harmony with the uncluttered lines of Modernism, typified at their most elegant by the bias-cut silk-satin sheaths of Madeleine Vionnet, and vulgarized with some flair by Jean Harlow. But eventually these gave way to more elaborate silhouettes and by the close of the decade accentuated shoulders, nipped waists and fuller skirts confirmed the new romanticism and anticipated the post-war New Look. This romanticism, like the optimism of the Futurama city of New York World's Fair in 1939, was a defiance of the forbidding realities of international politics.

Left New York World's Fair, 1939. This general view of the installations, showing the Trylon and Perisphere, gives some idea of the 'brave new world' architecture of the last great pre-war international exhibition.

127

INDUSTRIAL DESIGN

In this period, for a number of reasons, many of them purely economic, the concept of industrial design became far more widespread and effective. As a result, designers achieved a new status in society and, since design is so inseparable from commerce, it is hardly surprising that the first professional consultant designers should have emerged in the United States, the world's most commercial nation. Unlike Europe, design in the United States was rarely promoted by official or quasi-official bodies. Instead, it became an adjunct of marketing, a part of the communications business, neither more nor less important than advertising. It was in America that the independent 'design consultants' first appeared, and it was there that design found its true significance as a part of the modern economy.

The very concept of 'design' in America has always been somewhat different from that held in Europe. Travelling in the United States, Charles Dickens frequently remarked on how *temporary* everything looked, and ten years or so before, Alexis de Tocqueville had been struck by how restless the Americans seemed—almost, he said, as if they were searching for 'distractions from their happiness'. Edgar Allen Poe explained, 'We have no aristocracy of blood, and having . . . fashioned for ourselves an aristocracy of dollars, the display of wealth has . . . to take the place and perform the office of heraldic display in monarchical countries.'

American design, in its first phases, was largely about the display of wealth, and at the time that the first Model T Fords were appearing consumer design was directed to what were called 'women's tastes'. By the 1920s the economic boom of the early years of the century had been halted by the recession, and the Wall Street Crash of 1929 followed. Also, the success of Sears Roebuck's mail order service in supplying the needs of the nation had been such that a sort of stasis had been achieved and the production cycle had reached equilibrium. But in the modern economy, at least in the western system, commercial success, indeed survival, is dependent on constantly increasing consumption—that is to say growth. By the mid-twenties there was no growth, so manufacturers were forced to compete against each other in order to gain a place in the market. Also the National Recovery Act eventually stabilized prices and so removed yet another element from consumer choice.

Below The comparison between General Motors' 1926 Chevrolet and its 1932 successor (*opposite*) shows how design, now self-consciously a matter of 'styling', evolved to meet the needs of marketing.

The struggle for market share could have led to any number of disreputable practices. In fact, it led to the creation of the first generation of independent consultant industrial designers, for in these stagnant market conditions American manufacturers found they could increase their sales by adding *style* to their products. Goods were now competing on appearance alone, and design entailed not graceful form-giving, nor a quest for efficient function, nor indeed laudable social gestures: design was solely the manipulation of an object's character and appearance in order to stimulate more sales. Once dubbed by Henry Dreyfuss 'the silent salesman', the American designer separated himself entirely from his European colleagues to become a business consultant who specialized in taste.

The first generation of design professionals—Raymond Loewy, Norman Bel Geddes, Walter Dorwin Teague and Henry Dreyfuss—helped design America out of the recession, and working on everything from soft-drink bottles through duplicators to locomotives, they provided some of the most memorable imagery of the twentieth century. The term 'industrial design' was in use as early as 1919, but by the 1920s it was a topic of popular debate and American consumer magazines started running articles with such titles as 'Best Dressed Products Sell Best'. The designers became popular heroes, aided by their ability to market themselves as well as their products.

Initially Henry Ford resisted the idea of appearance for appearance's sake, and his Model T, despite criticism about its lack of style, continued to sell a million units a year. But in 1926 General Motors introduced a new Chevrolet that was deliberately stylish and colourful. In that year Chevrolet, for the first time, sold more cars than Ford, forcing Ford to reply with his 1927 Model A. At the same time, the DuPont chemical company (which had once owned General Motors) developed Duco synthetic paint whose wide range of colours at last released car manufacturers from the monochromatic strictures of Ford. Recognizing the implications of these innovations, Ford now declared, 'Design will take more advantage of the power of the machine to go beyond what the hand can do and will give us a whole new art.'

The challenge to General Motors had been brought about primarily by economic factors. Ford's efficient production lines had dropped the price of the Model T to only $290 and threatened

Right Bantam Special camera designed by Walter Dorwin Teague for Kodak, 1936. Teague remained closely involved with the design of Kodak products for the rest of his life.

Below Texaco filling station designed by Walter Dorwin Teague, 1930s. In his book *Design This Day* (1940) Teague compared the modern garage to the temples of the ancients.

the profits of other manufacturers. General Motors, therefore, had to find other ways of making a profit and they realized that styling could add value in the eye of the customer. In response to this need for styling, Alfred Sloan created an 'Art and Color' section within General Motors in 1928 and hired a Californian custom-body shop proprietor called Harley Earl to run it. Earl rose to become vice-president in charge of styling for the entire General Motors Corporation and had control

over the appearance of every General Motors product from cars and fridges to railway locomotives and buses until 1959. His period of greatest influence was in the fifties, but his initial appointment was an early indication of the national awareness of styling and design.

While Harley Earl did have some experience in car design, most of the other pioneer designers had very different backgrounds, in theatre, window-dressing and fashion illustration. Walter Dorwin Teague had been a graphic artist before setting up an industrial design consultancy in 1926. His first major client was Eastman Kodak and in 1936 he produced the Bantam Special camera. This, with its horizontal metal banding, apparently decorative but in fact essential in preventing the cracking of the body lacquer, is a skilful marriage of styling and function. His other work included industrial machinery, Pullman cars and Texaco service stations. He was also the author of an important

Left Duplicator designed by Raymond Loewy for Gestetner, 1929. This piece of streamlined office furniture stood for many years as a symbol of the designer's effectiveness.

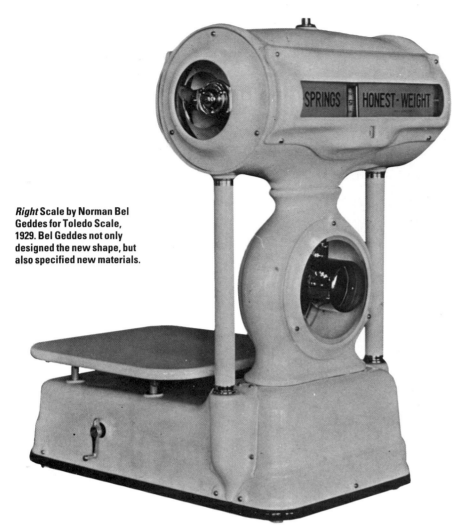

Right Scale by Norman Bel Geddes for Toledo Scale, 1929. Bel Geddes not only designed the new shape, but also specified new materials.

early book on industrial design, *Design This Day*, published in 1940.

Norman Bel Geddes, on the other hand, had been trained in the theatre, but under the influence of Modern Movement designers such as Erich Mendelsohn and Le Corbusier he saw that the world at large offered a broader canvas than the stage. Geddes actually designed very little, but his two visionary illustrated books, *Horizons* and *Magic Motorways*, and his countless appearances in magazines helped introduce the American public to a sort of Modernism in design.

He was also a pioneer of opinion polls and his 'consumer-use surveys' established a pseudo-scientific basis for his designs. Garnering his data from surveys done on, for instance, trans-continental trains, Geddes was able to determine the precise market requirements for any given product long before he actually began designing it.

It was Geddes who introduced Henry Dreyfuss to industrial design. Dreyfuss, who had been Geddes's assistant in a Broadway production, set up his own studio in 1929 and his first major job was perhaps his most successful, the design of the 300 telephone for Bell. Dreyfuss was a pioneer of the science of ergonomics and believed that objects

Right 300 telephone designed by Henry Dreyfuss for Bell Telephones, 1937. By paying careful attention to functional and ergonomic requirements, Dreyfuss was able to design a shape that lasted unchanged for decades.

Opposite above Refrigerator designed by Raymond Loewy, 1955. Loewy's first refrigerator for Sears Roebuck (1935) transformed sales; different models continued to appear over the following years.

Opposite below Lucky Strike cigarette packet designed by Raymond Loewy, 1942. The clean graphics suggested quality and became an international touchstone of successful commercial packaging.

should respond to the requirements of the human body. He also understood the idea, then novel, that a consumer product should, as it were, be designed from the inside out, so that its appearance was determined by the functional necessities of its components. The Bell management was at first sceptical, perhaps even incredulous, but Dreyfuss's elegant and efficient design went into production in 1937 and, manufactured in huge numbers to meet wartime demand, became an international symbol of modern America.

Unlike his contemporary Raymond Loewy, Dreyfuss was never seduced by streamlining and other styling gimmicks. But it is probably fair to say that Loewy better represented the real concerns of American consumer society between the wars. Loewy thoroughly understood the business of sales, and indeed his greatest sales success was his own personality and elaborately crafted life style— he even managed to appear on the cover of *Time* magazine. Paid annual retainers of between $10,000 and $60,000, he took full advantage of the commercial possibilities of his professional status, a business consultant specializing in taste.

Loewy, who trained as an engineer, was born in France, and as the only American pioneer consultant designer who was not a native he could see the phenomenon of American civilization afresh. He was very impressed, and his observations about the country are moving because they are so frank, original and uncomplicated: 'I have seen assembly line or spray booth operators that would make movie stars look like tired head waiters.'

Loewy thought of the American consumer as 'the working aristocracy of the world' and, rather as Edgar Allan Poe had suggested, he set about giving them the trappings of a democratic, mass-produced version of wealth. He created the heraldry of America. At one time it would have been possible for an American citizen to pass his entire day surrounded by products and packages designed by Loewy and his team: Studebaker cars, Pepsodent toothpaste, Schick razors, Greyhound buses, Lucky Strike cigarettes, Carling beer and, if he were the President, Air Force One.

It was in Raymond Loewy's work that the distinction between styling and design became marked. To the élite group of New York and New England architects and designers associated with the Museum of Modern Art, Loewy's slick commercialism was dishonest and vulgar. The Museum's director, Alfred H. Barr, condemned him for having a 'blind concern with fashion'.

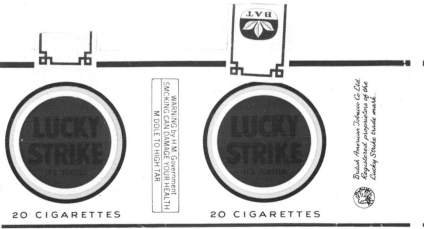

America: the romantic engineer

The futuristic images of Norman Bel Geddes's *Horizons* (1932) did much to popularize the concept of streamlining, which American industrial designers then evolved into a distinctive national style for product design which is generally labelled 'streamline Moderne'. The exaggerated aerodynamic styling, even of static objects, evoked the dynamism of speed and the machine, and in the thirties became the first widespread style for American consumer product packaging, applied on every scale from the locomotive to the office stapler. It was found that plastics, now widely used, could be readily moulded into streamlined forms.

Streamlining was an expression of the romance of the machine, and during this period American aero engineers, notably John Northrop and 'Kelly' Johnson, created some of the most unforgettable forms of the century. But their aeroplanes were not merely exercises in slick styling: they were imaginative applications of technology, using streamlining to reduce drag and increase stability in a manner that had first been explored by automobile designers at the beginning of the century. Flying machines have, of necessity, to respect the laws of physics but these engineers stretched the laws to their limits in their search for functional efficiency and aesthetic form.

It was John Knudsen Northrop whose aircraft did most to impress the concept of streamlining on the imagination of the public. He was co-founder of the Lockheed Aircraft Company and chief designer of the 1927 Lockheed Vega monoplane, a vehicle of astonishingly dramatic appearance, proportions and performance which Amelia Earhart used on her solo Atlantic crossing in 1932. George Hubert Wilkins, the first man to fly over the top *and* bottom of the world, saw one of Northrop's Vegas in 1927 and wrote of it in his book *Flying the Arctic*: 'I marked the beauty of streamline, angle of incidence, and attack of the wing in level flight. . . . As it turned towards me I realized the full beauty of its design. It apparently offered no head resistance except for the engine, leading edge and a slim landing gear. It had no flying wires; no controls exposed—nothing but a flying wing.'

Northrop was consistently thirty years ahead of his time, a pioneer of all-metal aircraft construction (hitherto wood and canvas had been used), but most importantly the pioneer of the tail-less plane, or 'flying wing'. He developed a multi-cellular structural system, using shaped and riveted alloy sheets to form sub-assemblies. These made up the spars and ribs of a structure that functioned like a series of torsion boxes.

The flying wing has technical advantages because it allows the airframe designer to dispense with all those components, including the tailplane, which contribute to drag. The result is more aerodynamic efficiency, and therefore more speed, greater payload or longer range, or a combination of all three. Northrop's first all-wing aircraft appeared in 1928, about the same time that Alexander Lippisch was finalizing designs for his own flying wing which he called the Delta: but the first true 'wing' did not fly until 1940. This aeroplane, the N-1M was very near to Northrop's own goal of ultimate simplicity in design—a favourite maxim of his was 'What you don't put into an airplane can't give you no trouble.'

It was when US generals and strategists began to fear German victory in Europe that they realized the demand for a long-range bomber for the Army Air Force. This became the magnificent Northrop XB-35. A wing weighing 165,000 lbs (75,000 kilos) and carrying a crew of fifteen, it did not fly until 1946, a year after the end of the war. The XB-35 was radical and successful but plagued by mundane mechanical faults. Northrop's vision went beyond the capacity of the available propulsion technology and the four 3000-horsepower Pratt & Whitney Wasp Major reciprocating engines that powered the XB-35 were replaced by jet engines in the YB-49, which first flew in 1947 and could fly faster and farther than any of its rivals.

Another American engineer, Donald Douglas, said, 'Every major aircraft in the sky has some Jack Northrop in it.' Despite this, Northrop retired demoralized in 1952 because his flying wing had been cancelled by the Air Force. Later, in 1979, NASA's Administrator, Robert A. Froisch, wrote to Northrop saying, 'Our studies of technology needs for potential large cargo . . . aircraft have led us to investigations of span-loaded configurations during which we have, in effect, rediscovered the flying wing.'

Clarence L. 'Kelly' Johnson fared better than Northrop, but his real achievements were not apparent until during and after the Second World War. Still, his aircraft designs show how stylistic concerns exist even among the most disciplined engineers, and the success of his designs proves that the dominant forms of the age trickle down into popular culture. Johnson's design for the wartime Lockheed P-38, with its dramatic twin tail-booms, was the inspiration for Harley Earl's General Motors tail-fins during the fifties. While Earl toyed with the symbolism of science fiction, Johnson made it reality; what Norman Bell Geddes could not even imagine, 'Kelly' Johnson was engi-

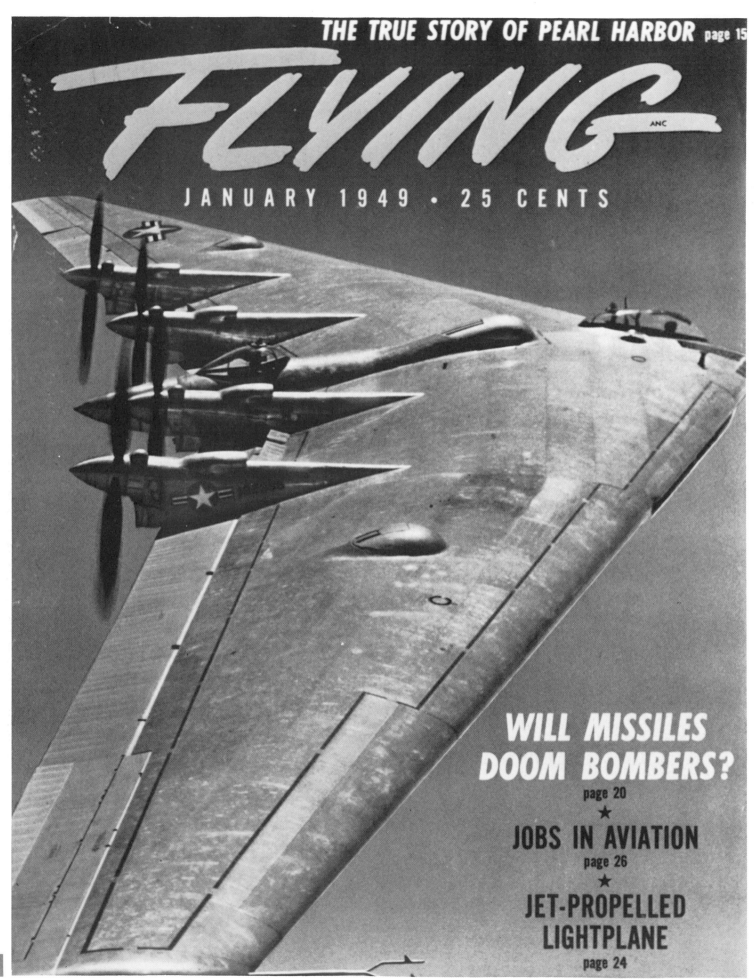

THE TRUE STORY OF PEARL HARBOR page 15

Flying

JANUARY 1949 · 25 CENTS

WILL MISSILES DOOM BOMBERS?
page 20
★
JOBS IN AVIATION
page 26
★
JET-PROPELLED LIGHTPLANE
page 24

neering. His other work of the thirties, which only flew in the forties and fifties, included the Lockheed P-80 Shooting Star, America's first jet aeroplane; as Lockheed's chief designer from 1952 Johnson was also responsible for the Starfighter, the U-2, the C-130 Hercules and the SR-71.

Johnson deplored specialization and revered the creative genius of the individual, practical engineer. He ran Lockheed's experimental 'Skunk Works' with no organization charts, and specialists swapped disciplines and exchanged opinions.

The rational tradition in Germany

At the end of the war the atmosphere in Germany was one of despair, with unemployed artists and architects banding together in radical groups. Revolution was in the air and a Bavarian Soviet was briefly established in 1919. The architect Hans Poelzig tried to turn the clock back, declaring at the Werkbund's Stuttgart conference of 1919 that industry was necessarily concerned only with business and that the true task of the Werkbund should be to promote art. Art, he said, should

Opposite **XB-35 designed by John Knudsen Northrop for the Army Air Force, 1946.** In the 1980s aero engineers are again recognizing the technological advantages of Northrop's 'flying wing'.

Above **P-38 designed by Clarence L. 'Kelly' Johnson for Lockheed, 1939.**

Near right Lamp by Marianne Brandt, around 1926. Brandt designed in the sparse, geometric style which characterized the self-conscious functionalism of the Bauhaus.

Far right Lamp designed by Marianne Brandt, around 1928. Such plain, unadorned desk lamps are typical of the break with the earlier tradition in which decoration was applied to functional objects.

Below Teapot by Marguerite Friedländer-Wildenhain, 1929-30. A simple, timeless, practical form, well adapted to industrial manufacture.

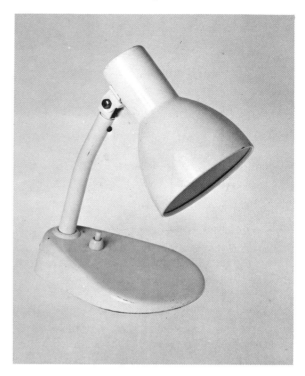

disclaim any contact with business and the Werkbund should be concerned with creativity, not with industry.

In this radical-reactionary atmosphere, Behrens believed he was witnessing 'the collapse of a technically and economically advanced civilization'. Indeed, two of Behrens' own studio assistants, Walter Gropius and Ludwig Mies van der Rohe, became involved in the revolutionary Arbeitsrat für Kunst and the Novembergruppe. But out of this revolutionary atmosphere Walter Gropius emerged to found the Bauhaus.

Although the Bauhaus has, quite correctly, the reputation for being the scriptural home of the Modern Movement, its first years in Weimar (discussed below in the context of Architecture) were expressionist in character. Gropius was motivated by genuine pedagogic and democratic concerns; his design theory was to stress aesthetic principles and encourage pupils to strive for geometrically pure forms. He did not, however, disdain the use of machines and one of the most important achievements of the Bauhaus was the development, largely by Marcel Breuer, of tubular steel furniture for series production. This was inspired by a remarkable early example of mass production: the furniture, of steamed and bent wood, made by the Thonet company in Austria since the mid-nineteenth century. One of Breuer's earliest tubular steel chairs, the B5 of 1926, was manufactured by Thonet.

Under Gropius the Bauhaus successfully promulgated ideas about modern design and its relationship to industry which had been originated by Peter Behrens; they had first found expression in his work for AEG and in the charter of the Werkbund. But Gropius's great advantage was that, unlike his mentor Behrens, he was not tied to the relatively narrow concerns of an electrical engineering concern, nor indeed to any commercial undertaking. Gropius, as Tilmann Buddensieg pointed out, was able to look upon his school as a laboratory, and 'he stood on the broad shoulders of Behrens as the apostles stood on the shoulders of the prophets'.

German industrial design in the inter-war years reflected the complex economic and political climate of the period, both in the troubled years of the Weimar Republic and in the National Socialist regime which grew out of its ashes.

Industrial production suffered in the period of social and revolutionary unrest which followed Germany's defeat, but by 1924 the economic crisis had passed as a result of American loans and investment, so industrial regeneration became possible. American notions of modern management in industry gave a fresh impetus to practicality in design, technology and production. Indeed Henry Ford's autobiography was an immediate bestseller when first published in Germany in 1924. The recovery of industry could be seen in the renewed activities of the Deutsche Werkbund, such an important body in German design circles

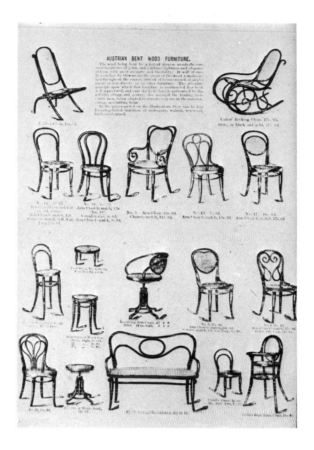

Left **Bentwood furniture by Thonet, 1885. Thonet's designs, a radical response to the demands of mass production, were an inspiration to Bauhaus designers.**

Below **Furniture by Marcel Breuer in the home of Erwin Piscator, 1927. This interior, with its chic minimalism expressed by 'industrial' components, underlines the ambiguities of the Bauhaus style.**

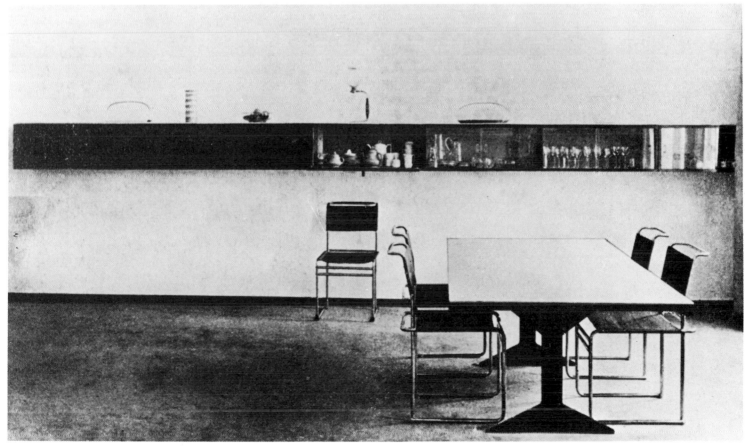

Right: Die Form, 1929. The Werkbund's journal was devoted to raising the standards of industrial design. Sanserif typefaces characterize the minimalist ambitions of German functionalism.

DIE FORM

ZEITSCHRIFT FÜR GESTALTENDE ARBEIT

4. JAHR

HEFT 21

1. NOVEMBER 1929

VERLAG HERMANN RECKENDORF G. M. B. H. BERLIN SW 48

DAS BUCH

before 1914, which once more became a rallying point for progressive ideas. It propagandized for a 'Neue Zeit' (New Spirit), as could be seen in its 'Form Ohne Ornament' (Form without Ornament) exhibition of 1924, where hand-crafted and machine-produced articles were shown alongside each other. Form was seen as a substitute for ornamentation, and standardized forms, geared to mass-production technology, epitomized simplicity, rationality and a machine aesthetic. Ferdinand Kramer, a leading designer of domestic equipment represented at the exhibition, exemplified these ideals in the clean, geometric forms of metal jugs and a cast-iron stove.

The mid-1920s was a period of renewed municipal patronage in a number of cities, including Breslau, Dessau, Frankfurt and Stuttgart. Progressive thinkers encouraged 'Neue Gestaltung' (New Design) and 'Neue Bauen' (New Architecture) as appropriate settings for the 'Neue Wohnen' (New Life-style). In Frankfurt, the magazine *Das Neue Frankfurt*, published from 1926 to 1933, sought to show how design and architecture could endow the city with a modern spirit. More revealing perhaps was the publication of the *Frankfurter Register* which listed approved mass-produced designs of a wide variety of domestic equipment and fittings, from lighting to telephones, a spiritual forerunner of the British Council of Industrial Design's Design Index, which evolved from planning for the 1951 Festival of Britain. However, this spirit of optimism was overtaken by yet another crisis in German industrial production, resulting from the decline in foreign investment and the withdrawal of US war loans in the wake of the Wall Street Crash. The social, economic and political crisis which followed led to the rise of the National Socialists under Adolf Hitler.

Although the Bauhaus was closed in 1933 and its leading figures emigrated, the rational tradition in Germany remained alive and a few industrial prototypes were put into production. These included pottery for the State Porcelain Factory in Berlin, lighting for Körting & Matthiesen of Leipzig and Schwintzler & Graff of Berlin, as well as tubular steel furniture, textiles and wallpaper for a number of other firms. Such items were insignificant both in terms of the income generated and the wider context of manufacturing output, but they demonstrate that the Modernist industrial aesthetic of the Bauhaus and other progressive design centres of the 1920s was not entirely swept away in the *völkisch* tide of the Third Reich.

Wilhelm Wagenfeld, a pupil and teacher at the Bauhaus during the 1920s and a member of the Deutsche Werkbund, continued to design in the same clean, geometric machine forms under the Third Reich as he had in the Weimar years. Such work included porcelain for the Fürstenberg and Rosenthal factories, cutlery for the Württembergische Metallfabrik, inexpensive pressed glass for the Lausitzer Glasverein, including the Kubus modular stacking containers.

Hermann Gretsch was another noted designer who also employed a Modernist aesthetic vocabulary under the Third Reich, as in his ceramic designs for Arzberg and Villeroy & Boch. From 1935 Gretsch led the Deutsche Werkbund division of the Kampfbund für Deutsche Kultur (Fighting

Left Cast-iron stoves by Ferdinand Kramer, 1931. These compact, efficient designs were part of an extensive programme to improve living conditions in Frankfurt.

Left Advertisement for Jena glass designed by Wilhelm Wagenfeld, around 1930. This inexpensive, functional glass, entirely compatible with mass production, reflects Wagenfeld's commitment to good industrial design.

Right Messerschmitt 109, 1935. Captured German aircraft were used by the RAF, hence the British insignia.

Right: The Flying Hamburger for German State Railways, 1933. Adopting the lightweight bodies and diesel engines of airships, this streamlined railcar was remarkably fast.

Opposite Zeppelin airship under construction, photographed by E.O. Hoppé and published by Deutsche Arbeit, 1930. In Germany transportation was seen as a symbol of national prestige and the Zeppelin was a favourite Nazi progaganda device.

League for German Culture) which aimed to promote German goods on the export market. Five years later he was responsible for the publication of the *Gestaltetes Handwerk* (Creative Handicrafts) which was close in spirit to the Deutsche Werkbund of the 1920s.

Engineering design was an important element of the German technological regeneration under the Third Reich. It was promoted in a number of contemporary exhibitions and by the award of the German Prize in 1938 to a quartet of engineer-designers: the aircraft designers Ernst Heinkel and Willy Messerschmitt, Fritz Todt the autobahn planner and Ferdinand Porsche the automobile engineer.

The foundations of an efficient transportation network had, in fact, been laid before Hitler came

to power. By the 1930s, Lufthansa, using the Dutch Fokker Trimotor, one of the most successful airliners before the advent of the American Douglas DC3, had the most comprehensive network of air routes in Europe. Railway design also developed at this time and German State Railways were able to boast a number of fast, well-designed trains such as the streamlined, two-unit, diesel electric railcars of 1933, including the celebrated *Flying Hamburger*. Count Kruckenberg's aerodynamic, air-conditioned railcars of 1937 featured even more expressive streamlining.

Porsche's design for the Volkswagen car is the outstanding example of the German rational tradition in design: it is a piece of popular machinery in which every detail betrays the character and ideals of the designers and engineers who produced

it. After a distinguished career as an engineer with Austro-Daimler, Porsche had opened his own design office in Stuttgart in 1930 and here he began work on his Volksauto, in every respect a forerunner of the Volkswagen. Although the specific performance of the prototype was encouraging, it was not taken into production because NSU, Porsche's clients, believed that the future lay with motorcycles. Hitler felt the same, but said at the 1934 Berlin motor show, 'What *I* want to see is a mass-produced car costing virtually the same as a motorcycle.' In the same speech the Führer coined the word 'Volkswagen', the people's car. Costing no more than one thousand marks, this project was to give the Reich a consumer product to accompany the 'Volksarchitektur'. Immediately after this speech Porsche submitted a specification of the Volkwagen to the German

Transport Ministry, and a contract for the project was signed in June 1934.

Hitler then suggested that Porsche visited the United States to observe Henry Ford's production. 'Remember', he said, 'the price is . . . fixed at a thousand reichsmarks, but you will not have to worry about any return on investment, or to allow vast sums for sales organization. We don't need any of that. I will get rid of all the middlemen and their unnecessary profits when selling the people's car.' Porsche's son, Ferry, described to Ford the car of the future: 'The future car in Europe is going to be of modest size, although a full four-seater, capable of carrying any size adults in comfort. It will be able to cruise without effort at a minimum of sixty to seventy miles per hour for almost indefinite distances, since we too are building super highways—the autobahns—in Germany.'

The design for the Volkswagen—by now re-christened by Hitler the 'Kampf durch Freude wagen'—was finalized in 1936 but the war interrupted production plans and only military versions were produced. The first true Volkswagens became available in 1946. They were designed by Porsche, with a body by Erwin Komenda and an engine by Josef Kales.

Other European developments: Italy and Britain

Mussolini's Fascist Italy, like Hitler's Germany of the Third Reich, saw many significant improvements in transportation, its most impressive legacy being the *autostrade*. And, just as Ferdinand Porsche had been experimenting in Germany on the Volkswagen (and Pierre Boulanger in France with the Michelin Company on what was later to become the Citroën 2CV), Italy's 'people's car' was

realized in Dante Giacosa's Fiat 500 of 1937, portrayed in the advertising as 'Bella, Comoda, Economica'.

The Italian railways were also modernized and electrified under Mussolini, with celebrated designs such as the ETR 200 express locomotive which went into service in 1936. The ability of Italian Fascism to accommodate progressive design and architecture alongside traditional forms is evident from the design by Michelucchi and others for Florence railway station. Here modern lighting, clocks, seating and other accessories were co-ordinated with the building, an ensemble expressing a Modernist spirit.

However, although it continued to be a live force throughout the period, Modernism never enjoyed a position of real dominance after Mussolini's rise

Opposite, above and below The Volkswagen prototype by Ferdinand Porsche, and the finalized design at the opening of the Volkswagen plant in 1936.

Above Citroën 2CV, 1939, the body by André Lefebvre and Flaminio Bertoni. The design, with its ostentatious geometry, unsophisticated materials and industrial finishes, suggests the influence of the Bauhaus.

Left Fiat 500 designed by Dante Giacosa, 1936. The Topolino with its radical design was only successful in Italy.

Right **Wedgwood ceramic vase designed by Keith Murray, 1930s. Murray worked for Wedgwood from 1935 and designed a range of ceramics in the purist Modernist mode.**

Below **Dressing-table by Heals, around 1930. The spartan lines of such pieces lent themselves to series production and anticipate the practical and austere look of furniture made under the wartime Utility programme.**

to power in the early 1920s. Nonetheless, it was an important force in debates about an aesthetic style appropriate for Fascism, and it emerged as Rationalism in 1926. Many of the Rationalists were receptive to the Fascist emphasis on youth and dynamism, since it promised to bring about a cultural revolution as its aesthetic counterpart. However, the fact that the movement was largely international, rather than national, in outlook was perhaps a strong reason why it failed to establish itself as *the* style of Fascism. The more progressive factions in 1920s design were rooted in the north of Italy, erstwhile home of Futurism and mainstay of the Italian manufacturing industry. Rome, on the other hand, sought to emphasize its links with the Roman imperial past, thus confirming a socio-cultural divide which resurfaced after Italy's defeat in the Second World War.

The Modernist aesthetic was continually promoted during the 1920s and 1930s by a vociferous and articulate minority, particularly at the Triennale exhibitions which, having been held at Monza until 1930, were moved to Milan in 1933 and have become focal points for design debates ever since. At the 1930 Triennale Italian designers and industrialists were exposed to progressive German design in an exhibit organized by the Berlin Werkbund, which included scientific apparatus manufactured by Siemens, tubular steel furniture by Mies van der Rohe and products of the Bauhaus. The most striking Italian exhibit was the Electric House, designed by Figini, Pollini and others for the Edison Company, which included a variety of electrical appliances. For the most part, however, the Triennali of the 1930s were showcases for rationalist design, rather than stimuli for production, since few manufacturers would put such progressive ideas into production on a large commercial scale.

Magazines were also important disseminators of progressive design and technological innovation, particularly *Domus*, founded in 1928 under the editorship of Gio Ponti, the father of modern Italian design; also *Casabella* which, from the early 1930s, carried articles on subjects as diverse as German tubular steel furniture, artificial fibres and resins, aluminium alloys and glass. Italy, like Germany in the 1930s, stressed the need for total control and therefore the development of altern-

Left Radio, Model AD65, designed by Wells Coates for Ekco, 1934. Earlier radios had tended to resemble cabinet furniture, but this was a serious attempt to apply the principles of modern design to the products of modern technology.

ative and synthetic materials became an important issue. Industry began to investigate the possibility of using home-produced, rather than imported, materials; Gio Ponti urged manufacturers to take note of the Triennali and other such exhibitions as proof of the economic (as well as aesthetic) potential of rationally produced Italian designs. As the economic climate became more fraught in the second half of the decade, there was a renewed interest in standardization as a key element in design.

A number of interesting designs were produced in this atmosphere, stimulated by the competitions sponsored by industry, such as that organized in 1936 by the National Gramophone Company in conjunction with *Domus* and *Casabella*. This called for radio designs which used Italian-produced woods and synthetic resins. Many of these radios evolved from acoustic and technological research, and were potent expressions of the modern, rational, industrial aesthetic.

British industrial design achievements of the inter-war period were very mixed. There were a number of apparently healthy signs of a growing respect for industrial design: the continual campaigning of the Design and Industries Association (DIA); the establishment of the Society of Industrial Artists (SIA); and increased governmental involvement in the field, with a number of committees set up to examine design matters, such as the Gorell Committee on Art and Industry which reported in 1932. Other promising signs included

the establishment of the Council for Art and Industry under the Board of Trade in 1933 and the staging of a number of important and well-attended exhibitions of industrial design during the decade.

The fact that most historians of British design have been individuals with intimate connections with many of the official bodies has tended to overemphasize their true historical significance. Many campaigners for better standards of design in British industry were still guided by the tenets of the Arts and Crafts movement rather than the economic realities of industrial production. The sad truth of the matter is that in most areas of British manufacturing the designer was valued neither in terms of status nor salary. In 1937 the Council for Art and Industry reported:

'Adequate prospects are essential if the liveliest intelligences are to be drawn into industrial designing, and the heads of businesses must learn to understand something about this side of their business and to maintain it in a high state of efficiency. As industry is now organized, the conditions of employment often appear to be insufficiently attractive and the prospects so uncertain. Industry must be prepared to pay adequately for design and to give the designer a position of standing and responsibility.'

Ekco (E. K. Cole Ltd), a plastics company, was a notable pioneer of industrial design in Britain. It commissioned a number of leading designers to produce wireless casings, an important growth field in the inter-war period. Wells Coates, Misha Black, Jesse Collins and Serge Chermayeff were among those who produced successful designs which recognized plastics as materials with specific aesthetic properties. PEL (Practical Equipment Limited), founded in 1931, manufactured tubular steel furniture on a large scale, including designs by Chermayeff, Wells Coates and others who were strongly influenced by progressive ideas from the Continent. It was not welcomed in Britain, though, and even John Gloag, usually a firm supporter of Modernism, wrote that 'It expresses the harsh limitations of the movement to which it belongs'.

There were, however, serious shortcomings in some of the best-known British designs of the period. The Spitfire, for instance, was a product typical of the culture which created it, just as the German Messerschmitt was of its own. In *The Audit of War*, an iconoclastic study of the industrial design process which created the aeroplane, Correlli Barnett has shown that the Spitfire was expensive and difficult to manufacture, relying on American machine-tools and guns, German aerodynamics and Swiss instruments. The carburettors on its Rolls-Royce Merlin engine would surge in high 'g' conditions, while Messerschmitts and Focke-Wulfs with their Daimler-Benz and BMW engines ran smoothly with their advanced fuel-injection systems. Its innovative wing design with a very narrow section did not allow it to carry adequate armament. Typically, Barnett adds, it was delivered to the RAF a year late. Unlike the German aeroplane, which, with its modular construction, was a rational industrial design, the Spitfire was an elegant piece of industrial *craft*.

During the thirties 'advanced' railway locomotive designs aped the shapes of aeroplanes, but without the scientific refinements of genuine aerodynamics, although Nigel Gresley's A4 *Mallard* of 1935 nonetheless set a world steam speed record of 126 mph in 1938. While car and aeroplane engineers created forms which had a wide influence, locomotive design was, at least as far as aesthetics are concerned, derivative.

Below Office desk, manufactured by PEL, around 1930; chromium-plated tubular steel and cellulosed wood. PEL were the leading industrial manufacturers of tubular steel furniture in Britain, and many of their designs were close to Bauhaus models.

Left Supermarine Spitfire VB, 1941. The fame and achievements of the Spitfire as a fighter plane belie certain technical shortcomings in terms of industrial design.

Left A4 Mallard designed by Nigel Gresley for the London and North Eastern Railway, 1935. Gresley insisted that the streamlined form should be functionally justified.

Installation of furniture
designed by Charles Eames
and Eero Saarinen for the
Museum of Modern Art, New
York, competition 'Organic
Design in Home Furnishings',
1940.

3/THE FORTIES AND FIFTIES

Austerity and reconstruction

Increased prosperity after the Second World War and attempts to restructure society in a new era led to a growth in consumerism. To Charles Eames and many other designers the pursuit of fine handcraft seemed increasingly anachronistic and they turned instead to design for mass production and to the packaging of mass-market goods. Many of the leading Modernists had emigrated from Europe to the United States and Modernism itself had become more commercial, the International Style of big business. At the same time a change in aesthetic was creeping into all areas of design: the sculptural and unpolished form of Le Corbusier's chapel at Ronchamp astounded his supporters, and strong organic shapes became fashionable in home furnishings. In both instances, the designers were attempting to reflect the nature of the materials with which they were working, Le Corbusier expressing the inherent, hitherto concealed, properties of concrete, and Eames exploiting the fluid, mouldable qualities of plywoods and plastics.

ARCHITECTURE AND URBAN DESIGN

Much more than the First World War, the years between 1939 and 1945 were a hiatus for European architecture. Apart from Speer's megalomaniac ambitions to remodel Berlin and Le Corbusier's indefatigable plan-making, carried on even in Vichy France, it was only in England that architects were in a position to give much continuous thought to the architectural and planning problems that would arise from post-war reconstruction. The Modernists of the MARS group produced a proposal that was radical in the extreme, totally recasting London and rebuilding everything but the historic core of Westminster and St Paul's on a scientific transport grid. Ironically, at about the same time the most badly damaged cities on the Continent were preparing to start a stone by stone reconstruction of lost landmarks as soon as hostilities ended.

The focus of modern architecture had now lost its European bias: it had become a world movement, and for the duration of the war at least, many of its leaders were in America. The experience was to change both them and it irrevocably. With the exception of Frank Lloyd Wright, whose boundless inventiveness and highly personal exoticism can be seen in his two key projects of the 1930s, the famous Falling Water house and the Johnson Wax Company headquarters in Racine, Moder-

Right **In 1936, when nearly seventy, Frank Lloyd Wright built the Falling Water house, Pennsylvania. With its series of concrete slabs cantilevered out from solid rock, it is a remarkable spatial and structural performance.**

Opposite above **Built in two stages, the Johnson Wax Company's buildings in Racine, Wisconsin, are an important departure from Wright's previous work, exploring new materials and geometries. The administration building of 1937-9 mixes brick, glass and mushroom columns to create a heroically scaled interior. The laboratory tower of 1949 is cantilevered from a central structural core.**

Opposite below **Van Alen's Art Deco spire for the Chrysler building of 1930 is rich in automobile symbolism and fine craftsmanship that have combined to make it a New York landmark.**

nism in America until this time had been dominated by European architects. Americans were familiar with planning and technological problems of a complexity that inflamed European imaginations, but the native style with which they clothed these projects, such as the Chrysler building and the Rockefeller Center in New York, was decorative and grandiloquent.

However, America was already receptive to the Europeans and they had such champions as Henry-Russell Hitchcock and Philip Johnson, the director of the architecture department in the Museum of Modern Art (MoMA) in New York. Also, the extent to which Americans were willing to accommodate themselves to the European current is demonstrated by Edward Durrell Stone's white liner of a building for MoMA in mid-town Manhatten, executed in the International Style.

When they arrived in America, the Europeans—notably Gropius, Mies, Aalto and Breuer—were able to build on a scale for which they had never before had either the resources or clients. But because their clients tended to be progressive businessmen in American corporations, Modernism's social underpinning quickly disappeared. It became the corporate style of enlightened business taste, and as such was able to reshape the skylines of all the major American cities. A decade or two later, by a process of imitation, it did the same for much of the rest of the world. It can be argued, though, that this very success later undermined much of the moral authority of Modernism and deprived it of its initial force.

When Mies van der Rohe arrived in America in 1938 he took up the post of director of architecture

Above **Crown Hall is the most monumental of Mies's buildings for the Illinois Institute of Technology's Chicago campus. Completed in 1956, it was built to house the architecture and industrial design departments.**

at the newly formed Illinois Institute of Technology in Chicago. He brought with him two Bauhaus teachers and quickly established a school in Chicago that was modelled closely on Bauhaus principles. He began work almost immediately on plans for a new campus for the IIT. The master plan was based on the repetitive use of key modules and a uniform planning grid, while architectural expression was provided by a simple vocabulary of expressed steel frames with brick infill walls, alternating with large sheets of glass. Critics of the development have since attacked the poverty of this vocabulary for expressing hierarchy within a development: the plant-room is treated with the same deliberation as the chapel, which itself is only distinguishable from the other buildings by its name, picked out in modest sanserif lettering.

Mies continued to work on buildings for the campus throughout his twenty-year tenure, but he also began to build on a larger and larger scale through his own office, in many cases realizing the themes anticipated by the drawings he had made earlier in Germany.

The Farnsworth house, designed between 1945 and 1950 as a weekend retreat at Plano outside Chicago, restated in perhaps the most perfect form the classical concerns that Mies pursued throughout his career. Walls, roof and floor were pared down to their essence, linking the house with its natural setting. Unfortunately, though, the client and architect fell out over the cost of the house and Mies faced a lawsuit which, despite his eventual victory, made him the target of press vilification.

During the building of the Farnsworth house Mies met the developer Herbert Greenwald, with whom he was to work on a series of apartment buildings, including his first realized high-rise project on Chicago's Lake Shore Drive. Commissions followed for more apartments in Detroit, giving Mies the chance of establishing his own office in Chicago. This, as much as the architecture school at IIT, was to give him a platform for his ideas and a group of disciples to practise them around the world. In 1947 his reputation was firmly established by an exhibition of his work at the Museum of Modern Art in New York, organ-

Left Mies's twin apartment blocks in Lake Shore Drive, Chicago, were built between 1948 and 1951. The composition depends on the careful juxtaposition of the blocks and the subtle proportional relationships between the structural frame and the glazing.

ized by Philip Johnson who at that time was Mies's leading champion in America.

Johnson's exhibition catalogue was the first English book ever published about Mies. As well as five seminal projects from just after the First World War, it contained a selection of his writings that brought the rigour and discipline of his approach to a general audience in the English-speaking world for perhaps the first time. In it, like Le Corbusier, Mies reiterated the argument that Modernism represented the ineluctable will of history and the spirit of the age, in a way that echoes the Marxist belief in the tide of history. In 1924 he wrote:

'Architecture is the will of the epoch, translated into space. Until this simple truth is clearly recognized, the new architecture will be uncertain and tentative. It must be understood that all architecture is bound up with its own time, that it can only be manifested in living tasks and in the medium of its epoch. In no age has it been otherwise. It is hopeless to try to use the forms of the past in our architecture. Even the strongest artistic talent must fail in this attempt. Again and again we see talented architects who fall short because their work is not in tune with their age. In the last analysis, in spite of their great gifts, they are dilettantes; for it makes no difference how enthusiastically they do the wrong thing. It is a question of essentials. It is not possible to move forward, and look backwards; he who lives in the past cannot advance. Ours is not an age of pathos; we do not respect flights of the spirit as much as we value reason and realism. The demand of our time for realism and functionalism must be met. Only then will our buildings express the potential greatness of our time. We are concerned today with questions of a general nature. The individual is losing significance: his destiny is no longer what interests us. The decisive achievements in all fields are impersonal, and their authors are for the most part unknown.'

Some of these words were to be quoted against Mies in the storm over the Farnsworth house. Yet they reflected not the authoritarianism of the Nazis or other totalitarians, as was claimed, but Mies's concern with the refinement of industrial building rather than the elaboration of the craft tradition.

Unfortunately for Mies his aphorisms became almost as well known as his buildings. 'Less is more' became particularly notorious. It expressed his way of refining buildings down to their fundamental elements, discovering in the process the richness that can only be found in real simplicity.

If any one building epitomizes this idea, it is the Seagram tower in New York, completed in 1959. Mies, not being registered to practise as an architect in New York State, formed an association with Philip Johnson for the project. In fact, Johnson had been instrumental in putting forward Mies's name for the consideration of the Seagram Corporation. In return, Mies gave Johnson the celebrated Four Seasons restaurant on the Seagram's ground floor to design. With the Seagram, Mies created a new form for the commercial skyscraper. Rather than build over the entire site and incorporate the daylight setbacks required by the New York City building code, Mies devoted much of the site to an open public plaza, enabling him to give the tower itself perfectly sheer walls. The Seagram's plaza became a dignified outdoor room for the city, but such was the damage done to New York street life by the legions of lesser imitators that have followed it that the local zoning laws have since been altered to prohibit this type of configuration. New buildings must now maintain the street wall.

Mies had developed his vocabulary of an expressed steel structure with large window-walls in Chicago with the IIT building and the Farnsworth house. In New York, with the Seagram tower, he took it to extremes of elegance, with sheer bronze units that run the entire height of the thirty-nine-storey building. These exposed beams do not, in fact, have a structural role to play, and it is a well-worn refrain to suggest that this in some way invalidates Mies's intention to use materials in an honest and truthful manner. This is to miss the point of what he was trying to do. With tall, glass-walled buildings, Mies had discovered by observation and experiment that the way to avoid monotony was to concentrate on the play of reflections and not 'the effect of light and shadow as in ordinary buildings'. In the Seagram tower the beams form an immensely subtle framework which gives the building grain and texture and creates a dense, massive impression.

Some have criticized the Seagram on grounds of consistency: the T-shaped plan includes a crop of additions at the rear, screening other buildings from sight. Fault-finding critics have called this a bustle; they also point to the difficulty that Mies experienced in continuing a regular window grid around a re-entrant corner. Equally, they have pointed out that in some areas travertine has been used to conceal a diagonal structural bracing grid. But for all this, and despite its many imitators, the Seagram does represent the highwater mark of a particular kind of Modernism.

It was quite clear with the Seagram that for Mies architecture had nothing to do with the social-engineering aspects of Modernism as represented by his predecessor at the Bauhaus, Hannes Meyer. Nor was he interested in technology for the sake of technology. Rather, he had a semi-mystical obsession with architecture as the perfect object. Yet even before the Seagram building was complete the curtain wall had become the universal symbol of the bureaucratic office block. This truly was the International Style, in a manner that the original users of the words had never envisaged.

On a site almost opposite the Seagram, completed a few years earlier but in fact representing a commercialization of its guiding principles, is the Lever Brothers headquarters designed by Gordon Bunshaft of Skidmore, Owings & Merrill. While lacking the purity and refinement of Mies's design, it nevertheless established a formula that was to be as much a part of the international phase of post-war Modernism as the Seagram's slab and plaza equation. Bunshaft split his building mass in two— a low block stepping forward to the street, topped by a tall slab set at right angles to the street front.

Mies's inspiration remained unclouded right up to the end of his career, when he was working on the design of a tower for the City of London. This project, never actually executed, was commissioned by an English developer, who in an act of homage had earlier acquired and lovingly restored the Farnsworth house.

Sadly, the same cannot be said of Walter Gropius, whose post-war work and position at Harvard's School of Architecture was to have as much influence on the course of events as Mies. After a number of modest commissions to build

Left Bronze glass and bronze-finished steel beams are used with consummate skill in Mies's Seagram tower of 1958 in New York. Philip Johnson collaborated on the project, being responsible for the interior spaces of the Four Seasons restaurant.

Right **With the Lever Brothers'**
building of 1952 in New York,
Gordon Bunshaft was the first
to turn the glass curtain wall
into the official uniform of
corporate America.

Left Walter Gropius acted as consultant for Emery Roth's plan for the Pan Am building of 1958 in New York. But the manner in which it destroyed the civilized scale of Park Avenue led to doubts about Gropius's judgement.

houses in the Massachusetts area after his arrival from London, Gropius established a practice under the name of The Architects Collaborative. Despite the genuflection in its name towards the spirit of the Bauhaus, the work of this large and productive office was indistinguishable from the mundane commercial architecture of its period. In at least one case—the Pan Am tower in Manhattan—Gropius's influence was to have the most malign consequences. It was he who insisted that this dominating slab over Grand Central Station was turned at right angles to block the axis of Park Avenue, brutally dwarfing its delicate and civilized architectural scale.

Another European who failed to live up to his earlier promise was Marcel Breuer, who had moved to the United States in 1937 to join Gropius at Harvard. His subsequent work included such projects as those for UNESCO in Paris and for IBM, but with the exception of the Whitney Museum of 1966 it was not distinguished.

For a couple of decades throughout the world, the International Modern Style became universal. From Japan, where the rising generation of architects were strongly influenced by Le Corbusier, to South America and to India, where Le Corbusier himself was building, the pre-war generation of Modernist masters triumphed. Throughout this period, it was possible to find a remarkable degree of agreement between architects throughout the world on a particular approach, an aesthetic vocabulary and a vague, but genuine, belief in the moral force of Modernism and the *Zeitgeist*.

This is exemplified in the work of Oscar Niemeyer, who had come under the spell of Le Corbusier during the planning of the Ministry of Education building in Rio de Janeiro. After Le Corbusier's brief visits, Niemeyer rose to lead the team of young architects working on the project. His first independent building was a nursery in Rio, designed in 1937 in a Corbusian idiom of white cubes. In 1942 he first became associated with Juscelino Kubitschek, then mayor of Pampulha. Here Niemeyer built a casino of exceptional geometrical purity and spatial complexity, again within the Corbusian mode, as well as a church and yacht club.

Kubitschek later became president of Brazil, determined to establish the country's image as a modern nation by the building of a new capital, Brasilia. Working within a master plan sketched in diagrammatic form by Lucio Costa in 1956, Niemeyer put the Corbusian vocabulary to work in a richer, ceremonial mode, particularly in his General Assembly building and Secretariat of 1962.

So, as never before, Modernism had become a world style. Certainly it was possible to find

Above In the 1950s Le Corbusier moved away from the white Purist cubes of the inter-war years and developed more sculptural expressions. The chapel at Ronchamp dismayed many of his supporters.

Opposite above Built between 1946 and 1952, Le Corbusier's Unité d'Habitation on the outskirts of Marseilles was imitated everywhere in the post-war years, usually without success.

Opposite below Pier Luigi Nervi exploited the expressive architectural potential of structural concrete with elegance and economy in a series of buildings. The Palazzo dello Sport in Rome dates from 1959.

regional differences in emphasis between the work of, say, Luis Barragan, the purist Mexican master, and Pier Luigi Nervi, the Italian engineer-architect who excelled in the aesthetic possibilities of re-inforced concrete; but these architects had much more in common than they had dividing them. Throughout the world there was, it seemed, a single spirit. To a Modernist this was inevitable, for if architecture was to be true to the spirit of the modern age, then it must be universally applicable.

This was true as much of individual architectural works as of planning principles, which had now become an integral part of the Modernist approach to architecture. A generation of Modernist pioneers had carved out a huge area of responsibility for architecture—Le Corbusier even called it an alternative to revolution. In this high Modernist phase the architect saw himself as a fit and proper person to hold sway over every aspect of life, from the city to the living-room: it was said of Mies that he placed furniture in a room with the same deliberation that he put buildings around a square.

The search for expression

The minimalism of Mies was adopted by big business as its own corporate house-style—a suitably modest, anonymous envelope that could be built at minimal cost—but some of Modernism's founding figures were still prepared to experiment with alternative modes. Le Corbusier particularly, while his plans for the Ville Radieuse formed part of the ideology of Modernism in the fifties and sixties, refused to ossify and constantly introduced new ideas and new motifs into his architecture.

Perhaps the single most influential building that Le Corbusier produced in the post-war period was the Unité d'Habitation in Marseilles, designed and built between 1946 and 1952. It was the closest he

ever came to realizing his plans for a utopian new city, and although only a fragment of what Le Corbusier intended, it did provide an irresistible model for planners throughout the world.

Unlike his imitators, Le Corbusier was able to make the Unité work on both a functional and poetic level. As a piece of architecture, it was a harmonious, sensitively proportioned, sculptural exercise in raw concrete, set up on pilotis in a green setting and planned according to Le Corbusier's modular system. As a piece of urbanism, it functioned well too: Le Corbusier's streets in the sky were real streets, creating a community with its own shops, schools and sports facilities. The model was to prove highly dangerous, however, particularly in the context of the English welfare state.

The Unité, in fact, with its delight in the 'as-found' possibilites of the concrete casting process, was to signal the start of a new theme in Le Corbusier's work, a theme that was to take it ever further from the technological classicism of the German-derived school of Mies.

The chapel of Ronchamp in southern France, completed by Le Corbusier in 1955, was greeted with shock and concern, not least by many of his own supporters. Until that moment, the Modernists had always presented their work as the scientific expression of the spirit of an age of reason, democracy and progress. There was a general consensus that the appropriate mode of expression in architecture was that derived from the machine and industry, the two forces which have done most to change the shape of life in this century.

At Ronchamp, however, Le Corbusier produced a wilful and highly sculptural design which deliberately set all that aside. Whereas most Modernist architecture had pointed towards the creation of standardized building types, Ronchamp was the deliberate creation of a unique, expressive building for that particular project. It took the Unité to establish Corbusier's vocabulary of Brutalism, that is, the acceptance of the accidents of the building process; Ronchamp gave it a poetic form and made it into a powerful work of art.

Le Corbusier said of the Unité, which was originally intended to have been built in steel, 'The defects shout from every part of the structure. Luckily we have no money. Exposed concrete shows the least incidents of the shuttering, of the joints of the planks, the fibres and knots of the wood. In men and women, do you not see the wrinkles and the birthmarks, the crooked noses, and the innumerable peculiarities? Faults are human; they are ourselves, our daily lives. What matters is to go further, to live, to be intense, to aim

high, and to be loyal.'

What Le Corbusier was doing with the Unité, with Ronchamp and with the other buildings that he designed at this time, such as the Chandigarh government centre in the Punjab, was to create a new vocabulary for twentieth-century architecture. His revisionism, for that is how it appeared to many, including such notable architects of the younger generation as James Stirling, found an echo in the change that was overtaking others during the 1950s.

Right and above In America Eero Saarinen was also searching for more expressive architectural forms. Dulles airport in Washington DC, 1959, is a symbolic evocation of flight.

The birth of a decorative, yet abstracted, specifically American architecture was given powerful impetus by the Cranbrook Academy, which also continued to shape the decorative arts. Eero Saarinen, the son of the co-founder Eliel Saarinen, was prominent among those attempting to find a more expressive model for architecture.

The younger Saarinen began in practice with his father with the design of the General Motors Technical Institute at Warren, Michigan, built between 1951 and 1955. Here the aesthetic is clearly rationalist, in sharp contrast to the romanticism of his father. But Eero Saarinen's subsequent buildings were to exhibit a radical change. With such works as the TWA terminal at Kennedy Airport in New York, designed in 1956, and the terminal at Washington's Dulles airport of 1959, he used the structural freedom offered by technology to express not technology, nor the nature of the material that he was using, but a symbolic embodiment of the purpose of the building.

Both buildings in different ways seem to express flight. The TWA building is recognizably birdlike, its two concrete-shell wings swooping towards a beak. Dulles, on the other hand, seems to leap skywards, in a gesture reiterated in other airports around the world. In this building some have seen the influence of remarkable shell forms of Jørn Utzon's design for the Sydney Opera House. The expressionism of Saarinen's work also reached Europe, for example in Gio Ponti's Pirelli skyscraper in Milan of 1955-8, with its elliptical form and bravura approach to structure.

The post-war work of the Finnish architect and designer Alvar Aalto, though different in form

Left The Pirelli tower in Milan (1955-8) by Gio Ponti and Pier Luigi Nervi is a rare and early example of a European skyscraper built with conviction. It is distinguished by the extreme attenuation of its forms.

from that of his former fellow-countrymen, does exhibit certain Scandinavian tendencies. Like the elder Saarinen, Aalto was attempting to fuse a vernacular tradition, derived from the Finnish experience of a severe climate, limited raw materials and a society based on a strong degree of social cohesion, with the order and discipline of classicism. And like Eero Saarinen, Aalto was prepared to deploy representational elements in his buildings at a time when the prevailing Modernist orthodoxy of the International Style was to totally condemn them.

Aalto was an intuitive, independent-minded architect, always distrustful of dogma and abstract theory. Yet, like the Modern Movement pioneers, he saw architecture as a potential force for social change. To him architecture could be used to humanize the man-made environment. 'It seems to me', he said in 1955, 'that there are too many situations in life in which the organization is too brutal: it is the task of the architect to give life a gentler structure.' Earlier, Aalto had written, 'Architecture should always offer a means whereby the organic connection between a building and nature, including man

and human life as an element of greater importance than others, is provided for.'

Unlike that of many of his contemporaries, Aalto's work shows an enduring concern for these preoccupations. After building the not entirely satisfactory Baker Hall of Residence for the Massachusetts Institute of Technology, where a serpentine block of bedrooms makes the most of the river views, Aalto returned to Finland, where he won a competition to design the Säynätsalo town hall.

At Säynätsalo his architecture assumed a dual role: it provided a complex of buildings which appeared to be linked inextricably with the site on which they were placed, rather than being imposed upon it; and it gave a physical form to an image of a democratic institution free of authoritarian rhetoric. Planned in rugged brick and timber around a series of courtyards, Säynätsalo became the inspiration of English liberal architects, who ransacked its images in their picturesque brick boxes with thin-lipped 'people's' detailing.

Aalto's National Pensions Institute in Helsinki of 1952 applied a similar approach to a large bureaucratic building. Here he tried to treat the small-scale detail of the scheme, such as doors and windows, as well as the street frontage, in a way that rendered the whole building accessible to visitors and passers-by. As at Säynätsalo, with its grassed earth steps and pavilions that seem to grow out of the landscape, the Pensions Institute campus is designed in a series of terraces. Around these are blocks of casually grouped buildings of varying

heights—a far remove from the doctrinaire Modernists' way of treating buildings as perfect, immutable objects isolated in a landscape. However, both approaches are fundamentally unsuitable to the pattern of existing cities, and it is this failure of Modernism to deal with its urban context which has aroused the strongest criticism in recent years.

In America, Louis Kahn's role in the attempts of the post-war generation to revise the principles of the Modern Movement without losing sight of its goals and ideals has parallels with that of Aalto. Kahn's career as an independent architect was brief. He only established his own office in 1947, already well into middle age. But within the space of about fifteen years he designed a series of highly influential buildings: the Yale University Art Gallery of 1951, the Richards Medical Research building at the University of Pennsylvania of 1957 and the Salk Institute at La Jolla, California. At the time of his death he was working on the government buildings in Dacca in Bangladesh, the Institute of Management in Ahmadabad in India and the Mellon Center for British Art in New Haven.

All these buildings responded to the need to redefine Modernism, to distance it from the utilitarianism and commercialism that were rife. Like Mies's, Kahn's influence was popularized by a series of aphorisms. In the Richards building he developed the concept of 'served' and 'servant' space, differentiating between the primary spaces and by

Left The Art Gallery at Yale University, New Haven, 1951, was the first of Louis Kahn's major works.

Below Kahn's architectural philosophy was encapsulated in a series of aphorisms. The Richards Medical Research building, 1957, with its laboratory spaces and brick service towers, expresses his concept of 'served' and 'servant' spaces.

Right Frank Lloyd Wright's Guggenheim Museum in New York has proved unsuited to the display of works of art, but it is a powerful sculptural space. The spiral ramp theme had been explored earlier by Wright in his Morris shop in San Francisco, 1948.

Right Frank Lloyd Wright's Guggenheim Museum in New York has proved unsuited to the display of works of art, but it is a powerful sculptural space. The spiral ramp theme had been explored earlier by Wright in his Morris shop in San Francisco, 1948.

those secondary ones reserved for mechanical equipment—a distinction which, in the case of the Richards building, was not without practical difficulties.

Frank Lloyd Wright's most powerful work had already been completed by the time the Second World War had ended. But as the dominant figure of native-born American architecture he still enjoyed enormous prestige and popular recognition, which was in no way diminished by the decline of his reputation among certain critics; his decorative and highly inventive buildings now seem to have inspired a new generation.

In the closing years of his career, Wright's primary preoccupation was to realize certain projects and themes which he had been working on in earlier decades. One of these was for the construction of a high-rise tower, a truncated form of which he built in Bartlesville, Oklahoma, in 1955. Another was his spiral theme, first seen in the Morris gift shop in San Francisco of 1948. This reappeared in the fatally flawed Guggenheim Museum in New York, completed in 1960 but designed in the 1940s. Nothing will ever make Wright's spiralling circular ramp a good place for the display of pictures: his strip glazing has had to be blacked out to cut down the glare, the curving walls that slope outwards do not allow the pictures to be properly hung and much of the detailing,

Right Designed near the end of his long career, the Marin County Center showed that Wright was still capable of remarkable invention. It was executed posthumously between 1959 and 1966.

Opposite above Buckminster Fuller's faith in the potential of technology inspired many architects to experiment with lightweight structural systems. His geodesic dome for Expo' 67 at Montreal was highly influential, but was destroyed by fire shortly after the exhibition closed.

Opposite below Charles Eames's only important realized architectural work was his own house in California. It was built as a demonstration project in 1949 and used prefabricated components with great sensitivity.

with its strident geometry of interlocking circles, simply suggests a science fiction fantasy. Yet the museum remains a powerful, compelling and highly individual image.

The Marin County Center dates from the late 1950s—when Wright was approaching ninety—and is a coarser mixture of similar motifs, using an equally insistent geometry and set on a hillside in suburban California like a beached flying saucer.

Not all the architects of the 1950s abandoned the inventiveness of the pioneers. There remained a group that neither accepted the commercialization of Modernism nor rejected the reformist impulses that had created it in the first place. Visionary utopianism was kept alive by Buckminster Fuller, the inventor, entrepreneur and engineer, who kept working on his modular, lightweight, prefabricated, geodesic structural systems throughout the decade. His aim was to provide mass-produced, low-cost, instant shelter, but ironically it was the United States Defense Department which turned out to be Fuller's largest customer. It used his system to house its early-warning radar system.

But Fuller's unquenchable technological optimism, his belief in the inescapable logic of industrialization for building and his habit of asking architects such unexpected questions as 'How much does your building weigh?' inspired designers to experiment with technology.

Another enthusiast for the positive power of technology was Charles Eames, who, though trained as an architect, was to become best known as a furniture designer. Eames completed just one major architectural work, his own home in California, designed in 1949, but for a project of modest size this has had a remarkably powerful influence ever since.

The Eames house was a deliberate celebration of the possibilities of prefabrication. It was built by ordering standard industrial building components from the catalogues of manufacturers and assembling them on site with a minimum of building skills. Yet there was a Miesian purity and elegance to its glass and steel facades. The frankness of its exposed steel trusses and diagonal bracing appealed particularly to the younger generation of English architects, who were looking for more inspiring models than the limply picturesque tradition that had grown out of the Festival of Britain. Its use of 'as-found' materials influenced the Hunstanton school of Alison and Peter Smithson almost as much as the original Miesian model. Even Le Corbusier was to adopt a similar vocabulary with the Fondation Le Corbusier building of 1966 in Geneva.

167

DECORATIVE ARTS

Opposite above Oak bedroom furniture illustrated in a catalogue of Utility scheme products. The furniture, though soundly designed and constructed, seems very drab.

Opposite below A typical Swedish living-room, photographed in 1954. This style found wide favour internationally in middle-class homes in the fifties.

Right Fashions improvised from recycled clothes, presented in the 'Make and Mend' exhibition, London, 1942. On the left is a lady's suit made from a man's old dinner suit; to the right, a cardigan from a man's waistcoat with knitted sleeves.

The Second World War halted progress in many of the purely decorative arts, just as it had in architecture. This was the result of the serious shortage of materials, the diversion of manpower and machinery to manufactures related to the war effort and the inappropriateness of indulgence in the apparently frivolous. Yet, style still had a role to play, and women's struggle to keep fashion alive underlined its value as a morale-booster. By contrast, the British Utility furniture scheme was a demonstration of the drab results of functionalism imposed by necessity rather than by choice.

The war effort did, however, give impetus to research and developments in materials and processes which were to be of lasting benefit in peacetime, notably in the exploitation of versatile new alloys and the development of a wide range of synthetic materials. Such wartime research was to help change the face of design and further emphasized the new-found influence of the engineer-designer, which had been heralded by the pioneers of Modernism and which has become a fundamental feature of the Modern Movement.

The emergence of a battle-scarred Europe from the restrictions of war was occasion for a renaissance in the applied arts. American designers, particularly those associated with the Cranbrook Academy, who had enjoyed a greater freedom of activity during the war than had their European counterparts, were to have a widespread influence on design in Europe. At the same time, Scandinavian design was to achieve international pre-eminence and the Scandinavian Modern style, a cohesive and mellow blend of the functional and the traditional, came to be regarded as an internationally recognizable measure of good taste in middle-class households. With the notable exception of its couture industry, France failed to re-establish its pre-war primacy in the applied arts. The new creative centres were the United States, Scandinavia, though in a restrained manner, Great Britain, where the 1951 Festival of Britain provided the focus for an exuberant new style, and Italy, where the immediate post-war period witnessed a remarkable outburst of creativity both in craft and in decorative design applied to series production and industry.

From these centres came a wide array of ideas and achievements, encompassing novel decorative styles, bravura craftwork, the refinement and adaptation of traditional themes, styles inspired by the new avant-garde in fine art and a continuation of the functionalist ideal.

The story of post-war design is a complex skein drawing together these often inextricably interwoven threads. It has been intellectually fashionable, however, to give particular emphasis to the story of functionalism and the Modern Movement, a viewpoint greatly encouraged by the polemical character of the movement and by the favour which it has enjoyed in institutional contexts, from the Museum of Modern Art in New York to the Design Council in London. The Modernist lobby has encouraged a view of post-war design history in which a rationalist élite is seen to pursue purist ideals in the face of the perverse rebuttals of expendable, fashionable, quirky, even vulgar decorative styles.

The 1983 exhibition 'Design Since 1945' at the Philadelphia Museum of Art was a stimulating and highly refined survey, but the manner in which it placed history into intellectually rationalized compartments was symptomatic of the increased emphasis since 1945 on the concept of 'good taste', as a tool of social mobility and as a language of social and intellectual status. In her introduction to the catalogue, Kathryn B. Hiesinger stated, 'The triumph of functionalism as the universal modern

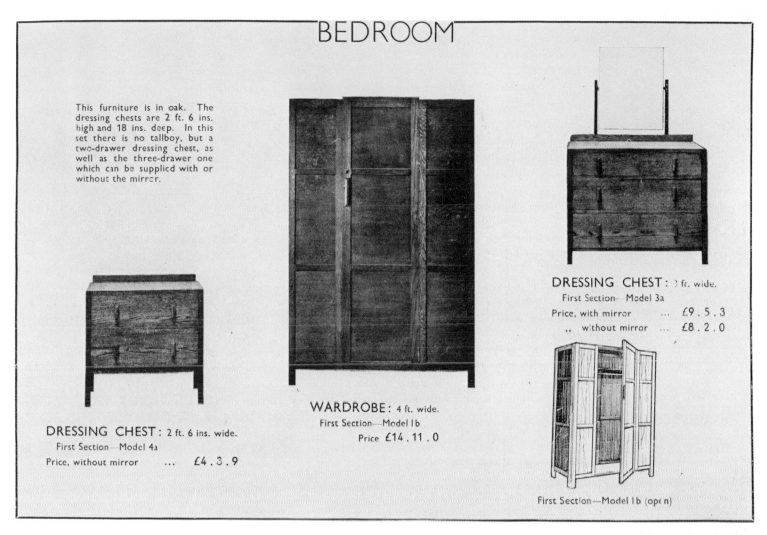

BEDROOM

This furniture is in oak. The dressing chests are 2 ft. 6 ins. high and 18 ins. deep. In this set there is no tallboy, but a two-drawer dressing chest, as well as the three-drawer one which can be supplied with or without the mirror.

DRESSING CHEST : 2 ft. 6 ins. wide.
First Section—Model 4a
Price, without mirror   ...   £4.3.9

WARDROBE : 4 ft. wide.
First Section—Model 1b
Price £14.11.0

DRESSING CHEST : 3 ft. wide.
First Section—Model 3a
Price, with mirror   ...   £9.5.3
    ,,   without mirror   ...   £8.2.0

First Section—Model 1b (open)

aesthetic in the 1950s—and the ways in which the vacuum left by its decline and collapse has been filled—is to a large extent the history of design since 1945.' The thread of functionalism was, indeed, a key factor in design in the forties and fifties, a theme carried through from before the war and still, in the mid-eighties, far from defunct. In the post-war years, however, functionalism was to evolve a new language. The angular Modernism of the years around 1930 was superseded by a new, organic style, and just as first-phase Modernism had co-existed with a variety of decorative styles, so post-war Organic Modernism co-existed with new decorative styles; indeed, it even became an ingredient within the fashionable repertoire of decorative motifs.

The decorative arts continued to derive many elements from the fine arts. Surrealism remained a rich source of ideas and motifs in the forties. Avantgarde abstract art suggested a new vernacular of forms and patterns. The sculptures of Arp, Moore and Hepworth, the mobiles of Alexander Calder, the motifs of Joan Miró, the splashed canvases of Jackson Pollock and other Abstract Expressionists provided inspiration to designers and decorators; they suggested ideas for the forms of glass vases, lamp bases, jewels and other objects, for the patterns and motifs of murals, textiles and carpets.

This pattern of borrowing from the fine arts was hardly new, but there was an invigorating new array of work from which to plunder.

Right Printed textile designed
by Renato Birolli, 1950s.
Birolli adapted the language
of abstract art to repeat
patterns for furnishing
fabrics.

Right Printed textile designed
by Renato Birolli, 1950s.
Birolli adapted the language
of abstract art to repeat
patterns for furnishing
fabrics.

Below 1958 advertisement for
Cadillac cars. The eye-
catching styling recalls
Reyner Banham's definition of
'massive initial impact' as the
principal ingredient of
popular consumer products.

In one major respect, however, post-war design differed from that of previous periods. Taste was no longer systematically imposed from above as the prerogative of a privileged few, nor was it the inevitable, immutable reflection of one's social level. A new middle-class market was becoming increasingly informal in matters of taste, and designers now had to face the demands of popular consumer culture.

It is a truism of post-war design that the principle of built-in obsolescence is in conflict with the concept of absolutes in pure design. The story of applied design illustrates the dichotomy between disposability and up-to-the-minute fashionable-ness, and the opposite notion of good design as a progressive evolution towards perfection on the basis of lasting values.

Long after a new Cadillac car has come into the family, the lady of the house continues to marvel at how delightfully easy it is to handle. On the open highway or in the city's traffic, her briefest gesture conducts the car in a perfect symphony of obedient motion. You ought to try it for yourself. Your dealer will be happy to put you behind the wheel—to explain the virtues of Cadillac's exclusive Fleetwood coachcrafting—and to familiarize you with all Cadillac models, including the Eldorado Brougham. FORWARD FROM FIFTY

CADILLAC MOTOR CAR DIVISION • GENERAL MOTORS CORPORATION

Cadillac

GOWN BY OLEG CASSINI

EVERY WINDOW OF EVERY CADILLAC IS SAFETY PLATE GLASS

This conflict was recognized by Reyner Banham, an informed and perceptive commentator on the phenomenon of Pop culture, in his essay 'A Throw-Away Aesthetic' written in 1955 and published in 1960 in *Industrial Design*. 'We live', he wrote, 'in a throw-away economy, a culture in which the fundamental classification of our ideas and worldly possessions is in terms of their relative expendability, [so] it is clearly absurd to demand that objects designed for a short useful life should exhibit qualities signifying eternal validity—such qualities as "divine" proportion, "pure" form.' Many facets of decorative design and styling were dictated by the demands of the mass market, by the consumers' appetite for the new and by the general preference for an eye-catching design exuding glamour and novelty rather than the subtle under-statement created to fulfil a designer's perception of the ideal. Such was the impact of proletarian values that there developed a new aesthetic of popular culture, which Banham defined as depending on 'massive initial impact and small sustaining power'.

From the whimsical excesses of the Festival style or the more frivolous extremes of Italian decorative styling, to the gaudy elaboration of American motor cars and the brash commercial architecture of Las Vegas, a new ingredient of populist vulgarity and exuberance entered the mainstream of decora-tive design in the optimistic era of reconstruction which followed the Second World War.

The United States

Apart from architecture, America's major contributions to design in the forties and fifties within the parameters of the Modern Movement were in the areas of furniture and interior design. The focal point of creativity around 1940 was the Cranbrook Academy, still under the direction of Eliel Saarinen. Comparable in certain respects with the Bauhaus, not least in the primacy given to the role of the architect, the Academy differed from the Bauhaus in its avoidance of dogma. Cranbrook encouraged free interdisciplinary experiment and the venerable Saarinen, with his wide practical experience within the Arts and Crafts movement and subsequently as a pioneer of Modernism, provided a distinguished example of the open-minded designer with a wide range of skills.

The Cranbrook Academy encouraged the talents of architects, artists, designers and craftsmen in a variety of media, including textiles, ceramics and metalwork, though by 1940 interior design and architecture were eclipsing the Academy's earlier emphasis on the crafts. Three outstanding designers emerged around 1940: Eero Saarinen, Eliel's son, who taught at the Academy between 1939 and 1941, Charles Eames, a student in 1938

and instructor between 1939 and 1941, and Florence Knoll, who graduated in 1941. Their subsequent development as designers owed much to the progressive attitudes of two furniture manufacturing and retailing firms, Herman Miller and Knoll, both of which set new standards in furniture design

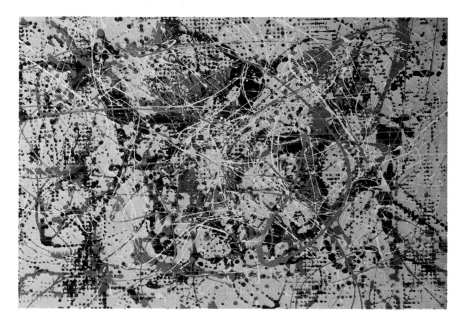

Above: Painting Number 21 by Jackson Pollock, 1949. Pollock was the most celebrated exponent of the splashed-canvas style of Abstract Expressionism.

Left 'Chickenwire' chairs and a stool, designed by the sculptor Harry Bertoia and manufactured by Knoll, 1950s.

for high-quality series production and had far-reaching influence in interior design within both the private and contract sectors. Eames was invited to work for Herman Miller by George Nelson, the firm's senior design consultant, and the relationship between designer and manufacturer was to prove extremely fruitful, with Eames given a free hand to develop new concepts in furniture design. Florence Knoll joined the Knoll Furniture Com-

pany around 1943 as head of the planning unit and guided the firm to a position of international pre-eminence by the mid-fifties, a position which it holds to this day.

The revolution brought about by Eames and Saarinen demanded a drastic re-working of the rationalist concepts of domestic design. For Eames, new materials and manufacturing techniques suggested fresh solutions to perennial problems, in furniture design as in architecture. With the potential of new plywoods, which allowed multi-directional curves, the strong mouldable fibreglass and the synthetic foams, the problem, wrote Eames, 'becomes a sculptural one, not the cubist, constructivist [one]'.

'It wasn't until I started to work for Eliel Saarinen and Eero that I had any conception of what "concept" was,' claimed Eames. His earliest collaborations with Eero resulted in dramatically new approaches to furniture design: both designers evolved an organic, sculptural version of Modernism which seemed subconsciously to fuse the curvilinear natural forms of Art Nouveau with the functionalist philosophy of pre-war Modernism. Their ideas and experiments, together and as individuals, extended beyond furniture to concepts of interior architecture—the term architec-

Below Lounge chair and ottoman designed by Charles Eames in 1956 and manufactured by Herman Miller; laminated rosewood on steel and aluminium base, upholstered in leather.

Right Womb chair and footstool designed by Eero Saarinen in 1948 and manufactured by Knoll; moulded fibreglass shell, covered in latex foam and upholstered in fabric, raised on steel rod legs. In their chair designs Eames and Saarinen treated the seat and the base quite separately.

ture, rather than decoration, is used advisedly, for Eames and Saarinen were sensitive and radical in their approach to interior space. They largely eschewed decoration, just as they avoided the cold and brittle chic of the pre-war Modernists, and they exploited light, fluid organic volumes to create spare but immensely inviting living and working spaces.

Florence Knoll, who had worked briefly for Gropius and Breuer in 1940, championed a mainstream Modernism in her own designs, which owed a debt to the minimalist elegance of Mies van der Rohe. She developed a corporate image for Knoll which, with its austerely elegant lines tempered by natural materials and colours, became an internationally adopted style for office and public spaces, and to a lesser extent for domestic interiors.

Exposure was given to the early work of Eames and Saarinen by the Museum of Modern Art, New York. They shared first prize for their joint projects in the museum's 1940 competition for 'Organic Design in Home Furnishing'. Exhibited the following year, their ideas for sculptured seat-shells on an independent substructure and for modular storage units provided inspiration to designers in the United States and in Europe. In 1946 MoMA presented a one-man show of Eames's work. By the end of the decade the influence of Eames and Saarinen was evident in the entries for MoMA's 1948 competition for 'Low-Cost Furniture Design'. The museum played an important didactic role through the public education programme conceived around the 'Good Design' shows inaugurated by Edgar Kaufmann Jr., in 1950.

Above Living-room furniture designed by Charles Eames and exhibited in the Museum of Modern Art, New York, 1948.

173

Organic Modernism became a fashionable style and inspired such refined expressions as the sculptor Isamu Noguchi's wood and glass table of around 1945 for Herman Miller, as well as such wild excesses as the skyline of Las Vegas. Both the physical appearance and the cultural significance of this extraordinary desert city have been well evoked by Tom Wolfe in his 1965 anthology *The Kandy-Kolored Tangerine Flake Streamline Baby*:

Below Low table of glass and curved wood designed by the sculptor Isamu Noguchi around 1945, and manufactured by Herman Miller. Noguchi's table is a fine example of the sculptural, organic tendency in post-war furniture design.

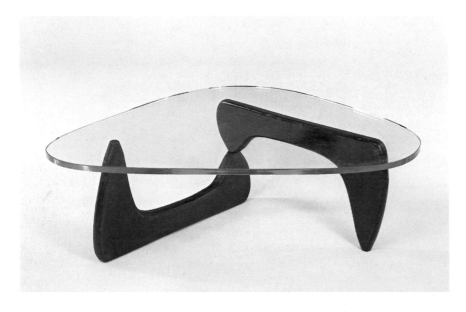

'That fantastic skyline . . . fifteen-story-high display signs, parabolas, boomerangs, rhomboids . . . they soar in shapes before which the existing vocabulary of art history is helpless. I can only attempt to supply names—Boomerang Modern . . . Flash Gordon Ming-Alert Spiral . . . Mint Casino Elliptical, Miami Beach Kidney. . . . The important thing about the building of Las Vegas [is] . . . not that the builders were gangsters but that they were proles. They celebrated, very early, the new style of life of America—using the money pumped in by the war to show a prole vision . . . of style.'

To European eyes the United States was a promised land of affluence and style in the post-war years. This vision was nurtured by the combined influences of the understated yet self-confident image of corporate prosperity, exemplified in the Knoll style, and the vulgar symbols of popular culture, the commercial architecture, custom-built cars, jukeboxes and neon signs which conformed to Banham's 'initial impact' theory.

In America, highly sophisticated and influential exponents of commercial art were to be found in the realms of photography and graphic design, notably in the inspired art direction of Alexei Brodovitch and in the incomparable photography of Irving Penn.

Right The Flamingo Hilton frontage, Las Vegas, photographed in 1977. Las Vegas architecture is characterized by its brash, overscaled signs and facades.

Brodovitch designed posters, books and record sleeves, created advertising campaigns, taught graphic arts classes and, for twenty–five years from 1934, was art director of *Harper's Bazaar*, in which capacity he revolutionized magazine layouts by creating visual excitement in a clever integration of text and images. Among the photographers to flourish under his direction was the talented young Richard Avedon.

Irving Penn had worked for and been inspired by Brodovitch before taking up a contract with Condé Nast. Penn formulated his distinctive approach in the late forties and, both in fashion and still-life work, raised commercial photography to new levels of dignity and sophistication.

Italy

Design in post-war Italy flourished in harmony with and as an essential ingredient of the rebirth of industry, each being dependent on the other. In Turin and particularly in Milan, designers and industrialists worked in close collaboration, laying the foundations for the enormous export success of Italian motor cars, furniture, lighting and office and domestic hardware. There was much discussion on the theory and practice of design; the intellectual climate was highly stimulating and many manufacturers reaped the benefits of putting their faith in the young generation of designers who sought and evolved a new aesthetic through the processes of product development.

The decorative arts in Italy enjoyed an explosion of verve and invention in the post-war years, in the work of artist-craftsmen working in glass, ceramics and other media, and in the work of designers working for large-scale industry or within more limited manufacturing or creative contexts, such as luxury furniture, textiles and interior design.

A central role in the story of Italian design was played by the architect-designer Gio Ponti, through the wide-ranging and ever inquisitive character of his approach to design, the inventive nature of his work in a wide variety of media, from architectural projects to decorative objects, and through his influence on the journal *Domus*. Since its establishment *Domus* has proved perhaps the most stimulating journal on design for over fifty years, both increasing the Italian design community's awareness of international achievements and promoting the work of Italy's progressive designers.

In the post-war years, *Domus* was a treasury of Italian and international design theory and practice, and confirmed the broad conceptual horizons which have characterized the Italian approach.

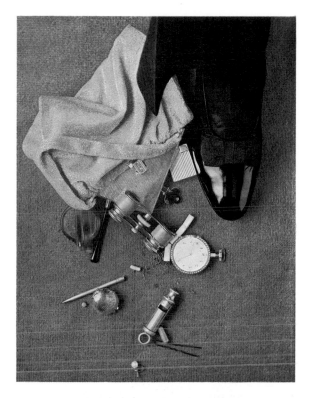

Left 'Theatre Accident', a sophisticated still-life study by Irving Penn, reproduced from *The Art and Technique of Color Photography*, 1951.

Below A director's office, designed by Gio Ponti, published in *Domus*, April 1951. The subtle use of streamlined curves give this furniture a sleek, sensual look typical of Italian design of the period.

The Italians have not been afraid to measure their achievements in international terms, and such comparisons have only confirmed the creative energy of Italian craft and design. The Milanese publishers Hoepli issued a series of volumes in the fifties, edited by Roberto Aloi, entitled *Esempi di Arredamenti, Architettura e Decorazioni d'Oggi di Tutto il Mondo*; covering various aspects of design, these anthologies underline the strength and variety of Italy's post-war design renaissance.

The new Italian styles were created by and for a young urban middle class and drew on a number of sources. Here are the sculptured forms and curvilinear sweeps of an organic, revamped Modernism, demonstrating an evolution of thought along similar lines to those followed by Eames and Saarinen; here are contrasts of full, often asymmetrical masses and slender structural elements; here is the pursuit of logic in materials and form, but also *brio* and wit, often courting eccentricity both in its literal and more usual sense. Here, too, are lively adaptations of current fine art styles and a fascinating revival of archaeological styles. All this, in a context far removed from the patrician or aristocratic tradition of Italian design, found new roots in an industrial urban environment, in which style was dictated by a young, professional middle class and vulgarized by an urban proletariat. Italian style encompassed rationalist design for industry, inventive interior and object design for both domestic and public spaces, and a popular visual culture which produced such evocative symbols as the Vespa, the sharply tailored mohair suit and the hissing Gaggia coffee machines of the newly fashionable meeting places, the coffee bars.

The late forties and fifties were years of economic growth in which exuberant style was a tangible expression of material prosperity for a bourgeoisie in pursuit of *la dolce vita*, a dream scrutinized in 1960 in the similarly entitled film by Federico

Below Enamelled decorative panel designed by Guido Gambone, 1950s. This combines elements of the fashionable 'archaeological' style with features of contemporary painting.

Right Milan Triennale, 1954, shallow velarium domes hung at varying heights over the Industrial Design section. The Triennale exhibitions were an important international forum for the exchange of design ideas.

Fellini. Through these years the Milan Triennale exhibitions, in 1948, 1951, 1954 and 1957, provided an international showcase for Italian design.

The Triennali demonstrated the sophisticated mix of rationalism and panache which characterized so much Italian design of this period. In the area of furniture design for series production certain relationships between designers and manufacturers deserve particular credit, notably the work of Osvaldo Borsani for the firm of Tecno, of Marco Zanuso for Arflex and of the venerable Gio Ponti for Cassina. Gino Sarfatti and the brothers Achille and Piergiacomo Castiglioni designed ingenious and expressive light fittings and the firms of Flos, Arredoluce, Arteluce and Fontana Arte were notable manufacturers in this field. The creative climate encouraged fruitful links between artists and manufacturers in the area of domestic and public interior design, and stimulated highly original solutions to special commissions.

No single character better represents the flair, the bravura mix of logic and stylish invention of this era than the Turin architect-designer Carlo Mollino. A remarkable man with a tremendous appetite for life, Mollino conceived dramatic shapes for architecture and furniture, sculpting plywood, oak or concrete into organic forms, taut with an implied energy, sometimes vaguely anthro-

Above Table of sculpted plywood and glass, designed by Carlo Mollino, around 1950. Mollino, the Turin-based architect, was an eccentric and versatile genius whose furniture displayed extraordinary invention.

Left Adjustable chaise-longue, designed by Osvaldo Borsani in 1954 and manufactured by Tecno.

Above The 'Belvedere' room in the Milan–Naples luxury express, a forward observation lounge with furniture designed by Renzo Zavanella, late 1940s, published in *Design*, September 1955.

Right Glass vase designed by Fulvio Bianconi in 1960 and made in the Venini glassworks, Murano, Venice.

Opposite right Neon ceiling-sculpture, designed by Lucio Fontana, above the grand staircase at the Milan Triennale, 1951.

ative arts, no motif would be more representative than the swirling asymmetrical lines of Lucio Fontana's neon ceiling-sculpture above the grand staircase of the 1951 Triennale, stylish, expressive and impermanent.

British design and the Festival of Britain

Design in Britain in the immediate post-war period was dominated by official endeavours to raise general design awareness and standards by educating the public and manufacturers; but there was also a popular need for whimsy, humour, style and decorative indulgence after the austerity of the war years. These two factors were not always compatible. The British design establishment set out on a crusading path with the worthiest of motives, but to a certain extent it was blinkered by a narrow concept of rightness in design. Echoes of Ruskinian idealism reverberated through the avowed aims of the new Council of Industrial Design, founded in 1944, as indeed in the visions of a new Britain perceived by Gordon Russell, design consultant to the Board of Trade, who foresaw a nation spiritually uplifted by the new consciousness of 'good' design. The British public, however, is by nature conservative, or indifferent, in matters of taste and there has remained a gulf between the

pomorphic and always drawn or modelled with inimitable zest. His contemporary Renzo Zavanella designed eccentric furnishing for hotel and railway-car interiors, and his architectural installations for the 1948 Triennale were an inspiration to the designers of the Festival of Britain three years later.

A new generation of designers and artisans brought about a veritable renaissance in the glassworks of Murano, Venice, adapting traditional Venetian techniques to new colours and sculptural forms. Flavio Poli, Carlo Scarpa, Archimede Seguso, Fulvio Bianconi, Paolo Venini, Dino Martens and Alfredo Barbini were leading figures in this revival of an ancient craft in lively modern guise. Guido Gambone, Lucio Fontana and Fausto Melotti were among the most talented of the artists who sought to translate the qualities of current abstract art to the medium of ceramics. Abstract Expressionist art also inspired bold, splashy fabrics by Fede Cheti and others, and a free, painterly quality characterized the enamel work of Paolo de Poli and of Eros and Luigi Genazzi.

If one were to seek a design symbolic of the energy, the artistic awareness and fashionable transience of this rich period in the Italian decor-

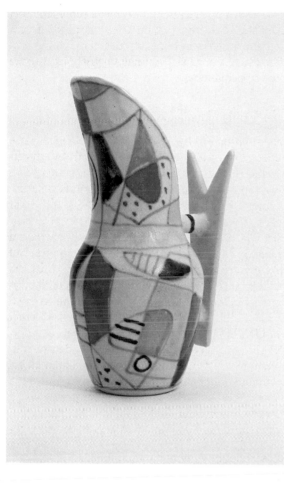

itions. The Festival of Britain sought to redress the balance, and it was symptomatic of the prevalent mood that a profile of Britannia within a quasi-heraldic motif was chosen as the Festival symbol.

The strengths of the Festival style were at once its weaknesses, for its unified decorative approach was destined to be short-lived by virtue of its very novelty and topicality. The fashionable contrasts of masses and slender lines could be seen everywhere,

Left Ceramic pitcher designed by Guido Gambone, 1950s. This exploits to decorative effect motifs drawn from the vernacular of abstract art.

'educated' designers' understanding of what the market needs and 'uneducated' popular and middle-class levels of consumer taste.

The Festival of Britain in 1951 succeeded in drawing together these elements, with designers responding to a deeply felt national mood and creating a decorative style that was truly popular. The whimsical, fanciful Festival style plucked ideas from Italy and from the United States but, in its most concentrated state, acquired a distinctive independent character and deserves to be regarded as one of the most lively stylistic manifestations of the post-war era.

The Festival of Britain can only be understood in its complex historical context. After the drabness of the Utility schemes as applied to furnishing and clothing, it was an attempt to re-establish a national style, to demonstrate the rebirth of British industry and creativity in a new mood of optimism, and to show that Britain was still capable of laying on a major exhibition of its design achievements. One hundred years had elapsed since the Great Exhibition had set the precedent for such displays, but Britain had since fallen behind and the French had come to dominate the grandiose exhib-

Right Antelope chairs designed by Ernest Race for use at the Festival of Britain, 1951; steel rod construction with plywood seats painted in primary colours.

Below: Abacus screen designed by Edward Mills for the Festival of Britain, 1951. This stood on the boundary of the administration zone and was intended to screen Waterloo Station.

in the architecture of the South Bank, the Dome of Discovery, the Skylon, Edward Mills' *Abacus* screen and in the design of furniture and various other exhibits.

Bright, joyous colour was in vogue, characterized by novel contrasts, clashing primaries, lime yellows and greys. The leitmotifs of the Festival style were the formal patterns derived from molecular structures, or more free-flowing motifs inspired by such artists as Miró or Calder and exemplified in the fabric designs of Lucienne Day. The Festival Pattern Group had been set up specifically to devise graphic patterns from the stylization of molecular structure as observed through the microscope. This bringing together of nature and science to suggest form and motif was in the finest tradition of Ruskinian theory, though Ruskin would surely have disapproved of the fashionable, rather than timeless, character of the resulting designs.

Meanwhile, certain craft traditions were revived and developed in a context that owed much to William Morris's ideals of the artist-craftsman. Fine work in silver was promoted by the patronage of the Worshipful Company of Goldsmiths; studio pottery was again raised to the level of an art form by Bernard Leach, strongly influenced by Japanese ceramics, and by Lucie Rie and Hans Coper who had emigrated from Germany in 1938 and 1939 respectively.

In 1952 the Utility scheme came to an end. By 1956, the year in which the Design Centre was opened, the Festival style seemed already outmoded; Scandinavian design and Italian decorative styles were attracting attention instead, and Britain's avant-garde was translating the symbols of American popular culture into a new artistic vernacular which was to have a considerable impact on the applied arts. It was in 1956 that Richard Hamilton first showed his collage painting *Just what is it that makes today's homes so different, so appealing* . Often cited as the first Pop picture, this collage underlined with considerable irony the new design values and criteria dictated by the popular consumer market.

Paris—haute couture and high style

Paris survived the occupation years but failed to regain after the war the position of supremacy in the decorative arts which it had enjoyed in previous eras. The Exposition Universelle of 1900 and the 1925 Exposition Internationale had marked pinnacles of achievement which, with one notable exception, were not to be repeated. The outstanding exception to this pattern of decline was in the

Left Printed fabric designed by Lucienne Day, 1950s. Day created a lively, decorative abstract idiom, in contrast to the more functionalist simplicity of her husband Robin Day's furniture designs.

Below left Silver coffee and milk pots, designed by Stuart Devlin and made by Wakely & Wheeler, London, 1959. The heat-resistant nylon bases eliminate the need for handles.

Below right: Just what is it that makes today's homes so different, so appealing?, collage by Richard Hamilton, 1956. This is an early landmark in the iconography of Pop culture.

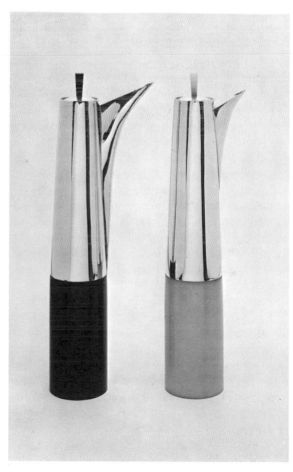

Right Illustration of a Balenciaga coat by Eric Stemp, published in British *Vogue,* November 1959.

Below Suit called 'Bar' from Christian Dior's 'New Look' collection, presented in February 1947 and destined to change instantly the face of fashion.

world of fashion. From the late forties through to the early sixties, Parisian haute couture was to dominate fashion headlines, Parisian couturiers were the unchallenged international arbiters of colour, cut and silhouette and Paris inspired brilliant achievements in the related arts of fashion photography, editorial design and illustration.

The central characters in this glorious flowering of the art of dress were the new generation of couturiers, most notably Christian Dior, Cristobal Balenciaga, Pierre Balmain, Jacques Fath and Hubert de Givenchy. The name of Dior has become almost synonymous with Paris fashion, not because he was a more talented designer than his contemporaries but through the fortuitous results of his impeccable timing. Dior found instant

success and attracted world attention to Paris couture with his New Look, launched in February 1947, just five months after the opening of his Avenue Montaigne salon. Dior sensed the need for a romantic reaction to the austerity imposed on fashion by war-time restrictions. His New Look was an exaggeratedly feminine, wilfully indulgent line, narrow-waisted and full-skirted, involving many yards of fabric in elaborate pleatings.

The New Look was the first of a series of fashion silhouettes suggested by Dior and his contemporaries over the next decade, reported religiously by the fashion press and accepted as law by Paris couture's wealthy clientele. Couture became a growth industry, expanding into and increasingly dependent upon more profitable affiliated marketing ventures, notably perfumes, and giving work to a wide array of highly skilled artisans.

Dior's death in 1957 was, by chance, as symbolic as his début a decade earlier, for new influences were undermining haute couture's dominance of fashion. A popular, youthful and increasingly self-conscious market was dictating its own styles and shifting the balance of power in fashion from the ivory tower to the street, a swing which Dior's successor, the young Yves Saint Laurent, acknowledged in 1960 with his revolutionary 'Beat' collection.

The genius of Paris couture was the Spaniard Balenciaga, who is widely acknowledged as the

supreme master of cut. He was an enigmatic figure who shunned publicity. His creations, typically the stiff, plain silks, dazzle by the confidence and sheer verve of their cut and construction. Balenciaga was a sculptor in cloth, a master of proportion with a highly sophisticated eye.

Paris fashion inspired brilliant photography, notably from American photographers on assignment for *Vogue* and *Harper's Bazaar*. The images of Penn and Avedon, the witty vision of William Klein, the stylish view of Henry Clarke and Louise Dahl-Wolfe survive as a gracious pictorial record of this era of elegance. The leading fashion illustrator was the talented René Gruau, who devised a style which expressed to perfection the spirit of Parisian fashion.

Couture flourished briefly in a small, albeit international, privileged world. But the former dominance of wealth and social status in matters of style was doomed and the post-war years of extravagance in fashion were the swansong of an already archaic life-style. Its final flowering was to be seen in the ritual of grand balls and costumed fêtes. The couturier Jacques Fath was a sparkling host and tireless party-giver in the tradition of Poiret, and no single event better evoked the romantic yearning for a fading past than the costumed ball held in Venice in 1951 by Charles de Bestegui. In a similar vein, Cecil Beaton had

evoked another age in his memorable 1948 study of slender models in extravagant satin ball gowns by Charles James, looking for all the world like courtly ladies in a canvas by Watteau.

Scandinavian design

It is a tribute to the achievements of Scandinavia's post-war designers, manufacturers and artisans that the term Scandinavian Modern has entered the international language of design and is widely acknowledged as signifying a distinctive aesthetic. Its basic elements have been well defined by David Revere McFadden in his introduction to the Cooper Hewitt Museum's 1982-3 survey exhibition 'Scandinavian Modern Design 1880-1980'. The elements which he lists, 'restraint in form and decoration, embodiment of traditional values, unity of form and function and reliance on natural

Above 'Chorus girl', preparatory sketch by René Gruau, 1950s, demonstrating the economy of line and liveliness of his graphic style.

Left Balenciaga fashion recorded with characteristic rigour by Irving Penn, reproduced from French *Vogue*, October 1950.

materials', suggest ground rules of sound design and manufacture not far removed from the Arts and Crafts ideal proposed by British theorists of the nineteenth century. The social context, however, was very different. Whereas in Britain the Arts and Crafts movement proposed an escapist ideology which was never a realistic solution to the debasement of design standards in a heavily industrialized society, in the Scandinavian countries Arts and Crafts ideas were an integral part of the social fabric. Respect for tradition and reliance on natural materials were almost inevitable within low-density, largely rural societies with limited scope for industrialization.

In the years before the Second World War, the Scandinavians had developed their own brand of functionalism, tempered by humanist concerns and quite different in character from the hard-edged, dogmatic approach of the Bauhaus purists. Kaare Klint, a designer and teacher at Copenhagen's Academy of Art, epitomized in his approach the respect for both functionalism and tradition which was the very basis of the Scandinavian aesthetic. In Sweden, the furniture of the architect Alvar Aalto and the glass produced by Orrefors were successful practical applications of the new functionalism.

After the war increased industrialization and consequent urbanization made new demands on Scandinavian design and manufacture. Industrialization has been a process of evolution rather than revolution, however, and Scandinavian manufacturers have been able to develop along rational lines, shunning exaggerated styling and responding instead to basic human needs for objects and environments, at once functional and inviting. Such was the character of the Scandinavian Modern aesthetic which made so considerable an impact internationally in the fifties.

The export success of Scandinavian design owed much to the publicity attracted by the Scandinavian exhibits at the Milan Triennali and by the various exhibitions of Scandinavian design held in Europe and North America in the fifties and early sixties. Exhibitions such as 'Design in Scandinavia', travelling in the United States and Canada between 1954 and 1957, and 'Formes Scandinaves' in Paris in 1958-9 encouraged awareness of the high quality of Scandinavian production in the applied arts and opened up new export markets. By the early sixties no major western city was without its distributors of Scandinavian domestic goods and this worthy design movement was in danger of becoming just another decorators' cliché.

Opposite **Mrs Charles James in an evening dress designed by her husband and photographed by Cecil Beaton in James's Madison Avenue salon, 1955.**

Left **interior of the Baker Hall of Residence designed by Alvar Aalto, with bent plywood furniture also designed by Aalto, 1940s.**

Above Glass vase designed by Tapio Wirkkala in 1946 and made in the Iittala glassworks.

Right Dumb valet chair designed by Hans Wegner in 1951, manufactured by Johannes Hansen from 1953.

often inspired by nature, and by a noble respect for his materials.

A focal point of Denmark's design achievements were the galleries of Den Permanente, established in Copenhagen in 1931 as a retail outlet and promotional display centre for the best of Danish design. The Danes have set and maintained high standards. Danish furniture manufacturers, for example, have their own Quality Control Board as a self-imposed monitóring system. Furniture has proved Denmark's forte and the soft contours of oiled teak have become one of the most distinctive elements of the Scandinavian look. Among the most distinguished Danish furniture designers of the fifties were Arne Jacobsen and Hans Wegner, the latter being joint winner, with Tapio Wirkkala, of the first Lunning prize in 1951, an award established by Frederick Lunning for excellence in Scandinavian design. The Danes also excelled in

The unified multi-national image of the Scandinavian Modern movement should not blind one to the national characteristics and specific strengths of contributor countries. The lead in the post-war period was taken by Finland and Denmark, but Sweden earned considerable acclaim, notably for its glassware, while Norway and Iceland played peripheral roles.

A central figure in the story of Finnish design was the talented Tapio Wirkkala. A sensitive and versatile designer and an inspiring teacher, Wirkkala was responsible for the design of the Finnish installation at the 1951 Triennale and led his country's team to a triumphant success. He played an influential role in shaping the development of Finnish design as director of the Institute of Industrial Arts between 1951 and 1954. His own work, in wood, metal, glass and other media, is characterized by a fondness for curvilinear forms,

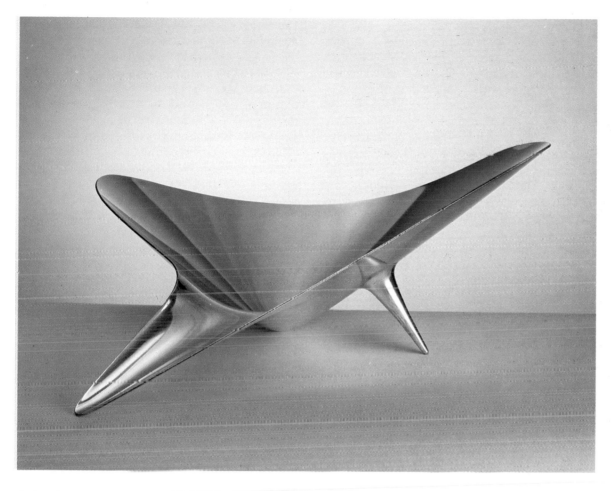

their silverware, typified in the fifties by simple, usually soft-contoured forms and unadorned surfaces. The firm of Georg Jensen flourished under the new functionalist design influence of Count Sigvard Bernadotte, and the designer Henning Koppel developed forms for Jensen in the late forties and fifties that are outstanding sculptural essays in Organic Modernism. Other silver designers of note included Tias Eckhoff, a Norwegian who worked for Jensen, Nanna Ditzel, who designed jewellery for Jensen, and Bent Gabriel Pederson for the firm of Johannes Hansen

Scandinavian, and particularly Swedish, decorative glassware attained new standards of sculptural and expressive form in the post-war era and became a major luxury export. The leading Swedish factories of Orrefors and Kosta, and smaller workshops such as Stromberg, produced heavy-walled vessels, often with internal decoration which emphasized the natural clarity and translucence of the medium. Vicke Lindstrand, with Kosta from 1950, was an outstanding designer. Wirkkala, Timo Sarpaneva and, until her untimely death in 1948, Gunnel Nyman designed for the leading Finnish glass factory Iittala.

Stig Lindberg, artistic director of the Gustavsberg ceramics factory, and the potter Berndt Friberg represent the high quality of Swedish post-war ceramics in both the commercial and studio sectors. It was characteristic, though, of the Scandinavian approach in this medium, as in every other, that there should be no distinction between the artistic validity of the individually crafted or the manufactured item. Scandinavian design of the fifties was centred around the concept of domestic furnishing and a not insignificant element of the typical Scandinavian interior was the use of textured fabrics and hangings in mellow, muted natural colours. The traditional Norwegian wall-hanging, the rya, enjoyed a revival and for a while rough, knobbly-textured, loose-weave wools in shades of oatmeal, beige, cream and brown were essential ingredients of 'good taste' interiors.

The Scandinavian Modern movement, though it avoided style as an end in itself, was adopted internationally in the fifties and inevitably fell victim to the vagaries of fashion. The values at the basis of the Scandinavian aesthetic, however, remain eternal and have continued to evolve a rich form language.

INDUSTRIAL DESIGN

During the Second World War many technological developments took place, particularly in communications and aerospace, which were later applied to industrial design, and after the war, which devastated many of the combatant nations, industrial design was promoted both in Europe and Japan as a means of national and economic regeneration. At the same time the role of the designer began to change, and he was less likely to exert an influence over a whole industrial empire. With relatively simple machines and straightforward organizations, one designer could have a considerable effect, but the explosion of communications and electronics that eventually took place in the sixties brought about a new generation of machines and systems that were simply too complicated for any one individual to comprehend.

This phenomenon is illustrated by the fate of the Mini, which first appeared in 1959. For although the design by Alec Issigonis was radical and successful, it made demands to which British management could not, or would not, respond. Huge numbers of these cars were produced, but the extra manufacturing capacity was created simply by duplicating existing production lines rather than investing in new technology. As a result the car sold at a loss for seventeen years despite its continued popularity.

The design establishment: Italy, France, Germany, the United States and Japan

The many important initiatives—governmental, private and institutional—of the 1940s and 1950s did, however, further the status of both the industrial design profession and particular aesthetic values. The founding of the International Congress of the Societies of Industrial Design (ICSID) was a consolidating force.

Milan, home of the Triennale and other important design exhibitions, continued to be a focal point for developments in Italian design after the Second World War. The leading department store chain La Rinascente played an important role in design propaganda. As Cesare Brustio remarked, 'La Rinascente is not only a department store chain, but has also been a marketing, management and design school.' The Milan branch reopened in December 1950 to great press publicity, and set out to improve public taste through the mounting of exhibitions (including participation in the Triennali) and the commissioning of products from leading designers such as Gio Ponti and Franco Albini. After a successful exhibition entitled 'The Aesthetics of the Product' it was decided to institute the Compasso d'Oro awards for well designed Italian products in 1954, extending the competition two years later to include international

Right **British Motor Corporation's Mini first appeared in 1959. The design by Alec Issigonis was technically ingenious and influenced every succeeding small car.**

designs. Among the early award-winners were Gino Colombini's plastic bucket for Kartell; Piergiacomo Castiglioni's REM vacuum cleaner; Dante Giacosa's Fiat 500 motor car and Marcello Nizzoli's Olivetti Lettera 22 typewriter. In 1959 Britain's Council of Industrial Design (COID) received the Compasso d'Oro Gran Premio for its services to design.

In 1956 the Associazione per Il Disegno Industriale (ADI) was founded in Milan to raise the status of the design profession and stimulate a greater awareness of design in industry and education. Prior to assuming overall responsibility for the scheme, the ADI collaborated with La Rinascente in the running of the Compasso d'Oro between 1959 and 1965. Italy also had her own magazine concerned with industrial design, *Stile Industria*, founded in 1953 and edited by Alberto Rosselli until its demise in 1962. It was concerned with the relationship between design and industry, new materials and processes, and the nature of good design.

In France, there was no state organization comparable with Britain's COID. The Union des Artistes Modernes, an organization of architects, decorators and designers, sought to improve public taste through publications and the 'Formes Utiles' exhibitions but was of little real national signifi-

Left Formes Utiles catalogue, 1954. The Formes Utiles exhibitions provided a showcase for the work of members of France's U.A.M., whose concerns, in the post-war years, were increasingly dominated by industrial design questions.

FORMES UTILES

Left In the Citroën DS of 1955 the front-wheel drive (developed from Boulanger's Traction Avant of 1934) gave the passengers a great deal more space. For twenty years it was the most advanced large car in production.

cance. The Institut de l'Esthétique Industrielle was of greater importance; it was established in 1950 by Jacques Viennot (the founder of Technès, the most important French industrial design concern of the period) and published a magazine also called *L'Esthétique Industrielle*. In 1955 the Ministry of Commerce initiated an awards scheme, Beauté-France, for well designed goods ranging from domestic products to heavy engineering. Similar in many respects to the Italian Compasso d'Oro of the previous year it nonetheless excluded the decorative arts and placed no limit on the number of awards which could be made. It was followed by a Belgian scheme, the Signe d'Or, in 1956 and the British Council of Industrial Design's Design Centre Awards Scheme in 1957.

Although post-war German industrial design is often associated with the Hochschule für Gestaltung, Braun products or Volkswagen and Mercedes-Benz cars, there were also a number of organizational initiatives. The West German parliament approved the establishment of the Rat für Formgebung in Darmstadt in 1951, close in spirit to the British COID. Industry sponsored the Darmstadt Institut für Neue Technische Form and Haus Industrieform at Essen. Their aims were to forge links between manufacturers, public and retailers and to establish a policy which woud lead to the acceptance of better standards in design. The Neue Sammlung Gallery in Munich also showed the work of both German and foreign designers and mounted travelling exhibitions to educational establishments.

In 1960 Reyner Banham's article 'A Throw-Away Aesthetic' called for a recognition of the realities of a flourishing consumer society—obsolescence, styling, novelty and change were all characteristic of industrially produced goods, whether automobiles, refrigerators, juke-boxes or food-mixers. There were, however, concerted attempts to counter this consumerist tide, mainly by individuals such as Edgar Kaufmann Jr. and organizations like the Museum of Modern Art (MoMA) in New York which had, in the 1930s, initiated a policy of collecting 'mass-produced objects made to serve a specific purpose'. Despite the sponsoring of design competitions in the 1940s and the holding of a conference on 'Industrial Design as a New Profession' in 1946, MoMA was ultimately more important as a tastemaker than as a propagator of design initiatives. Edgar Kaufmann, along with his series of shows of 'Good Design' (discussed in the previous chapter) introduced Good Design awards and labels which manufacturers could attach to selected products, an idea of

Opposite above **Suzuki Diamond Free motorcycle of 1953. Suzuki were originally a textile manufacturing company, but such was the success of their first motorcycles that within a decade they were infiltrating European markets.**

Opposite below **The Toyota SF of 1951 was introduced when the Japanese economy was beginning to revive. At first Japanese cars were rather primitive, but they then began to imitate European styles.**

Below **Sewing machine designed by M. Katsuyama and K. Hamada for the Japanese Sewing Machine Co. Ltd. This won first prize in the 1959 Industrial Design Competition organized by the Mainichi Press.**

which retailers approved. The dominant aesthetic, however, was closely related to that of the European Modern Movement, typified by clean, purist external appearances devoid of superficial styling or decoration, as in Marcello Nizzoli's Olivetti Lettera 22 typewriter. In 1952 the Museum held a highly successful show of Olivetti designs, and in 1958 it organized a permanent display of Braun products, a company whose work has been associated with 'good taste'. As Russell Lynes indicated in his book *The Tastemakers* of 1954, 'good design' was very much a status symbol for American consumers, endorsing as it did an anti-consumerist, anti-obsolescent stance.

This period also saw the organization and consolidation of the industrial design profession in the United States. In 1944 the Society of Industrial Designers (SID) of America was founded by a dozen or so leading figures, including Egmont Arens, Raymond Loewy, Walter Dorwin Teague and Russel Wright. Their main aims were to establish a climate of professionalism and understanding among designers, to develop industrial design education strategies and to educate industrialists and consumers in the social and economic value of design. In 1949 the SID's annual publication *US Industrial Design* was launched, by which time membership had risen to one hundred, and by 1959 to over two hundred, revealing the growth of the profession. The magazine *Industrial Design* was first published in 1954 and has become the leading American journal of design.

The launching of the Aspen conferences in 1951 was another landmark in design identity in the United States. Held in June on the theme 'Design—A Function of Management', the first conference initiated an important facet of post-war design debates, with designers campaigning for proper recognition within business management structures. The conferences were organized on an annual basis and in 1954 became incorporated as the International Design Conference in Aspen (ICDA), a major discussion forum for design practice and theory.

The 1950s was an important decade for the development of industrial design in Japan, with an intensive design promotion campaign by government and industry. The Ministry of Trade and Industry (MITI) played a key role, sponsoring design-related research and advising manufacturers. In 1957 the Industrial Design Promotion Council of MITI initiated a Good Design awards scheme, known as the G Mark, which was originally intended to act as a stimulus to manufacturers. Later, in the 1960s, it was directed more to the general public. In 1959 a Design Division was newly created in MITI, and in the following year the Japan Design House was established as a permanent exhibition centre and information source for well designed Japanese products.

The profession began to organize itself in 1952 with the establishment of the Japanese Industrial Designers Association (JIDA). With an initial membership of twenty-five the Association sought to establish a professional identity for industrial designers and to develop appropriate educational training courses. By the end of the decade membership stood at about sixty. A landmark in encouraging young talent in the field was the Industrial Design Competition launched in 1953 and sponsored by the Mainichi Press, a company of some significance in the development of post-war Japanese design potential.

The foundations of Japanese industrial design

The prime objective of the Japanese government was to reconstruct the national economy after the humiliating defeat in the Second World War. The many economic, social and political reforms that had been initiated in the late 1940s under the aegis of the Allied forces became the foundations of Japan's post-war recovery. The existing power-base in Japanese industry, now associated with Japan's war efforts, was restructured and the dominant élite of leading industrialists was replaced by a younger generation who were responsible for the introduction of new, more democratic management techniques. In the 1950s, American industrial design techniques, products and business management all played an influential role in this economic recovery, and by the end of the decade a new breed of industrial designers had emerged. By this time there were also six faculties of industrial design in the higher education sector.

Raymond Loewy had visited Japan to design a cigarette packet in the early 1950s, a time when industrial design was viewed as an activity analogous to fashion design. But as the decade unfolded many Japanese businessmen went on organized study tours of the United States to learn about business management techniques and were able to see at first hand the value of design to product development. From the mid-fifties onwards the Japanese Export Trade Organization (JETRO) sent five or six students abroad every year to study design, partly funded by the government and partly by business or individual sponsorship. Most students were attracted to the United States but others went to study in Germany and

Right The Sony TR-55, the world's first mass-produced transistor radio, came on the market in August 1955. This radio, an early example of the Japanese ability to miniaturize technology, was the first to bear the name Sony.

Italy. JETRO also invited American and European designers to Japan to participate in a highly popular series of seminar programmes.

The role of 'design' in Japanese industry is not well understood. The Japanese experience demonstrates the ambivalence of the word: as the success of industries in Nagoya, Yokohama and Kawasaki suggest, design is not one subject, but a great many. Yet naive western commentators anxious to imitate Japanese success frequently cite 'design' as the means of oriental industrial pre-eminence. This is misleading because, for the first twenty or so years after the Second World War, Japanese efforts were directed not at design, but at achieving high efficiency in the manufacturing process, their *kan-ban* (or 'just-in-time') systems eliminating bottlenecks from factories.

As Marx knew, the means of production influence the fruits of industry. Although the traditional reverence for quality and miniaturization inevitably confers certain attractive characteristics on Japanese products, Japanese excellence depends not on having the best designers, but the most efficient factories. Quality and innovation arise from the factory floor.

In the late 1950s and early 1960s, however, some company presidents began to promote design as an element of company development. An important figure in this context was Konosuke Matsushita of the Matsushita Electric Industrial Company (founded in 1918 and now embracing National, Panasonic, Technics and Quasar), who had been to the United States in 1951. On his return, enthused by what he had seen, he set up the industrial design department at Matsushita, said to be the first in Japanese industry. Consisting of a handful of designers, it was to grow, by the end of the decade, to more than fifty strong.

This innovation was soon followed by other firms: in 1953 the Canon Camera Company set up its industrial design unit to develop the subsequently successful Canon V camera of 1956; Toshiba established its design section in the same year; the Sharp Corporation introduced a systematic industrial design policy in 1957; the Sony company, now well recognized for its enlightened attitude towards design, appointed its first full-time designer in 1954 and, seven years later, instituted its design department.

Today the Sony Corporation has an established international reputation for design and innovation in audio-visual equipment, a reputation which reflects its development in the context of post-war economic growth in Japan. Founded in 1946 under the name of Tokyo Tsushin Kogyo (TTK), the company was quick to profit from a report published by the US Army about the development of tape-recording technology in Germany during the war. TTK was soon manufacturing the first Japanese tape-recorder, the Type G, in 1950. This was followed by the Type H recorder, the first intended for general use, which also marked Sony's first use of consultant design expertise. It was marketed between 1952 and 1953.

In 1954 TTK obtained a licence to manufacture transistors, new components which had been developed in the Bell Telephone Laboratories in 1947. TTK's first mass-produced transistor radio, the TR-55, appeared in 1955 and was the first product to bear the name Sony, later to be adopted as the company's own name. It was also the first of a number of related Sony developments, being followed by the first pocket radio, the TR63, in 1957 and the first portable miniature television, the TV-8-301, in 1959. However, it was not until the 1960s, after the creation of its design department, that Sony adopted a consistent design image to complement its technological innovations and imaginative marketing.

Germany's Economic Miracle

Like Japan, Germany was appallingly desolate after the war; the scene in Nuremberg, for instance, has been described by Richard Mayne in his book *Postwar*: 'Only the bleak new suburbs and a few isolated buildings remained intact. Along streets still strewn with rubble, a few tramcars threaded their way, linked together in threes and crowded to suffocation with pale, cowed, angry people . . . who turned away when they passed American or British soldiers.'

Fortunately, under the guidance of Konrad Adenauer, Germany's economic recovery was remarkably rapid, so much so that it became known as the *Wirtschaftswunder* or 'economic miracle'. This was aided by two factors: the strong base of applied design that had been established before the war, and the character of the German people who, it was once remarked, look upon life itself as if it were a mathematical problem. The rigorous German approach to design in the fifties is epitomized by one celebrated educational establishment: the Hochschule für Gestaltung (College for Design), located in Ulm on the banks of the Danube.

The school was founded in 1955 by Inge and Grete Scholl, two sisters whose family had suffered under the Nazis. Inge Scholl was already married to a graphic designer, Otl Aicher. They chose the Swiss architect and minimal sculptor Max Bill as their first director and the designer of the school buildings. At this stage the Hochschule was intended to do no more and no less than revive the ideals of early Bauhaus, which, if not entirely extinguished by the Nazis, had certainly been strongly discouraged by them.

Max Bill believed in the value of individual creativity and an artistic, intuitive approach to design, with the aim of humanizing the products of modern industry. These ideals brought him into conflict with Tomás Maldonado, an Argentinian polymath who joined the school and replaced Bill as director in 1956. Maldonado was influenced by the Hannes Meyer regime at the Bauhaus and believed, like so many others in this period, that the individual was no longer of much value in the design process. Instead, design was to be explored by systematic teamwork and rigorous intellectual enquiry. With Maldonado's belief that design should be studied in a broader context, the Ulm school's curriculum grew to include the study of psychology, semiotics, games theory, sociology and anthropology.

Below Domestic appliances by Braun, around 1960, including the HE1 kettle by Reinhold Weiss, the F60 flash gun (1959) by Dieter Rams, SK1 radio by Artur Braun and Dr Fritz Geichler, the M1 food-mixer (1960) by Gerd Alfred Muller, the H1 fan heater (1958) by Gerd Alfred Muller, and the SM3 electric razor (1960) by Gerd Alfred Muller.

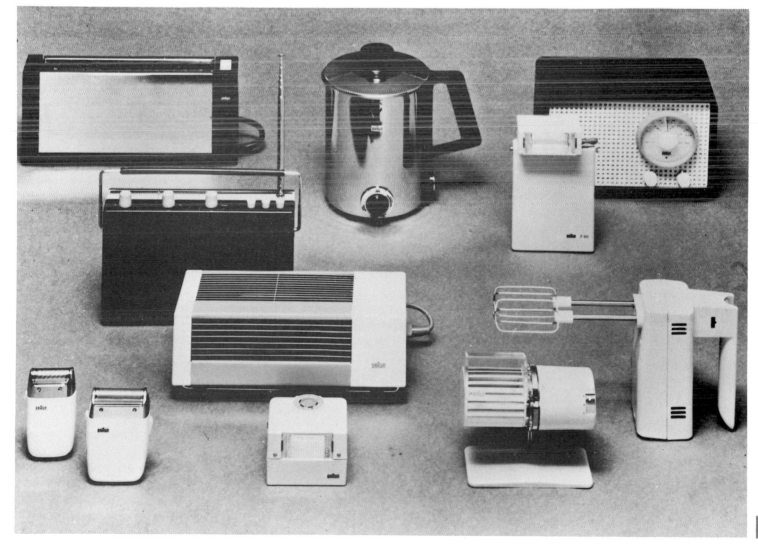

Opposite, above left **Wall clock for Junghans designed by Max Bill, 1957. This is a typically German expression of 'gute Form', a clean shape apparently derived from purely functional considerations.**

Opposite, above right **Lexicon 80 typewriter designed by Marcello Nizzoli for Olivetti, 1948. This and the calculator overleaf display Nizzoli's characteristically elegant and sculptural approach.**

Opposite below **Vespa motor-scooter, around 1960, the first version of which was designed in 1946. This became a symbol of Italy's post-war optimism.**

The Hochschule für Gestaltung was more successful than the Bauhaus in establishing real links with industry. When, as part of the post-war reconstruction, the Frankfurt radio manufacturer Braun diversified into household appliances, Artur Braun turned to the Hochschule. He hired Otl Aicher, the product designer Hans Gugelot, and, later, a younger product designer, Dieter Rams. All these were clearly influenced by Maldonado's systematic approach to design and they gave a distinctive form to Braun's electrical household goods. After their appearance in the 1955 Radio Show in Düsseldorf, the Braun products soon became internationally recognized as images of perfection in design.

The Braun style was very sophisticated, depending for its effect on geometrical simplicity, harmony of detail, superb graphics and high-quality mouldings. An American journalist, Richard Moss, summed up this achievement: 'Three general rules seem to govern every Braun design— a rule of order, a rule of harmony, and a rule of harmony.' Dieter Rams himself added, 'I regard it as one of the most important and most responsible tasks of a designer today to help clear the chaos we are living in.'

His success was such that the highly stylized and formal Braun goods have become perfect symbols of the industrial civilization that the Hochschule initially set out to humanize. Like the Bauhaus before it, the Hochschule für Gestaltung was forced by political pressure to close in 1968, but not before its influence, through the graphics of Otl Aicher and the products of Dieter Rams and Hans Gugelot, had turned its pedagogic theories into an almost universally acceptable style, one which became influential throughout the world, particularly in Japan.

The Italian *Ricostruzione*

Luigi Barzini, in his book *The Italians* (1964), observed that never has a modern nation been so uninfluenced by technology as Italy. This assertion is both bold and justified because Italy, like Germany, is a modern political creation that lacked the unity which in Britain, during the eighteenth century, had allowed the arts and sciences to flourish in the interests of commerce. Moreover, while certain areas of Italy have maintained craft traditions since the Roman era, others were essentially agricultural until the end of the Second World War.

Italy's industrial revolution occurred in the late 1940s. It was a social revolution, known as the *Ricostruzione* because it entailed both a material

and a symbolic rebuilding of the country after the years of Fascism. It resulted in perhaps the first coherent consumer style, and, as a result of the changes taking place in the post-war years, 'Italian Design' became a synonym for stylish living. *La dolce vita* was given form by Italy's new industrial designers and Gio Ponti, the founder of *Domus*, summarized the mood in an editorial in 1947. *Domus* promoted a version of the Modern Movement that was peculiarly Italian: lacking the austere social purpose of Germany, Italian design was based on luxury and consumerism. Ponti wrote: 'Our ideal of the good life and a level of taste and thought expressed by our homes and manner of living are all part of the same thing.'

Milan and Turin were the centres of Italy's industrial revolution. The school of architecture in Milan Polytechnic was turning out architects at a rate that the country's appetite and capacity for building could not match, despite the government-backed INA-Casa housing initiatives. Many of these young architects turned to local industries, either the new generation of electrical manufacturers, such as Brionvega in Milan and Olivetti in Turin, or to the local furniture industries.

One of the most powerful symbols of the *Ricostruzione* was the Vespa motor-scooter, a stylish, democratic form of transport. This was designed by Corradino d'Ascanio, a pioneer of Italian aviation who had devoted the earlier part of his career to the design of helicopters. In 1934 he joined the Genoese engineering firm of Piaggio and eleven years later was asked to design a radical, two-wheeled motor vehicle. The Vespa was conceived on aeronautical principles, for it had a streamlined shape and was constructed in drawn steel like an aeroplane's 'monocoque' structure. Eighteen thousand Vespas were manufactured in the first year of production and the design brought about a revolution in Italian private transport.

The same interest in streamlining influenced Olivetti, the makers of business equipment and one of Italy's leading industrial groups. This company had become interested in design in the thirties, when the MP1 typewriter was produced to the design of Aldo Magnelli and his brother Alberto, an abstract painter. Through Adriano Olivetti, the son of the founder, Olivetti came to world prominence as a symbol of modern Italian culture during the years of the *Ricostruzione*. Adriano, like Emil Rathenau, was a cosmopolitan Jewish intellectual who brought the influence of art to bear in every aspect of Olivetti's production. Employing Marcello Nizzoli as the leading creative figure, Olivetti had artists and sculptors to create the appearance of

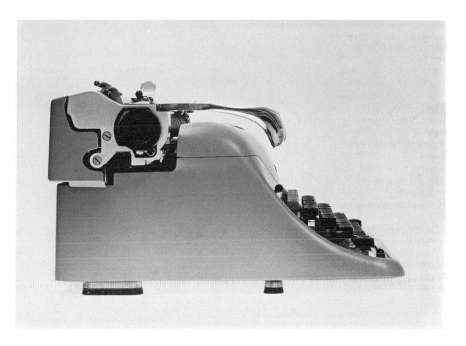

Right Divisumma 24 calculator designed by Marcello Nizzoli for Olivetti, 1956.

Below left The Mirella sewing machine, designed by Marcello Nizzoli, won the Grand Prize at the Milan Triennale of 1957. The sophisticated form of this product is a telling contrast with the Japanese sewing-machine on page 192.

Below right Sanitary ware designed by Gio Ponti for Ideal Standard, 1954, a demonstration of the Italian ability to endow even the most mundane articles with formal harmony.

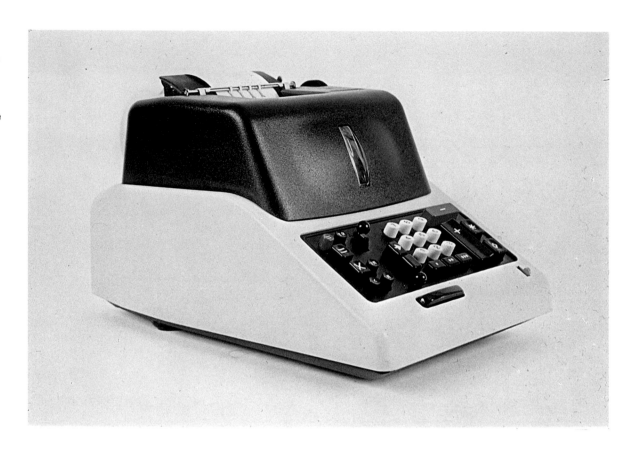

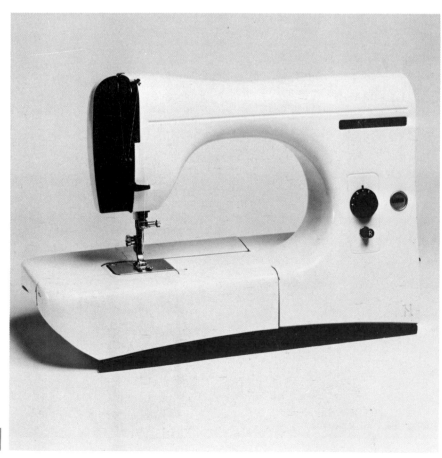

its products, to work in the publicity departments, and to design showrooms and exhibitions in the world's major capital cities.

Among Olivetti's most successful products in this period was Nizzoli's Lexicon 80 typewriter, an elegant, streamlined machine that attracted attention in Olivetti showrooms throughout the world. Thomas Watson, the chairman of IBM, was so impressed that he instructed Eliot Noyes to bring about a similar result in his own company. In 1952 Olivetti's achievement was recognized by an exhibition at the Museum of Modern Art in New York.

It was during the fifties that Italian Design became a widely recognized phenomenon. In furniture, although the designers were strongly influenced by Charles Eames's work for Hermann Miller and by the abstract forms of contemporary sculpture, the style they created was original and unique. Manufacturers deliberately publicized their relationships with specific designers and individuals established close links with certain companies: Nizzoli with the sewing-machine manufacturer Necchi, Marco Zanuso with Arflex, and Ettore Sottsass Jr. with Olivetti. One of the most versatile was Gio Ponti who, as well as designing furniture for Cassina, was responsible for the chrome-plated coffee-machine for La Pavoni and expressive, sculptured sanitary ware for Ideal Standard. Meanwhile Alfa Romeo used the automobile design studio of Giuseppe 'Nuccio' Bertone, based in Turin, to provide designs for their car bodies, and in the giant Fiat company Dante Giacosa developed a line of sophisticated small cars, including the Nuova 500 of 1957, a replacement for his highly successful 'Cinquecento' of 1937.

Below Coffee-machine for La Pavoni designed by Gio Ponti in 1949. This gleaming cult object brought the styling of Detroit car studios into the fashionable new coffee bars.

The United States

The mid-fifties in America was a period of great confidence and economic expansion and most people believed that life would simply get better and better in this 'dynamic economy', as Harley Earl called it. Others, notably the playwright Arthur Miller and the social critic Vance Packard, preferred to call it 'planned obsolescence'; in Miller's play *Death of a Salesman* the hero, a victim of hire purchase and the dynamic economy, mournfully declares, 'Once in my life I would like to own something outright before it's broken! I'm always in a race with the junkyard!'

In pursuit of economic growth, American industry in the forty years since the First World War had used up more of the earth's resources than all of civilization in the preceding four thousand years. This produced irate reactions from sensitive commentators. Vance Packard in his book *The Waste Makers* of 1960 and Ralph Nader in *Unsafe at Any Speed* of 1962 both singled out the automobile industry as the chief culprit. This was not unreasonable, for in the automobile industry planned obsolescence was an integral part of styling.

Harley Earl had made a significant contribution to this phenomenon, particularly through his 'Motorama', a travelling circus of automobile design conceived by Earl and Alfred P. Sloan as a testing ground for future car designs. The 'dream' cars in the exhibitions were displayed in theatrical spectacles with dancing girls and live music, and the superficial design details, if liked by the visitors, would eventually reach the production line. Earl's first post-war 'dream' car was the Le Sabre which first took shape in 1949 and emerged as a running prototype in 1951. It was modelled in clay, a technique developed by Earl and now used throughout the car industry, and styled to look somewhat like its namesake, the F-86 Sabre jet. Inspired by the 'plane's military canopy, Earl gave his car the first ever wraparound windshield, and scoops, vents and ducts that were more the product of his fertile imagination than functional necessity. Earl then went on to apply this vocabulary of aerospace imagery to General Motors' next generation of private cars.

The consumers, unsophisticated citizens of a new industrial economy, were delighted by these

Right **IBM Selectric typewriter, model 721, designed by Eliot Noyes & Associates, 1961. Noyes eschewed excessive styling and favoured clean, functional design.**

stylistic gimmicks. So much so that by the late fifties even European architect-designers such as George Nelson were arguing in favour of planned obsolescence and the dynamic economy. In *Problems of Design* Nelson said that however absurd the concept of private cars looking like rocket ships was, it was still a formula that pleased the public and generated huge wealth for the economy.

One of the ironies of design history is that the Bauhaus style, which had been conceived as an instrument of libertarian social change, actually found its fullest expression in the service of corporate America. The impact of European standards of design in the States is epitomized by the re-design of IBM by Eliot Noyes, an architect who had trained under Gropius and worked at the Museum of Modern Art. Though inspired by the example of Olivetti, Noyes's work at IBM was less individual and more conformist in approach. Telling the chairman, 'You would prefer neatness', Noyes took in hand the architecture, product design, graphics, packaging and signage. He rejected superficial styling and planned obsolescence, and believed instead that a clean, modular,

Left Armchair, 1950, designed by Charles Eames, moulded fibreglass and steel. Eames was an inventive designer who conceived forms and developed materials ideally suited to mass production.

Left 'E.S.U.' (Eames Storage Units), 1951.

201

Right Harley Earl at the wheel of the Buick Le Sabre, which he designed in 1954. The stylistic indulgences of these 'dream' cars found their way into less exclusive models.

Right The Chevrolet Bel Air convertible of 1955, designed by Harley Earl, was a characteristic product of planned obsolescence.

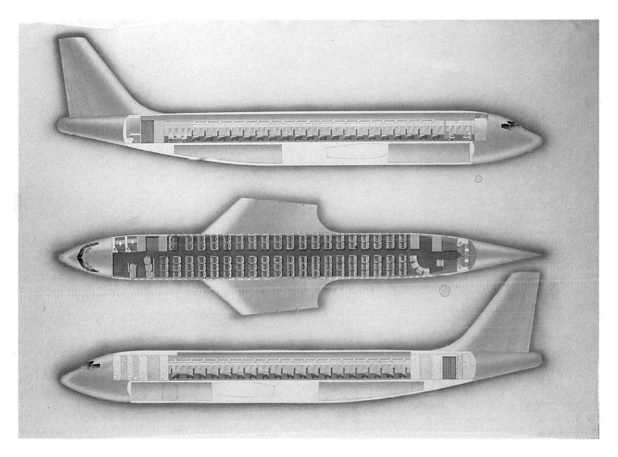

Left Interior of the Boeing 707 designed by Walter Dorwin Teague and Frank de Giudice, 1957. Teague had an enormous influence on aircraft interiors and was even consulted on exterior features of the aircraft.

Below Interior of the Lockheed Super Constellation designed by Henry Dreyfuss, 1953. To many people in the 1950s aircraft interiors offered a first real taste of the environmental possibilities of modern design.

functional house style with a considered use of technology would be respected by the consumer.

An important concern of the period was that of ergonomics, originally pioneered by Henry Dreyfuss. As air travel became cheaper and more popular, designers turned their attention to the interiors of aircraft and both Dreyfuss, for Lockheed, and Walter Teague, for Boeing, developed seating that was both economical in its use of space and comfortable. Teague used expensive, but effective, full-scale models of aircraft interiors to perfect the seating, lighting, storage and safety systems. Charles Eames, too, was interested in ergonomics and applied this science to his furniture designs for Herman Miller (discussed in the previous chapter). Experimenting with new lightweight materials, such as plywood, plastics and aluminium, he also took mass production into account and developed forms that could be moulded and stamped.

Britain

Although British industrial design in the 1940s and 1950s was not particularly distinguished, there were nonetheless a number of important developments in the field. The Council of Industrial

Design was established, the design profession consolidated its position, and there was greater respect for design in everyday life.

Wars have often proved to be important catalysts for accelerated scientific and technological change. The Second World War was no exception: it stimulated new mass-production techniques in a number of key industries and led to the rapid development of man-made materials as substitutes for traditional ones such as rubber and metals. Plastics technology was significant in this respect (polythene was an essential element in the development of wartime radar and other high-frequency equipment). Many commercial applications were adopted in the post-war years, helped by the British Plastics Design Advisory Service set up under A. H. Woodfull in 1947. The important pioneering efforts of Frank Whittle in the introduction of jet-propulsion engines during the war led Britain to challenge the United States' supremacy in airliner design in the early 1950s with the commercial debut of the De Havilland Comet in 1952 and the Vickers Viscount turbo-prop medium-haul airliner in 1954. But it was not only new materials and technologies which were generated through wartime activity: ergonomic and anthropometric data, major considerations in many branches of post-war industrial design, were also developed by research groups in the armed forces which had been set up to analyze man/machine/task efficiency.

Before the Second World War few people in Britain were aware of the success of industrial design in the United States. During the 1940s, anticipating the competitive nature of post-war markets, more attention began to be paid to the phenomenon with the publication of articles by leading figures such as Harold van Doren and George Nelson in the British design press. Raymond Loewy, perhaps the most successful and publicity-conscious American industrial designer, had opened a London office and lectured on 'Selling Through Design' at the Royal Society of Arts in 1941. At a critical time for British design, November 1945, he wrote a letter to *The Times* expressing his views of British industry, an assessment of some perspicacity:

'The high quality of British goods is known throughout the world. There are, however, many occasions when it is difficult to detect quality or the lack of it through the very nature of the product, the ersatz looks as good as the original (until you learn later). The high quality of many items is often obscured by such trivia as an irritating colour scheme or a disorganized appearance. Problems such as this are a professional matter with the industrial designer. Quality can and should be made apparent, for British quality will not remain unchallenged.'

At this time Loewy Associates were consultants to more than seventy-five companies and the office staff included architects, stress analysts, plastics specialists, mechanical engineers, business psychologists and marketing specialists. Their success encouraged the development of the design consultancy profession in Britain during the 1940s. Among the most important practices was the Design Research Unit, established by Herbert Read, Misha Black, Milner Gray and others to offer 'a service so complete that it could undertake any design case which might confront the State, Municipal Authorities, Industry or Commerce'. During the 1950s, however, a new generation of British designers emerged who tended to work on the Scandinavian model of the artist collaborating with industry—designers such as Robert Welch, David Mellor and Robert Heritage—rather than the American. It was not until the late 1950s and early 1960s that a further breed of British design consultancies emerged, such as the Conran Design Group, Fletcher, Forbes & Gill and, later, Minale

Above and left. Oriana, owned by P&O, the interior designed by the Design Research Unit, 1960.

Right Victory ware designed by Victor Skellern for Wedgwood, 1940.

Below 'From War to Peace', a section in the 1946 'Britain Can Make It' exhibition. This display demonstrates ways in which wartime scrap metal could be recycled into new industrial products for peacetime.

VICTORY SHAPE. 4573.
UTILITY WARE.

JUG. 2 PINT SIZE
See Tpot 2pins-sgt
re lid.

Tattersfield and Wolff Olins. These were to offer a wide range of services and expertise, although product design, at least in the early stages, was not in high profile.

The more fruitful climate for design resulted in the reorganization of the Society of Industrial Artists (SIA) which until then had been a largely ineffective body. The membership was disbanded in 1945 and a more vigorous system of entry devised. Members had to be involved in design for mass production and two membership groupings emerged: industrial design and marketing/publishing. Important steps were taken to improve the professional status of designers, especially with regard to contracts and fees, and to establish a code of professional conduct. By 1955 there were over one thousand members and in 1965 it was renamed the Society of Industrial Artists and Designers (SIAD).

The war years were not only important in terms of accelerating new technologies, processes and approaches for design matters. Acute shortages of materials induced the Board of Trade to introduce its Utility Furniture Scheme in 1942, stipulating

that all future production should conform to specific forms, materials and modes of construction. Gordon Russell, a member of the Utility Advisory Committee and chairman of the Design Panel, must have relished the opportunity to promote his Arts and Crafts inspired notions of good design to a captive market. Utility was, as one contemporary writer put it, 'applied democracy'.

The wartime restrictions led to similar moves in other industries. The ceramics industry, although not formally part of the Utility programme, conformed to the utilitarian aesthetic as in Victor Skellern's Victory ware for Wedgwood: sound construction, clean shapes devoid of superfluous decoration, practical in use and geared to mass-production technology. Russell, who became director of the Council of Industrial Design (COID) in 1947, was determined to pass on the moral earnestness of the design reform circles of the 1920s and 1930s to the post-war design establishment.

The COID (renamed the Design Council in 1972) was established in 1944 and represented an important commitment by government to promote better standards of design in British industry. Set up by the Board of Trade with an initial grant of £55,000, its immediate concern was to develop strategies for the manufacture and marketing of British industrial goods, both at home and abroad, in the competitive economic climate of the reconstruction period. On a longer-term basis it sought to advise, inform and educate manufacturers, government and the public in design matters.

The public debut of the newly formed Council was the 1946 'Britain Can Make It' exhibition, which was intended to demonstrate that 'the brains, ingenuity and taste which long gave Britain her place as leader of world industry had not deserted her'. Although important as a shop-window for buyers from home and abroad, the exhibition concerned itself with many issues relating to the development of industrial design in post-war Britain. Included were sections such as 'From War to Peace', which showed designs springing from wartime innovations in materials and production, 'Designers Look Ahead' and 'What Industrial Design Means'. The latter exhibit, designed by Misha Black, suggested how the industrial designer could liaise with management, engineers and salesmen and make decisions about design based on an understanding of mass-production technology.

The Festival of Britain of 1951 was a further major opportunity for the COID to promote its propagandist cause. The Council was represented on the planning committees and responsible for selecting all the industrially manufactured goods on site. The Festival's influence on industrial design was, however, strictly limited to the light industrial sector—tableware, lighting equipment, furniture and domestic appliances. This, to a large extent, reflected the major concerns of the COID at the time, since it was not until the 1960s that engineering and heavy industrial design were taken into account.

Of more lasting importance was the establishment of the COID's Design Centre in the Haymarket, London, in 1956. Although there had been a long-standing campaign for such a centre it was not until Britain's share of world trade was in decline in the early 1950s that it bore fruit. The intention was to display exemplars of good contemporary British industrial design which could be viewed by the

Below Catalogue to the Festival of Britain, 1951. The Festival was a rallying point for British designers and provided a morale boost to industry; the note of patriotic optimism was well expressed by the quasi-heraldic Festival symbol.

public, manufacturers, retailers and buyers for both domestic and export markets. The annual Design Centre Award Scheme was initiated in 1957 with the selection of twelve utilitarian domestic torch-bearers of the official good design aesthetic. Two years later the Design Centre Labelling Scheme was introduced, which enabled manufacturers whose products had been on show to apply labels to that effect. Early award-winners included David Mellor, Robin Day, David Ogle, Kenneth Grange, Hulme Chadwick and Robert Welch. The scheme was extended in 1962 to include all products on the Centre's Design Index.

Although the Centre was admired by many at home and abroad and had a strong effect on the shape, direction and organization of similar bodies elsewhere, it also attracted hostile criticism from many quarters with regard to its narrow definitions of what constituted good design. A sense of moral righteousness pervaded some of its public utterances, particularly through its propagandist *Design* magazine, launched in 1949. Good design was seen as conforming to a Modern Movement inspired norm of clean, pure forms; bad design as that which embraced notions of obsolescence and the application of cosmetic styling in all kinds of products from aerodynamic toasters to chrome-encrusted juke-boxes. Incurring particular wrath

was the iconography of American mass-produced goods in which space-age technology was a major inspiration for styling. *Design* magazine expressed concern over the meaningless (in functional rather than symbolic terms) array of dials which spread themselves in ever-increasing numbers across all types of consumer appliances: 'A single hotplate, for instance, instead of being controlled by one turn switch clearly graded for different temperatures, has anything up to seven push buttons. Add to these the oven and boiler controls, and automatic timing devices, and you have a scene which has been likened to the cockpit of an aeroplane.'

Popular imagery in design, stimulated by the introduction of commercial television in 1955, Hollywood films and glossy magazines, became a force far too powerful for the COID to hold in check. John Berger, Reyner Banham and other critics felt that the approved aesthetic represented the perpetuation of a class-based code of values; also one which was inappropriate in a media-orientated world of rapid change.

Scandinavian developments

In essence much Scandinavian design of the 1920s and 1930s had been characterized by the successful collaboration of the artist-craftsman and industry, most notably in the fields of ceramics, glass and

Right Symbol, a stainless steel place setting designed by David Mellor, 1960.

furniture. The late 1940s and 1950s, however, saw a growing consciousness of the importance and nature of industrial design, particularly in Sweden, with the emergence of a number of designers with an engineering background. Among these were Ralph Lysell, who had worked in the United States, Sixten Sason, designer of the famous Saab 92 automobile of 1950, Rune Monö, Hugo Lindstrom, best known for his design programmes at Electrolux (the electrical equipment manufacturer), and Rune Zernell, a tool designer. It is perhaps significant that their names are far less widely known than those of their craftsmen-designer counterparts, achieving recognition through the names of the companies for which they worked as members of a team, rather than as individual celebrities in their own right.

One of the most notable achievements in postwar Scandinavian industrial design was the planning and production of the highly successful Saab 92, which evolved from the necessity to redeploy the aeronautical expertise and manufacturing capacity of the Saab aircraft company. The project brief was to build a light Swedish car, a concept developed by a team headed by an engineer, Gunnar Ljungstrom. Sixten Sason, Saab's technical illustrator who had an engineering and artistic background, transformed the whole appearance of

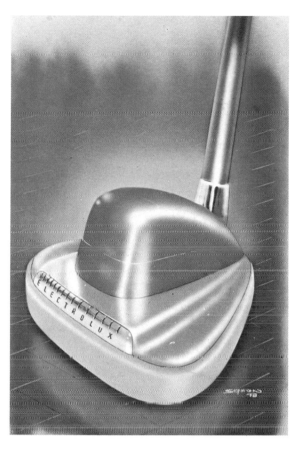

Left Floor polisher for Electrolux designed by Sixten Sason, 1950. In domestic appliances streamlined styling remained popular well into the 1950s.

Below Vacuum cleaner for Electrolux designed by Sixten Sason, 1950. This is influenced by the more functionalist style of Braun domestic products.

Right Glass flasks, around 1955, designed by Timo Sarpaneva for the Iittala glassworks.

Right Airline meals service designed by Sigurd Persson for SAS.

the design into its characteristic aerodynamic shape. The Saab 92, launched in 1950, provided the basis for the subsequent series of Saab models which continued into the late 1970s. Another enduring, though less aesthetically and technically innovative, Swedish automobile design of the 1950s was the Volvo Amazon of 1953 by Jan Wilsgaard, which remained in production until the sixties.

As has already been indicated in the discussion on the decorative arts, the quality of Scandinavian design in the 1950s achieved widespread international recognition through successful exposure at a number of exhibitions: the Milan Triennali of 1951 and 1954; the impressive exhibition of architecture, industrial design, home furnishing and crafts mounted at Hälsingborg in Sweden in 1955 (known as H55), which was viewed by 1,100,000 visitors; also the 'Design in Scandinavia' exhibition, with exhibits drawn from Denmark, Finland, Norway and Sweden, which toured North America between 1954 and 1957.

There were concerted efforts to promote design in mass production. In Norway, for example, the National Design Organization (founded in 1918) sought to effect this through design propaganda

exhibitions and publications, schools education programmes and industrial liaison. A number of design departments, such as those at the Porsgund porcelain factory and the Hadlands glassworks, were reorganized, resulting in products such as Tias Eckhoff's oven-to-tableware range of 1955 and Willy Johansson's everyday Siri pressed glassware of 1953. In Sweden attempts were made to bring design into more fruitful contact with heavy industry, particularly by the Svenska Slöjd-foreningen (the Swedish Society of Industrial Design), which adopted the slogan 'Profit by Design', one similar to that taken up by the Department of Industry and the Design Council in Britain in the 1980s, 'Design for Profit'. Another Swedish pressure group for industrial design was founded in 1957, the Föreningen Svenska Indus-triedesigner (Society of Swedish Industrial Designers). This was a small and select body but had good international contacts.

Despite such initiatives it was, nonetheless, a transitional period in the development of Scandinavian industrial design and was characterized by many designers working across a wide range of media: Stig Lindberg, Kåge's successor as design director at Gustavsberg, worked in fields as diverse as tableware, sanitary ware and plastics; Sigvard Bernadotte designed silverware as well as office equipment for the Facit company; Sigurd Persson's work ranged from a plastic meals service for SAS, stainless steel saucepans for the Swedish Co-operative Union and Wholesale Society, to designs in precious metals. In Finland diversification was also apparent, with leading designers such as Timo Sarpaneva and Tapio Wirkkala working on products ranging from glass to cutlery.

Below The aerodynamic body of the Saab 92 was designed by Sixten Sason. After the war Saab's aerospace engineers turned their attention to the design of this advanced light car, which remained in production for almost thirty years.

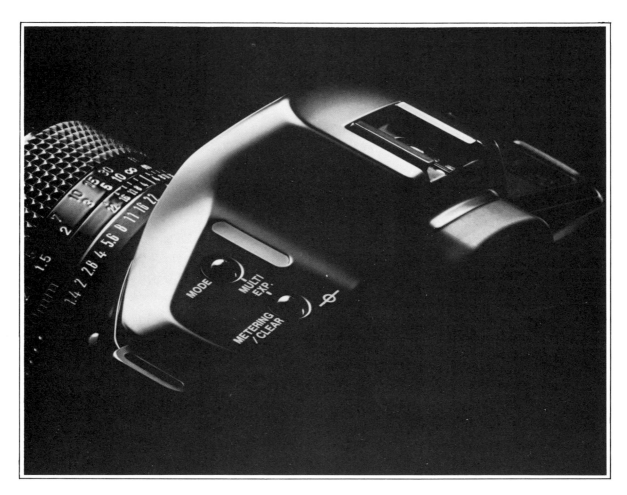

**Detail of a T-90 camera
manufactured by Canon, 1985.
The styling is influenced by
the organic designs of Luigi
Colani.**

4/THE SIXTIES TO THE PRESENT

Experiment versus continuity

Today, the form of a high-technology product is the end result of a variety of processes which include a detailed analysis of consumer requirements and responses, a scientific study of ergonomic factors and the development of state-of-the-art technology. The air of technical superiority in this camera, however, owes as much to fashion as to functionalist ideals. Now, when Modernism has been deemed a failure and the world is threatened by an ecological crisis, Behrens' belief in the power of technology to create a brave new world is no longer invincible. Memphis and other recent debates have overturned many of the conventional tenets of good design, and in all areas, including architecture, the expression of technology has simply become a stylistic mode, competing with historicist, popular and anti-rational trends.

ARCHITECTURE AND URBAN DESIGN

Disenchantment with Modernism as it was being practised in the 1960s took different forms in different countries. In America and Western Europe, the curtain-wall minimalism adopted by large commercial architectural offices had become completely identified with the big corporations. It was, therefore, inevitable that this style would come under question when the values of the society which produced it were themselves challenged in the revolt against materialism that beset prosperous western economies during the 1960s.

The fact that such buildings were as essential as a steelworks and a national airline to the self-image of emerging Third-World countries also helped to bring the style into disrepute: the International Style was being used to reduce every city in the world to a crude copy of the Manhattan and Chicago of Mies van der Rohe. To add to the problems facing architects, the values of all the professions came under increasing attack in the 1960s. Public faith in the competence of every professional was undermined by a series of spectacular failures. Architects had promised new utopias that would sweep away the squalor of the old slums, if only they were allowed to plan the new communities that would take their place. In fact, especially in the provision of public housing, the utopian promises turned out to be hollow.

Far from providing healthy new communities, high-rise flats and Ville Radieuse inspired housing layouts were quickly becoming the slums of the future. When new forms of housing ran counter to cultural norms, they disrupted the fragile social rules which alone make it possible for large numbers of people to live together in close proximity in towns. Kenzo Tange might be able to make Corbusian models work for the highly disciplined Japanese, but in England a similar formula led to disaster. By the late 1960s, the image of technocratic architecture was tarnished, apparently beyond repair. Not only were the residents of high-rise flats discovering the drawbacks of such a life, but the very buildings which had promised so much were turning out to be technically flawed. Condensation and rot caused by insufficient understanding of the porosity of materials were bad enough. But when Ronan Point, a factory-made high-rise block in an eastern suburb of London, collapsed like a pack of cards in 1968 in the aftermath of a minor gas explosion, less than two years after it had been built, public confidence in technocratic architecture in all its aspects was shattered. A popular outcry followed, only partially quietened by a crash programme to strengthen existing high-rise blocks.

If the technical problems were serious, the social ones appeared to be insoluble. High-density flats and redeveloped communities, in which a rigid segregation was enforced between housing, shops and industrial zones, turned out to be unpleasant, even dangerous places in which to live. Jane Jacobs' seminal book *The Death and Life of Great American Cities* amounted to a frontal assault on the planned modern city, with its rejection of the street and traditional patterns of life. Oscar Neuman's *Defensible Space* focused on one aspect of the problem, the difficulty of coming to terms with the Modernists' ideal of communal living. Large, open, parkland settings sounded attractive in theory, but in practice when no individual felt able to identify with them sufficiently to care for them, they quickly deteriorated into arid squalor.

Le Corbusier's ideal of streets in the sky, that is, of high-density apartment buildings serviced by enclosed, or partly enclosed, access corridors turned out in practice, when adopted by others, to be a grim device. In these anonymous spaces, intruders could prey upon residents, unchecked by the social restraints automatically exerted by normal streets, with pavements and under continual scrutiny from passers-by, upper-floor windows and ground-floor shops. Such housing configurations invariably lead to stress in societies which have developed no tradition of living in such a way. In such blocks, litter, petty vandalism and graffiti are the milder manifestations of disorder: robbery and violence are associated with more serious social breakdowns. In extreme cases, and there has been a disturbingly large number of them, complete housing developments may be shunned altogether by the people for whom they were intended.

In both America and Britain, there are all too many large public–housing developments which have been abandoned to dereliction within a decade of completion. By the 1970s, the problem had become so serious that it was no longer a novelty for troublesome teenage buildings to be dynamited. In some countries a complete ban has been placed on the construction of any further high-rise housing using public funds. But the problem is not simply one of height. Indeed, tall slender buildings tend not to suffer so seriously from intruders and the squalor they cause. It is those very buildings which were designed to encourage social interaction, by including communal areas of landscaped grounds, high-level walkways through medium-rise blocks and so on, that have failed most disastrously.

The effect of all this on the morale of an entire generation of architects was devastating. It triggered what can only be described as a collective crisis of conscience among architects. From being treated as heroic form-givers and respected social engineers, they suddenly found themselves cast as the most vilified of professionals.

Even before this, however, the architectural profession itself had begun to question the validity of some of the principles upon which Modernism had been founded. In particular, it seemed to a growing number of architects that the issue of architectural context had been largely ignored—context both in the sense of the culture in which the building was being designed and in the sense of its physical setting.

The idealistic Modernist approach had always preferred the green-field site, in which a building could exist as a three-dimensional object. In those settings in which such a context did not exist, such as a street or an existing pattern of squares, the Modernist solution was to erase what had gone before and to start afresh. In time, it became only too apparent that such an approach was having a tragically coarsening effect on the grain of city life.

The other aspect of Modernism that was coming increasingly under suspicion was the view that the pioneers, like Gropius, had of the style in which they were working. Modernism, as far as he was concerned, was not an architectural style at all. Rather it was the application of scientific analysis to a given formal problem. It was becoming clear that such a view could no longer be maintained. There was no clean break between Modernism and the rest of architectural history; Modernism was a style, no more, and no less, than all the others.

A new generation

Responses to this crisis were varied. Some young architects, for example James Stirling, were quick to perceive the continuity of architectural tradition and to explore ways in which Modernism could be enriched to take this into account. By 1959, Stirling had already embarked on his first major building, the engineering faculty at the University of Leicester, with his partner James Gowan. Leicester exhibits a knowing kind of Modernism, one that is aware of its own past, containing as it does references to Constructivism as well as to the patent glazing and engineering brick of Victorian industrial tradition. Buildings such as Stirling's—he was to restate similar themes in his Cambridge history faculty of 1966 and the Florey building at Queen's College, Oxford, of 1968—represented in a way the coming of age of Modernism, an emergence from naive, uncorrupted innocence into sophisticated awareness.

For other architects in this period the historicist turn of events took other directions. The Italian studio of BBPR produced the remarkable Torre Velasca, designed in 1958, a high-rise tower which clearly expresses its division into two parts, one

Left The engineering faculty building at Leicester University by James Stirling and James Gowan is a wholly original fusion of Constructivism with the nineteenth-century vernacular.

Below After the break-up of his partnership Stirling went on to design the Cambridge history faculty building. Its reading room is a dynamic fan-shaped, glass-roofed space which contrasts with the red-brick seminar block.

containing offices, the other made up of flats, in a manner that clearly recalls Milan's medieval towers. Minoru Yamasaki in America took this decorative historical revivalism to extremes, with his filigree Gothic fretwork at the Federal Science Pavilion for the Seattle World Fair of 1962, and, even more curiously, in certain aspects of his World Trade Center in New York.

A more significant, and far more influential, response to the architectural crisis of the 1960s is represented by Robert Venturi, author of *Complexity and Contradiction in Architecture*, published in 1966 and perhaps the most significant book written by a practising architect since *Vers une architecture*. Venturi was himself a product of the Modern Movement and had worked for both Eero Saarinen and Louis Kahn before setting up in practice with his wife Denise Scott-Brown and John Rauch as Venturi & Rauch. He mounted a cogent, damaging attack on simple-minded functionalism and the reductionist aesthetics of Mies van der Rohe. Instead, he wrote in *Contemporary Architects*, 'We promote an architecture responsive to the complexities and contradictions of modern experience, the particularities of context, the varieties of the users' taste cultures, and the symbolic and decorative dictates of the programme.

Left Robert Venturi's house of 1963 in Philadelphia for his mother reflects his belief in 'complexity and contradictions' rather than the Miesian tenet of 'less is more'.

Below From a distance the twin towers of Yamasaki's World Fair Trade Center in New York of 1974 read as a gigantic, minimalist sculpture. Close up his predilection for Gothic ornament reasserts itself.

Complexity and Contradiction, and even more the book which followed, *Learning from Las Vegas*, preach the need for architecture to grow from popular culture as well as from high art, to incorporate the symbolic values with which users like to invest buildings and to absorb the unconscious vernacular of those buildings that have never seen an architect. Venturi's influence would have been even greater had he had the opportunity to build more himself. The few realized projects, notably Guild House, an old people's home in Philadelphia designed in 1963, a series of private houses, the Dixwell Fire Station in New Haven of 1970 and his bicentennial exhibition structures in Philadelphia of 1976, explore the issues addressed in his theoretical writings, never with complete success.

However, especially in the light of the wholehearted revolt against simple-minded functional Modernism that is taking place in the eighties, Venturi's polemics have taken on a crucial role in the birth of the so-called Post-Modern sensibility. In fact, Venturi has always regarded himself as part of the Modern Movement, albeit from the faction that rejected the purist functionalism of Gropius. For Venturi, the precept held by Gropius that 'Firmness plus Commodity equals Delight' was never enough; delight in architecture needs to be sought after for itself and is by no means the outcome of the other qualities.

This was a stand that attracted considerable hostility from some of the older generation of Modernists and went a long way to shaping the emergent Post-Modernist school. Also important was the way in which Venturi was to borrow from linguistic theory the concept of signs, that is, the meanings implicit and explicit that are embodied in the form of a building and its ornament. Venturi attempted to provide a commentary on Modernism while continuing to work within the conventional architectural framework. There were many others in the 1960s who remained faithful to the social conscience of Modernism but demanded a total rejection of the traditional role of the architect.

In some cases, this involved an attempt to resurrect the forms of vernacular architecture; in others, it meant a wholesale reappraisal of working methods and professional identity. Some architects even attempted to work entirely outside conventional society. Paolo Soleri, for instance, the Italian-born former disciple of Frank Lloyd Wright, established his own semi-mystical community in the Arizona desert, in which the devotees actually pay to work on the master's designs. Despite this hierarchical approach, Soleri was, during the 1960s, the model for a number of 'alternative' builders who rejected conventional society to the extent of attempting to create their own communities. Others switched their allegiance within the urban context, working not for large bureaucratic organizations but offering their skills directly to the users. Tenants' groups were set up and local community activists emerged with the professional back-up to fight unsympathetic redevelopment plans. Attempts were made to upgrade run-down public housing rather than demolishing it, thereby avoiding the clean-slate approach that inevitably destroyed existing communities.

The most thorough-going theoretical exposition of this trend was postulated by the Dutch architect and planner John Habraken. In his book *Supports: an alternative to mass housing* Habraken took a jaundiced look at the failure of design professionals to produce housing that met the constantly changing needs of its users:

'As architects we still operate in a social role bestowed on us in the Renaissance. We dream of monuments and try—by building—to stop time; we try to erect a symbol that transcends everyday life. Simultaneously, we embrace the whole built environment as worthy of our attention or service. But the built environment is a living thing. Change within durable patterns is its primary characteristic. Although one can design for it, it cannot be designed, but wants to be cultivated. Thus we find ourselves in conflict with our chosen subject matter. Neither our theories, nor our methods, nor our education give us the understanding or the tools needed to operate in the broader realm of the everyday world.'

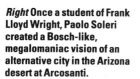

Right Once a student of Frank Lloyd Wright, Paolo Soleri created a Bosch-like, megalomaniac vision of an alternative city in the Arizona desert at Arcosanti.

Left Conceived as a political response to the brutal conformity of the existing buildings, Lucien Kroll's work on the campus of the Catholic University at Louvain mixes materials in a collage of user-participation.

His response in the mass-housing field was to postulate a division between the role of the architect, who would provide the basic structures with all the necessary services, and that of the occupant, who would have free rein in each home. Habraken saw the fitting out of a home as being akin to the process of acquiring consumer durables: a home could be altered, expanded or contracted by the occupant to meet his changing circumstances by the addition or subtraction of accommodation kits.

Though concrete realizations of this theory were few—limited to a few experimental estates in London—it provided an influential new way of looking at the design process. The striving for architectural form was finally abandoned, and instead the buildings were to cater for every changing whim of the user.

The work of the Belgian architect Lucien Kroll provides a powerful demonstration of similar concerns. Kroll saw a symbolic as well as a procedural failure in Modernism. To his eyes, regular curtain-walled office buildings presented a 'fascist facade to the world', and mirror-glass corporate building recalled 'the sunglasses of American policemen'. In other words, not only were such buildings planned in an oppressive way, their very appearance formed part of that oppression. Kroll's alternative was not simply to make every individual responsible for his own part of the environment, reducing the role of the architect to a mere enabler, but also to create buildings which consciously and defiantly *look* anarchic. Yet, as is demonstrated on the Catholic University of Louvain's campus in Brussels,

Kroll's major built work, these two approaches contain inescapable contradictions.

Kroll was commissioned to undertake the design of student residences at the university's medical school in 1969, in the wake of the worldwide student uprisings of 1968. His appointment was a sop to student demands for participation in the running of the university, and was seen as a calculated reaction against the brutal and repetitive concrete massing of the university teaching hospital that had already been completed on the campus.

Below **An anglicization of Corbusier's Unité, Darbourne Darke's flats in Lillington Street, London, of 1961 onwards represents a picturesque and humane form of welfare-state housing.**

Kroll spent six years working with students on the design of the residences, allowing each individual to plan his own room and inventing a system of flexible partitions to allow for changes in the future. The builders, too, were encouraged to play a full part in determining the detail of the facades, which now look like a surrealist collage of different materials and motifs, reminiscent of Gaudí's work. The result is a powerful architectural statement, one that is entirely the product of the architect and has little to do with the occupants, who inevitably had little in common from year to year, let alone with the original participators. In some ways, Kroll succeeded all too well: his aesthetic caused such deep offence to the university's administrators that once student fervour had evaporated in the 1970s, they made persistent attempts to curtail its extremes of expression.

The idea of participation enjoyed a vogue throughout the West in the closing years of the 1960s and the early 1970s, especially in the field of public housing, but also in many urban redevelopment schemes. Often the element of participation was more symbolic than real. It was assumed by the proponents of the movement that by involving would-be tenants at the design stage of a housing scheme, the dismal housing failures of the previous generation could be avoided. In fact, architectural leadership was not so easily abdicated. Nor were the mysteries of architectural design so readily converted into a multiple-choice check list as was once thought. As far as architectural expression was concerned, 'participatory' design usually took the form of somewhat condescending evocations of industrial revolution vernacular. In Britain this involved the extensive use of brick, asbestos-cement slates, pitched roofs and high-density picturesque layouts.

An early proponent of this style was the architectural practice of Darbourne & Darke, whose much-imitated Lillington Street flats in London initiated a whole school of local authority housing design. In fact, Lillington Street was based on a Corbusian block with streets in the sky, but camouflaged behind handmade bricks and a complicated silhouette. Later Darbourne & Darke schemes were more suburban in inspiration, but these proved no more socially successful than the ugly concrete tower blocks which they were intended to replace. Doubts were expressed in some quarters as to the wisdom of any architectural involvement in mass housing, and researchers such as Conrad Jameson and Alice Coleman have argued that market forces are a healthier influence than any amount of utopian planning.

Ralph Erskine, a British-born architect now living in Sweden, is often quoted as a member of the participatory school, notably on account of his large housing scheme at Byker in Newcastle. In fact this view misrepresents Erskine's work. Participation at Byker only extended as far as the opening of a branch office of Erskine's architectural practice in the old Byker area before demolition for the new scheme started. Potential residents of the new buildings were made aware of what was to be built, but the degree to which they were involved in the design was minimal. Nevertheless, Erskine's casual layout and his use of cheerful colour schemes and patterns has come to be identified with 'participation' and the demystification of the planning process.

Mainstream Modernism

When compared to other movements in architectural history, it becomes apparent that Modernism has remained a vigorous force for an unusually protracted period. It was founded by a pioneering group of remarkably creative and forceful individuals, and above all, it has been sustained by its

Left In Sir Denys Lasdun's Royal College of Physicians, London, the mosaic cladding was used to signify the ceremonial aspects of the building, while blue engineering brick indicates the functional areas.

Below Lasdun wishes his National Theatre in London to be read as a series of geological strata. Constructed of board-marked concrete, it addresses the riverside site with confidence.

moral certitude and commitment to the spirit of the age. Thus, despite increasing evidence of the gap between the promises and the reality of modern architecture, the majority of architects in the sixties saw no viable alternative to Modernism. They continued to work in a Modernist mode, and indeed many of the third generation of Modernists built some of their best and most uncompromising work during this decade.

In England Denys Lasdun, who before the war had built one of the most sophisticated examples of a Corbusian house in Britain, and who had been involved with Berthold Lubetkin and the Tecton group, now produced a series of buildings which continued to explore a monumental architectural language consistent with the machine age. Lasdun's buildings, from the Royal College of Physicians in London (1960), to the University of East Anglia at Norwich (1962-8), to the National Theatre in London (1967-76), have a common theme of terraces cast in concrete which suggest the forms of a natural landscape. Strongly sculptural and spatially articulate, they are far removed from the simple-minded functionalism of so much utilitarian Modernism.

Yet for all this, and his other achievements, Lasdun came under fierce attack for his schemes to extend the University of London by demolishing the squares of Georgian Bloomsbury to make way for his large-scale megastructural buildings. Similarly, in his residence for Christ's College, Cambridge, of 1966 he presented a particularly severe, blank concrete facade to the modest domestic streetscape of Cambridge. This solution may have been diagrammatically elegant, but it was inappropriate to this context. At the start of the decade, there would have not been the slightest doubt that his priorities were perfectly correct, but by the end of it he and many other architects found it hard to justify such decisions.

Alison and Peter Smithson's 1964 redevelopment of part of St James's Street in London for *The Economist* has suffered from the same critical reappraisal. When completed, it was hailed around the world for the humanity of its contextual gestures and its sympathetic relations with its dignified eighteenth-century neighbours in London's clubland. By the 1980s, such was the change in public attitudes that it was inconceivable that any form of tower development, not even one as modest in its height as the Economist building, would be permitted by the planning authorities in a historic street.

Initially at least, the climate against Modernism did not harden with such speed in other parts of the

Opposite above Ralph Erskine conceived these blocks in Byker, Newcastle, as a wall to shelter a large-scale housing estate from the noise of a nearby motorway, which in fact never materialized.

Opposite below Lasdun's residence for Christ's College, Cambridge, is oriented towards the college rather than the outside world: a blank facade faces the street and the ziggurat-like cascade of study bedrooms is at the rear of the building.

Left Despite its faults Utzon's Opera House, designed from 1959, is a masterpiece that immediately became a symbol for the city of Sydney.

Left Bruce Graham of SOM turned the Miesian vocabulary in a new direction with the 1970 Hancock tower in Chicago. The structural steel bracing and tapering profile gave it a distinctive form.

world. In Australia, for example, the Danish architect Jørn Utzon was able to win an international competition with his flawed, but breathtaking, structure for the Sydney Opera House. The resulting fiasco over its building led to huge cost over-runs, Utzon's resignation from the project and a compromised interior which has never been ideally suitable for the performance of opera. It is still a rare example of a genuinely popular landmark conceived in an abstract Modernist aesthetic.

Also in Australia, Harry Seidler, trained by Gropius and Breuer at Harvard, continued to build in a highly polished, unabashedly purist manner, apparently oblivious to any doubts concerning the International Style. He was even able to take the style back to Europe for the building of the Australian embassy in Paris, but instead of the stucco favoured by his teachers he used stark white concrete.

But in America, Skidmore, Owings & Merrill, by the 1960s the world's largest independent architectural organization, employing hundreds of architects in dozens of offices, was still under the unbending creative direction of Gordon Bunshaft. If there were any changes at all, it was in the direction of a still greater expertise and suave fluency with technology and engineering. This stemmed from SOM's Chicago office, which under the direction of Bruce Graham produced two

Right Moshe Safdie's Habitat project for the Expo '67 world fair in Montreal was a heroic but flawed attempt to realize the dream of the Modern Movement: production–line housing.

remarkable skyscrapers. The Hancock tower with its tapering shape and conspicuous diagonal structural bracing marked an early attempt to provide the high-rise form with a greater range of expression than that of the Lever building and the Seagram tower. In fact, with its mixture of apartments, offices and retail outlets spread over one hundred floors, the Hancock represented in many ways a realization of the writings of Le Corbusier. An even greater structural achievement was the Sears tower which, with 110 floors and a height of 1400 feet (426 metres), remained the world's tallest building for fifteen years after its completion in 1974. Together, these two buildings could be said to constitute the principle ornaments of a new Chicago school.

One of Gropius's former Harvard students, the Chinese-born American I.M. Pei, has been dedicated to architectural abstraction throughout his career. During the 1960s his works at Philadelphia and for New York University in Manhattan looked like polished and elegant restatements of Corbusian precedents. Later, however, Pei moved more and more to an entirely formalist approach, in which all other aspects of building were subordinated to the dictates of pure form, but accompanied by the stripped idioms and blandness of the Modern Movement pioneers. It was an ironic completion of the circle, a return in a new guise to the formalism of the academic tradition which the Modernists had once decried.

Paul Rudolph, also a pupil of Gropius, veered towards a similar approach, but his prolific output of buildings lacks the polish of Pei, or the inventiveness of Kevin Roche, who with John Dinkeloo took over the remains of Eero Saarinen's practice after the untimely death of the latter. Rudolph talked of the need to design buildings that took expressiveness and symbolic values into account, but such works as the Boston Government Services Centre and the architecture faculty at Yale merely demonstrate an overbearing structural elaboration.

In some cases, the gathering doubts aroused by Modernism produced a response that pushed design to a theoretical extreme not envisaged even by the Futurists. Fuelled by a booming economy in Europe, Japan and America, together with ever-increasing technical and technological possibilities, some of these theories even began to be realized. Mass-produced housing could be envisaged on an ever greater scale, not as a utopian dream but as a bureaucratic reality. One manifestation of this tendency was Moshe Safdie's Habitat project for Montreal's 1967 world fair, Expo '67. Safdie created a crumbling ant-hill, made up of factory-produced, concrete, trough-shaped units stacked together in different configurations to create a strictly limited range of apartment types. The idea was to provide a dramatic demonstration of the possibilities afforded by industrial techniques when applied to building; Safdie believed that standardization and production line methods could produce the kind of cost savings that Henry Ford had exploited to bring motoring within reach of the mass market.

In reality, Habitat proved that the opposite was true of industrial building. Conventional houses could have been built far more cheaply than Habitat's costly apartments, which had to bear the burden of establishing the plant and equipment needed for a production line that would have to be written off after producing a very short run. The genuine flexibility of a rationalized traditional technique, such as the timber-frame system, would have far outshone the much vaunted advantages of these heavy concrete components. Standardized, ready-made units could not be adapted to the structural demands of the building, in which the materials at the bottom had, of course, to carry far greater loads than those at the top.

However, as far as Safdie and many of his fellow architects and planners were concerned, none of this really mattered. Habitat embodied the image and the rhetoric of industrialized building, and these were so powerful that in the short term at least they swamped the mundane technical shortcomings.

The pessimists

The 1970s were a difficult period for most architects—or at least for those who regarded architecture as something other than a business. The depressing evidence of cities all around the world brutalized by post-war redevelopment was inescapable: despite the unprecedented opportunities offered by the 1960s building boom, Modernism had failed to deliver its promises. Technical defects were rife, city centres were being drained of life by the flight to the suburbs and, at the most fundamental level of all, there was evidence of a popular yearning for a richer means of aesthetic expression. A tidal wave of nostalgia in all forms burst over the 1970s, and in interior decoration, advertising and many other indexes of popular taste there was ample evidence of the demand for natural materials and tradition.

Yet, because they were educated in the Bauhaus ethic, which had by this time percolated throughout the world's schools of architecture, most architects found it impossible to respond. They had been trained to believe that any approach other than functional Modernism was not only wrong, but downright immoral as well. Decoration, historical references and any kind of elaboration were a complete anathema.

The reappraisal of planning policies was equally traumatic, after so many years of struggle to realize the ideals of Le Corbusier's Ville Radieuse. Along with the changes in planning policies came a fundamental shift in architectural values, and the disenchantment with comprehensive redevelopment was no longer a minority view. So successful were the campaigns in countless cities to safeguard both individual buildings and complete neighbourhoods from the bulldozer, that the clean-slate redevelopment of existing cities came to be recognized as both wasteful and counterproductive. Instead of attempting to impose order on the organic layout of ancient cities and adapt them to the demands of the motor car and the tower block, political protests now forced architects and planners to tackle urban decay in a more sensitive way.

The success of campaigns mounted from within communities, aided by advocacy work by professionals, influenced official bodies to adopt such policies themselves. Old buildings were to be retained and restored wherever possible; new developments were to be carried out with a minimum of disruption to existing communities and on a scale that could be accommodated within the existing urban fabric. These concerns fitted in well with the changing perceptions of society that resulted from the ecological campaigns of the early 1970s. The oil crisis which followed the Arab-Israeli war of 1973 brought home with brutal clarity just how finite mankind's resources really were.

This ecological revolution caused a profound change in the way that some architects perceived buildings. In the first place, it became glaringly apparent that many of the devices of Modernism were profligate in their use of energy. Single-skin glass-curtain walling, for example, made buildings costly to heat in winter and even more costly to cool in summer. Equally, it brought a new awareness of the value of buildings as resources. Rather than demolishing buildings which had outlived their original purpose, there was a growing interest in recycling them for new uses. It was a move which was to have much wider repercussions than was initially realized: it helped to keep the existing pattern of towns and streets intact, and it forced architects to reconsider the value of historical detail and traditional planning, which had been ignored in the utilitarian functionalist period. Indeed, in the course of remodelling a building behind an existing facade, architects were forced to abandon the Modernist tenet that the elevations of a building should be the direct expression of its plan.

Charles Jencks, popularizer of the term Post-Modernism in its architectural application, has gone so far as to claim that modern architecture

225

Above The AT&T tower in New York by Philip Johnson, once the most devoted of Mies's disciples, was seen as an act of apostasy, but it marked the acceptance of Post-Modernism in America's corporate style.

Right Arup Associates' 1973 conversion of the Maltings at Snape, Suffolk, into a concert hall was an early example of the now common practice of adapting redundant buildings rather than simply clearing them away.

shopping centre rather than pulling them down. When Arup Associates were invited to convert an old maltings in Aldeburgh, Suffolk, into a concert hall, they found no theoretical objections to this.

A more decisive step was taken by Charles Moore in 1978, when he embellished a new urban square for a run-down inner-city area of New Orleans with a fountain symbolizing in three dimensions a map of Italy and adorned with cut-out Tuscan orders picked out with neon. Historicism, acceptable again, became a stronger and stronger force in the work of many architects. In some cases, such as Andrew Derbyshire of the London-based practice of Robert Matthew, Johnson-Marshall & Partners, it was historicism as camouflage. In 1971, Derbyshire and his team were commissioned by the London Borough of Hillingdon to build a new civic centre in a style that would be accessible and unintimidating. To this end, they devised an elaborate brick and tile facade, based on the suburban London vernacular of semi-detached Victorian houses, to disguise a deep, open-plan interior—a dichotomy that gave particular offence to the more puritanical Modernist critics.

In America, Philip Johnson's design for the AT&T headquarters in New York of 1978 proved a symbolic landmark. It was the most conspicuous and celebrated example of the new mood that had overtaken architecture. Unlike the halting, cartoon-like examples of early Post-Modernism, this design reflects Johnson's intention to build a

died during the 1970s. Indeed, he gave its death a precise moment: the day that Minoru Yamasaki's Pruitt-Igoe housing project in Saint Louis was dynamited in 1972. In reality, the changes that have taken place in architects' perceptions of architecture have been at a much more gradual pace. Nor, barring a few individuals who have deliberately overstated their positions in the cause of polemics, has the architecture of the 1980s been such a clean break with the Modernist tradition as is sometimes claimed. Architects responded quite readily to a situation in which they would adapt buildings, such as Boston's old market, into a

Left Once an orthodox Modernist office, Robert Matthew, Johnson-Marshall produced a design for Hillingdon Town Hall which caused considerable surprise. They camouflaged a large bureaucratic building with a facade of brick-and-tile domesticity.

historical high-rise building in all seriousness. For one of the designers of the Seagram tower and a founder of the Museum of Modern Art, it was an act of apostasy, as well as a challenge to one of the biggest taboos of the Modern Movement. Johnson planned the AT&T in stone—granite quarries had to be reopened specially for the project—and in keeping with the classic skyscrapers of the Art Deco period he split his design into three elements: a base, loosely modelled on Brunelleschi's Pazzi chapel, a shaft that rises up the main facade of the building and a broken-pedimented top. It was a device that not surprisingly invited comparison with a Chippendale tallboy.

When unveiled, the design attracted enormous interest, featuring on the front pages of both the London and the New York *Times*. While it was not the first example of historicism—James Stirling, for example, had already produced a series of projects inspired by contextualism—Johnson's design marked its commercial acceptance. By the time it was completed, the AT&T's shock value had worn off, and indeed far more flamboyant examples of the new historicism were being built, many of them by Johnson himself.

Michael Graves, who in the 1960s had worked within a design vocabulary derived from Le Corbusier and Terragni's Purism, moved in a decisively new direction towards a highly decorative, allusive architectural language, full of spatial complexity and poetic and historical references. In *Contemporary Architects* Graves has written of his disenchantment with architectural abstraction, calling it a 'self-conscious rejection of historical precedent in favour of an interest in machine technology and its symbolism. The building is seen as a technical artifact whose abstract geometric devices are generally unadorned and read as minimal. The loss of those figurative elements thought to be derived from classical analogies of man and nature leads to a sense of alienation or a lack of association with the architecture.' By contrast, Graves suggests, 'If we are to increase the participation in and identification with architecture by the culture at large, we must begin to re-establish the former, somewhat classical mode of thinking which is capable of representing in physical form the symbolic and mythic aspirations of that culture.'

Graves's first major realized work in this new mode was the City office building in Portland, Oregon, begun in 1980. With its garlands, giant keystones and representational sculpture, the Portland building sparked off fierce hostility from conventional Modernists in Oregon. Graves went on to develop similar themes in his Humana tower in Louisville, Kentucky. His militant rejection of the purist Modernists made him a fashionable public figure, celebrated well outside the confines of the architectural world.

The Catalan architect Ricardo Bofill has developed an even more flamboyant form of monumental historicism. Working with precast concrete, Bofill has set out to recreate in the most literal way classical landmarks. His largest project to date, just outside Paris, endeavoured to provide the sterile satellite town of Marne-la-Vallée with a sense of identity: it resembles the Colosseum. Huge columns are applied to the outside of the structure, which is pierced by a series of monumental triumphal arches. Inside this grandiloquent exterior are utilitarian flats, whose layout has been subordinated to a plan that includes giant half-detached columns that double as bay windows. Another of Bofill's schemes near Paris takes the form of a viaduct set within a lake, while in the centre of Montpellier he has completed the design of a housing scheme with a layout modelled on the floor plan of St Peter's in Rome.

The justification for all this flamboyance is a somewhat naive faith in the civilizing powers of

Right Michael Graves beat Norman Foster in a competition to build Humana's skyscraper headquarters in Louisville. Graves's building, completed in 1985, is a confident attempt to endow high-rise buildings with formal values.

Left above and below The Spanish-born architect Ricardo Bofill now works mainly in France, and his recent buildings use a classical mode in precast concrete. The viaduct at St Quentin-en-Yvellines evokes Piranesian grandeur and the flats at Marne-la-Vallée Versailles-like spendour.

Below Bofill's early buildings in Barcelona were exercises in structural gymnastics and geometry, as in the Walden 7 block of 1970-75.

classicism. Bofill began his career in Barcelona towards the close of the Franco era, and his early architecture played its part in the cultural upsurge that accompanied the Catalan nationalist revival at that time. Bofill established a studio in a half ruined cement factory on the outskirts of Barcelona, converted in a florid neo-Romanesque style and decorated with furniture designed by Antonio Gaudí, a figure with whom Bofill clearly feels much sympathy. The studio was originally run as a type of commune, housing not simply architects but also—in Bofill's words—philosophers, composers and poets. On a site adjacent to the old factory, Bofill built an apartment block, known somewhat self-consciously as Walden 7. A wilful, individualistic design, its constituent apartments are subordinated to the overall image of the block, a Piranesian, cavernous atrium carved out of the middle of a large vivid orange cube, with its

entrance in the form of a vertiginous crack that opens up the two narrower end walls.

Bofill's monument to the Catalan people, at the motorway crossing-point on the frontier between France and Spain at Le Perthus, is a mixture of landscaping brick and stone. The monument takes the form of a pyramid topped by four broken and twisted columns, a moving and powerful vision. Bofill has established an office in Paris, where he has pursued the theme of mass-produced housing first proposed by the early Modernists. In his case, this involves working in close collaboration with a mass-market private house builder, using prefabricated concrete-panel constructional systems. How-

ever, Bofill's use of prefabrication is motivated by its ability to create low-budget classicism, since it is his belief that the language of classicism has now been shorn of the authoritarian associations that it acquired during the Fascist era. In fact, many of Bofill's clients have been socialist French mayors eager to create architectural landmarks that will reflect well on their periods in office.

The extent to which the aesthetic uniformity of the 1950s and 1960s had broken down by the 1980s can be judged by the fact that by 1980 it was possible to find a serious revival of interest in academic classicism. In England, for example, such figures as Quinlan Terry, building Palladian villas for rich patrons with a taste for nostalgia, were no longer seen as historical anomalies, but were emerging to take on large-scale developments that included offices in a style that would have been quite familiar to Sir William Chambers. Yet it would be misleading to see this as the triumph of one school against another. The extent to which those architects who had once been regarded as aggressively modern had themselves shifted their architectural emphasis without abandoning their allegiance to the Modern Movement can be seen in the later work of James Stirling.

Stirling had come to international prominence in the 1960s and his buildings of that period, with their harsh, crystalline surfaces and striking, faceted geometries, combining brick and tile with aluminium factory glazing, invented an aesthetic vocabulary that enjoyed a considerable vogue for two decades. But Stirling himself has proved to be too restless and questioning an architect to remain locked within a single vocabulary for long. The late 1960s and early 1970s saw him experimenting with a variety of styles and approaches, which usually grew out of different constructional techniques.

For the Olivetti training centre at Haslemere of 1969, Stirling made extensive use of fibre-glass cladding panels that provided a sleek, sensuous look attuned to the mood of Pop Art. The Olivetti building has most often been described as a large-scale piece of industrial design. But had it been built in the colours that Stirling originally intended, blue and green, which were vetoed by the local planners, the image would have been much closer to that of a marquee pitched in an Edwardian garden. The glazed link connecting Stirling's work with the Edwardian country house on the site underscores the same theme, with its suggestions of a conservatory. An altogether sterner, grimmer idiom appeared at Runcorn, in Stirling's large-scale housing project. Around a pattern of squares and mews, he laid out a

Below **Stirling's Olivetti training centre of 1969, in Haslemere, uses glass-reinforced plastic panels to create a sleek and sensuous image. It demonstrates Stirling's continuing interest in exploring technological as well as stylistic avenues.**

Left Bofill's flats outside Paris are popular and technologically impressive, but they are also disturbingly theatrical.

repetitive group of medium-rise flats and maisonettes in a heavy concrete prefabricated system.

After this project was completed, Stirling's career went through something of a hiatus: for nearly ten years he built nothing. This fact does much to explain the apparent discrepancy between the work of the earlier part of his career and his next major building, the Stuttgart Staatsgalerie, opened in 1984. At first sight the gallery, designed after a limited competition in 1977, appears to be as heretical as Philip Johnson's AT&T building. The design, with its huge open central drum, its references to Egyptian, Romanesque and classical precedents, appeared to critical observers to have

Right The manner in which the heavy precast concrete panels are deployed by Stirling at Runcorn (1967-76) evokes the regular formality of Georgian squares and terraces.

Opposite At the centre of the Stuttgart design is a roofless, open-air drum, part of a new pedestrian route that carves its way through the middle of the museum. Faced in banded stone, it has proved a great success with the public.

Right Having not built anything for ten years, Stirling won a competition for the extension to Stuttgart's Staatsgalerie. This gave him an opportunity to build in a style that took more account of context than his earlier buildings.

entirely abandoned the challenging, innovatory concerns with which Stirling had begun his career. There was bitter opposition from certain German architects, notably Frei Otto, the engineer-architect who had designed the striking lightweight tent structure at the Munich Olympic stadium of 1977. Opponents claimed that Stirling's gallery was authoritarian, even fascist in its imagery.

Stirling himself refused to be drawn into these polemics, preferring to keep verbal explanations of his buildings to a minimum. In his book *Buildings and Projects* he simply said of Stuttgart, 'I hope that this building will evoke an association of Museum, I'd like the visitor to feel it looks like a museum. In its built details, it may combine traditional and new elements, though old elements are used in a modern way. For instance, the historic coving is not a cornice used throughout, but is confined to the sculpture terraces. Similarly, there are assemblages of constructivist canopies which define a hierarchy of entrances.' Stirling acknowledges Schinkel's Altes Museum, the quintessential nineteenth-century museum, as a strong influence. 'It has attributes which I find more appealing than those from the twentieth century, for instance a parade of rooms, as against freely flowing space; also, even when

small, nineteenth-century museums have a certain monumentalism. In the city, it's essential to have a hierarchy of landmarks, a city without monuments would be no place at all. For me, monumentalism has nothing to do with size or style, but entirely to do with presence.'

In his increasing feeling for the importance of architectural context, Stirling came under the influence of a former associate, Leon Krier, the Luxembourg-born architect and teacher who has also had a strong impact on on the work of Michael Graves. With a savagery that recalls Pugin's *Contrasts*, Krier rejects the modern city as a denatured purgatory, in which identity and sense of place have been banished by a fascination with machinery. He abhors the anti-urban tendencies of the Modernists for their insistence on separating functions into distinct zones, and for their neglect of the spaces between buildings in favour of the creation of the isolated object. Despite his implacable pessimism—Krier has renounced building altogether in favour of developing a strategy to resist the destruction of the European city, which he sees as one of the great achievements of civilization—his polemics and powerful drawings have had a profound effect. In *The Presence of the Past* he wrote: 'Considering the magnitude of destruction and the

Right The tent-structure roof of the Munich Olympic stadium of 1972 was inspired by the work of Frei Otto's lightweight-structures team. It used acrylic panels fastened by a net to shelter the stadium seats.

Above Leon Krier has conducted a polemical campaign, as bitter as that of Pugin, against what he sees as the barbarism of the modern city. In place of motorways and skyscrapers he proposes a picturesque pedestrian city.

theoretical confusion which agitates the most enlightened professionals, building today can only mean a greater or smaller degree of collaboration in the process of the self-destruction of civilized society. . . . Each project that I have done is a manifesto about a particular tactic of reconstruction, either on the scale of architecture and building, or on the scale of the entire city. All these projects lead me to formulate very simple theses which are the basis of all reconstruction work. A city can only be reconstructed in the form of streets, squares and urban quarters. The quarters must integrate all functions of urban life in areas which cannot exceed thirty-five hectares and 15,000 inhabitants. The streets and squares must present a familiar character. Their measures and proportions must be those of the best and most beautiful pre-industrial cities. The city must be articulated into public and domestic spaces. Monuments and urban fabric, classical architecture and vernacular building, squares and streets, and in that, hierarchy.'

Krier is not entirely pessimistic about the pro-

spects for his campaign. He sees it possible to co-opt the communities who have already adopted political action to prevent the destruction of existing communities, to take up similar tactics to revive those that have already disappeared. 'It is possible to ally the great majority of the citizens around a "common sense", which is not dictated by industrial mass media, but which is still profoundly rooted in the surviving traces and the overwhelming memory of the pre-industrial European cities.' Krier could well be correct, although it is uncertain how the majority would react were they fully to understand the content of his programme, which appears to include the abolition of the motor car and the aeroplane in favour of the tram and the dirigible.

There is now a substantial body of architects whose buildings betray a similar disquiet. To the work of such diverse characters as Bofill, Stirling and Graves must be added that of Aldo Rossi. The fact that Rossi's book *L'Architettura della Città* was not translated into English until long after it was written in 1966 may have limited his influence in

Right Mario Botta's houses, mainly in Switzerland, adopt a geometric form and make much of the precision with which the materials are assembled. The Viganello house dates from 1981-2.

Below In the 1970s the architect and engineer John Portman made the atrium an almost obligatory part of American urban life. Used internally, as with this San Francisco hotel, it offered little to the outside world.

Britain, where there is in any case an inbuilt Anglo-Saxon suspicion of the lyrical, metaphysical tone of principal Italian discourse on architecture. However, the essence of Rossi's message is not far removed from Krier's, namely that there are principal elements within the city—street, arcade, piazza and monument—which must form the basis of architectural composition. As realized, Rossi's building, such as the Gallaretes housing development on the outskirts of Milan, built in stages after 1970, have the starkness of a De Chirico painting.

Rossi's architecture not unnaturally attracted the label of rationalism, and claimed a continuity with the work of eighteenth-century architects such as Boullée. A similar theme can be seen in Mario Botta's buildings, mainly executed in the Ticino area of Switzerland. Botta creates a monumentality that depends on simple stark geometries.

The optimists

Despite the vehemence of the reaction against Modernism, there remains a vigorous school of practising architects who have directed their criticism towards its more commercial manifestations, rather than the principles of its founders. In America this response has taken many forms. In the case of such large architectural practices as John Portman and Welton Becket, the answer to public dissatisfaction with the restraint and lack of ornament of Modernism was to accentuate and exaggerate its forms. Thus Portman built a series of hotel developments centred around spectacular indoor spaces which, in American cities with rotting downtown areas, took the place of public squares. Welton Becket's mirror-glass Reunion Hotel in Dallas adopted a similarly flamboyant approach. For other Americans, Richard Meier in particular, the early days of Modernism provided a continuing inspiration. His High Museum in Atlanta of 1983 and his Frankfurt Museum of Decorative Art of 1985 have the geometric purity of Le Corbusier's buildings of the 1920s.

In Britain too, there are those who have attempted to update the tradition of Modernism. And, partly because the pace of technological change during the 1970s and 1980s has been far greater than anything experienced by the early Modernists, this proposition has a certain validity. Throughout the 1960s London was a centre for those who wanted to explore an architecture that was responsive to change, emphasizing the use of technology to transform buildings into mechanisms capable of interacting with their users.

Among the leading proponents of this approach was the Archigram group, centred on the Archi-

Left Le Corbusier's Purist vocabulary of the 1920s is the inspiration for Richard Meier's series of museums in which, as in the High Museum in Atlanta, he abstracts forms and spaces.

Below The aviary at the London Zoo of 1961 is Cedric Price's first major work and an early example of his optimistic espousal of technology rather than form in buildings.

tectural Association and in particular on Peter Cook, along with Warren Chalk, Ron Herron and Dennis Crompton. In the pragmatic English scene architectural manifestos are few and far between, but Archigram managed to produce one, based on a hedonistic commitment to changing technology and—inevitably in the 1960s—fun. Archigram never quite managed to build anything, but even on paper its theories were a heady mixture. Cedric Price, whose ideas about Fun Palaces and the gulf between intentions and bricks and mortar were closely related to Archigram, did build a few projects, notably the aviary at the London Zoo and the Interaction Centre in north London, an ad hoc assembly of materials in a design that was deliberately as open-ended and unfinished as possible.

The most striking realization of this variety of architecture is the Beaubourg in Paris, officially known as the Centre Georges Pompidou and completed in 1977 by the Anglo-Italian partnership of Piano & Rogers. Built after an unexpected competition victory, it takes the form of a giant steel exoskeleton structure, which acts as a con-

Above The anglicized Futurism of the Archigram group influenced Cedric Price's Interaction Centre of 1972 in London. Its low-budget structural frame and units of portable accommodation could be deployed as required.

Right and above right A similar approach can be seen in Piano & Rogers' much more monumental Beaubourg Centre in Paris. The colour-coded pipework and exquisitely designed structure transformed the architecture into a machine whose purpose was to create street life.

tainer or climbing frame. Within it are slung a collection of separately expressed units of accommodation, air-conditioning, lifts and escalators. The original intention was that the structural framework should provide for a completely flexible interior: not only would the deep steel trusses span clear across the exhibition floors, leaving column–free space, but the floors themselves would be relocatable, allowing for shifts in ceiling heights as required. In the event, this latter feature was not incorporated. Nor was the planned system of electronic screens and noticeboards that was to have adorned the exterior.

But for all this somewhat unnecessary trimming, the impact of the technocratic, but romantic, styling of the Beaubourg has been powerful. Piano & Rogers brought into being the 'High Tech' school, a movement characterized by the frankly decorative and picturesque treatment of functional elements. The Beaubourg has, in keeping with the tenets of Modernism, no applied ornament, nor even a facade in the conventional sense; yet the elements of structure and servicing have been detailed and positioned with all the care that once might have been lavished on the facade of a Palladian palace. One criticism raised against the Beaubourg is the over-simplification of its interiors. The huge open floors are subdivided only by demountable partitions, so losing, in the opinion of some critics, the richness and complexity that come from the careful composition of rooms and corridors within a plan.

Above Norman Foster, formerly Rogers' partner in Team 4, used an exposed structural system for Renault's Swindon warehouse of 1981. This enriched the basic industrial shed and provided a distinctive landmark.

Right The £500-million Hong Kong and Shanghai Bank, with its suspended steel structure and extensive prefabrication, is nothing less than Foster's attempt to reinvent the skyscraper.

Rogers' next major building, the Lloyds head-quarters in London, completed in 1986, attempted to come to terms with this problem. In contrast to the colour-coded ductwork of the Beaubourg, Lloyds is a restrained silver and grey. It combines a nine-storey glass-vaulted atrium, that recalls the Crystal Palace or the Galleria of Milan, around which are arranged tiers of office floors.

Norman Foster, Rogers' former partner in Team 4 in the late 1960s, took the modern tradition in a different direction. Like Rogers he produced large, open, flexible spaces, but where Rogers is interested in the decorative possibilities of exposed structure and servicing, Foster often uses tense, taut skins, sleek and carefully detailed. Perhaps the most original of Foster's early works was the Willis Faber Dumas office building in Ipswich of 1974. Here Foster attempted to create a contextually responsive building from high-technology components. In a medieval town brutalized by crude concrete buildings in the 1960s, Foster's building ingratiates itself into its setting with a sleek, undulating, glossy black glass facade that wraps itself around the existing street frontage. In a quiet way, the building recalls Mies's experiments with glass skyscrapers in the Berlin of the 1920s.

Foster's next major work, the Sainsbury Centre on the Lasdun-designed University of East Anglia campus in Norwich, was an attempt to create a classical modern building. Set in the midst of a park and overlooking a lake, the Sainsbury Centre, part art gallery and part university department, is contained within a gleaming aluminium-skinned tube, a single gesture as forceful as a Doric temple. The structure is enclosed within a thick wall section which also houses the service spaces and air-handling plant. With an admirable economy of means, the same section is curved up to form the roof, which is itself skinned with cladding panels identical with those used on the walls. At each end, sheer sheets of glass from floor to ceiling appear to unite interior with exterior.

Foster followed these two buildings with the Hong Kong and Shanghai Bank tower, completed in 1985. Built at enormous cost, the bank is one of the very few completely convincing skyscrapers

Left In the Lloyds building, London, Rogers developed Kahn's ideas on 'served' and 'servant' spaces. The circulation and service towers, differentiated from the main fabric, create an array of technological ornament.

Right, above and below Attached to Lasdun's concrete buildings at the University of East Anglia by the narrowest of umbilical cords, Foster's Sainsbury Centre, Norwich, of 1978, adopts high-technology, superplastic aluminium panels. The hangar-like interior is domesticated by trees and restaurants, but almost dominates the art collection.

Left Foster's earliest attempt at a large-scale urban office was the Willis Faber Dumas building in Ipswich. The undulating glass skin recalls Mies van der Rohe's glass skyscraper project of 1914.

Left Many new museums were built in Japan in the 1970s. Arata Isozaki's Prefectural Museum at Gunma, completed in 1974, is the most polished.

Right **Kisho Kurokawa's Sony tower of 1976 in Osaka, with its prefabricated service capsules, clearly anticipates elements of Rogers' and Foster's work. Indeed some of the same subcontractors were involved in the Hong Kong and Shanghai Bank.**

Below **Kenzo Tange's Kagawa Prefectural Centre, completed in 1964, combines Corbusian references with traditional Japanese forms.**

designed by an architect from outside North America. Its floors are suspended from tubular steel masts that rise the whole height of the building. For once, because of Hong Kong's isolated geographical position and lack of heavy industrial manufacturing capacity, a large number of components were prefabricated and assembled on site—from necessity rather than rhetoric. This was, in any case, a technique which Foster prefers: his chosen method of working involves extensive prototyping and the use of full-scale mock-ups, in a manner that echoes the car industry.

From the 1950s Japan has begun to take a significant place in contemporary architecture. The works of Le Corbusier proved a powerful inspiration for Kenzo Tange and his students, expressed in such buildings as the Kagawa Prefectural Centre. But in the 1960s Japanese architects began self-consciously to create a specifically Japanese school. Kisho Kurokawa formed a group named the Metabolists, which owed much to the 'served and servant spaces' concept of Louis Kahn. Arata Isozaki was never a committed Metabolist,

Left Arata Isozaki's Museum of Contemporary Art in Los Angeles, under construction in 1986, marks the emergence of the Japanese school as a prime mover rather than an isolated school.

but he was very much in sympathy with its ends and in later years he and Kurokawa have emerged as Japan's principal architectural innovators. Isozaki is perhaps the more exportable of the two: he has moved from the metallic perfectionism of the Gunma Prefectural Museum at Takasaki to the Los Angeles Museum of Modern Art, which attempts to fuse oriental motifs with more figurative architectural elements. Kurokawa's Sony tower in Osaka of 1976 with its machine-like imagery and its plug-in capsule towers echoes the preoccupations of the Archigram group. Since then his work has begun to show more traditional Japanese motifs. In Japan both Kurokawa and Isozaki have been able to work in a great range of styles without being charged with inconsistency in the way that their European contemporaries would have been.

Few decades can have seen such a variety of architectural expression or such a rapid change in sensibilities as the 1980s. It is a decade which has accommodated almost any architectural style, from the surrealism of James Wines and the SITE group, to the Art Deco revivalism of Helmut Jahn, to the sober historicism of César Pelli. After nearly sixty years of moral certainty, a new orthodoxy is not easily established.

Left César Pelli's immaculate facade for the United States embassy in Tokyo, designed in 1972 when he was at Gruen Associates, was to prove a highly influential model.

245

DECORATIVE ARTS

The story of style in the applied arts since the mid–to late fifties has been dominated by various new forces, including social and economic factors and certain aspects of technical and scientific progress. A major shaping force has been the complex pattern of consumerism in our society, creating new markets for design. A significant new voice has made itself heard—that of the young, who for the first time, in the mid-fifties, staked their own claim as creators of style, found their own heroes and music, and therefore were recognized as a rich market by designers and manufacturers. As jet travel and television became an integral part of life in the affluent countries of the world, the greater cosmopolitan awareness and rapid dissemination of information and ideas which they have encouraged have had a marked impact on the pace at which style is absorbed at a popular level.

Below: Playboy, **French edition, July 1981, cover photograph by James Baes.**

In the fifties a new affluence was generated by the growth economy and revitalized post-war industry. As the pattern of consumerism became essential to the economic structure of highly industrialized manufacturing nations, it engendered a cycle of obsolescence and renewal. The wheels of industry and commerce, oiled by the increasingly sophisticated techniques of advertising, both in print and on television, were kept in motion by a wide middle-class market whose appetite for the new was constantly stimulated.

This market was enjoying the luxury of disposable income and its style consciousness, nurtured and exploited by designers and manufacturers, was the very cornerstone of consumerism. A demand was created for constant stylistic evolution within a vast array of luxury goods and labour-saving devices, and, indeed, within categories of basic household goods and appliances, the form of which should in theory be impervious to fashion.

In a society based on growth, few products escape the cyclical force of fashion. Today's Design Centre approved object rapidly becomes démodé, but ironically a very small number of designs achieve the glory of being dubbed 'classics', in recognition of the supposedly timeless qualities for which they are revered. Our society demands a rapid turnover in styles and ideas, and since the late fifties the applied arts have been dominated by middle-class consumerism, led by an ever inventive avant-garde of designers whose ideas have often only found popular acceptance in a somewhat diluted form.

Style consciousness and design awareness have been greatly stimulated by the proliferation of colour magazines dedicated to materialistic concerns. The British *Sunday Times* newspaper launched its colour magazine in 1962 and set a rapidly followed precedent for mass-circulation supplements, providing instant information on questions of fashion and style. The fluid integration of advertising and editorial features in such magazines has proved a clever marketing device. More specialized publications have targeted specific sectors of the market, and by proffering images of a sophisticated life-style attainable through consumer goods have done much to promote fashionable styles and to perpetuate the cycle of consumerism. Prominent among such magazines are the up-market fashion journals *Vogue* and *Harper's Bazaar*, more popular women's magazines such as the French *Elle* and *Marie Claire*, men's magazines such as *Playboy*, launched in 1953, and the French *Lui*, launched in 1964, the last two being almost as much concerned with selling

ary centre, inspiring international counterparts, for the activities of the new professionals, the copy-writers, art directors and account executives who were to play so crucial a role in this age of new-found affluence.

A significant new market category was the urban young, who around 1955 began to assert their own stylistic ambitions in the United States and in certain European countries, notably Britain. They found a collective identity through the rhythm of the new Rock and Roll, through rebellious young celluloid heroes such as James Dean and Marlon Brando, and through certain aspects of style, particularly fashion and dance.

1955 was a key point in this explosion of youthful style, the year in which James Dean starred in *Rebel Without a Cause* and met his tragic death, the

products, style and gadgetry as with selling female glamour; design magazines such as the British *Design* or the Italian veteran *Domus*, and interior design magazines such as French *Art et Décoration*, British *House and Garden* and American *House Beautiful*.

The late fifties saw the birth of advertising as we know it today, a high-powered business dedicated to the development of insidiously effective marketing techniques; it involved new design concepts and a whole new professional jargon of product packaging, market research, corporate images and house styles. Madison Avenue became the legend-

Above: I wonder what my heroes think of the space race, **by Derek Boshier, oil on canvas, 1962.**

Opposite left **Marlon Brando in** *The Wild Ones* **(1955), silkscreen on canvas by Andy Warhol, 1963.**

Opposite right: Hat stand, **mixed media sculpture by Allen Jones, 1969.**

leadership. The youthful heroes and style-setters of this 'swinging' London of the early to mid-sixties were chronicled by the young photographer David Bailey in his 1965 'Box of Pin-Ups'. These heroes included pop stars, film producers, art directors, advertising executives, photographers and models, an ephemeral pantheon of media figures.

Pop Art—pop culture

No art movement of recent decades has been so inextricably interwoven with the applied arts at a popular level than that which took form in the late fifties and early sixties in New York and London, and which acquired the label 'Pop Art'. In his study *Pop as Art*, published in 1965, the critic Mario Amaya examined the sources of the movement's imagery and found fundamental correlations between the iconography of Pop as a fine-art style and the symbols of throw-away popular culture. He defined the new, quintessentially urban art as relying upon the 'widely accepted trivia of the commonplace world, as seen in movies, television, comic strips, newspapers, girlie magazines, "glossies", high fashion, "high camp", car styling, billboards and other advertising.' Pop artists scrutinized, usually without direct comment, the strange visual vernacular of the new mid-century urban 'folk' art of commercial signs, symbols, emblems and imagery, which was being absorbed within the collective subconscious. 'These artists', wrote Amaya, 'are not painting "life" itself so much as about an ad-mass attitude to a way of living, as experienced through certain commercial idioms.' Pop was an exploration, at times even a glorification, of the gaudy, the transient and the superficial aspects of a consumer society. Icons of the Pop movement held a mirror to all those objects and styles which Reyner Banham had identified in 1955 in his analysis of the new throw-away aesthetic. By immortalizing the ephemeral on canvas or as sculpture, Pop artists have both forced their public to take stock of the inherent qualities of objects which would otherwise be taken for granted, and have refined the vernacular of Pop, transmuting a largely anonymous, spontaneous art form into a new and self-conscious design language.

The movement had its roots in the activities of the Independent Group in the Institute of Contemporary Arts in London. Founded in 1952, this discussion group included Reyner Banham, Eduardo Paolozzi, the architects Alison and Peter Smithson, Richard Hamilton and John McHale. Their evolution was chronicled by Jasia Reichardt, who recorded the Group's preoccupation with

year in which Brando established a stylish prototype for subversive youth in *The Wild Ones*. In 1955 Rock and Roll hit the headlines: a taste, rooted in ethnic American rhythm and blues, became a popular cult and gave birth to an industry which has been at the forefront of stylistic innovation, not just in music itself but in affiliated areas, including graphic design, fashion and, recently, video imagery. In 1955 Mary Quant opened her first Bazaar boutique in the King's Road, Chelsea, a highly symbolic event in the story of fashion. For fashion was to become dominated by the tastes and demands of a popular young market whose priorities were novelty and stylishness and London, in the so-called Swinging Sixties, was to seriously undermine Paris's former popular culture and focused the crystallization of their aesthetic on the return from America in 1955 of John McHale. He brought with him a trunk full of magazines including *Esquire*, *Mad* and *Playboy*, which opened up a new world of imagery and revealed America as a promised land, 'the source of a new and unexpected inspiration, as a romantic land with an up-to-date culture, a hotbed of new sensibility in art'.

In 1956 Pop was born. The Whitechapel Art Gallery held an exhibition, 'This is Tomorrow', in which Richard Hamilton showed his painting *Just what is it . . .* His exhibit included a giant front-of-house cinema publicity cut-out of a robot carrying an unconscious girl and superimposed with a film still of Marilyn Monroe, her first appearance as a Pop cult figure. The following year Hamilton defined the ingredients of Pop Art as he perceived them—popular, transient, expendable, low-cost, mass-produced, young, witty, sexy, glamorous and Big Business.

The Pop Art movement embraced the work of a new generation of artists on both sides of the Atlantic. In Britain, in addition to the Independent Group, there were Peter Blake, Allen Jones, Derek Boshier, Gerald Laing and Peter Phillips. In the United States, Jasper Johns, Roy Lichtenstein, Claes Oldenburg, Robert Rauschenberg, Andy Warhol, Tom Wesselman and others formalized the language of product packaging, from beer cans to Campbell's Soup tins, of strip cartoons, fast food, advertising hoardings and pin-ups.

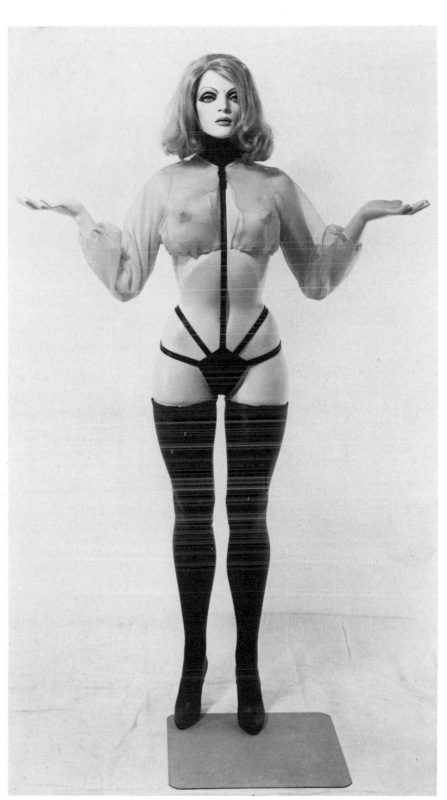

Pop Art at once reflected and glorified mass-market culture and injected a new vigour into the applied arts. Pop and the art styles which were its natural successors, notably American Hard-Edge Abstraction and the Hyper- or Photo-realist

Right Bikini by Fiorucci in plastic zipped pouch with plastic bag and label, 1981. The product and the packaging share the same bright Pop graphics and imagery.

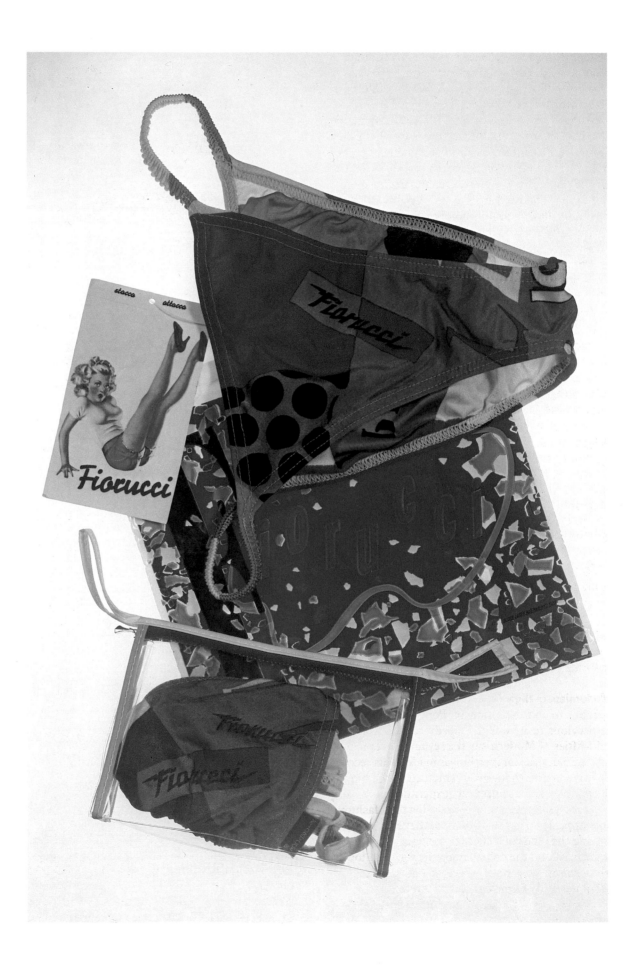

school of around 1970, suggested a new palette of colours and gave a fresh, ironical edge to the imagery of popular culture. The Pop ethic positively encouraged designers to exploit vulgarity, brashness and bright colour, and to use synthetic or disposable materials in contexts in which they would formerly have been unacceptable. Pop has had a lasting effect on design in a wide variety of media, including interiors, graphics and fashion.

Pop has spawned furniture in bright, primary-coloured plastics and in boldly printed fold-away cardboard; it has inspired, notably in Britain and Italy, witty sculptural furniture in brash, synthetic materials reminiscent of the sculptures of Claes Oldenburg. The fashion and furniture shop Mr Freedom, opened in London in 1969 by Tommy Roberts, was a veritable shrine to the Pop cult, with lively furniture designs by Jon Weallans. Italian Pop furniture was one aspect of the Italian design community's wide-ranging intellectual approach which, since the sixties, has made Italy the most progressive country in many areas of the applied arts.

The influence of Pop can be seen in graphic design in the sixties in the work of the American Pushpin Studios, founded by Milton Glaser and Seymour Chwast. Pop and the Hyper-Realists also inspired the slick airbrush work of a number of graphic artists working in the seventies and eighties, notably the British artists Philip Castle and Michael English. Pop imagery is still, today, a part of the staple diet of graphic design.

Pop's most notable impact on the world of fashion was in London in the late sixties and early seventies, and in Italy in the achievements of Elio Fiorucci in the seventies. Fiorucci brought fun into fashion, and his shops, first in Milan and then internationally, became known for their Pop-inspired clothes and graphics.

Modernism to High Tech

Parallel to the explosion of Pop, and seemingly impervious to it, was the steady revival from the mid-fifties of Modernism in a revamped version of its original, pre-war, rectilinear mode. This second phase of purist Modernism emerged as the highly decorative and sculptural experiments of the euphoric post-war period were losing their fashionable appeal. So at the same time that Pop Art was sowing the seeds of a counter-culture based on the superficial and the ephemeral, a new generation of Modernists was once more debating ideas of absolutes and of timeless good design.

The pursuit of pure lines and forms, unclut-tered, unadorned surfaces and rigidly rationalized

Left Prototype chair in moulded and painted polyurethane, designed by Piero Gilardi for Gufram, 1970.

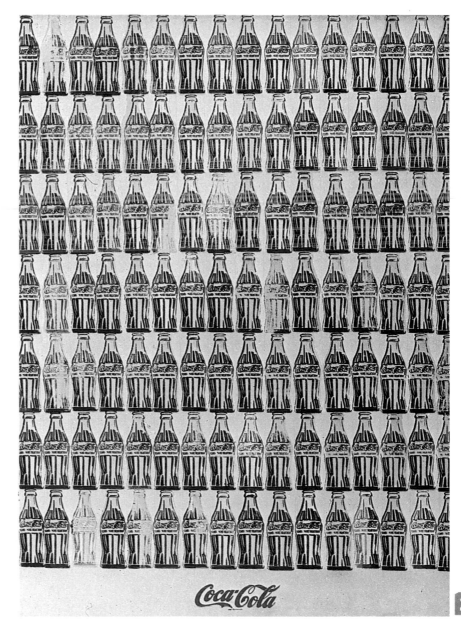

Below: Green Coca Cola Bottles, by Andy Warhol, oil on canvas, 1962.

grids was increasingly evident from the mid–fifties, in furniture and interior design, in various aspects of product design and in graphics, notably in the layout of the printed page.

Circumstances had changed, however, since the pioneer days of Modernism, and those designers who took up the rationalist, functionalist ideas of the Bauhaus were no longer leading the avant-garde but were trading in an established currency. Modernism now found favour within the mainstream of applied art and represented an educated, cosmopolitan modernity. The new Modernism became the adopted style of big business around the world, expensive understatement symbolizing success in the reception areas of corporate offices. In an age of jet travel, it provided the conceptual basis for the large commercial design projects of an increasingly urbanized society within such contexts as contract office-planning and the design of airport concourses. The style was taken up by a professional middle class which considered itself the arbiter of good taste. In furniture, object or graphic design the new Modernism implied an

Above Table and credenza designed by Florence Knoll, 1961, and chair designed by Eero Saarinen, 1957, all manufactured by Knoll. In the post-war period both the architecture and the furniture of large corporations tended to be in the Modernist style.

Right Interior designed by the architect Peter Womersley, Port Murray, near Maidens, Ayrshire, Scotland, in the purist Modernist taste revived in the late fifties and early sixties.

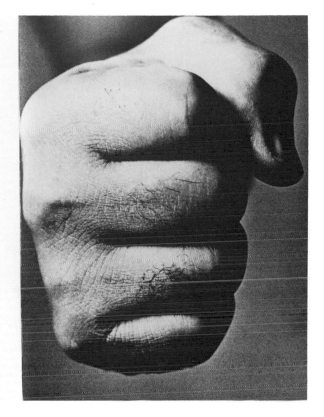

interest in ideals and standards which rose above the vicissitudes of mere fashion.

Instrumental in promoting this new Modernism was the design company Knoll Associates, still under the direction of Florence Knoll, and the design institution Hochschule für Gestaltung. The latter was founded at Ulm in Germany around 1950 under the aegis of the hard-line Modernist Max Bill, and it is best considered within the context of industrial design. Knoll expanded its operations through the fifties and sixties, opening showrooms internationally and becoming the world's largest design service and manufacturing retailer of prestigious Modernist furniture. Knoll International, as the corporation eventually became known, evolved new designs in the Modernist tradition, none more purist than those of Florence Knoll herself. In 1955 the firm started a programme of putting back into production the classic furniture designs of the first generation, pre-war Modernists, notably Mies van der Rohe and Marcel Breuer.

The new Modernism found able exponents internationally, notably the furniture designers Robin Day, working for the British company Hille, and Poul Kjaerholm for the Danish manufacturers E. Kold Christensen. A new rationalsim also entered the rich language of design in Italy in the sixties, within an open-minded and experimental climate which was to give Italian designers an international pre-eminence from the sixties into the eighties.

In graphic design the new Modernism became manifest around 1960 in the trend towards a clean, even clinical, style for magazine and book design, and for promotional and corporate graphics. The new graphics owed much to the Constructivist style advocated by the Bauhaus, and ranged from the purist grid-structured austerity of layouts by Max Bill to more dramatic or witty uses of type in

Right Interior detail of Joseph, Sloane Street, London, designed by Norman Foster Associates, 1979. The retailer Joseph Ettedgui has acquired a reputation in the 1980s for the chic Modernist/ Industrial Style décor of his various premises.

the work of the British design team of Alan Fletcher, Colin Forbes and Bob Gill.

Modernist ideas have enjoyed a constant following since their reappraisal in the fifties, despite the movement's detractors of the late seventies and eighties and the evolution of the Post-Modernist movement, a conscious reaction to the absolutism, purism and minimalism of the Modernist ethic. Modernism has to some extent changed its character. Utopian pretensions have been cast aside and the movement has come to represent a somewhat élitist approach to design, blending intellectual rigour and concern with style.

The form-language of Modernism has evolved and, in the late seventies, embraced a new style, born as a curious offshoot of functionalism. 'High Tech', or the Industrial Style, was christened by

Joan Kron and Suzanne Slesin in their highly successful design source book, published in 1978. They popularized the concept of using available industrial products, such as metal shelving, medical trolleys, studded rubber flooring and laboratory glassware, in domestic or commercial contexts. The style has been used with considerable chic in the design of shop interiors, notably in London by the entrepreneur Joseph Ettedgui, whose Sloane Street shop was fitted in a sophisticated version of the style by the architects Norman Foster Associates.

Youthful influences on style

Since the mid-fifties the influence of the young has made itself felt in those aspects of style—self-adornment and dance—that are central to what a

Left 'Way-In', Harrods, London, refurbished in 1985 in a highly sophisticated Industrial Style version of Modernism by Eva Jiricna, who is also responsible for the various interiors for Joseph Ettedgui.

social anthropologist might describe as the mating ritual. The young, that is to say teenagers and those in their early twenties, an age group not yet so concerned with the creation of domestic environments, have been encouraged to spend their disposable income on personal adornment, fashion accessories and make-up, and on pop music and its affiliated products. The young have also proved an eager market for fashionable sporting paraphernalia, from hula-hoops, through surf boards, skateboards, roller skates, to the fitness-fad workout fashions of the eighties.

Though they soon had their counterparts in Europe, in the Teddy Boy dandies of Britain and the Existentialist students of Paris, it was the American young who first attracted attention as a market force. This style-conscious generation of

the late fifties has been glorified in such films as *American Graffiti* (1973), and their clothes, hairstyles, cars, music and drive-ins have been romanticized as part of the folklore of adolescence.

London became a focal point for the young in the sixties. The phenomenon of Swinging London was the end-product of a pursuit of style by a loose-knit group of young, classless, ambitious professionals, artists, designers and performers, who created a hub of excitement in music, fashion, photography, graphic art and other aspects of design.

This British counter-culture owed much to the Pop Art movement for it too was characterized by a brashness of colour and approach, a sense of impermanence and a delight in novelty and the superficial. Its most obvious symbols were cheap, eye-catching fun fashions and the bold, gaudy Pop

frontages of the new boutiques in Chelsea and Carnaby Street, most notably the series of facades created by Michael English for Granny Takes a Trip, a boutique in the King's Road.

In April 1965 *Harper's Bazaar* devoted an issue to the explosion of youthful talent on both sides of the Atlantic, presenting features on Pop Art, Space-age and Op-Art fashions and the new heroes, among them Bob Dylan and Jean Shrimpton.

Paris, bastion of traditional values in fashion, was not impervious to the powerful voice of youth. Two young couturiers evolved dramatically new fashion concepts: André Courrèges with Op-Art, Science Fiction Clothes of the Future, launched in 1965 amid enormous publicity, and Paco Rabanne with his provocative metal and plastic clothes which hit the headlines the following year.

Space-age images were very topical in the mid- to late sixties, the years in which America's youngest president, John Kennedy, had vowed to set a man on the moon. Futuristic styles could be found in fashion, in furniture design, in advertising and, in their purest form, on celluloid in such lavish productions as *Barbarella* and *2001*.

Pop music and its associated drug culture were a rich source of inspiration for graphic imagery in the psychedelic art of the late sixties. Characterized by hallucinogenic clashing colours and complex, often virtually illegible, organic lettering, this art was drawn from various cult sources. It included Art Nouveau, Surrealist, mystical, Pop, Op, cartoon and other motifs and found its most brilliant exponents in London and San Francisco. Wes Wilson, a San Francisco graphic artist, is credited with having invented the style in 1967 in his posters for rock concerts at the Fillmore Auditorium. In London, the artists Michael English and Nigel

Above Metal trouser suit designed by Paco Rabanne, 1969.

Right 'Hilton Space Station', a set from Stanley Kubrick's visionary film *2001*, 1968.

Opposite The designer Verner Panton in a multiple exposure portrait, around 1970. The soft, sculpted seat units conform to the fashion in the late sixties for furniture that constituted a self-contained environment.

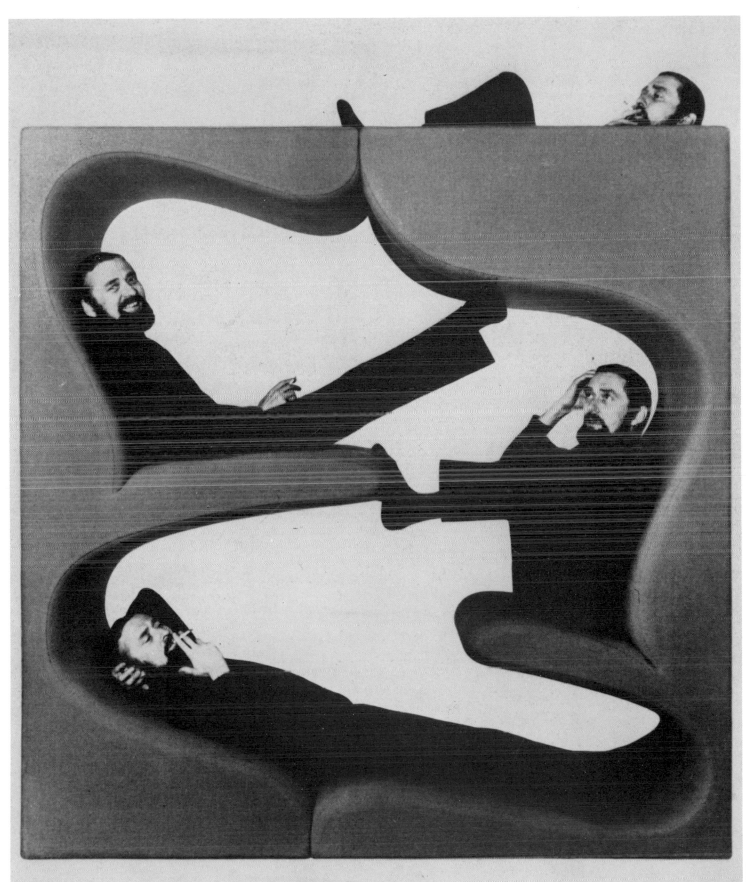

Right Psychedelic poster for
The Who record 'I can see for
miles', by Hapshash and the
Coloured Coat, published by
Osiris Visions Ltd, 1967.

Weymouth produced extraordinary psychedelic graphics under the name Hapshash and the Coloured Coat. The Beatles promoted the psychedelic style as patrons of the group of young Dutch artists who called themselves Fool and who created rich, colourful graphics, with more than a hint of Surrealism. They are best remembered for decorating the Apple store opened by the Beatles in Baker Street. The Beatles' animated film *Yellow Submarine* of 1968 was a remarkable synthesis of fashionable graphic imagery, including purely psychedelic sequences.

The most forceful manifestation of young style after psychedelia and the hippie cult had had their day was the British punk phenomenon of around 1976-7. Punk was a counter-culture founded on raw-edged music and half-formed nihilistic philosophies. Its impact on fashion and graphics was considerable and it rapidly entered the vernacular of avant-garde design, suggesting a cynical visual language with a quasi-subversive chic. Zandra Rhodes' torn silk dresses of 1977 were a sophisticated version of the aggressive punk uniform and one was acquired by the Victoria and Albert Museum for its costume collection—street style to museum within a season. The deliberate haphazardness of punk graphics became the basis for so-called New Wave graphics which, in a highly polished and stylish form, have had a lasting

Left The first issue of *Anarchy in the UK*, 1977, a short-lived publication expressing the subversive, but stylish, nature of the British punk movement.

Left Poster for *Yellow Submarine*, the animated film based on the Beatles' album 'Sergeant Pepper's Lonely Hearts Club Band', 1968.

Right 'Conceptual chic' silk jersey dress, designed by Zandra Rhodes, 1977, photographed by John Swannell. A chic adaptation of punk styles.

influence into the eighties, as part of the on-going radical or anti-design movement which found its most vociferous exponents in Italy.

Italy—the new domestic landscape

In 1972, the Museum of Modern Art in New York presented an exhibition, 'Italy: The New Domestic Landscape', in recognition of the major contribution made through the previous decade by Italy's design avant-garde, not only in terms of its tangible products, but above all in terms of its radical intellectual debate. There is some irony in the fact that MoMA, a decade later the butt of criticism for its dogmatic allegiance to International Modernism, should have provided the opportunity for so perceptive a survey of style, design and design philosophy in Italy at this period. In the introduction to the exhibition catalogue, Emilio Ambasz gives a first-hand analysis of the forces at work in Italy in the sixties:

'The emergence of Italy during the last decade as the dominant force in consumer-product design', he wrote, 'has influenced the work of every other European country and is now having its effect in the United States. The outcome of this burst of vitality among Italian designers is not simply a series of stylistic variations of product design. Of even greater significance is a growing awareness of design as an activity whereby man creates artifacts to mediate between his hopes and aspirations and the pressures and restrictions imposed upon him by nature and the man-made environment that his culture has created. . . . Many designers are expanding their traditional concern for the aesthetic of the object to embrace also a concern for the aesthetic of the uses to which the object will be put. Thus the object is . . . conceived . . . as an integral part of the larger natural and socio-cultural environment.'

Ambasz distinguished three tendencies, though these were far from clear-cut categories since so many designers applied different approaches according to the nature of the design problem. These were the Conformist, Reformist and Contestation tendencies: the first was concerned with objects for their own sakes, experimenting with new materials, techniques and colours, yet working in a traditional, rationalist, isolated way; the Reformist tendency was aware of the many contradictions in design and expressed these unresolved questions through ironical or rhetorical references

in objects; and the Contestation tendency was socio-politically motivated and more often concerned with the theory and implications than with the practice of design.

Ambasz's Conformists represented the rationalist continuum in Italian style and design. These were the designers who worked in close harmony with Italy's manufacturers, developing designs for furniture, light fittings, domestic and office equipment for series production. Their collective approach might be characterized as a kind of neo-Modernism, motivated by a desire to find rational and aesthetically satisfying solutions to design problems without feeling restricted by dogmatic functionalism such as that associated with the Hochschule für Gestaltung. For the Italian rationalists, style, visual and tactile quality, elegance and a certain understated panache have tempered the austerity of pure functionalism.

Firms renowned for this distinctive Italian look, which combined practical serviceability and

Above Cab chair designed by Mario Bellini, 1977, manufactured by Cassina; hide fitted over a steel carcase.

Left MT lamp of white-painted metal, designed by Giancarlo Mattioli, 1969, and manufactured by Sirrah from 1970. This design featured in 'Italy: The New Domestic Landscape' exhibition, 1972.

261

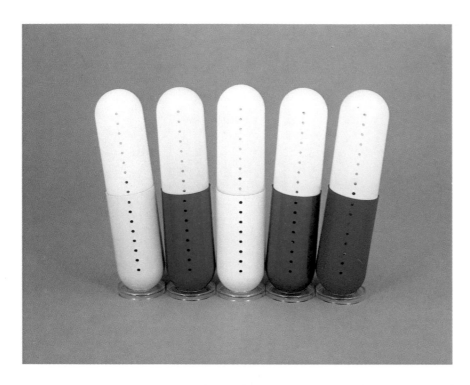

considerable stylishness, were the furniture manufacturers Cassina, Tecno and Kartell, the lighting manufacturers Flos and Artemide, and manufacturers of electrical goods, metalwork and plastics including Olivetti, Brionvega and Alessi.

The Milanese firm of Cassina achieved an outstanding synthesis of unfussy, elegant modern design and a respect for traditional materials, incorporating leather, wood and marble, as well as steel and glass. Its team included Tobia Scarpa, Vico Magistretti and Angelo Mangiarotti; Achille Castiglioni and Gae Aulenti continued to develop inventive lighting designs; Joe Colombo and Anna Castelli Ferrieri practical designs in plastics for Kartell; Richard Sapper stylish electrical goods and metalware for Brionvega and Alessi. Their story is as much a part of the evolution of industrial design concepts as of the history of style.

The counterpoint to this evolution of mainstream rationalist values and discreetly elegant styling were the provocative, witty and eccentric artifacts of the Reformist movement, variously

Above **Pillola lamps, plastic and acrylic, designed by Cesare Casati and Emanuele Ponzio, 1968, manufactured by Ponteur from 1969; included in the 'Italy: The New Domestic Landscape' exhibition in the category of 'objects selected for their socio-cultural implications'.**

Right **Sinbad armchair designed by Vico Magistretti, 1981, manufactured by Cassina. This design was inspired by the idea of a horse-blanket thrown over a frame.**

Opposite **Interior project by Joe Colombo, around 1970. The functional, cellular concept was explored with considerable invention by Colombo.**

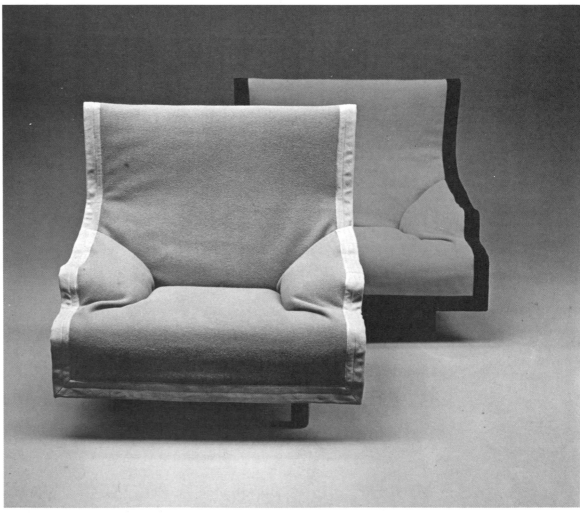

described as 'anti-design' and 'radical design'. The movement gained momentum in the sixties through the work of several designers and design studios who saw one of their prime responsibilities as the stimulation, if necessary by shock tactics, of debate on the purposes of design. In the vanguard were Ettore Sottsass Jr., regarded as the father-figure of the radical design movement, Gaetano Pesce and the two experimental design studios founded in Florence in 1966, Archizoom and Superstudio. Andrea Branzi, an associate of the Archizoom studio, has conceived many

Right Arco lamp designed by Achille and Piergiacomo Castiglioni, 1962, manufactured by Flos; marble, aluminium and steel.

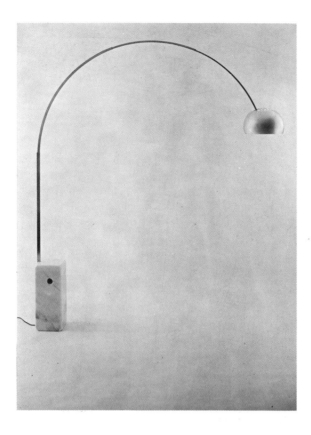

Right Capitello chair, designed by Studio 65 for Gufram, 1971; moulded and painted polyurethane. Many Pop objects shared the Surrealist characteristic of their function contradicting their initial appearance.

Opposite Drawers in irregular form, designed by Shiro Kuramata, 1977. Kuramata expresses in a contemporary idiom the Japanese love of modularity and fine craft.

thought-provoking designs, and in his 1984 publication *The Hot House* has brought up to date the story of conflicts and achievements in Italian avantgarde design.

The Venice Biennale of 1964 had been crucial in bringing American Pop to Italy, and the radicals drew on Pop imagery as if to underline the transient character of all design. Sottsass was also influenced by the iconoclastic character of British Pop, publishing a photo essay on London Pop in *Domus* on his return from a trip to the British capital in the autumn of 1966. Pop was the inspiration for the overscaled Pillola lamp designed by Cesare Casati and Emanuele Ponzio for Ponteur in 1968, and for the moulded-foam sculptural furniture designed by Piero Gilardi and others for Gufram around 1970. There was an almost Dadaist element of provocation in the radicals' determination to create objects which broke the accepted canons of design. Sottsass was both the most stylish and subversive, as in the series of prototype cupboards in printed laminates which he designed in 1966. Monolithic totems, closer to Hard Edge Abstractionist sculpture than to any recognizable furniture form, these designs brought into question traditional rationalist concepts and aesthetics.

The 'Italy: The New Domestic Landscape' exhibition paid tribute to the versatile, visionary talent of Joe Colombo, a gifted, practical designer with a flair for dramatic, back-to-the-drawing-board concepts of environmental design. Colombo's career was cut short, after less than a decade, by his untimely death in 1971. He personified the best qualities of progressive Italian design—concern for function and for human needs, a sure eye for form and boundless imagination.

Japan

Japanese culture was discovered by the western world in the 1860s. Not until a century later did Japan, on the foundations of a flourishing economy, start significantly to absorb aspects of western and particularly American culture. The 1964 Olympics, staged in Tokyo, and the Osaka World Fair of 1970, the last grand-scale international fair, were crucial in encouraging cultural exchange. In the past two decades there has been a distinct polarization of Japanese philosophy on questions of style and design in the applied arts: on the one hand, Japan has been anxious to preserve and adapt to modern contexts her traditional values and styles, a process of enlightened evolution; on the other hand, she has learned valuable lessons from the West, and many Japanese designers have shown a strong appetite for all the superficial symbols of western Pop culture and have recycled these symbols in their own iconography.

Traditional features of Japanese design include fine craft, love of compactness, modularity and simplicity, even decorated objects having a quality of clarity and an almost mystical respect for the forms and symbols evolved through history. Many of these features can be seen in the impeccable miniaturization of Japanese technological designs: an informative parallel might be drawn between the compactness of a Sony Walkman and a traditional lacquer *inro*. Traditional qualities in modern guise characterize the simple, modular furniture of Shiro Kuramata. The Japanese spirit is evident in designs by the sculptor Isamo Noguchi for lamps, created for American manufacturers and much copied, notably his wire and paper 'Akari' of 1966. In the *mingei* (folk craft) movement, Japan has attempted to keep alive traditional skills in ceramics, textiles, lacquer and other crafts.

A young generation of Japanese fashion designers has, in the eighties, made a considerable impact in the West with styles evolved from the Japanese cultural heritage. Issey Miyake is the most celebrated and the most talented. His rattan corsage epitomizes the character of this movement;

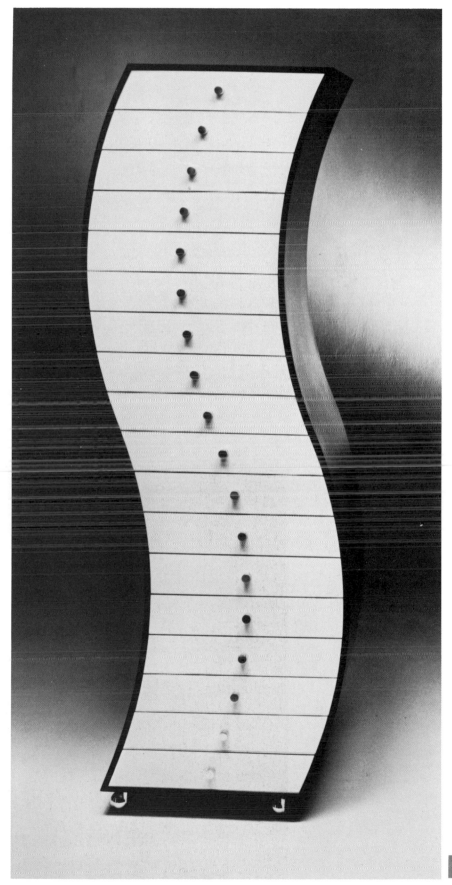

Right Tokyo street scene, 1982. Japanese typography blends with the international street vernacular of American consumer-product branding.

ISSEY MIYAKE

it is an exciting sculptural form, adapting a traditional craft technique and laden with oblique cultural references, not least to samurai armour.

In contrast, signs of western influence are widely apparent at street level, in the ubiquitous international language of petrol stations, fast-food outlets, neon signs and advertising hoardings. The Japanese display a seemingly insatiable appetite for slick western commercial photography and for the symbolic brand images of western society, from Coca-Cola to McDonald's. Young Japanese graphic artists and illustrators, working in Japan and the United States, have developed styles which draw together many of the features of western culture. Prominent among these artists are Pater Sato, Harumi Yamaguchi, Hajime Sorayama and Yosuke Ohnishi. Motifs from American Pop culture, Hyper-realism and western erotic photography are fused in hybrid graphic works with a polish that is distinctly Japanese.

The crafts revived

The craft revival which has gained increased momentum internationally in the last ten to fifteen years has provided a haven of direct creative involvement for artists. This is, to some extent, an idealistic retreat from increased mechanization in

Left Corsage designed by Issey Miyake, 1981. The traditional craft of lacquered rattan is adapted to a modern fashion in a design that makes reference to an ancient cultural heritage.

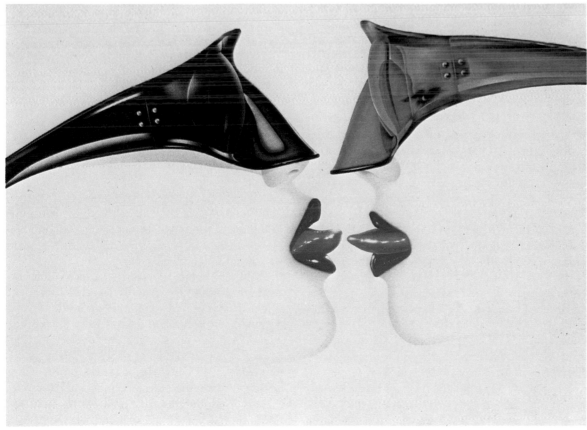

Left: Visor Love greetings card, published by Paper Moon Graphics Inc., Los Angeles, from an airbrush drawing by Pater Sato. This artist is among the slickest exponents of airbrush illustration.

Right Stoneware vase by Hans Coper, around 1970. The form is derived from Greek Cycladic sculpture of the Bronze Age.

our society and from the reliance on machine rather than handwork in the production of objects; it is also an antidote to the design profession's allegiance to industry rather than to craft.

The current craft revival, however, unlike the Arts and Crafts movement, makes no attempt to promote utopian philosophies, but rather acknowledges its role as a privileged and in many respects anachronistic service sustained by a small, wealthy market. It makes a valuable contribution to our culture in providing successive generations of designer-craftsmen with a framework of traditional artisan skills within which to seek a contemporary form language. There is no attempt to put back the clock; the aim is rather to extend the possibilities within the various craft media, emphasizing their artistic rather than purely practical potential. Self-expression has taken precedence over function as the goal, and certain crafts formerly associated primarily with the production of functional objects have developed closer affinities with the fine arts. This is particularly true in studio glass and ceramics where many artists are deliberately abandoning any traditional functional form and creating instead works of pure sculpture.

The movement has found a strong following in the United States; in Britain, where the Crafts Council, set up in 1971, does much to promote interest and encourage high standards through a publishing, exhibition and sponsorship programme; in France, where the Métiers d'Art exhibitions at the Musée des Arts Décoratifs celebrate national achievements; in other European countries and in Japan. The Scandinavian countries do not suffer the extreme dichotomy between craft and industry of the more heavily industrialized countries, and their crafts have followed an unbroken, consistent path and flourish within a broader manufacturing context, as in the studio ceramics made under the auspices of the Gustavsberg factory, or the studio glass of Ann Warff at Kosta and of Ovia Toikka at Iittala.

The media to benefit most from this revival have been studio ceramics and glass, jewellery, textiles and furniture. Studio ceramics have the longest history and strong British roots, the contemporary movement owing much to the continuing influence of Bernard Leach, active since before the war, and to the example of Lucie Rie and Hans Coper. Ruth Duckworth, who left Britain in 1964 to set up a studio in Chicago, and Peter Voulkos were influential figures in American studio ceramics.

The studio glass movement, on the other hand, had its roots in the United States, in the experiments of Dominic Labino and Harvey Littleton at

the Toledo Museum of Art in 1962. Littleton's pupil Sam Herman graduated in 1965, moved to London and founded The Glasshouse in 1969. He played a crucial role in giving initial impetus to the British studio glass movement.

The most notable creators of handcrafted contemporary furniture include Wendell Castle and Michael Coffey in America and the British designer, craftsman and teacher John Makepeace, whose Parnham House workshop and school characterizes the fundamental problem facing craftsmen today. At Parnham, a generation of young artisans pursue the craft of cabinet-making to the highest possible standards and evolve inventive forms, yet they work in isolation from the realities

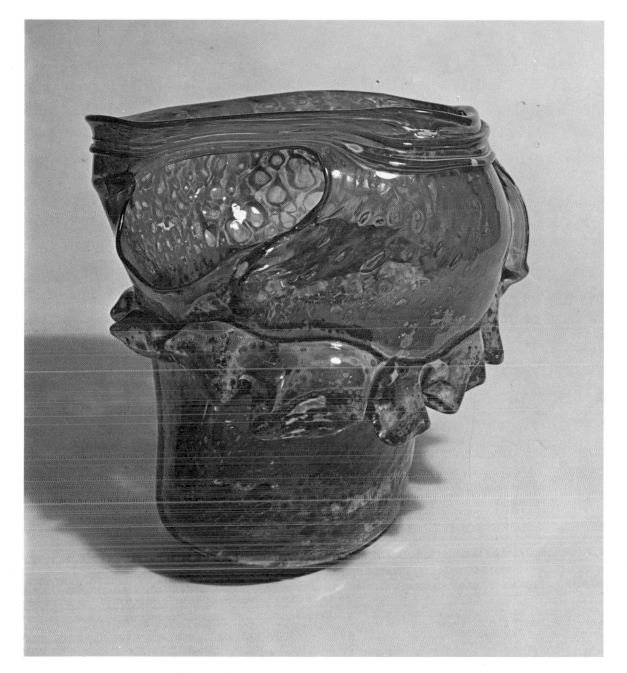

Left Free-form blown and applied glass vase by Sam Herman, 1973. Herman has played an influential role in promoting the revival of studio glasswork in Britain.

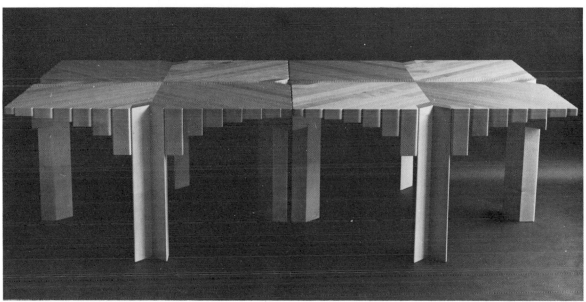

Left Pair of tables by John Makepeace, 1975, with a built-up construction of solid white sycamore.

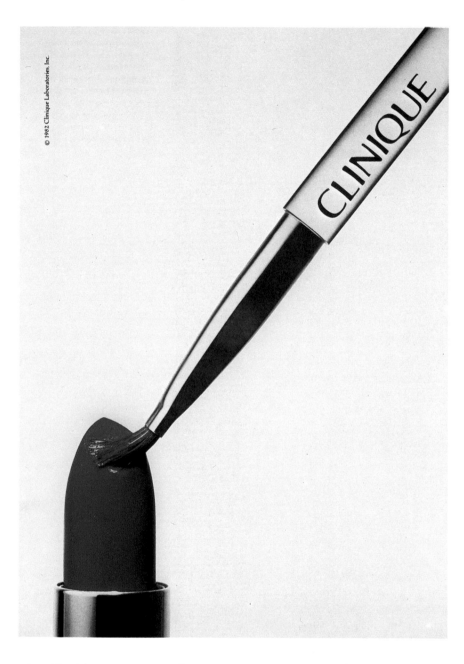

© 1982 Clinique Laboratories, Inc.

Above Advertising photograph by Irving Penn for Clinique, 1982. This demonstrates Penn's skill in creating memorable images of deceptive simplicity.

of mainstream design. There is a risk that their achievements may be regarded not as an integral part of contemporary design, but as an intriguing footnote to the central theme of design for industrial series production.

Commercial photography

Commercial photographic images are a major ingredient of our visual diet, assimilated from magazines, hoardings and such contexts as brochures, catalogues, calendars, packaging and point-of-sale promotional material. Commercial photography thrives as a means of creating highly polished images of a stylized, glamourized and idealized view of the world in order to sell a product

or a service. It owes its development to the post-war boom in consumerism, the increased scale and sophistication of advertising, the refinement of colour film, colour separation and printing processes, and the increased quality and popularity of colour magazines.

The major categories of commercial photography are advertising in its countless guises, including product photography and photo-illustration, fashion, beauty and certain categories of photography which are neither reportage nor aspire to be fine art, yet which can be fascinating social documents of considerable aesthetic quality.

Irving Penn has continued to be a master in each of these genres and has set standards to which many aspire. His career has spanned forty years, during which his work, from his early fashion and still-life compositions to current still-life product studies such as his series for the cosmetics manufacturers Clinique, has shown an inimitable vision and consistent aesthetic rigour.

Bert Stern, though far from being Penn's artistic equal, became the archetypal commercial photographer in the fifties and sixties, running a vast studio in New York and showing considerable skill and versatility in interpreting the briefs of art directors and clients.

In the sixties the profession of commercial and, in particular, fashion photography became greatly glamourized: the successful young photographer became a popular folk hero, as if the camera were a passport to the illusory world which it could depict—Antonioni's film *Blow-Up* (1966-7) defined the role model. Among the most interesting magazines to be launched in the sixties, the photography of which captured the youthful excitement of that period, were the British *Nova*, which commissioned some of the best fashion photography of its day, and the German *Twen*, brilliantly art directed by Willy Fleckhaus.

In the sixties advertising played a secondary role to editorial photography in magazines. Today the reverse seems true, for the character of many magazines is dictated by the market needs of advertisers and many photographers bemoan the greater restrictions this imposes. The seventies and eighties have, nonetheless, brought forth a new roll-call of talent. Outstanding contemporary figures include Helmut Newton and Guy Bourdin, who have dominated the field of fashion photography; Hans Feurer, Arthur Elgort, Denis Piel, Peter Lindberg and Deborah Turbeville, to name but a few of the less celebrated but talented fashion photographers; advertising and glamour photographers such as Francis Giacobetti,

FEB.
FEV.
FEB.
FEB.
•
1
2
3
4
5
6
7
8
9
10
11
12
13
14
15
16
17
18
19
20
21
22
23
24
25
26
27
28
•
•
•

ASAHI PENTAX

Left Calendar for Pentax with photographs by Hans Feurer, 1978. The Japanese manufacturers of photographic goods have commissioned calendars from a number of top commercial photographers including Helmut Newton, Guy Bourdin and Hans Feurer.

James Baes and Cheyco Leidman, inventor of garish surrealistic imagery in saturated colours; and Bruce Weber, who has recently attracted wide attention for his advertising campaign for Calvin Klein and for his fresh ideas in fashion photography.

Commercial photographers play a crucial role in our consumer society, creating the images of a lifestyle to which we are constantly encouraged to aspire. They create glamourized images of women and give a heightened visual appeal to the products which are the economic mainstay of our society, be it a hamburger, a perfume or an automobile.

Post-Modernism and style today

The fashionable, and often controversial, topic of Post-Modernism is central to the applied arts today. This label has been used for a variety of decorative styles which have in common the designer's reaction against what is seen as the sterility of Modernism. Post-Modernism represents a search for a vernacular of design to enrich and entertain the spirit with visually legible socio-historical points of reference, and to stimulate aesthetic responses with the shock of novel forms, patterns, colours and contrasts.

Sottsass Jr., a key figure in the Italian Radical Design movement of the sixties, has become a spokesman of the influential Italian Post-Modernist movement, particularly as it affects domestic design. As a member of the Alchymia design

Right **Chair of bird's-eye maple and ebony, designed by Michael Graves for Sunar, 1981. There are clear historicist allusions in this Post-Modernist design.**

studio, founded in Milan in 1976 by the architect Alessandro Guerriero, Sottsass, together with the designers Andrea Branzi, Alessandro Mendini and Michele de Lucchi, suggested a new language of furniture and object design. The Alchymia style was characterized by bright, playful colours and lively contrasts, laminates printed with patterns like magnified noodles or granules, and logic-defying forms—sloping shelves, asymmetrical chairs and tables.

In a catalogue of projects for Alchymia, dated June 1980, Sottsass explained how he drew his motifs and reference from 'a figurative iconography found in spaces uncorrupted by the sophistication of the standard culture of private interior design'; he derived textures and patterns 'from areas . . . abandoned . . . by any intellectual intent or expectation . . . the mosaics of public conveniences . . . tight wire-netting of suburban fences . . . spongy paper of government account books'.

The Alchymia project was superseded in 1980-1 by the foundation of the Memphis design studio in Milan. Led by Sottsass and including Nathalie du Pasquier, George Sowden, Andrea Branzi, Michele de Lucchi and Peter Shire, Memphis transformed a subversive, avant-garde concept into high fashion and this chic version of Post-Modernism has, in five years, had a considerable influence on style in design. The Memphis group create costly limited-edition prototypes, but their ideas have filtered through to many areas of design for mass-production and have inspired a new international style in graphic and object design.

Sottsass, ever ready to open philosophical debate on the topic of design and its language, expressed the underlying spirit of Post-Modernism in his comments in the Philadelphia 'Design Since 1945' catalogue: 'Design should be removed from the acid mechanism of industrial needs and programs to be taken into a wider area of possibilities and necessities. Design starts when you design the metaphor of life, which means that so-called anti-design in fact was "anti" nothing at all, it was all just for enlarging and deepening the design event.' His aim was 'to deliver to design a larger catalogue of communications, more meaning, a wider linguistic flexibility, and a wider awareness of the responsibilities towards private and social life'.

Post-Modernism has found its advocates internationally in such figures as the American architect-designer Michael Graves, who has created eclectic furniture for Memphis and other manufacturers; and in the British architectural historian Charles Jencks, who should be credited with giving

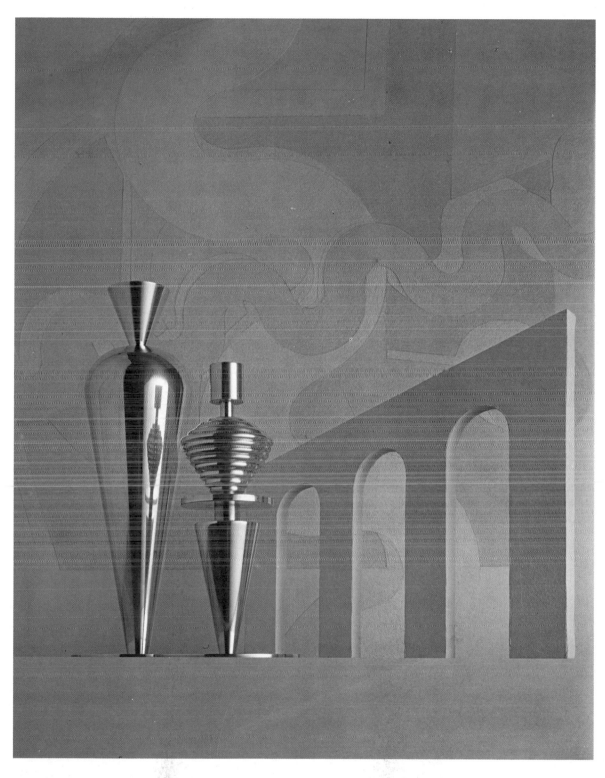

Left **Composite of metalwork and graphics by Studio Alchymia, published on the cover of *Décoration Internationale '69*, 1984.**

the movement its label and whose London home is an elaborate exercise in the metaphors of Post-Modern decoration.

Contemporary decorative graphics owe much to Post-Modernism, and also to the diverse influences of British New Wave graphics, fifties revival motifs and perennially fashionable Pop imagery. The Los Angeles company Paper Moon Graphics has, since the late seventies, produced a wide range of ephemeral graphics, including greetings cards and stationery, which encompass the full gamut of current fashions.

Modernism meanwhile is far from defunct. Its considerable commercial success in the eighties is

Opposite Memphis showroom window display, Milan: Treetops floor lamp, designed by Ettore Sottsass, 1981; Brazil table, 1981, and Anchorage tripod teapot, 1982, silver, metal and wood, designed by Peter Shire.

Left: April, a greetings card designed by April Greiman, 1981, published by 'Look Out', Los Angeles.

Right Pileo floor lamp, designed by Gae Aulenti, 1972, manufactured by Artemide; plastic on metal column. The design also exists as a table lamp, without the column.

Below Paper bag with printed slogan, designed by Katharine Hamnett, 1985. Hamnett's fashion designs have included a range with political slogans printed in giant letters.

proven by the re-issued designs by René Herbst, Eileen Gray, Robert Mallet-Stevens and other first-generation Modernists, swelling the list of 'classic' designs by Le Corbusier, Mies van der Rohe and Marcel Breuer already available. Modernism today can be a chic decorator's style, as practised by Andrée Putman and her Paris-based design company Ecart, or by the fashion entrepreneur Joseph in his London, Paris and New York shops. Modernism flourishes in the Knoll International style, and the rationalism of the movement's founders is perpetuated in the work of designers internationally, including such outstanding talents as David Mellor and Kenneth Grange in Britain,

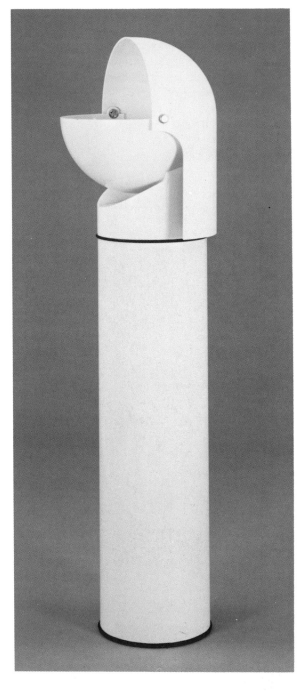

STAY ALIVE IN 85

the Italians Gae Aulenti and Richard Sapper, the Dane Erik Magnussen and, of course, the German purists Dieter Rams, Dietrich Lubs and their colleagues.

In the world of fashion, the more interesting phenomena of the last few years include the translation by a group of Japanese designers of ethnic traditions into international high fashion, and the enormous success of western fashion styles based on the current cult of fitness. The 1984 Olympics gave an added spur to this fad. Exciting newcomers to the field of fashion design include

Calvin Klein and Norma Kamali in America, the former known for classic, easy styles, the latter for stylishy cut day and evening wear and swimwear; the British designer Katharine Hamnett, whose slogan-printed clothes have been widely copied; and the Paris designer Azzedine Alaïa, who cuts leather and jersey with a verve rarely seen since the heyday of Balenciaga.

The story of style today is a complex blend of seemingly contradictory tendencies, and any at-tempt to tidy creativity into neat compartments is, surely, to render a disservice to the individuality of designers. The greatest achievements are precisely those instances where individuality triumphs over the predictable to create the unexpected, be it the design of a piece of furniture by Sottsass, stage sets by David Hockney, a jacket by Azzedine Alaïa, a graphic design by Pater Sato, a fashion illustration by Antonio Lopez, a glass sculpture by Dominic Labino or a new lamp by Achille Castiglioni.

Left **Illustration by Antonio Lopez of a design by Sylvano Matta for Lux Sport, 1979. Lopez has kept alive the finest traditions of fashion illustration in work that combines a self-assured graphic style and an innate chic.**

277

INDUSTRIAL DESIGN

The 1960s and early 1970s saw great tensions within the industrial design profession. These were publicly and vigorously debated in Italy particularly, where many leading figures reacted against design which conformed to notions of good taste and high style. As discussed in the previous chapter, these designers sought to explore cultural and linguistic references in design through kitsch and popular culture. The Milan Triennali, which for thirty years had provided a forum for the discussion and exhibition of design ideas, came under increasing attack and many progressive designers felt that they were paying excessive homage to products which epitomized good taste and style at the expense of examinations of design as a process and socio-cultural activity. This culminated in the closure of the fourteenth Triennale in 1968, following protests by students, architects and designers who objected to the manner in which it had been organized.

It was, nonetheless, a period in which mainstream industrial design continued to prosper in Italy. The Italian design consultant enjoyed considerable status as a tastemaker whose name stimulated product sales in a wide variety of mass-produced goods. Firms such as Arteluce, Artemide, Brionvega, Fiat, Kartell, Olivetti and Sambonet developed successful working relationships with leading designers and saw the enhancement of their reputations not only through the ensuing production but also through the many design awards accorded them, both national and international. This was consolidated further by wide coverage in the design press.

Arteluce, founded by Gino Sarfatti, helped to establish the reputation of modern Italian lighting. Sambonet underlined the aesthetic possibilities of design in kitchen equipment and utensils, especially through Roberto Sambonet's series of products, including oven dishes, saucepans, cut-

Below **Hi-fi unit designed by Achille Castiglioni for Brionvega, 1966. Before the age of sleek electronics designers achieved novelty with strikingly curious sculptural forms.**

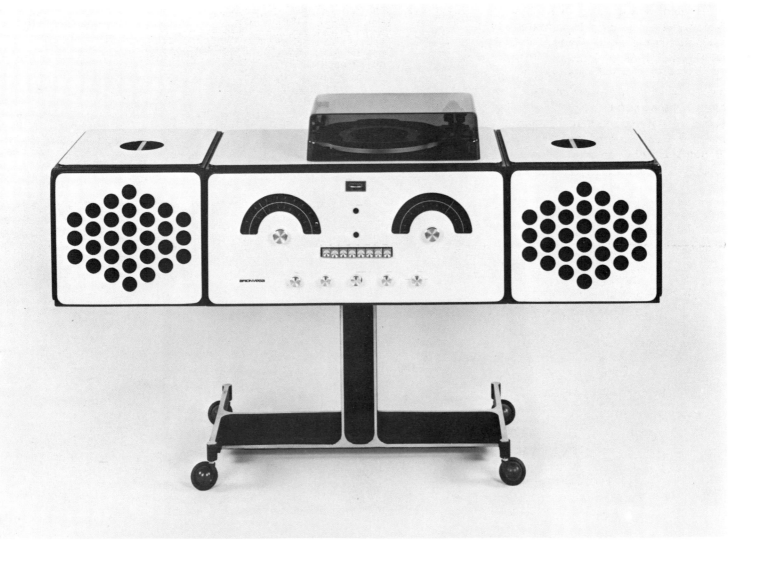

lery and steel trays, which depended on his close liaison with the engineering and technical staff. Kartell became a leader in the field of plastics—public, domestic and industrial.

Kartell is internationally acknowledged as a company which has exploited plastics for their own aesthetic and formal, rather than imitative, qualities. Founded by Giulio Castelli in Milan in 1949, its growth reflected both the emergence of Italian design as an international force and the importance of Milan as a major centre for design initiative.

By the mid-1950s the company had established itself as a propagandist for high standards of design, gaining a Compasso d'Oro award for Gino Columbini's plastic bucket with lid. It had also embarked upon a series of collaborations with many leading architects and designers, including Gae Aulenti, Rodolfo Bonetto, Achille and Piergiacomo Castiglioni, Joe Colombo, Anna Castelli Ferrieri, Ignazio Gardella, Richard Sapper, Ettore Sottsass and Marco Zanuso. Over the years there were a number of sections within the company: Car Accessories (1950–67), Housewares (1951–79), Lighting Fixtures (1958), Industrial Plants (1960–68), Habitat (1963–9), Labware (1958). They were all sustained by considerable research, investment, technological experimentation and, most importantly, emphasis on design. In the early 1960s Kartell moved into furniture manufacture, producing Zanuso and Sapper's award-winning injection-moulded polyethylene chair, followed by such key products as Anna Castelli Ferrieri's ABS square,

Left Television designed by Richard Sapper and Marco Zanuso for Brionvega, 1970. This austerely minimal design was one of the first consumer products to make black chic.

Below left Valentine typewriter designed by Ettore Sottsass and Perry King for Olivetti, 1970. The Pop styling was used to undermine popular prejudices about office machinery.

Below right Plastic waste-bins manufactured by Kartell, around 1983. Using injection-moulding techniques, Kartell produces a wide range of stylish domestic goods.

279

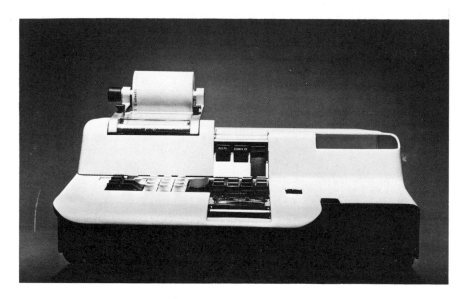

Above Programma 101 desk-top computer designed by Mario Bellini for Olivetti, 1966. The size and weight (64 lbs) of this computer were a remarkable achievement at this period.

coloured portable Valentine typewriter of 1969 to the DE700 data entry machine which was designed after careful analysis of ergonomic and anthropometric data.

Another figure, important in the more industrially orientated range of Olivetti products, was Rudolfo Bonetto who, before being put in charge of machine tools produced by ONC (the Olivetti Numerical Control Division), had been a consultant to Pininfarina and other car-body builders and had lectured for four years in product design at the Hochschule für Gestaltung at Ulm in Germany.

Ettore Sottsass has perhaps been the dominant figure in Italian design over the past fifteen years, contributing to radical design ideology as well as mainstream industrial practice. Another celebrated figure in the design world is Giorgio Giugiaro, who studied painting in Turin and at the age of twenty-one joined Bertone's *carozzeria*, where he immediately designed the bodywork of the classic Alfa Romeo Giulia GT. He then became chief executive of Ghia, a rival to Bertone, but left the following year to set up his own firm ItalDesign in 1968. Here Giugiaro was able to develop that razor-

stacking units in 1967, Centrokappa's school system of 1978 and other products equally impressive for their strikingly colourful, technologically sophisticated and aesthetically pleasing designs.

The Olivetti company, which had built up a formidable reputation for high standards of design in the inter-war years and had re-established itself so successfully as a leading design force during the *Ricostruzione*, underwent a change of direction following the death of Adriano Olivetti in 1960. Reflecting the technological innovations that had been taking place since the 1950s, there was a distinct shift of emphasis from the mechanical to the electronic in a wide variety of products, exemplified in the development of equipment such as Mario Bellini's Programma 101, the first desktop computer in the world. Although new technologies offered a potentially new set of design solutions since the designer was no longer constrained by heavy mechanisms, as in Nizzoli's Lexicon 80 typewriter of 1948, there were other factors that needed to be observed in the design of office and business equipment. Increasing emphasis on modularity (for compatability with other related equipment) and greater attention to anthropometric and ergonomic factors were important influences in formal configurations.

The company continued to develop close working relationships with many leading designers and architects of the day, including Mario Bellini who began working for Olivetti in 1963 (and also worked with other firms such as Lancia, Brionvega, Artemide and Cassina). Ettore Sottsass was another eminent figure in the history of Italian design who worked with the firm on a number of products from 1957 onwards, ranging from the light-hearted, fashion-conscious, brightly

Right Synthesis office chair designed by Ettore Sottsass for Olivetti, 1969. Chunky and brightly coloured, it was deliberately intended to introduce an element of play into the office.

Left Fiat Panda designed by Giorgio Giugiaro, 1980. Styled as a successor to the utilitarian French cars (the Citroën 2CV and the Renault 4), this car is now sold in a variety of sporty and four-wheel-drive models.

Left Volkswagen Golf, first produced in 1974. The Golf, for which Giugiaro designed the body, became Europe's most popular modern car.

edged clarity that had made his early designs for Alfa Romeo so sensational.

The landmarks in ItalDesign's work have been the design of the Alfa Romeo AlfaSud of 1971 and the highly influential Volkswagen Golf of 1974. For the next major project, the Fiat Panda of 1980, ItalDesign presented two full-scale models, four alternative side elevations and a range of comparative data, so the manufacturer could decide for himself how ItalDesign would best interpret the various options. The company then built prototypes for Fiat and even designed some of the necessary tooling. In 1983 Giugiaro reinterpreted his Volkswagen Golf concept in his design for Fiat Uno, an upright, boxy, city car which confirmed his break from the low-slung, sporty styles of his earlier work.

ItalDesign is an international rarity in that, while it specializes in cars, it has now developed from being a *carozzeria* into a consultancy that can take any product from conception to prototype. The range of its design activity now rivals that of the great American studios of the thirties; since it was founded, the company has designed sewing-machines for Necchi, cameras for Nikon, watches for Seiko and even pasta for Voiello. These product designs appeal to consumer psychology through their eloquent aesthetic that depends on technological symbolism for its effect. In fact, ItalDesign has been consistently stylish and innovative in its approach to form, as well as remarkably professional in the execution of its clients' briefs.

By the mid-eighties, Italian design was in a hiatus: successful but somewhat directionless. Its prestige was immense, so much so that in 1984 General Motors announced an agreement with Pininfarina that the Turin body shop would supply bodies for the forthcoming Cadillacs. Yet, at the same time that the Italian body shops were attaining international status, the radical ideology of Studio Alchymia and Memphis promised yet another major conflict in Italian culture which, no doubt, will stimulate a debate as interesting and as ultimately fruitful as all the others that have preceded it.

Below and opposite below **Such is the range of ItalDesign's expertise that it has now designed cameras for Nikon, watches for Seiko, and pasta for Voiello.**

Japan

Japanese industrial design has, since the 1960s, established itself in a wide variety of areas, including the motorcycle and automobile industries, audio-visual equipment, domestic products, office and factory automation systems, telecommunications, advanced medical electronics equipment and many commodities within the heavy industrial sector. Over the years Japanese design has shaken off its dependence on foreign, especially American, models of the 1950s and 1960s and has become a technologically sophisticated, high-quality and economically competitive sphere of activity. However, in the 1980s many of those involved have recognized the importance of user needs in product development, assessing the extent to which technological change genuinely improves the product. As Kyoshi Sakashita, of the Corporate Design Centre at Sharp, wrote in 1982, 'Many successful corporations are shifting their strategy emphasis from merchandizing to need-orientation. So, naturally the roles of designers have been redefined.

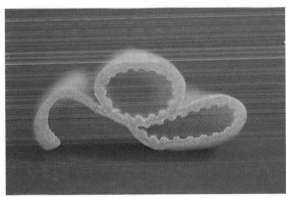

Designers in the past only wanted a human touch in product creation. Today, in addition to that, they need to think of the total living environment and to design life-styles accordingly.'

Companies such as Honda, Canon, Matsushita, Toshiba, Sharp, Sony and Japan National Railways have all set high standards of design and quality. A number of representative examples of design development within the past twenty-five years will indicate how the design climate evolved. GK Industrial Design Associates, the largest design consultancy in Japan with over two hundred full-time designers, was founded in the 1950s with less than ten. Its progress in the following decade mirrored Japan's rapid economic growth, capitalizing on the increased emphasis placed on design

Right Honda C50 motorcycle, in production from 1958. The success of Honda's lightweight motorcycles equalled that of their cars, and they soon sold widely throughout the world.

by manufacturing industry. Among their many clients at that time were Hitachi, Yamaha and the Nissan motor company. GK's research activity continued throughout the 1970s, a decade in which there was much greater emphasis on social and environmental issues, and in the 1980s it has introduced a new department to deal with systems engineering and computer hardware and software. Since its inception GK has been awarded many design prizes in fields as diverse as prefabricated housing, street furniture, sign systems, design for the handicapped, audio equipment, electrical industrial machinery, machine tools, shop display and research studies.

Honda has sidestepped import quotas by licensing production abroad. The Triumph Acclaim, a re-badged Honda Ballade, appeared on the British market in 1981. This marked the reversal of the position of the Japanese motor industry at the end of the Second World War, when Nissan was producing cars under licence from Austin. Automobile production at Honda commenced in 1962 with the introduction of the lightweight T-360 truck and the S-360 sports car, but it was not until the launch of the highly successful Honda Civic small saloon of 1972 that the company could rightly, in industrial design terms, be said to have matured. Over a number of years the Honda Civic series won many awards for car and styling design from all over the world, culminating in 1984 when the Civic three-door model was presented with the Ministry of Trade and Industry's Good Design Grand Prize, the first such award to a Japanese motor manufacturer.

During the 1970s Honda introduced a system called SED (Sales, Engineering and Development). Geared to the presentation of new products onto the market, small project teams were selected from the three relevant departments to evaluate consumer needs and to develop the products together with appropriate mass-production technology. The first item to evolve from this system was the 1976 Honda Accord, which was aimed at an older and more affluent market than that catered for by the Civic. It must be remembered, however, that there were many other factors which underlay Japan's industrial renaissance in the 1960s and 1970s. The Japanese car industry developed new systems of factory organization and production which were less labour-intensive than those of its international competitors; it managed at the same time to maintain high levels of manufacturing accuracy and flexibility in adapting to market requirements.

The Sony Corporation has built up a reputation for design and innovation since the 1950s, when it began to train its own designers. After bringing together the management of advertising and product-planning in a single design department in 1961, a consistent design image was soon established, characterized by clean, satin-finished steel fascias and casings. As the company grew in size, designers were dispersed into the separate company divisions (as was the norm in most other Japanese firms), but in 1978 the design direction was refocused on the Sony PP Centre and fully re-integrated under one management in 1985. Much emphasis has been placed on research and

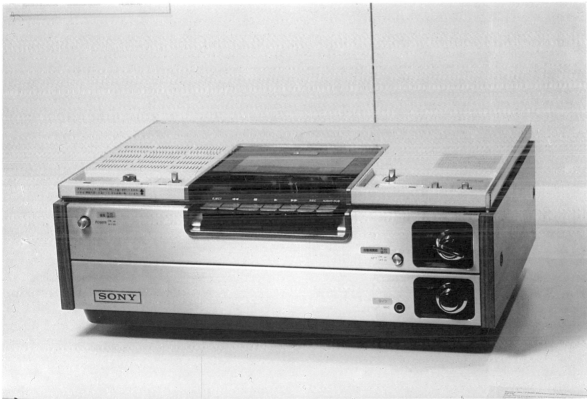

Above and left Walkman cassette player (1979), ICF-111 radio (1970) and SL-7300 Betamax video cassette recorder (1975). These products demonstrate Sony's crisp 'technological' styling and marketing acumen.

development (R and D) as a means of maintaining a hold on the market, particularly as Sony does not have tied retail outlets on the scale of its major competitors: Matsushita, for example, has 26,000 'National' shops selling only Matsushita brands. Mr Norio Ohga, president of Sony Corporation, speaking at the 1985 Japan-USA Design Management Conference in Tokyo, declared that 'industrial design has no meaning, no matter how attractive it is, unless it is backed by technical excellence. In our case we spend about 10% of sales for R and D. I must emphasize that, although great importance should be placed on industrial design, it cannot bear fruit without the state-of-the-art technology.'

So it is that Sony, like the Sharp Corporation, has developed a number of highly successful, imaginative and pleasing designs which have heavily influenced other manufacturers in the consumer electronics field. The ubiquitous Sony

Walkman was introduced in 1979, the Profeel component television system in 1981 (with separate tuner, monitor and tape deck) and the compact disc player in 1982, all three products being widely imitated soon after their market debut. The latter, which has set new standards in sound fidelity, was developed jointly with Philips, CBS/Sony (formed in 1969 to develop software capability) and Deutsche Grammophon.

A number of important governmental initiatives have also helped to give Japanese design a more prominent profile. The most significant, the Japan Industrial Design Promotion Organization (JIDPO), was set up in 1969, inspired in many ways by Britain's Council of Industrial Design (COID). Responsible to the Ministry of Trade and Industry, JIDPO has several key duties: the dissemination of information about design through exhibitions, publications and the organization of seminars; the promotion of better standards of design in regional industries; the selection of Good Design Products (the G Mark); and the mounting of the Japan Good Design exhibitions, which show the chosen products to the public in department stores and other venues.

Good Design is seen as not only concerned with appearance, but also function, safety, price and after-sales service. The G Mark scheme, between its inception in 1957 and 1985, has endorsed 11,324 products in a number of areas, including industrial equipment, transportation equipment, audio-visual items, information equipment, articles of everyday use, medical/health/welfare design and leisure. In 1984 the rules were amended to allow foreign products to be entered and a Good Design for Foreign Products Award was created to stimulate awareness of design standards elsewhere.

Since 1975 JIDPO has been responsible for the Design Development Programme for regional industries. This (funded by both national and local governments) programme sets out to introduce design awareness and product development in small- and medium-scale enterprises. To help bolster this line of activity a Good Design (G Mark) Prize for Products in Small Industry was created in 1984. In 1985 JIDPO initiated a register of industrial designers to put small-scale industries in touch with professionals, their aim being to have by 1990 two thousand names on their books. Consideration is also being given to the future inclusion of foreign designers in the listings.

The Japan Design Foundation, another major body for the promotion of Japanese design, was formed in 1981 and based in Osaka, a key centre of manufacturing and design. Established with the approval of the Ministry of Trade and Industry, the JDF was funded by a combination of national government, local government, commerce and industry. The main purpose was to organize a biennial International Design Competition and festival in Osaka which would make Japan a new centre for design and a focal point for international exchange. The first well-publicized and successful competition was held in 1983 and attracted 1,367 works from fifty-three countries for preliminary inspection. The International Award winners were Chermayeff & Geismar Associates (USA), Maris Benktzon and Sven-Eric Juhlin (Sweden), Paola Navone (Italy), Pentagram (UK) and Mrs Margaret Thatcher, for her public encouragement of design in Britain. The International Award winners for contributions to culture and society at the second International Design Competition included Bang & Olufsen of Denmark, Bruno Munari of Italy, Philip Johnson of the USA, Douglas Scott of the UK, and also Tadashi Tsukasa of Japan.

This awareness of design has certainly born fruit for in recent years Japanese design has not merely copied the West but has also begun to challenge its supremacy. The Japanese are now producing designs as stylish and sophisticated as many of their Italian equivalents.

Britain and Scandinavia

The decline of British manufacturing industry has, paradoxically, been paralleled by a growth in design consultancies, although it is worth emphasizing that these consultancies—Fitch & Co., McColl, the Jenkins Group, Wolff Olins, for instance—tend to work on retail environments and corporate images rather than major industrial design projects. This reflects the preoccupations of a country moving into a service economy. It is significant that Terence Conran, among the most successful influences in British design during the last twenty years, merged his own independent design consultancy with his retail empire in 1985, recreating the original Conran Design Group (which had been the source of the Habitat idea in the early 1960s). Some British design consultancies have, of course, responded to the needs of industry. Pentagram, for example, was formed in 1972

Right 'Chef' food-mixers designed by Kenneth Grange for Kenwood, 1950s–1960s. Grange was one of the first British designers to be influenced by the Braun style.

Above Plastic tableware designed by David Queensberry for BEA, 1964.

from the amalgamation of two successful offices, Crosby, Fletcher Forbes and the Kenneth Grange Industrial Design Consultancy, and their commissioned industrial designs have ranged from Bendix washing-machines and Wilkinson Sword razors to Parker 25 pens and cabs for British Rail high speed trains.

The Council of Industrial Design (COID) has attempted to reflect the changing industrial and economic climate, though with limited success. During the 1960s the COID was under pressure to broaden the spectrum of its interests to include heavy engineering, machine tools and other capital equipment. In 1967 the Capital Goods Awards Scheme was introduced. Among the early winners were Marconi's Mark IV colour television camera, Lancer Brothers' Boss Mark III fork-lift truck and

Rhymney Engineering's Hy-Mac excavator.

Meanwhile, with increasing desperation as its hermetic concept of design in industry was undermined by the loss of manufacturing capacity, the Design Council initiated a 'funded consultancy scheme' in 1982, in co-operation with the Department of Trade and Industry. This partially successful gesture hoped to take advantage of the supposed wealth of design talent in Britain by subsidizing manufacturers to hire consultancy advice. It was a characteristically British whim, too little coming too late, rather like strapping an outboard motor to a drifting raft.

In Scandinavia, with its homogeneous, middle-class societies, worthy, wholesome design was prevalent at a time when the rest of European industry was restructuring itself after the Second World War. Seen and admired by Paul Reilly of the Council of Industrial Design, Scandinavian design was brought back to Britain as an aesthetic which could be applied to industry. However, as soon as Germany, Italy and Japan achieved comparable economic and social stability Scandinavian design showed itself to be lacking in stylistic novelty and technical innovation.

In the past two decades Scandinavian industrial and domestic design has been characterized by a growing concern for more systematic approaches to product development, and regard for ergonomic and environmental factors, as well as for the context of the product. During this period, many of the larger manufacturing enterprises, such as Electrolux, Gustavsberg, Saab and Volvo, have engaged their own design staffs, while others have turned to design consultancies, such as Designgruppen. In 1975 the Swedish National

Left Mark IV television camera, Marconi, 1968.

Below Scanner, Toshiba, 1983. Designed with careful attention to human needs, this won a JIDPO Good Design Award.

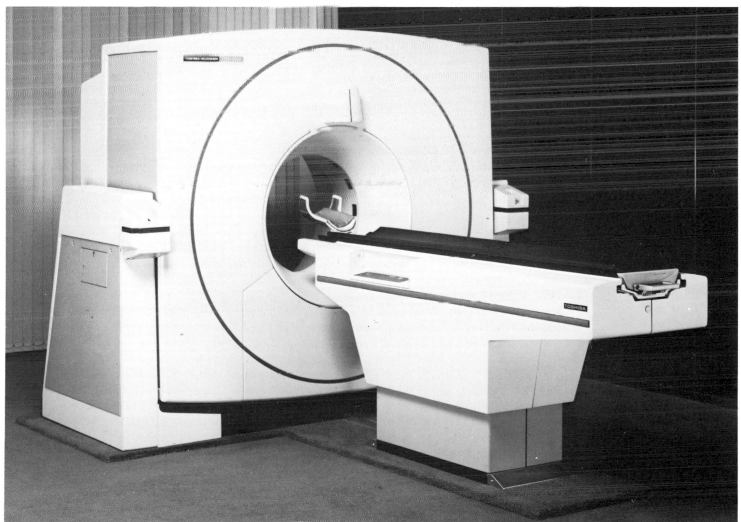

Right 610 vacuum cleaner manufactured by Electrolux, 1985. In this upright vacuum cleaner the hose is an integral part of the design and the various attachments are built into the rear of the body.

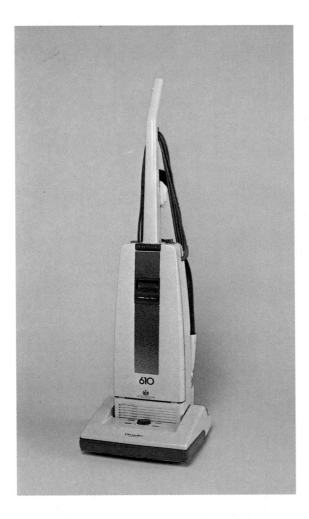

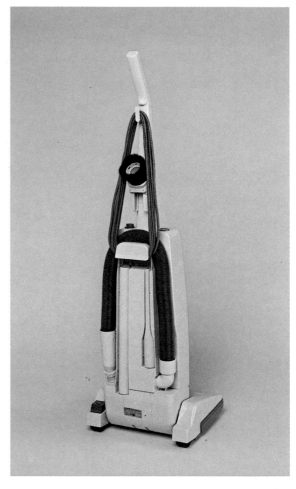

Board of Industry started an information service about designers for small- and medium-sized companies, many of them unaware of the potential role that design could play in the market place. At the same time, as in Europe and North America, many designers were becoming disillusioned with the restrictions of working for profit-orientated rather than socially motivated industries. As a result, they became involved with socially related design projects, often working with medical and handicap problems. A typical example is Ergonomi Design, founded in 1970. It is perhaps this responsiveness towards both the user and society as a whole that characterizes the best in Scandinavian design, as well as architecture.

New technology: design and products

As we have seen, the very concept of 'design' is an essentially modern one, the result of the industrial revolution which separated makers, sellers and users. Industrial design now combines engineering, materials science, inventions, art, commerce, anthropology, ergonomics and social science. The concept of 'good' design was born in the thirties

and came to prominence in the fifties, at a time when people were attempting to integrate industrial production into the existing values of taste by ascribing to a certain style particular moral attributes. It is no wonder that people became perplexed by the issue of 'good' design: the tastemakers of the period failed to recognize that as technology is now our culture it should dictate our politics.

John Ruskin, in *The Two Paths*, compared unfavourably his nightmare perception of industrialized Britain with his idealized view of Britain in the Middle Ages. Today there are two paths again; but the alternatives to growth, change and the reorganization of the means of production are not those of Ruskin and Morris, but poverty and despair. Nineteenth-century morality, aesthetics and politics will have no part to play in the future, since the restructuring of work and society is now the corollary of technological change, not mere political expediency.

Technology will bring about huge structural changes in the organization of work, means of communication, services and patterns of travel. If

in the past design was about *appearance*, then in the future it will be more concerned with *experience*. This is inevitable because the old technological revolution that brought about the system of values which created 'good' design is being replaced by one which is affecting the shape of life itself, not just the means of manufacturing. Structural changes in the means of production have produced fundamental changes in aesthetic criteria—both Marx's theories of political economy and the Modern Movement were the result of mass production and the division of labour—and the present revolution in technology, particularly in communications, will be no less important in making old values redundant.

Up to now mass production has used specialized equipment to produce standardized goods, but in the future factories will employ a more versatile robot under the control of a designer. The Japanese are pioneering the use of robots; they had, in 1979, 14,000 industrial robots, while the United States had 3,255, West Germany 850 and Great Britain 185. These robots will be capable of making infinite varieties of different products and will challenge the former assumption that economical production depends on long lead times, high volumes, low unit costs and standardization. In effect, technology is going to make a new form of 'craft' production economically feasible for the first time since the early eighteenth century.

Above A robot-operated Fiat production line in 1983.

With the computer-controlled 'flexible manufacturing systems' (FMS) of modern factories, manufacture and assembly will be so sophisticated, so flexible and adaptable to so many different roles, that a factory will not necessarily produce one particular type of merchandise. Indeed, it may not even be the property of a single manufacturing corporation, but merely an installation, owned by a service company, which will turn out furniture one day and electronic widgets the next.

These computerized factories will also be more sensitive to fluctuations in demand, for computerized tills will capture sales data from the stores and send it back to the factory. As soon as one line becomes less popular, it will be replaced by another one. Already this is happening to some extent in car production, where computer stock controls allow manufacturers to keep efficient inventories and order parts 'just in time' (a translation of the Japanese term *kan-ban*). One manufacturer says that by 1990 he will be turning over his parts stock twenty times annually against once or twice a year, as he did a few years ago.

These changes will naturally affect the role of the designer. The closer relationship between consumption and production, for instance, will re-

quire the designer constantly to monitor sales returns and modify the products in response to every variation in the consumers' tastes and demands. Also, it is now agreed that there will be structural changes in the manner in which design is practised. The old consultancies, which grew up out of the pioneering New York studios of the twenties, will have to adapt to the changing political and financial climate and become more closely involved with retailing and manufacturing—just as the advertising agencies, such as Saatchi & Saatchi, or accounting firms, such as Coopers & Lybrand, are now offering a wider range of services too. A polarity will develop in which the capital-rich interests on one side will be taking creative advice from the other.

One designer who has responded positively to these new conditions is Emilio Ambasz, an Argentinian architect living in New York. Ambasz no longer expects commissions to come to him, instead he develops his products himself. With his Vertebra chair of 1979, for instance, he sold a part of the future business to tool-makers, die-casters and upholsterers, persuading them to make tools and dies at no cost in anticipation of a share of the profits. He also carried out his own market projections, and so was able to approach the manufacturers, Castelli, with a fully costed programme. The company therefore was able to undertake the manufacture of the chair, itself a design of some ingenuity, with virtually no risk because the designer had removed much of the uncertainty from the design process. On the other hand, Ambasz took the division of labour even further with this ingenious system and reduced the role of the manufacturer. Emilio Ambasz is a quixotic figure and it is not to be expected that every other designer would wish, or even be able, to emulate this initiative. But new technology is going to lead increasingly to this kind of approach.

In the products of the future, too, there will be profound changes, especially in electronics, ground transport and aerospace. The first generation of electrically driven communications and entertainment appliances was highly derivative in style: the 1930s telephone had a neo-classical stylobate, radios and record players were initially given the mass and detailing of architecture, and early television sets resembled 1950s 'contemporary' style furniture. The arrival of the Japanese in the world market, with their taste for techno-glamour and ability to miniaturize, brought about radical changes in styling: their transistorized boxes, first in satin steel and then in black, cluttered with knobs and dials, shimmering with

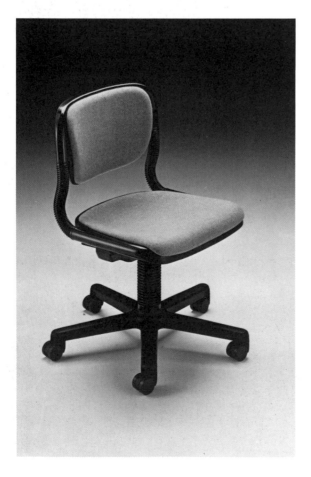

Right Vertebra chair designed by Emilio Ambasz and Giancarlo Piretti, manufactured by Castelli, 1979. This chair adapts to the shape and movement of the human body.

diodes, spawned a multitude of high-style boxes in the shops.

The pressure of market forces required the Japanese to make ever more innovations, sometimes real, sometimes apparent, in their consumer products. They were, in effect, practising planned obsolescence just as the Americans had in the fifties, but instead of Harley Earl's styling they exploited slickly packaged technology. It is already possible to predict that, instead of the array of interconnected boxes, the next generation of hi-fi and television will be integrated into one discrete unit. All the manifestations of audio and video equipment will be operated from one box, and the thin, electro-static speakers, connected by radio waves, will be visually insignificant. The video screen will also carry a teletext of the daily newspapers, of which a printer will provide a hard copy on request.

Many developments await the car of the future, for despite the problems of the oil crisis, congestion

Left Stereo radio receiver by Panasonic, 1984. Their achievements in process efficiency have enabled the Japanese to innovate new products at a rate that bewilders western competition.

Below Ford Sierra, launched in 1982. In response to the public appetite for technology, aerodynamics played a large part in the conception and promotion of this car.

Opposite **SR-71 Blackbird designed for Lockheed by Clarence L. 'Kelly' Johnson for Lockheed, 1964. One of the most sophisticated of all aircraft, its astonishing shape and performance are paradigms of industrial design.**

and pollution the car remains one of the most potent and symbolic consumer products, and the car industry fundamental to most western economies. Changing environmental and legislative conditions will force the internal combustion engine to become more efficient, for it is still at the beginning of its evolution.

The relationship between the changing preoccupations of the consumer and the intense, concentrated process of car design can be seen in the creation of the Ford Sierra in the early 1980s. The designers of the Sierra recognized that consumers had become enamoured of technology, and they therefore stressed the aerodynamic qualities of the car. Similarly, they knew that consumers are impressed by the internal environment in cars, which is often better co-ordinated and designed than that of their own homes—hence the brief, 'Make the driver feel important'.

The effect was novel, but the Sierra still used traditional technology; by 2000 aerodynamics will have been considerably improved. Wind resistance is one form of friction which bedevils efficiency,

but internal friction in the engine and other mechanisms require attention too. Weight compounds the detrimental effect of high drag and more and more components, including engines, will be of plastics.

Inside, analogue clockwork or electro-mechanical instruments will be wholly replaced by what in aerospace is called the 'glass cockpit'. Crucial information, including warnings, will be signalled to the driver when necessary via a head-up display which projects data onto the windscreen directly in front of the driver. The vehicle will be controlled by a solid-state side-stick with electronic rather than mechanical links with the steering. A voice-activated computer will control other functions and there will be sensors, linked to a radar, to warn the driver of obstacles and emergencies. Other forms of data transmission and control will be in the form of fibre-optics, instead of crude, current-carrying electrical cable which might interfere with the car's central computer.

Many of these innovations in car design will be inspired by existing practice in aerospace, but

Right **McDonnell Douglas's computer-generated 'glass cockpit', 1985. The flight path and other information are projected onto a screen directly in front of the pilot.**

meanwhile the aircraft themselves will also have changed. Plastic aircraft, the LearFan and Beech Starships, will be on the market before 1990, and new airframe configurations, with 'canard' front elevators, will make light, general aviation craft incapable of spinning. In the cockpit, electronic co-pilots will talk pilots down through the tricky parts of approaches, and there will be fewer possibilities of pilot error when the new 'glass cockpit' computers can differentiate between advisory and emergency information.

The United States Air Force is planning the development of Trans-Atmospheric vehicles (TAVs) designed for military reconnaissance from outer space (above 400,000 feet or 122,000 metres) at speeds of up to Mach 30. A TAV has the performance and capabilities of the space shuttle, but can launch itself rather as a conventional aeroplane. These will be the first genuine space-ships and, as this high technology reaches the ordinary consumer, innovations in the design of TAVs will find expression in everyday objects, just as in the past Corning's Pyroceram high-strength ovenware and Alcoa aluminium foil were developed from the Echo commercial satellite.

These are just some of the predictable developments in technology, examples of how applied science will transform our experience of the world and extend our understanding of it. But technology alone cannot create a more attractive environment. It must be applied to human purposes, and in the twenty-first century, just as in the eighteenth, the task of matching the capabilities of industry to human needs will fall to the designer.

Right **Beech Starship, 1983. Composite plastics and advanced aerodynamics create a high-performance aircraft whose shape may prove to be as influential in domestic design as Lockheed aeroplanes were in the 1940s.**

SELECT BIOGRAPHIES
SELECT BIBLIOGRAPHY
INDEX
ACKNOWLEDGMENTS

SELECT BIOGRAPHIES

ALVAR AALTO (Finnish, 1898–1976) An architect and designer of furniture and light fittings, Aalto has been a major influence on twentieth-century design, particularly in his innovative and expressive use of timber. He graduated in architecture from Helsinki Polytechnic in 1921, attended the Congrès Internationaux d'Architecture Moderne in 1929, and built his first major building, the Paimio sanatorium, between 1929 and 1933. For the sanatorium he designed the Paimio chair of bent and moulded plywood, and in 1935 he and his wife Aino Marsio established the furniture company Artek in Helsinki. Artek continues to manufacture his designs, including the tea-trolley of 1936 and the three-legged stool of 1954. Aalto's major buildings include the Baker Hall of Residence at the Massachusetts Institute of Technology (1947–9), the town hall at Säynätsalo (1949–51), the National Pensions Institute in Helsinki (1952–7) and the Hall of Culture in Helsinki (1958).

EMILIO AMBASZ (Argentian-American, b. 1943) Ambasz trained in architecture at Princeton and from 1970 was curator of design at the Museum of Modern Art, New York, where he organized the 'Italy: The New Domestic Landscape' exhibition in 1972. In 1976 he left MoMA and set up as an independant industrial designer. His award-winning designs include the Vertebra chair for Castelli of 1979 and the Osiris low-voltage spotlight for Erco (1983), both designed with Giancarlo Piretti.

PETER BEHRENS (German, 1869–1940) Initially a painter, Behrens became an architect, an industrial designer and a pioneer of the concept now known as 'corporate identity'. In the 1890s he was based in Munich, where he was a member of the Munich Sezession and a founder of the Munich Vereinigte Werkstätten. In 1899 he moved to the artists' colony at Darmstadt, where he designed not only his own house but also everything in it. From 1903 to 1907 he was director of the Düsseldorf School of Applied Art. In 1907 he became the architect for the electrical company AEG, where he remained until 1914, designing buildings such as the turbine factory of 1908–9 as well as lamps, kettles, fans, advertising and graphics. (Gropius, Mies van der Rohe and Le Corbusier all worked in his office at this period.) In 1907 he also became a founder-member of the Deutsche Werkbund. From 1922 to 1936 he taught architecture at the Vienna Academy; his house of 1925 in Northampton is one of the earliest examples of the Modern style in England. Throughout his career Behrens designed graphics, book-bindings, domestic ware, fabrics and furniture.

NORMAN BEL GEDDES (American, 1893–1958) Bel Geddes studied painting at the Art Institute of Chicago and later became an advertising draughtsman. As an industrial designer he is significant more for his polemics than his products, which were few. His designs include streamlined prototype cars, coaches, locomotives and aeroplanes, also interiors, theatre designs and radios. He published two highly influential books, *Horizons* (1932) and *Magic Motorways* (1940), and was able to realize some of his visionary ideas in the General Motors Futurama in the New York World's Fair of 1939.

MARIANNE BRANDT (German, b. 1893) Brandt studied painting in Weimar and from 1923 taught in the metalwork section run by Moholy-Nagy at the Bauhaus. At this period she designed teapots and other domestic ware, as well as light fittings, of which the most important are the wall light with a folding arm (1927) and the Kandem bedside table lamp (1928). Although her Bauhaus designs were craft prototypes, several were produced industrially. In 1949 Brandt became professor of industrial design in Dresden and later returned to her birthplace, Karl-Marx-Stadt, in East Germany.

MARCEL BREUER (Hungarian-American, 1902–81) After a brief period in Vienna Breuer moved to the Bauhaus as a student in 1920, where he became director of furniture design in 1925. Here he developed new forms for furniture, including modular storage units and chairs. His most important chair designs of this period were the Wassily of 1925 (the first tubular steel chair) and the cantilevered Cesca of 1928. Breuer moved to England in 1935, where he practised as an architect with F.R.S. Yorke and designed laminated plywood furniture for Isokon. In 1937 he emigrated to the United States to join Walter Gropius, with whom he was in partnership until 1941. He also taught architecture at Harvard until 1947. He continued to design furniture and one of his best known architectural projects is the Whitney Museum, New York, of 1966.

ACHILLE CASTIGLIONI (Italian, b. 1918) Born in Milan, Castiglioni qualified as an architect in 1944 and set up an office with his brothers Piergiacomo (1913–68) and Livio. They concentrated on exhibition and product design, and their Phonola radio was made from 1939–45. Achille became a leading champion of industrial design and was heavily involved in the Milan Triennali. From 1969 he taught industrial design in Turin Polytechnic. His designs, many of which have won Compasso d'Oro awards, include lighting for Flos (the Arco lamp, 1962), stereo equipment for Brionvega, flatware for Alessi, furniture for Kartell and the Mezzadro stool for Zanotta (1957).

SERGE CHERMAYEFF (Russian, b. 1900) Chermayeff was educated in England and worked as a journalist before becoming a designer in 1924. In 1928 he became director of Waring & Gillow's Modern Art Studio. He set up as an architect in 1931, collaborated with Erich Mendelsohn on the De La Warr Pavilion at Bexhill (1935–6), and emigrated to America in 1939 to teach design and architecture. His furniture designs include stacking tubular steel chairs for PEL, the plastic AC74 radio case for Ekco and Unit furniture for Plan Ltd.

JOE COLOMBO (Italian, 1930–71) Colombo studied painting at the Brera and architecture at Milan Polytechnic. He then became involved with avant-garde painting and sculpture before setting up his own office in Milan in 1962. A highly influential industrial designer, his projects include lights for O-Luce, furniture for Kartell, plastic storage trolleys and a complete kitchen on wheels. The 4801 armchair (1963) for Kartell was formed from three interlocking pieces of plywood, and the 4860 armchair (1967) was the first injection-moulded plastic chair.

HENRY DREYFUSS (American, 1904–72) Dreyfuss started his career as a stage designer but established an industrial design office in New York in 1929. Later he opened another branch in Pasadena, California, and the company became known as Dreyfuss Associates. Believing in designing for people, he became interested in ergonomics and developed systems of anthropometrics to analyze the needs of the human body. These theories were the basis of his books *Designing for People* (1955) and *The Measure of Man* (1959). He designed a wide range of products including ships, aircraft interiors, farm equipment and household appliances, but his most famous product is the 300 Bell telephone, which later developed into the classic model 500 of 1950.

CHARLES EAMES (American, 1907–78) One of the most influential and innovative designers of the century, Eames was the first to explore fully the potential of new materials and manufacturing techniques. He initially trained as an architect and from 1936 was first a student and then a lecturer at the Cranbrook Academy of Art. In 1940 he and Eero Saarinen won first prize for their moulded and curved plywood seating in the Museum of Modern Art's 'Organic Design in Home Furnishings' exhibition. He and his wife Ray then moved to California and established a company, Plyformed Products, to develop plywood furniture, and in 1948 Herman Miller began manufacturing his designs. In the same year Eames won second prize in the MoMA 'Low-Cost Furniture Design' competition for his stamped metal chairs which were eventually made in moulded fibreglass-reinforced polyester shells on metal legs; from 1951 the same chairs were made in woven wire. Eames's own house of 1949 was built in prefabricated industrial components as a 'case study'. In 1956 Eames produced his famous rosewood and leather lounge chair and ottoman for the film director Billy Wilder. As well as chairs, Eames designed tables and storage units, toys and exhibitions.

HARLEY EARL (American, 1893–1969) Earl was born into a family of coach builders who set up the Earl Automobile Works in 1908 and provided customized cars for Hollywood film stars. After studying at Stanford University Earl returned to car design and developed a technique of modelling car bodies from clay. In 1925 he was hired by Alfred P. Sloan of General Motors, where he remained in charge of the Art and Colour section until 1959. His most notable car designs include the La Salle of 1927, the Buick Y Job, a 'dream car' of 1937 and the Eldorado of 1959, but he also designed many other Cadillacs, Chevrolets, Pontiacs and Buicks of the period. As the motor industry's most influential stylist Earl gave expressive form to the concept of planned obsolescence.

RICHARD BUCKMINSTER FULLER (American, 1895–1983) A visionary designer with little formal training in design, Fuller was significant for his experiments in alternative technology. His few realized projects include the Dymaxion house (1927, a tensile domed structure), the Dymaxion car (1932), and a number of geodesic domes including one at Baton Rouge, Louisiana, of 1958 and that at the Expo 67 exhibition at Montreal.

EMILE GALLE (French, 1846–1904) A highly innovative and artistic glassmaker, Gallé was born in Nancy where his father had a faience and glass studio. From 1860 to 1866 he studied design, botany and mineralogy in Nancy and Weimar, and glassmaking at the Burgun & Schwerer factory at Meisenthal. He returned to Nancy to make glass and set up his own factory in 1874, later expanding into furniture manufacture. In 1901 he founded the Alliance Provinciale des Artistes, known as the Ecole de Nancy. An anthology of his writings, *Ecrits pour l'Art*, was published in 1908.

ANTONI GAUDI Y CORNET (Spanish, 1852–1926) A Catalan who worked largely in Barcelona, Gaudí was an architect and designer of furniture and fittings which combined Moorish, Art Nouveau and Gothic elements in a highly idiosyncratic manner. From 1873 to 1878 he studied architecture at Barcelona University. In 1879 he designed street lamps for Barcelona, but otherwise most of his designs were for his own buildings. His major works were the Güell Palace (1885–90), the Calvet House (1898–1904), the Batlló and Milá houses, the Güell Park (completed 1914) and finally the Sagrada Familia church, which was begun by Gaudí in 1883 and is still unfinished.

GIORGIO GIUGIARO (Italian, b 1938) After studying at the Academy of Fine Arts in Turin, Giugiaro worked for Fiat, Bertone and Ghia before setting up his own company, ItalDesign, in 1968. He is known principally for his car designs, which include the Alfa Romeo Giulia GT (1968, for Bertone), the Alfa Romeo Alfasud (1971), the Volkswagen Golf (1974) and the Fiat Panda (1980) as well as experimental and sports cars. Ital Design has also designed sewing-machines, cameras, watches and pasta.

MICHAEL GRAVES (American, b. 1934) An architect and furniture designer, Graves studied architecture at Harvard and has taught at Princeton since 1962. In the early 1970s he was included in the 'New York Five' (a group of architects at that time dedicated to re-exploring the Purism of Le Corbusier) and was largely known for his architectural drawings. Since then his career has taken a very different direction. He is now the leading American Post-Modernist and his many commissions include the Public Services Building in Portland, Oregon (1982), and the Humana building, Louisville, Kentucky (1982–5); also furniture for Memphis and Sunar, and a tea service for Alessi.

EILEEN GRAY (Irish, 1878–1976) Gray was born in Ireland and studied at the Slade School of Art, London, before moving to Paris in 1902, where she remained until her death. She studied lacquer under the Japanese master Sagawara and designed furniture in the Art Deco style for the couturier Jacques Doucet, including the screen *Le Destin* of 1914. She then progressed to interior design and between 1922 and 1930 had her own shop, the Galerie Jean Désert. Her work became more Modernist and she designed an abstract interior for the Salon des Artistes-Décorateurs in 1923 as well as three houses in the south of France, notably E–1027 at Roquebrune (1927–9). In the 1960s there was a modest revival of interest in her work and her designs are now in production again.

299

WALTER GROPIUS (German-American, 1883–1969) A highly significant figure in twentieth-century design, Gropius was a designer and teacher who sought to incorporate into architecture and design the methods of mass production and the needs of society. He studied in Berlin and Munich before becoming a pupil of Behrens in 1907. Three years later he set up his own practice with Adoph Meyer, designing the Fagus shoe factory in 1910 and a model factory for the Deutsche Werkbund exhibition in 1914. On the recommendation of van de Velde he became director of the Bauhaus in Weimar in 1919 and in 1925 he designed the new Bauhaus building in Dessau. Another important project of this period was the working-class housing scheme in Siemensstadt, Berlin. He resigned from the Bauhaus in 1928 and emigrated to Britain in 1934, where he set up practice with Maxwell Fry and built the Impington Village College near Cambridge. Gropius then went on to America and was professor of architecture at Harvard from 1938 to 1952. He also had a practice with Marcel Breuer and established The Architects Collaborative (TAC) in 1946. His early work was influenced by Expressionism but later he adopted the International Style wholeheartedly. He also designed furniture, including some for Isokon, and domestic ware.

AMBROSE HEAL (British, 1872–1959) Heal was educated at Marlborough College and apprenticed to a cabinet maker before joining the family firm of furniture and bedding retailers in 1893. Three years later he began to sell his own furniture in the store and in 1898 published his first catalogue, *Plain Oak Furniture*. He became chairman of Heal's in 1913 and was one of the founders of the Design and Industries Association in 1915. Until the 1930s he adhered to the principles of the Arts and Crafts movement, but he then began to sell and design furniture in the Scandinavian and Modern styles.

JOSEF HOFFMANN (Austrian, 1870–1956) Hoffmann studied architecture in Vienna and Munich, and was a pupil of Otto Wagner. In 1897 he was one of the co-founders of the Vienna Sezession and in 1903 of the Wiener Werkstätte. From 1899 to 1941 he was professor of architecture in the School of Applied Arts in Vienna. Influenced by Mackintosh he developed a strictly rectilinear version of Art Nouveau, of which the most notable examples are the Purkersdorf sanatorium of 1903 and the Palais Stoclet in Brussels of 1905–11. He also designed the Austrian pavilions for the 1914 Deutsche Werkbund Cologne exhibition and the 1925 Paris exhibition. His other work includes furniture, glass and metalwork, the latter executed by the Wiener Werkstätte.

VICTOR HORTA (Belgian, 1861–1947) As an architect and designer of furniture and decorative fittings, Horta was one of the initiators of the Art Nouveau style. He studied architecture in Ghent, Paris and Brussels. His Tassel House of 1892–3 was the first full-blown expression of Art Nouveau, followed by the Hotel Sôlvay (1895–1900) and the Maison du Peuple (1896–9) in Brussels. He also designed a shop front for Samuel Bing which was never executed. Later Horta's work became more classical and he taught rather than practised architecture.

CLARENCE L. JOHNSON (American, b. 1910) The aircraft designer 'Kelly' Johnson studied aerodynamics and structures at Michigan University and joined Lockheed as a tool designer in 1933. He then became chief engineer, chief designer and finally, in 1969, senior vice-president of Lockheed. His designs include the Lockheed P–38 (1938), the P–80 Shooting Star (the first American jet fighter, 1943) and the C–130 Hercules transport plane and the SR–71 Blackbird. The revolutionary forms of his aircraft greatly influenced other designers in the styling of a wide range of objects.

PHILIP JOHNSON (American, b. 1906) In 1932 Johnson, with Henry-Russell Hitchcock, organized an exhibition at the Museum of Modern Art in New York that was to be the first major representation of the International Style in the United States. Ten years later he completed his studies at Harvard and graduated as an architect, building his own Miesian house in 1949. From 1946 to 1954 Johnson was director of the architecture and design department in MoMA. Johnson was Mies's leading champion in the English-speaking world and thus played a major role in spreading the International Style. But later he rejected this style and advocated a return to historicism. His major buildings include the New York State Theater for the Lincoln Center (1962–4) and the AT&T building (1978) in New York, one of the first and most controversial monuments of Post-Modernism.

FLORENCE SCHUST KNOLL (American, b. 1917) A close friend of Eero Saarinen, Knoll trained at Cranbrook and at the Illinois Institute of Technology under Mies van der Rohe. With her husband Hans Knoll she set up the Knoll Furniture Company (later Knoll Associates) in 1943 and ran the company after his death in 1955 until her retirement in 1965. Through Knoll she produced furniture for corporate interiors – her own designs as well as revivals of Bauhaus classics and new work from Harry Bertoia, Eero Saarinen and others. Florence Knoll's own interiors include the Connecticut General Life Insurance Company, Hartford, and the CBS headquarters, New York (1964).

RENE LALIQUE (French, 1860–1945) Working in a naturalistic Art Nouveau manner, Lalique was a successful jewellery designer supplying such firms as Boucheron and Cartier, and also the shop of Samuel Bing. After his appearance at the 1900 Paris exhibition he was much imitated by other designers, but having been commissioned to design a range of scent bottles for François Coty he gradually turned his attention to glass. He set up a glass factory in Combes-La-Ville near Paris in 1909, and founded another in Alsace in 1918. He had his own pavilion at the 1925 Paris exhibition and in 1932 supplied glass and chandeliers to the *Normandie*; but he is best known for his vases, lights, scent bottles and car mascots of pressed glass.

LE CORBUSIER (CHARLES-EDOUARD JEANNERET) (Swiss-French, 1887–1965) An architect, furniture designer, theorist and abstract painter, Le Corbusier had enormous influence on twentieth-century design. He studied architecture and worked in the offices of Auguste Perret in Paris (1908–9) and Peter Behrens in Berlin (1910). His first publication was *Vers une architecture* of 1923, followed by *L'art décoratif d'aujourd'hui* (1925), *La ville radieuse* (1935) and others. In 1917 he settled in Paris, where he became associated with Amadée Ozenfant with whom he formed the concept of Purism and published a periodical, *Esprit Nouveau*. It was at this period that he assumed the name Le Corbusier. In his Pavillon de l'Esprit Nouveau for the 1925 Paris exhibition Le Corbusier displayed furniture by Thonet and other mass-produced items. He then went on to design furniture with Charlotte Perriand. Their designs for the 1929 Salon d'Automne employed tubular steel and combined modernity with luxury; they included the 'siège à dossier basculant' and the 'fauteuil grand confort'. Le Corbusier designed little furniture after the 1930s. Le Corbusier's architecture can be divided into two phases. In the first, Purist phase he concentrated on mass-produced housing (e.g. the Dom-ino system, 1914), town-planning (e.g. the Ville Contemporaine of 1922) and private houses, usually raised on pilotis, such as the villas at Garches (1927) and Poissy (1929–31). Other buildings from this period include the Salvation Army Hostel in Paris, the Maison Swisse for the Cité Universitaire in Paris (1930–2), consultancy work for the Ministry of Education building in Rio de Janeiro, and, in 1947, work on the United Nations headquarters in New York. The most notable buildings of Le Corbusier's second, more sculptural and expressive phase include the Unité d'Habitation in Marseilles (1946–52), the chapel at Ronchamp (1950–5) and the Law Courts and Secretariat at Chandigarh, India (1951–6). The Unité was based on Le Corbusier's Modulor system of harmonic proportions derived from the human figure.

ARTHUR LAZENBY LIBERTY (British, 1843–1917) The son of a draper, Liberty became an assistant in Farmer & Rogers' shop in Regent Street, London, becoming manager of their Oriental Warehouse in 1862. In 1875 he opened his own shop in Regent Street, selling goods in a variety of oriental and revivalist styles. In 1884 he supplied stock to Serrurier-Bovy in Belgium and in 1889 opened a shop in Paris. He became a leading figure in the English Arts and Crafts movement and, under the influence of E.W. Godwin, the dress reform movement. His stock included fabric designs by C.F.A. Voysey, silver by Archibald Knox and, from 1894, the Cymric range of silver. Though he was not a designer, the Liberty style was readily recognizable and in Italy Art Nouveau is often called 'Stile Liberty'.

RAYMOND LOEWY (American, 1893–1986) Born in Paris, Loewy studied electrical engineering at Paris University and the Ecole de Lanneau before emigrating to New York in 1919. He worked as a window dresser for Macy's, as a fashion illustrator and as a commercial artist before setting up his own industrial design company in 1929. His first important design, the Gestetner duplicating machine, was marketed from 1933 to 1949; his first car design dates from 1930; his highly successful Coldspot refrigerator for Sears Roebuck was marketed from 1934 and in the same year a full-scale mock-up of his office featured in the Museum of Modern Art, New York. In 1947 he appeared on the cover of *Time* magazine and four years later wrote his autobiography, *Never Leave Well Enough Alone*. Loewy virtually established the industrial design profession in the States and proved the benefits of styling in successful marketing; his work includes the Lucky Strike cigarette packet (1940), the Pepsodent toothpaste packet (1945), the Dole Coca-Cola dispenser (1948), the streamlined S–1 locomotive for the Pennsylvania Railroad and designs for the Greyhound bus company.

ADOLF LOOS (Austrian, 1870–1933) An architect and designer of furniture and other domestic objects, Loos is best known as a theorist who decried the use of ornament in any modern design. He studied building and from 1893 to 1896 visited America. He then returned to Vienna to work as an architect in Otto Wagner's office; his best known buildings include the Goldmann & Salatsch store of 1910 in Vienna and the Café Museum of 1899. In 1897 he began to write for various periodicals and his famous article 'Ornament and Crime' dates from 1908. From 1920 to 1922 he was chief housing architect in Vienna. Although a pioneer of Modernism, he also exhibited neo-classical tendencies and his entry for the 1922 Chicago Tribune Tower competition took the form of a giant Doric column.

EDWIN LUTYENS (British, 1869–1944) Working in a number of historicist styles, including neo-Palladian, neo-Baroque and medieval, Lutyens was the leading British official architect in the first three decades of the twentieth century. His large output includes country houses in the Arts and Crafts manner (notably Munstead Wood for Gertrude Jekyll, 1896, and Deanery Gardens, 1899), buildings in Hampstead Garden Suburb and flats in Westminster, London (1928). Between 1912 and 1927, in collaboration with Sir Herbert Baker, he was architect of the imperial capital in New Delhi, India, built in a monumental classical style but with details taken from Moghul architecture.

CHARLES RENNIE MACKINTOSH (British, 1868–1928) An architect and designer, Mackintosh was educated at the Glasgow School of Art and qualified as an architect in 1899. He designed a series of houses in the Glasgow area, including Windyhill, Kilmacolm, (1899–1901) and Hill House (1902–3), but his major work was the Glasgow School of Art of 1897–9 with its extensions of 1907–9. He also designed four tea rooms in Glasgow for Miss Cranston, including the Willow Tea Rooms of 1904. He began designing metalwork and graphics in 1893, inspired by the work of Voysey, Beardsley and Jan Toorop illustrated in *The Studio*, and subsequently, along with his wife Margaret Macdonald, he designed furniture and fittings for his own interiors. His work, in a delicate, rectilinear Art Nouveau manner, was scorned by the Arts and Crafts movement but much admired on the Continent. In 1900 he participated in the Vienna Sezession exhibition, where his work had a particular impact on Josef Hoffmann, and in 1901 he was awarded a special prize in a competition organized by Alexander Koch's magazine *Zeitschrift für Innen-Dekoration* to design a house for a connoisseur. His work was also exhibited in Budapest, Munich, Dresden, Venice, Moscow and Turin, and was widely featured in art journals on the Continent. Mackintosh left Glasgow in 1914 and settled in London, where he designed textiles for Foxtons and the interior of a house in Derngate, Northampton, in 1916. In 1923 he moved to France and devoted himself to painting.

ERICH MENDELSOHN (German-American, 1887–1953) Having studied in Berlin and Munich, Mendelsohn set up in practice in 1912. His early work, notably the Einstein Tower in Potsdam of 1921, was Expressionist in style, but he later became influenced by the International Style. He completed a number of stores and other buildings in Germany before moving to England in 1933, where he built the De La Warr Pavilion in Bexhill (1935–6) with Serge Chermayeff. He moved to Israel in 1934, and then to America in 1941, where he built the Maimonides Hospital in San Francisco (1946–50).

LUDWIG MIES VAN DER ROHE (German-American, 1886–1969) A pioneer of Modernism in architecture and furniture design, Mies was the son of a stonemason and studied architecture informally in Berlin. From 1908 to 1911 he worked in Behrens' office along with Le Corbusier and Walter Gropius. He then worked in Holland, where he was impressed by the work of H.P. Berlage, and in 1919 joined the revolutionary Novembergruppe in Germany. His work at this period was influenced by Expressionism and includes projects for glass skyscrapers. In 1926 he became vice-president of the Deutsche Werkbund and the following year organized their Stuttgart exhibition. Here he showed his tubular steel cantilevered MR chairs influenced by the work of Mart Stam. In 1929 he designed the German pavilion for the International Exhibition in Barcelona, installing his own X-framed, steel, glass and leather furniture. The Barcelona chair is still in production and has been made by Knoll Associates since 1947. Mies's Tugendhat house in Brno of 1928–30 also included furniture of his own design. From 1931 Mies's furniture and that of Lilly Reich, his collaborator, was produced by Thonet-Mundus. In 1930 Mies succeeded Gropius as director of the Bauhaus where he remained until its closure in 1933. In 1938 he emigrated to the United States (becoming a citizen in 1944) to be director of the Illinois Institute of Technology in Chicago. His later buildings include Crown Hall (1952–6) for the Institute, the Farnsworth house, Plano (1950), the Lake Shore Drive apartments, Chicago (1948–51), and the Seagram tower, New York (1958). In 1947 Philip Johnson organized a retrospective of his work at the Museum of Modern Art, New York.

LASZLO MOHOLY-NAGY (Hungarian, 1895–1946) After the First World War Moholy-Nagy abandoned his law studies and took up painting in Budapest. In 1919 he moved to Vienna and Berlin and over the following few years was in close contact with members of the Constructivist, De Stijl and Dada groups. In 1923 Gropius invited him to join the Bauhaus, where he ran the metal workshop and later the primary course. At the Bauhaus he made films, edited books on design theory and designed typography for Bauhaus publications. He moved to London in 1935, where he worked as a designer for the *Architectural Review*, and then settled in Chicago as director of the New Bauhaus, later the Chicago Institute of Design. He set up his own school in 1939 and also practised as an industrial designer.

KOLOMAN MOSER (Austrian, 1868–1918) From 1888 Moser studied painting at the Academy in Vienna and then design in the School of Applied Arts. In 1897 he was a founder-member of the Vienna Sezession and he designed stained glass and other decoration for the Sezession building of 1898. From 1900 to his death he was a professor at the School of Applied Arts and in 1903 he and Josef Hoffmann founded the Wiener Werkstätte. Although best known as a painter and book illustrator (he contributed to *Ver Sacrum*), he also designed furniture, glass, textiles and jewellery in a rectilinear Art Nouveau style, much of it executed by the Wiener Werkstätte.

GEORGE NELSON (American, 1907–86) Having graduated in architecture from Yale University in 1931, Nelson travelled to Europe where he became familiar with the work of the Modern Movement; in 1935 he published articles in *Pencil Points* about Le Corbusier and other European architects. In 1945 he became the design director of Herman Miller and later he introduced Charles Eames to the company. Nelson's own work includes the Storagewall (1945), which first brought him to the attention of Herman Miller, the Sling sofa and the Action Office (1964), as well as other articles such as lamps and dinnerware. He was also an influential writer and a leading figure at the International Design Conferences at Aspen.

MARCELLO NIZZOLI (Italian, 1887–1969) Nizzoli studied painting, architecture and decoration at the School of Fine Arts in Parma and made his first public appearance as a painter in the Nuove Tendenze exhibition of 1914 (which included the work of Sant'Elia). His Art Deco silk shawls were shown at the Monza Biennale in 1923 and later at the 1925 Paris exhibition. At this period he also designed posters and from 1938 he worked in the advertising office of Olivetti. Later his product designs for Olivetti included the Summa 40 adding machine (1940), the Divisumma 24 adding machine (1956), and two typewriters, the Lexicon 80 (1948) and the Lettera 22 (1950). He also designed sewing-machines for Necchi and lighters for Ronson (1959). For Olivetti he also worked as an architect and an exhibition designer.

ELIOT NOYES (American, 1910–1977) After graduating from the Harvard School of Architecture, Noyes worked in the office of Marcel Breuer and Walter Gropius. On Gropius's recommendation he then became first director of industrial design at the Museum of Modern Art in New York and in 1940 was responsible for the 'Organic Design in Home Furnishings' exhibition, featuring the work of Eames and Eero Saarinen. After the war he worked briefly for Norman Bel Geddes and then set up his own office in 1947. Among his earliest clients was the IBM corporation and in 1956 he was appointed corporate design director of IBM, responsible for product development and the appointing of architects and other designers for the company; his own work for IBM included the Selectric typewriter of 1961. Noyes also worked for other major corporations, including Mobil, Xerox and Westinghouse, and from 1965–70 was president of the International Design Conference at Aspen. His belief in the efficiency and value of Modern functional design was highly influential.

JOSEPH MARIA OLBRICH (Austrian, 1867–1908) From 1890 Olbrich studied architecture at the Academy of Fine Arts in Vienna and from 1893 he worked as an assistant to Otto Wagner, along with Josef Hoffmann. In 1897 he and Hoffmann, Wagner and Moser established the Vienna Sezession and the following year Olbrich designed the exhibition building. In 1899 he moved to the artists' colony in Darmstadt, where he became in effect the leader of the group and designed many buildings including the Ernst Ludwig House (1901) and the Wedding Tower of 1908. He also designed the Darmstadt exhibit at the 1900 Paris exhibition. His last major building was the Tietz department store in Dusseldorf (1907–8). He also designed furniture, posters, cutlery, lighting and fully integrated interiors.

CHARLOTTE PERRIAND (French, b. 1903) Perriand studied interior design at the Ecole de l'Union Centrale des Arts Décoratifs, attending courses by Paul Follot and Maurice Dufrène. In 1927 she exhibited her design for a avant-garde roof-top bar at the Salon d'Automne and on the strength of this was employed in Le Corbusier's atelier, where she worked until 1937 and collaborated in his designs for metal furniture. In 1938 she went to Japan to advise on industrial design, staying until 1945. She designed a prototype kitchen for Le Corbusier's Unité d'Habitation in 1951 and was also responsible for interiors for Air France.

PAUL POIRET (French, 1879–1944) Born in Paris, Poiret was apprenticed to an umbrella maker and became a dress designer after meeting Jacques Doucet in 1896. He later worked for Worth and set up on his own in 1904. In 1910 he visited Vienna, where he met Josef Hoffmann, and in 1912 he established the Atelier Martine for the design and manufacture of textiles and wallpapers by working girls. At the 1925 Paris exhibition Poiret had three barges decorated with hangings by Dufy. A keen self-publicist, he commissioned brochures of his work, *Les Robes de Paul Poiret racontées par Paul Iribe* (1908) and *Les Choses de Paul Poiret vues par Georges Lepape* (1911). Poiret was a major influence on the development of Art Deco, popularizing the new colours introduced by the Ballets Russes and rejecting the stiff, formal clothes of the nineteenth century for a looser, often vaguely oriental, style.

GIO PONTI (Italian, 1892–1979) Trained as an architect, Ponti is known as an architect, industrial designer and design propagandist. From 1923 to 1930 he produced ceramics for Richard-Ginori Doccia; his later work includes the Superleggera chair for Cassina (1957), the coffee-machine for La Pavoni (1949), a garden light for Arredoluce (1957) and sanitary ware for Ideal Standard (1954). His major architectural work is the Pirelli tower in Milan of 1955–8. In 1928 he became the founder editor of *Domus*, which he edited until his death as well as writing numerous books and articles. From 1925 he was director of the Monza Biennale, which moved to Milan in 1933 to become the Milan Triennale; he was an instigator of the Compasso d'Oro award, a co-founder of the Associazione per il Disegno Industriale and, from 1936, a professor of architecture at Milan Polytechnic.

DIETER RAMS (German, b. 1932) Having begun work as a joiner Rams trained as an architect and interior designer at the Werkkunstschule in Wiesbaden. As a result of his involvement with the Hochschule für Gestaltung he joined Braun as chief designer in 1955. His work for Braun includes many domestic appliances, such as food mixers, razors and radios, and he pioneered the concept of 'product families' in which products such as hi-fi units are separate yet interchangeable. The clarity of approach and detail of his work has had considerable influence in Japan.

GERRIT RIETVELD (Dutch, 1888–1964) Rietveld was the son of a cabinet maker and established his own business in Utrecht in 1911. At the same time he studied architecture under P.J. Klaarhamer, a follower of H.P. Berlage. Through Klaarhamer he met Bart van der Leck and Robert van't Hoff, founder-members of De Stijl, and in 1916 he designed furniture for the latter, influenced by Frank Lloyd Wright. In 1917 Rietveld joined De Stijl and in the same year designed the celebrated red-blue chair. His other furniture and architectural designs of the period (e.g. the plywood sideboard, 1919, and the Schröder house, 1924) are close in spirit to De Stijl. As an architect he was a founder-member of the Congrés Internationaux d'Architecture Moderne in 1928. He continued to experiment with materials and methods in furniture design throughout his life, producing designs which were sculptural and deliberately un-functional, for instance the zigzag chair of 1934. Since 1971 Rietveld's furniture has been produced by Cassina.

JACQUES-EMILE RUHLMANN (French, 1879–1933) A leading furniture and interior designer of the 1920s, Ruhlmann trained as a painter and began making furniture in 1901. He exhibited at the Salon d'Automne from 1913 and established his own company, Etablissements Ruhlmann et Laurent, in Paris after the First World War. The work of the company was of very high quality and included all the traditional skills of upholstery, japanning etc. Ruhlmann also designed silks, carpets, textiles, lighting and interiors. At the 1925 Paris exhibition he displayed his wares in the Hôtel du Collectionneur and he also designed the study in the Ambassade Française.

GORDON RUSSELL (British, 1892–1980) Russell was reared in the tradition of the Cotswolds Art and Crafts, going to school in Chipping Campden where Ashbee's School of Handicraft was established, and later working in his father's antique repair workshop. He then came in contact with the Design in Industries Association and in 1926 founded his own furniture company in Broadway, Worcestershire. In 1929 he opened a shop in Wigmore Street, London, for the sale of his furniture and also that of Thonet, Aalto and others. At this period he became more interested in Modernism and in mass production. His work became plainer, and was no longer entirely handmade, and he manufactured a series of radios in the Modern style for Murphy. In 1942 he joined a Board of Trade commission on the establishment of the Utility furniture scheme and in 1947 became the second director of the Council of Industrial Design, opening the Design Centre in 1956.

EERO SAARINEN (Finnish-American, 1910–61) The son of Eliel Saarinen, Eero moved to the United States in 1923 with the rest of his family. He studied sculpture in Paris and architecture at Yale, graduating in 1934. After this he worked as a furniture designer for Norman Bel Geddes and in 1936 returned to the Cranbrook Academy of which his father was director. With Charles Eames he won prizes in the 1940 'Organic Design in Home Furnishings' competition in the Museum of Modern Art, New York. As a teacher at the Cranbrook Academy from 1939 to 1941 he met Florence Knoll, and his later designs for Knoll Associates included the Womb chair of 1948, the elegant plastic and aluminium Tulip chair of 1957 and the Pedestal furniture of 1958. The organic shapes and experimental use of materials and technology that characterize his furniture could also be seen in his architecture. Until 1950 he worked in his father's practice and his later, better known, projects include the General Motors Technical Centre at Warren, Michigan (1951–55), the TWA terminal at the John F. Kennedy airport, New York (1956–62), and Dulles airport, Washington DC (1958–62).

ELIEL SAARINEN (Finnish, 1873–1950) Having studied architecture at Helsingfors Polytechnic Saarinen set up his own partnership in 1896. He designed the Finnish pavilion at the 1900 Paris exhibition and between 1904 and 1914 built his most notable work, the railway station in Helsinki. At this period he was in contact with Olbrich, Behrens and Julius Meier-Graefe and in 1913 he joined the Deutsche Werkbund. In 1923 he moved to the United States, having won second prize in the Chicago Tribune Tower competition. Two years later he joined the Cranbrook artistic community and in 1932 became president of the Cranbrook Academy of Art, for which he designed the buildings. With his wife Loja he also designed his own house with its furniture, textiles, lights and metalwork. His later work in the States includes Christ Church, Minneapolis (1949).

RICHARD SAPPER (German, b. 1932) Born in Munich, Sapper studied engineering and economics and worked for Daimler-Benz before moving to Milan in 1958. There he worked in Gio Ponti's office and collaborated with Marco Zanuso in designing for Brionvega. From 1970 to 1976 he was consultant to Fiat and Pirelli, and in 1972, with Gae Aulenti, he began an investigation of new systems of urban transport. In 1980 he became product design consultant to IBM. Though primarily interested in high-technology products such as microprocessors, his domestic designs include work for Kartell, Alessi (the Bollitore kettle, 1983) and Artemide (the Tizio lamp, 1972).

SKIDMORE, OWINGS & MERRILL One of the largest architectural practices in the United States, with branches in New York, Chicago and elsewhere, SOM combines commercial success with technical excellence. Its most distinguished designer is Gordon Bunshaft (b. 1909), who became a partner in 1945 and whose work is Miesian in style. SOM's best known buildings include Lever House, New York (one of the first curtain-walled skyscrapers, completed 1952), the Hilton Hotel, Istanbul (begun 1952), the United States Air Force Academy, Colorado Springs (begun 1955) and the Banque Lambert in Brussels of 1959.

ETTORE SOTTSASS JR. (Italian, b. 1917) The son of an architect, Sottsass was born in Innsbruck and studied in Turin Polytechnic, graduating in 1939. In 1947 he opened his own office and in the following years worked on interior design and housing projects for the INA–Casa scheme. In 1956 he visited America and worked for George Nelson and the following year became a design consultant for Olivetti. In the 1960s he became interested in alternative and 'anti' design. In 1980 he formed Sottsass Associati with a number of young architects and in 1981 started the Memphis movement, manufacturing furniture, lights and ceramics by designers all around the world, including Michael Graves and Arata Isozaki. The impact of Memphis was profound and brought about a reassessment of conventional ideas of good taste. Sottsass's work (for Olivetti, Knoll, Memphis, Studio Alchymia, Arredoluce and Alessi) combines – sometimes in the same product – practical functionalism and symbolic, provocative expressionism.

MART STAM (Dutch, b. 1899) Stam studied drawing in Amsterdam and worked as an architectural draughtsman in Rotterdam until 1922. In the following years, moving to Berlin, Switzerland and Paris, then returning to Amsterdam, he was associated with Bruno Taut, Hans Poelzig and El Lissitsky. In 1923 he contributed to a Bauhaus exhibition and from 1925 to 1928 wrote articles for the Constructivist journal *ABC*. In 1924 he invented the first tubular steel cantilevered chair, but this was not produced until 1926. In 1927 he designed three houses for the Deutsche Werkbund's Stuttgart exhibition and in the same year was a co-founder of the Congrès Internationaux d'Architecture Moderne. He was involved in the 'Neue Frankfurt' project in the 1920s and in similar town-planning projects in the Soviet Union in the 1930s. From 1948 he taught and then retired in 1966.

WALTER DORWIN TEAGUE (American, 1883–1960) Born in Indiana, Teague studied art in New York and worked in an advertising agency before setting up his own graphic design office in 1911. In the mid-twenties he began working as an industrial designer and in 1928 acquired his first major client, Eastman Kodak, for whom he designed the Baby Brownie camera in 1933. Other clients included Ford and Texaco, and his most notable designs include the Scripto pen and Pullman coaches for the New Haven Railroad. In 1939 he designed six pavilions, including Ford's, for the New York World's Fair. His influential book *Design this Day* was published in 1940 and in 1944 he was a founder-member and first president of the American Society of Industrial Designers. After the Second World War his office, by then large and successful, was run by Frank de Giudice who was responsible for designing interiors for Boeing.

HENRY VAN DE VELDE (Belgian, 1863–1957) A theorist, architect and prolific designer of furniture, graphics, textiles, porcelain etc, van de Velde was one of the instigators of Art Nouveau in Belgium. He was born in Antwerp and studied painting at the Antwerp Academy (1881–84) and in Paris. As a painter he was associated with the work of such Post-Impressionists as Seurat, Signac, Van Gogh and Gauguin. In 1892 he abandoned painting and began designing embroideries, book-bindings and book illustrations. His first architectural project was his own house of 1895 in Uccle for which he designed furniture influenced by William Morris and the English Arts and Crafts movement. In the same year he designed interiors for Samuel Bing's shop in Paris. His designs were widely acknowledged, published in progressive journals and exhibited successfully over the following years. He established his own decorating firm and factory near Brussels and projects in this period included an office for Meier-Graete's Maison Moderne and the Habana Company shop in Berlin. In 1900 van de Velde moved to Berlin and he remained in Germany until 1914, becoming artistic advisor in Weimar in 1901 and professor of the School of Applied Art two years later. (His successor when he resigned in 1914 was Walter Gropius.) In 1907 he was a founder-member of the Deutsche Werkbund but he failed to reach an agreement with Hermann Muthesius over the principles of the Werkbund, believing that the standardization and extensive mechanization advocated by Muthesius would curtail artistic expression in design. In 1926 he settled in Brussels, where he founded the Institut Supérieur des Arts Décoratifs in 1926. He was professor of architecture at Ghent from 1926 to 1936 and his last notable project was the Kröller-Müller Museum at Otterlo in Holland (1937–54). In 1947 he retired to Switzerland and in later years he preferred to stress his role in the creation of Modern design rather than his Art Nouveau work for which he is chiefly remembered.

ROBERT VENTURI (American, b. 1925) Educated at Princeton and the American Academy, Rome, Venturi is now a partner in his own architectural practice Venturi & Rauch. His buildings include Guild House, Philadelphia (1963), and the Dixwell Fire Station, New Haven (1970), but he is better known for his publications, *Complexity and Contradiction in Modern Architecture* (1966) and *Learning from Las Vegas* (1972), which were a major influence on the development of Post-Modernism. In 1983 he designed a silver tea service for Alessi and in 1984 furniture for Knoll.

CHARLES ANNESLEY VOYSEY (British, 1857–1941) Voysey trained as an architect in the offices of J.P. Seddon and others before setting up his own office in 1882. At the same period he began designing wallpapers, under the influence of William Morris and Arthur Mackmurdo. He joined the Art Workers' Guild and in 1888 exhibited wallpapers and fabrics at the Arts and Crafts Exhibition Society. He continued to design furniture, metalwork, wallpapers, printed textiles, carpets and tiles up to the 1930s. Between 1888 and the outbreak of the First World War Voysey also built a series of houses, notably The Orchard, Chorleywood (1899), for which he often designed all the furniture and furnishings. His unassuming and informal vernacular style was much admired on the Continent, particularly by Hermann Muthesius and Henry van de Velde, and it influenced the development of both Art Nouveau and the Modern Movement.

WILHELM WAGENFELD (German b. 1900) Having trained as a silversmith Wagenfeld joined the Bauhaus in 1923 and studied metalwork under Laszlo Moholy-Nagy. There he designed lamps and tea services, the latter manufactured by Walter & Wagner of Schleiz from 1925 to 1930. He taught at the Bauhaus from 1926 to 1931 and then moved to Berlin where he taught at the Berliner Kunsthochschule until 1935. His work for the Jenaer Glasworke commenced in 1930 and includes the celebrated glass tea service of 1932 which is still in production. From 1935 he also worked for Vereinigte Lausitze Glaswerke, designing their glassware and devising a campaign for its promotion. From 1932 he was chief designer for the Fürstenberg porcelain factory and in 1950 he moved to Stuttgart. His later work includes porcelain for Rosenthal and plastic tableware for Lufthansa. Wagenfeld has been steadfast in his belief in Modernism and the role of mass production and his work has been highly influential.

OTTO WAGNER (Austrian, 1841–1918) Initially a pupil of Gottfried Semper, Wagner became professor of architecture at the Academy of Vienna in 1894. As a teacher he was an important influence on Josef Hoffmann, Joseph Maria Olbrich and Adolf Loos and therefore contributed to the Sezession movement. His dislike of ornament and belief in the rational use of materials and building techniques are demonstrated in his buildings, notably Karlsplatz Station, Vienna (1894), the Post Office Savings Bank, Vienna (1904–6), and the Steinhof Asylum church (1906).

TAPIO WIRKKALA (Finnish, 1915–86) Wirkkala studied sculpture at the Helsinki Institute for Arts and Crafts (of which he was later director from 1951–4) and then worked as a sculptor and graphic artist. In 1947 he began his long association with the Iittala glassworks and in 1955 worked for a short time for Raymond Loewy. His work includes cutlery, lighting, silver for Christofle, ceramics for Rosenthal and others and glassware for Venini; for this he has won many prizes at the Milan Triennali.

FRANK LLOYD WRIGHT (American, 1869–1959) Wright worked as a draughtsman in the office of Louis Sullivan from 1888 to 1893. In 1889 he built his first house in Oak Park, Illinois, which was followed by a series of houses in the Chicago area (including the Winslow house, 1893, the Charnley house, 1891, and the Robie house, 1908) which established the form of the 'prairie' house. Believing in totally integrated interiors, he designed the furniture, lights, stained glass and all other fittings for his houses and other buildings. Wright's highly original approach to form, space and ornament, usually in an uncompromisingly geometric style, was influenced by Sullivan, the English Arts and Crafts movement and Japanese design. He visited Japan in 1905 for the first time and Europe in 1909, where his work, through the Wasmuth publications of 1910–11, was admired by the pioneers of the Modern Movement. The major buildings of his long and prolific career include the Larkin building, Buffalo (1904), for which he designed the first metal office furniture, Midway Gardens, Chicago (1913), the Imperial Hotel, Tokyo (1916–20), the Johnson Wax building, Racine (1936–9), and the Guggenheim Museum, New York (designed in 1942 and completed in 1960). He was influential as a teacher and writer and founded an educational establishment, the Taliesin Fellowship, in 1929.

SELECT BIBLIOGRAPHY

Aloi, Roberto. *Esempi di arredamenti, architetture e decorazioni d'oggi di tutto il mondo*. 6 vols. Milan, 1950–3.

Amaya, Mario. *Pop as Art*. London, 1965.

Ambasz, Emilio (Ed.). *Italy: The New Domestic Landscape*. New York, 1972.

Arnell, D., and Bickford, T. *James Stirling: Buildings and Projects*. Introduction by Colin Rowe. London, 1984.

Banham, Reyner. *Theory and Design in the First Machine Age*. London and New York, 1960.

Banham, Reyner. *The Architecture of the Well-Tempered Environment*. London, 1969.

Banham, Reyner. *Age of the Masters: A Personal View of Modern Architecture*. London, 1975.

Banham, Reyner. *Megastructure: Urban Futures of the Recent Past*. London, 1976.

Banham, Reyner. *Design by Choice*. New York, 1981.

Battersby, Martin. *The World of Art Nouveau*. London, 1968.

Battersby, Martin. *The Decorative Twenties*. London, 1971.

Battersby, Martin. *The Decorative Thirties*. London, 1969.

Bayley, Stephen. *In Good Shape: Style in Industrial Products 1900 to 1960*. London, 1979.

Benton, Tim and Charlotte, with Sharp, Dennis. *Form and Function: A Source Book for the History of Architecture and Design 1890–1939*. Milton Keynes, 1975.

Branzi, Andrea. *The Hot House: Italian New Wave Design*. London, 1984.

Brunhammer, Yvonne. *1925*. Paris, 1976.

Bush, Donald J. *The Streamlined Decade*. New York, 1975.

Clark, Robert Judson (Ed.). *The Arts and Crafts Movement in America 1876–1916*. Princeton, 1972.

Clark, Robert Judson et al. *Design in America—The Cranbrook Vision 1925–1950*. New York, 1983.

Conrads, Ulrich (Ed.). *Programmes and Manifestos on 20th-century Architecture*. London, 1970.

Curtis, William. *Modern Architecture since 1900*. Oxford, 1982.

De Noblet, Jocelyn. *Design: introduction à l'histoire de l'évolution des formes industrielles de 1820 à aujourd'hui*. Paris, 1974.

Doblin, Jay. *One Hundred Great Product Designs*. New York, 1970.

Dorfles, Gillo. *Il disegno industriale e la sua estetica*. Bologna, 1963.

Drexler, Arthur, and Daniel, Greta. *Introduction to Twentieth Century Design from the Collection of the Museum of Modern Art*. New York, 1959.

Drexler, Arthur. *Charles Eames: Furniture From the Design Collection, the Museum of Modern Art*. New York, 1973.

Drexler, Arthur. *Transformations in Modern Architecture*. New York, 1979.

Emanuel, Muriel (Ed.). *Contemporary Architects*. London, 1982.

Farr, Michael. *Design in British Industry: A Mid-Century Survey*. Cambridge, 1953.

Ferebee, Ann. *A History of Design from the Victorian Era to the Present Day*. New York, 1970.

Frampton, Kenneth. *Modern Architecture: A Critical History*. London 1980; revised and enlarged 1985.

Garland, Madge. *The Indecisive Decade*. London, 1968.

Garner, Philippe (Ed.). *Phaidon Encyclopedia of Decorative Arts 1890–1940*. Oxford, 1978.

Garner, Philippe. *Contemporary Decorative Arts from 1940 to the Present*. New York, 1980.

Giedion, Sigfried. *Mechanization Takes Command: A Contribution to Anonymous History*. New York, 1948.

Giedion, Sigfried. *Space, Time and Architecture*. Cambridge, Mass., 1971.

Grassi, Alfonso, and Pansera, Anty. *Atlante del design italiano: 1940–1980*. Milan, 1980.

Gropius, Walter. *The new architecture and the Bauhaus*. London, 1935.

Herbst, René. *25 Années U.A.M.*. Paris, 1956.

Heskett, John. *Industrial Design*. London, 1980.

Hiesinger, Kathryn B., and Marcus, George H. (Ed.). *Design Since 1945*. New York, 1983.

Hitchcock, Henry-Russell. *Architecture, Nineteenth and Twentieth Centuries*. London, 1958.

Hoffmann, Herbert. *Intérieurs Modernes de Tous les Pays*. Paris, 1930.

Hogben, Carol. *British Art and Design 1900–1960*. London, 1983.

Jencks, Charles. *Modern Movements in Architecture*. London, 1973.

Jencks, Charles. *The Language of Post-Modern Architecture*. London, 1977; 4th edition 1984.

Jencks, Charles, and Chaitkin, William. *Current Architecture*. London, 1982.

Jervis, Simon. *The Penguin Dictionary of Design and Designers*. London, 1984.

Kron, Joan and Slesin, Suzanne. *High-Tech: The Industrial Style and Source Book for the Home*. New York, 1978.

Lampugnani, V.M. (Ed.). *The Thames and Hudson Encyclopaedia of Twentieth-Century Architecture*. London, 1986.

Le Corbusier. *Towards a New Architecture*. London, 1937; reprinted 1946.

Lenning, Henry F. *The Art Nouveau*. The Hague, 1951.

Lorenz, Christopher. *The Design Dimension*. Oxford, 1986.

MacCarthy, Fiona. *All Things Bright and Beautiful*. London, 1972.

McFadden, David Revere (Ed.). *Scandinavian Modern Design 1880–1980*. New York, 1982.

Madsen, Stephen Tschudi. *Sources of Art Nouveau*. New York, 1956.

Moreau, Charles (Ed.). *L'Art International d'Aujourd'hui* (20 vols). Paris, n.d. (circa 1930).

Pevsner, Nikolaus. *Pioneers of Modern Design from William Morris to Walter Gropius*. London, 1949.

Philadelphia Museum of Art (Ed. Kathryn B. Hiesinger). *Design Since 1945*. Exhibition catalogue, 1983; London, 1983.

Quénioux, Gaston. *Les Arts Décoratifs Modernes*. Paris, 1925.

Schmutzler, Robert. *Art Nouveau*. New York, 1962.

Schweiger, Werner J. *Wiener Werkstätte Kunst and Handwerk 1903–1932*. Vienna, 1982.

Selle, Gert. *Ideologie und Utopie des Designs. Zur Gesellschaften Theorie der Industriellen Formgebung.* Cologne, 1968.
Spaeth, David. *Mies van der Rohe.* New York, 1985.
Sparke, Penny. *Consultant Design.* London, 1983.
Tafuri, Manfredo, and Dalco, Francesco. *Modern Architecture.* London, 1980.
Venturi, Robert. *Complexity and Contradiction in Architecture.* New York, 1967.
Watelet, Jacques-Gregoire (Curator). *Art Nouveau Belgique.* Brussels, 1980.
Watkin, David. *Morality and Architecture.* Oxford, 1977.
Wingler, Hans M. *The Bauhaus.* Cambridge, Mass., 1969.
Windsor, Alan. *Peter Behrens, Architect and Designer, 1868–1940.* London, 1981.
Wolfe, Tom. *The Kandy-Kolored Tangerine-Flake Streamline Baby.* London, 1968.

INDEX

ABS stacking units (Castelli Ferrieri) 280
AEG (Allgemeine Elektrizitäts Gesellschaft) 6, 9, 9, 72-4
A4 *Mallard* (Gresley) 149
AT & T tower, New York (Johnson) 226-8, *226*, 231
Aalto, Alvar 105, 121-2, *122*, 153, 162-4, *164*, 185, *185*
Abacus screen (Mills) 180, *180*
Academy of Art, Copenhagen 185
Adenauer, Konrad 194
Adler, Rose 110, 112
Adnet, Jacques 124
advertising 6, 247, *270*, 292
aerospace industry 68, 134-7, 142, 200, *204*, 296
Aesthetic movement 40
'Aesthetics of the Product, The' exhibition, Milan 188
African art 112
Agnès 113
Ahlers-Hesterman, Friedrich 40
Ahmadabad 164
Aicher, Otl 195, 196
Air Force One 133
airbrush illustration *267*
aircraft 71, 133, 134-7, 142, 148, *149*, 200, *203*, 204, *204*, 294-6, *295*, *296*
airline meals service, SAS (Persson) *210*, 211
Akari lamp (Noguchi) 265
Alaïa, Azzedine 277
Albers, Josef 120
Albert, Prince 19
Albini, Franco 188
Alchymia, Studio 272, *273*, 282
Alessi 262
Alfa Romeo 199
Alfasud (Giugiaro) 281
Giulia GT (Giugiaro) 280
Alix 124
Alix, Charlotte 118, 122
Aloi, Roberto 176
alphabet, Bauhaus 91-2, 120
Altes Museum, Berlin (Schinkel) 234
aluminium *118*, 120
Amaya, Mario 248
Ambasz, Emilio 260-1, 292, *292*
America, South 159
America, United States of
and architecture 6, 10, 25-6, 28, 36, 82, 87, 99, 101, 151, 152-9, 162, 164-7, 214, 216-18, 226, 228, 236, 245
and decorative arts 43, 58-60, 107, 114-16, 168, 171-5, 179, 181, 249, 251, 255, 268, 270
and industrial design 81, 76-9, 128-37, 145, 192, 200-4, 264, 291, 293-6
American Graffiti 255
Amsterdam 36, *36*

Anarchy in the UK 259
Anchorage teapot (Shire) 275
Antelope chairs (Race) *180*
'anti-design' 263-4
Antonioni, Michelangelo 270
Apple store, Baker Street, London (Fool) 259
April greetings card (Greiman) 275
Apslund, Gunnar *26*, 27, 105
Arab-Israeli war 225
Aram 264
Arbeitsrat für Kunst 138
Arbus, André 124
Archigram group 236-7, *238*, 245
Architects Collaborative, The 159
Architectural Association 236-7
Architectural Review 60
architecture and urban design 10-37, 82-105, 116, 152-66, 214-45
L'Architettura della Città (Rossi) 235-6
Archizoom 263
Arcosanti 218
Arens, Egmont 192
Arflex 177, 199
Arizona project (Soleri) 218, *218*
Arnold, William 70
Arp, Jean *88*, 91, 167
Arredoluce 177
art, fine 117, 169, 178
Art Deco 81, 62, 63-7, 102, 106-13, *152*, 228, 245
L'Art Décoratif 45
Art et Décoration 45, 247
Art and Industry (Richards) 115
Art and Industry exhibition, Stockholm 74
Art Nouveau 6, 9, 28-35, 40, 43-62, 74, 256
Art and Technique of Colour Photography, The 175
Art Workers' Guild 60
Artek 121-2
Arteluce 177, 278
Artemide 261, 276, 278, 280
Arts and Crafts movement 14-17, 38-43, 185, 268
in America 59, 115-16, 171
and Deutsche Werkbund 74
and Hoffmann 34
influence 32, 34, 56, 58, 62, 67, 68, 70, 147, 207
and Lutyens 27
and Mackintosh 32
and Morris 28, 38
and Voysey *11*
Arup Associatees 226, *226*
Ashbee, C.R. 39, *39*, 53
Aspen 192
Association of Austrian Visual Artists 32
Associazione per Il Disegno

Industriale (ADI) 189
Atelier Martine 64, 67, 112
Atelier Pomone 111
Atelier Primavera 110
Atlanta 236, *236*
atrium *236*
Audit of War, The (Barnett) 148
Aulenti, Gae 262, 276, *276*, 279
Austin 284
Australia 162, 223, *223*
Australian Embassy, Paris (Seidler) 223
Austria 29, 57 *see also* Vienna
Austro-Daimler 144
autobahns 145
autostrade 145
Automobile Association showroom, Southampton (Fitch) *286*
Avedon, Richard 175, *253*
aviary, London Zoo (Price) 237

BBPR 215
BEA plastic tableware *288*
BMW engine 148
Bacon, Francis 121
Baes, James *246*, 272
Bagge, Eric 111
Bailey, David, 248
Baker Hall of Residence, Massachusetts Institute of Technology (Aalto) 164, *185*
Bakst, Léon 62, 64, *64*, *65*
Baldwin, James *253*
Balenciaga, Cristobal 182-3, *182*, *183*, 277
Ballets Russes 63, *64*, 118, *119*
Balmain, Pierre 182
Bang & Olufsen 286
Banham, Reyner 23, 170, *170*, 174, 191, 208, 248
Bantam Special camera (Teague) 130, *130*
Barbier, George 110, *110*
Barbini, Alfredo 178
Barcelona 29, *29*, 229, *229*
exhibition 81, *81*, *94*, 95, 120
Barlow & Ordish 20, *20*
Barnett, Correlli 148
Barnsley, Sidney 39
baroque style 126
Barr, Alfred H. 133
Barragan, Luis 159
Barry, Sir Charles 10, 19
Bartlesville tower, Oklahoma (Wright) 166
Barzini, Luigi 196
batik 62, *62*
Battersby, Martin 63
Bauhaus 6, 91-4, 146, 159, 196
in America 201
closure 141, 196
foundation 14, 138
and furniture 120, 138, *139*
influence *145*, *148*
manifesto 14, *14*

and Modernism 81, 82, 116, 118
origins and forerunners 57, *68*, 117
principles 81, 95, 138, 185, 195, 225, 252, 253
and Russia 89
Bavarian Soviet 137
Bayer, Herbert 91, 120
Bazaar boutique, Chelsea, London 248
Beardsley, Aubrey 43, 48, 58, 59
'Beat' collection (Saint Laurent) 182
Beatles 259, *259*
Beaton, Cecil 124, *124*, 183, 185
Beaubourg (Centre Georges Pompidou), Paris (Piano & Rogers) 237, *238*, 239, 241
Beauté-France scheme 191
Becket, Welton 236
Bedford Park, London (Shaw) 15, *15*
Beech Starship 296, *298*
'Beggarstaff Brothers' 39
Behrens, Peter 6, 9, 9, 36-7, *37*, 213,
and applied arts 71, 72-4, *73*
and colleagues 82, 94, 96, 138, 139
in Darmstadt 57-8
early work 32, 33, 35, 56
Bel Air convertible (Earl) 202
Bel Geddes, Norman 129, 132, *132*, 134
Belgium 9, 29, 50-2, 53, 191, 219-20 *see also* Brussels
Bell, Vanessa 67, *67*
Bell Telephone Laboratories 194
Bell 300 telephone (Dreyfuss) 132-3, *132*
belle époque 27
Bellini, Mario 261, 280, *280*
'Belvedere' room, Milan-Naples express (Zavanella) *178*
Bendix washing machines 288
Benito, Edouard Garcia *112*, 113
Benktzon, Maris 286
Benois, Alexandre 62
Benson, W.A.S. 40
bentwood furniture (Thonet) 138, *139*
Benz Patent Motor Car *72*
Bérard, Christian 'Bébé' 124
Berger, John 208
Berlage, Hendrikus Petrus 36, *36*, 86-7
Berlin 37, *37*, 82, 92-3, 105, 152
Motor Show 144
Berliner Tageblatt building (Mendelsohn and Neutra) 101
Berman, Eugène 124
Bernadotte, Count Sigvard 187, 211
Bernhardt, Sarah 48
Bertoia, Harry 116, 171

Bertone, Giuseppe 'Nuccio' 199, 280
Bertoni, Flaminio *145*
Bestegui, Charles de 125, 183
Betjeman, John 60
Bexhill 102, *102*
Bexleyheath *13*
Bianconi, Fulvio 178, *178*
Biennale, Venice 264
Bijvoet, Bernard 98, 99
bikini (Fiorucci) *250*
Bill, Max 195, 196, 253
Bing, Samuel 32, 43–4, *43, 44*
Birolli, Renato *170*
Bismarck, Count Otto von 77
Black, Misha 148, 205, 207
Blake, Peter 249
Blast 67
Blomfield, Sir Reginald 104–5
Blow-Up 270
Boeing 204
    707 aircraft *203*
Bofill, Ricardo 228–30, *229, 231,* 235
Bogardus, James 17
Boldini, Giovanni 48
Bon Marché 111
Bonetto, Rodolfo 279, 280
book-binding 110
book design 253
Booth, George C. 115–16
Bordeaux 99
Borsani, Osvaldo 177, *177*
Bosch, Hieronymus 218
Boshier, Derek *248,* 249
Boss fork-lift truck 288
Boston
    Government Services Center (Rudolph) 224
    old market 226
Botta, Mario 236, *236*
Boulanger, Pierre 145, 189
Boullée, Etienne-Louis 89, 236
Bourdin, Guy 270, *271*
Bouval, Maurice 47
'Box of Pin-Ups' (Bailey) 248
Bradley, Will 58, *58, 59*
Brando, Marlon 247–8, *248*
Brandt, Edgar 106, 108, 109
Brandt, Marianne 118, 120, *138*
Brandt, Paul 122, *123*
Branzi, Andrea 263–4, 272
Brasilia 159
Braun 191, 192, *195,* 196, 209, 288
Braun, Artur *195,* 196
Brazil 105
Breslau 141
Breuer, Marcel *118, 139,* 173
    in America 153, 159, 223
    at the Bauhaus 116, 120, 138
    in England 102, 120
    influence 253, 276
    at Weimar school 91
brick 95
brick house design (Mies van der

Rohe) 94
Brionvega 196, 262, 278, *278,* *279,* 280
Britain
    and architecture 10, 12–17, 19–20, 26, 29, 34, 152, 214, 215, 221, 230–1, 236–42
    and decorative arts 38–43, 116, 168, 178–81, 185, 246–9, 251, 254, 255
    and industrial design 69–71, 147–9, 204–8, 286, 287–8, 290, 291
'Britain Can Make It' exhibition 206, 207
British Motor Corporation *188*
British Plastics Design Advisory Service 204
British Rail high speed trains (Pentagram) 288
Brno 95
Brodovitch, Alexei 174–5, 253
Brunel, Isambard Kingdom 19
Brunelleschi, Filippo 228
Brunhammer, Yvonne 63
Brussels 28, 29, *30,* 32, 34, *34,* 43, 219–20, *219*
Brustio, Cesare 188
Brutalism 160
bucket, plastic (Colombini) 189, *279*
Buddensieg, Tilman 73, 139
Buffalo 82
Bugatti, Carlo 50
Buick Le Sabre (Earl) 200, *202*
Buildings and projects (Arnell & Bickford) 234
Bullerswood *39*
Bunshaft, Gordon 156, *158,* 223
Burkhalter, Jean 111, 122
Burnham, Daniel 25
Burton, Decimus 19
Buthaud, René 110
Butterfield, William 13
Byker housing scheme, Newcastle (Erskine) 221, *223*

CPS/Sony 286
cabinet (Süe et Mare) *110*
Cadillac cars *170,* 282
Café l'Aubette, Strasburg (van Doesburg) 87, *88*
Café Unie, Rotterdam (Oud) 87
calculator, Olivetti (Nizzoli) *196*
Calder, Alexander 169, 180
calendar, Pentax (Feurer) *271*
California *99, 166, 247*
Cambridge, University of
    Christ's College, residences (Lasdun) 222, *223*
    history faculty building (Stirling) 215, *215*
cameras 130, *130,* 194, 213, *213*
    television 288
Canon Camera Company 194, 283

Canon T–90 *213*
Canon V camera 194
Capital Goods Awards Scheme 288
Capitello chair (Studio 65) *264*
Carling beer 133
carpet design (Gray) *118*
Carson, Pirie, Scott building, Chicago (Sullivan) 10, *24,* 25
Casa Batlló, Barcelona (Gaudí) 29, *29*
Casa del Fascio, Como (Terragni) *105*
Casa Milá, Barcelona (Gaudí) 29
Casabella 146, 147
Casati, Cesare 262, 264
casino, Pampulha (Niemeyer) 159
Cassandre, A.M. 122
Cassina 177, 199, 261, *261,* 262, *262,* 280
Castel Béranger *45*
Castelli 292, *292*
Castelli, Giulio 279
Castelli Ferrieri, Anna 262, 279, 280
Castiglioni, Achille 177, 262, 264, 277, *278,* 279
Castiglioni, Piergiacomo *177,* 189, 262, 279
Castle, Wendell 268
Castle Drogo, Devon (Lutyens) 26
Catalan monument, Le Perthus (Bofill) 230
Catalogue of Plain Oak Furniture (Heal) 40
Catholic University of Louvain, Brussels (Kroll) 219, *219*
Central School of Art and Design, London 70
Centre Georges Pompidou *see* Beaubourg
Centrokappa school system 280
ceramics
    in America 268
    in Britain 39, *146,* 180, 207, 268
    in France 45–7, 110
    in Italy 178, *179*
    in the Netherlands 62
    in Sweden 74–5, 187, 211
    in Vienna 114
Chadwick, Hulme 208
Chagall, Marc 91
chair(s)
    Antelope (Race) 180
    Barcelona (Mies van der Rohe) 81
    Cab (Bellini) *261*
    'Chickenwire' (Bertoia) *171*
    dumb-valet (Wegner) 186
    (Eames) *172, 201*
    (Graves) *272*
    Gufram (Gilardi) *251*
    Gufram (Studio 65) *264*

Kartell (Zanuso and Sapper) *279*
    (Kjaerholm) *253*
    (Le Corbusier and Perriand) *122*
    '1919' (Rietveld) 116, *116*
    red-blue (Rietveld) 87, *88, 116*
    (Saarinen, Eero) *172, 252*
    Sindbad (Magistretti) *262*
    Synthesis, Olivetti (Sottsass) *280*
    Vertebra, Castelli (Ambasz and Piretti) 292, *292'*
chaise-longue
    (Borsani) *177*
    (Breuer) *118*
    (Le Corbusier and Perriand) *122, 123*
Chalk, Warren 237
Chambers, Sir William 230
Chandigarh government centre, Punjab (Le Corbusier) 162
Chanel, Gabrielle 'Coco' 118, *119*
Chanin building, New York 116
Chap-Book, The (Bradley) 58
chapel, Ronchamp (Le Corbusier) 160, 162, *151*
Chareau, Pierre 98, 99, 101, 112, 122
Charpentier, Alexandre 47
Chasnik, Ilja *118*
Chatsworth, Derbyshire 19
Chéret, Jules 48
Chermayeff, Serge 102, *102,* 120, 148
Chermayeff & Geismar Associates 286
Cheti, Fede 178
Chevrolet *128, 129, 202*
Chiattone, Mario 84–5
Chicago 23, *24,* 25, 29, 93, 154, 156, 214, 223–4, 268
    Hancock tower (SOM) 223, 224
    Illinois Institute of Technology (Mies van der Rohe) 154, *154,* 156
    Lake Shore Drive apartments (Mies van der Rohe) 154, *155*
    school 25
    Tribune tower 28, *28, 36,* 93, *93*
'Chickenwire' chairs and stool (Bertoia) *171*
Chorleywood *11*
'Chorus Girl' (Gruau) *183*
Choses de Paul Poiret vues par Georges Lepape, Les 64, 65
Christensen, E. Kold 253, *253*
Christiansen, Hans 58, *58*
Christ's College, Cambridge, residences (Lasdun) 222, *223*
Chrysler building, New York (Van Alen) *115,* 116, *152,* 153
Chwast, Seymour 251
cigarette-case (Brandt) *123*
Cité Industrielle (Garnier) 24, 24–5

Citroën
2CV 145, *145*, *281*
DS *189*
Type A *78*
Città Nuova 85
City office building, Portland (Graves) 228
Clarke, Henry 183
classicism 10, *10*, 37, *37*, 230, 240
Cléopâtre 64
Clinique 270, *270*
clock, wall, Junghans (Bill) 196
Clutton Brock, Arthur 70
Coard, Marcel 106, *111*, 112
coat (Balenciaga) *182*
Coates, Wells 104, 120, *147*, 148
Cobden-Sanderson, T.J. 39, *41*
'cockpit, glass' 294, *295*
Cocteau, Jean 125
coffee-machine, La Pavoni (Nizzoli) 199, *199*
coffee and milk pots (Devlin) *181*
Coffey, Michael 268
Colani, Luigi *213*
Cole, E.K. Ltd (Ekco) 147, *147*
Cole, Henry 19
Colefax; Lady 124
Coleman, Alice 220
Colin, Paul 122
Collins, Jesse 148
Cologne 35
exhibition 82, *83*, *84*, 85
Colombini, Gino 189, 279
Colombo, Joe 262, *262*, 265, 279
Colonna, Edouard *43*, 44, 47
Colosseum 228
Commerce, Ministry of (France) 191
Como *105*
compact disc player, Sony 286
Compagnie des Arts Français, La 109
Compasso d'Oro awards, 188, 189, 279
Complexity and Contradiction in Architecture (Venturi) 216, 217
computer, desk-top, Olivetti (Bellini) 280, *280*
computerized factories 291–2
computers, 'glass cockpit' 294–6, *295*
'conceptual chic' *260*
concrete 17, 23, 24, 95, 151, *152*, 160, *221*, 222, 223, 232
Conformist tendency, Italy 261
Congrès Internationaux d'Architecture Moderne 101
Conran, Terence 287
Conran Design Group 205, 287
Constructivism *88*, 89, 90, 91, 93, *116*, 117, 215, 253
consumerism 6, 151, 246, 272
Contestation tendency, Italy 261–2
Contemporary Architects

(Emanuel) 216, 228
Contrasts (Pugin) 234
Cooper Hewitt Museum, New York 183
Cooper & Lybrand 292
Copenhagen 185, 186
Coper, Hans 180, 268, *268*
Corning 296
corsage, rattan (Miyake) 265, *267*
Costa, Lucio 159
Council for Arts and Industry 147
Council of Industrial Design 141, 168, 178, 189, 191, 204, 207, 211, 286, 288
Country Life 60
Cournault, Etienne 112
Courrèges, André 256
couture *see* fashion
craft revival 267–70
Crafts Council 268
Craftsman, The 59
Craftsman Workshops 59
Cranbrook Academy 116, 162, 168, 171
Cranston, Miss 31
credenza (Knoll) 252
Cretté, Georges 110
Creuzevault, Louis 110
Crompton, Dennis 237
Crosby, Fletcher Forbes 288
Crown Hall, Institute of Technology, Chicago (Mies van der Rohe) *154*
Crystal Palace (Paxton) *18*, *19*, 19–20, 23, 240
Cubism 67, 87, 97, 106, 117
Culture and Anarchy (Arnold) 70
curtain wall, glass 156, *158*, 214, 219, 225
cutlery 211
'Cymric' silverware 40
Czaky, Josef *111*, 112, 122
Czechoslovakia 95, 105
Czeschka, Carl Otto 114

Dacca government buildings, Bangladesh (Kahn) 164
Dadaism 264
Dahl-Wolfe, Louise 183
Daimler 72
Daimler, Adolf *72*
Daimler, Gottlieb 72
Daimler-Benz engine 148
Dali, Salvador 125, *127*
Dammouse, Albert-Louis 45–7
Danese 262
Darbourne & Darke 220, *220*
Darmstadt 32–3, 37, *37*, *41*, 57–8, *58*, 72–3, 91, 191
d'Ascanio, Corradino 196
Daum brothers 50
Davis, Arthur J. 27, 60, *60*
Day, Lucienne 180, *181*
Day, Sir Robin *181*, 208, 253
day nursery, Rio de Janeiro (Niemeyer) 159

De Havilland Comet 204
De La Warr Pavilion, Bexhill (Chermayeff and Mendelsohn) 102, *102*
de Lucchi, Michele 272
De Stijl group 67, 86–90, 93, 94, 101, 116, 117, 118, *118*, 120
Dean, James 247
Death and Life of Great American Cities, The (Jacobs) 214
Death of a Salesman (Miller) 200
Decœur, Emile 110
decorative arts 38–67, 106–27, 168–87, 245–77
Decorative Twenties, The (Battersby) 63
decorators, interior 123–6
Décorchemont, François 109
Defensible Space (Neuman) 214
Dekorative Kunst 57
de Giudice, Frank *203*
Delamarre, Jacques 116
Delta aircraft (Lippisch) 134
Den Permanente galleries, Copenhagen 186
Denmark 121, 185, 186–7, 253
Depression 6, 122–3
Derbyshire, Andrew 226
Dernière Lettre Persane, La 112
Derry & Toms, Kensington, London 116
Design 178, 208, 247
Design Centre 181, 207–8, 246
Award Scheme 191, 207
Labelling Scheme 207
design consultants 128–37, 278, 283–4, 287–8, 292
Design Council *see* Council of Industrial Design
'Design—a Function of Management' 192
Design Index 141, 208
Design and Industries Association 40, 70–1, 116, 147
Design Research Unit 205, *205*
'Design Since 1945' exhibition, Philadelphia 168, 272
'Design in Scandinavia' exhibition 185, 290
design studios 6, 110–11
Design This Day (Teague) *130*
Designgruppen 288
desk (Ruhlmann) *107*
Dessau 92, 93, *93*, 141
Destin, Le, screen (Gray) 112
Deutsche Arbeit 142
Deutsche Grammophon 286
Deutsche Kunst und Dekoration 57
Deutsche Normen Ausschuss 74
Deutsche Werkbund
conference 137
exhibitions 64, 82, *83*, *84*, 86, 95, 146
and *Die Form* 140
formation 74
influence 40, 63, 70, 116

in inter-war years 139–40
members 141
principles 85
Devlin, Stuart *181*
Diaghilev, Serge, 62, 64, *64*, 118, *119*
Dickens, Charles 128
Dinkeloo, John 224
Dior, Christian 182, *182*
dish, silver (Koppel) 187
Ditzel, Nanna 187
Dixon, James, & Sons 68
Dixwell Fire Station, New Haven (Venturi) 217
Documents de Bijouterie et Orfèvrerie Modernes (Follot) *44*
Documents Décoratifs (Mucha) *45*
Dome of Discovery 180
Dom-ino system (Le Corbusier) 97
Domus 146, 147, 175, *175*, 196, 247, 264
Dorn, Marion 118, 121
Doucet, Jacques 64, 65, 111, 112–13
Douglas, Donald 134
Douglas DC3 aircraft 142
Douro Bridge, Portugal (Eiffel) 21, *21*
Doves Press 39, 40, *41*
Drawers in irregular form (Kuramata) *264*
dress (Rhodes) *260*
Dresser, Christopher *68*
dressing-table (Heals) *146*
Dreyfuss, Henry 129, 132–3, *134*, *203*, 204
Duckworth, Ruth 268
Duco paint 129
Dufrène, Maurice 45, 63, 111
Dulles airport, Washington (Saarinen) 162, *162*
Dunand, Jean, 107, *107*, 109, *109*, 110, 112, 113
Dupas, Jean 108, 112
duplicator, Gestetner (Loewy) 131
Dupont company 129
Düsseldorf 72, 196
Dymaxion house (Fuller) 97

E.S.U. (Eames Storage Units) *201*, 204
ETR 200 locomotive 145
Eames, Charles 116, 151, *151*, *166*, 167, 171, *172*, 173, 176, 199
Eames house, California *166*, 167
Eames Storage Units *201*, 204
Earhart, Amelia 134
Earl, Harley, 81, 130, 134, 200, *202*, 293
East Anglia, University of, Norwich (Lasdun) 222, 240, *242*

East Aurora 60
Eastman Kodak 130, *130*
Ecart 276
Echo satellite 296
Eckhoff, Tias 187, 211
Eckmann, Otto 56
Ecole des Beaux-Arts, Paris 23, 24
L'Ecole de Nancy 49–50
Economist, The 222
Ecrits pour l'Art (Gallé) 48
Edison, Thomas 72, 77
Edison Illuminating Company 77, 146
Eiffel, Gustave 21–2, 29
Eiffel Tower, Paris 21–3, *22*, 88
Einstein Tower, Potsdam (Mendelsohn) *86*
Ekco (E.K. Cole Ltd) 147, *147*
Electric House (Edison Company) 146
electricity 72
Electrolux 209, *209*, 288
610 vacuum cleaner *290*
Elgort, Arthur 270
Elle 246
Elliot & Fry *71*
Elvira Photographic Studio 56
Elvis (Warhol) 247
enamelling 47, *48*
Endell, August 56
England *see* Britain
Englische Haus, Das (Muthesius) 14–15, 74
English, Michael 251, 256, *256*
English Art & Design 1900–1960 (catalogue) 38–9
English school 14–15
ephemera 273
Ergonomi Design 290
ergonomics 204, 213, 280
Ernst, Grand Duke, of Darmstadt 32, 33
Ernst Ludwig House, Darmstadt (Olbrich) 33, *33*
Erskine, Ralph 221, *223*
Erté (Romain de Tirtoff) 113
Esempi di Arredamenti, Architettura e Decorazioni d'Oggi di Tutto il Mondo (ed. Aloi) 176
Esquire 248
Essen 191
L'Esthétique Industrielle 191
Ettedgui, Joseph 254, *254*, 255
excavator, Hy-Mac 288
Existentialism 255
Expo '67, Montreal 166, 224, *224*
'Exposition Cinquantenaire de l'Exposition de 1925' 63
Exposition Internationale des Arts Décoratifs et Industriels Modernes, Paris 6, 81, 88, 99, 106–9, 122, 181
Exposition Universelle, Paris 43, *44*, 49, 181

Expressionism 6, 14, 84, 85, 86, 91, 116, 138
    Abstract 169, *171*

F–86 Sabre jet 200
Fabergé, Carl 62
Facit 211
Fagus shoe factory, Alfeld (Gropius) 82
Falling Water house (Wright), Pennsylvania 152, *152*
fan, electric, AEG (Behrens) *73*
fan heater, Braun H1 (Muller) *195*
Farnsworth house, Plano (Mies van der Rohe) 154, 156
Fascism *105*, 145–6, 196, 230
fashion 117–18, 124, 127, 272
    in America 277
    in Britain *168*, 259, *260, 276*, 277
    in France 6, 64–5, 112–13, 125, 168, 181–3, 256, 277
    in Japan 265–7, *267*, 276–7
    in Vienna 114
Fath, Jacques 182, 183
Favier, Louis 109
Federal Science Pavilion, Seattle World Fair (Yamasaki) 216, *216*
Feininger, Lyonel 14, *14*, 116
Fellini, Federico 176
Festival of Britain 6, 102, 141, 167, 168, 170, 178, 179–81, *180*, 207
    catalogue *207*
Festival Pattern Group 180
Feuillâtre, Eugène 47, *48*
Feuillets d'Art 113
Feure, Georges de *43*, 44, 47
Feurer, Hans 270, *271*
Fiat company 24, *24*, 199, 278, 280, *291*
Fiat
    'Cinquecento' 199
    500 Topolino (Giacosa) 145, *145*, 189, 199
    Nuova 500 199
    Panda (Giugiaro) 281, *281*
    Uno (Giugiaro) 281
fibre-glass 230, *230*
Figini 146
Fillmore Auditorium 256
film industry 124
Finland *105*, 121, 162–4, 186, 187, 211
Fiorucci, Elio *250*, 251
First World War 86, 94, 104, 117
Fitch & Co. *286*, 287
Flamingo Hilton, Las Vegas *174*
flash gun, Braun F60 (Rams) *195*
Fleckhaus, Willy 270
Fletcher, Alan 254
Fletcher, Forbes & Gill 205, 245, *286*
flexible manufacturing systems 291–2

Flöge, Mathilde *56*
floor polisher, Electrolux (Sason) *209*
Florence 228, 263
    railway station 145
Florey building, Queen's College, Oxford (Stirling) 215, *216*
Flos 177, 261
Flying the Arctic (Wilkins) 134
Flying Hamburger 142, *142*
'flying wing' 134, *137*
Focke-Wulf aircraft 148
Fokker Trimotor aircraft 142
folios, illustrated 108
Follot, Paul *44*, 45, 63, 111
Fondation Le Corbusier, Geneva 167
Fontana, Lucio 178, *178*
Fontana Arte 177
food mixer(s)
    Kenwood Chef (Grange) 288
    Braun M1 (Muller) 195
Fool 259
footstool (Saarinen) *172*
Forbes, Colin 254
Ford, Henry 76, 77–9, *78*, 129, 139, 145, 225
Ford
    Model A 129
    Model T 77–9, *78, 79, 128*, 129
    Sierra *293*, 294
'Fordism' 79
Foreign Office, London (Scott) 13
Föreningen Svenska Industriedesigner 211
Form, Die 74, *140*
Form ohne Ornament 140
'Formes Scandinaves' exhibition 185
'Formes Utiles' exhibitions 189
    catalogue *189*
Forstner, Leopold 57
Foster, Norman 228, *239*, 240, *242, 243*, 244, *244*, 254, *254*
Fouquet, Georges 47
Fouquet, Jean 122
Four Seasons restaurant, Seagram tower, New York (Johnson) 156, *157*
Fourrures Max, Les 112
France
    and architecture 21–4, 29, 91, 99–101, 152, *229*, 230, 237–9
    and decorative arts 43–50, 60, 63–6, 106–13, 117, 122, 168, 268
    and industrial design 145, 189–91
Francis Little house (Wright) 60
Frank, Jean-Michel 124
Frankfurt 141, *141*, 196
    Museum of Decorative Art (Meier) 236

Frankfurter Register 141
Frechet, André 111
Friberg, Berndt 187
Friedländer-Wildenhain, Marguerite *138*
Frognal house, Hampstead, London (Lucas, Connell, Ward) 104
Froisch, Robert A. 134
Fry, Maxwell 102
Fry, Roger 67
Fuller, Loïe 48, *51*
Fuller, Richard Buckminster 96, *166*, 167
Fun Palaces 237
functionalism *140*, 168–9, 187, 209, 216, 222, 252, 254, 261
Furness, Frank 25
furniture
    in America 59, *59*, 124, 171–4, *171–4*, *185*, 268
    in Britain *43*, 60, *70*, 120, 148, 168, *168*, 180, *180*, 251, 253, 268–70
    in France 62, 65, *66*, *70*, 107–9, *107*, 110, 112, 113, 124
    in Germany 118, 120, *139*, 146
    in Italy 50, 175, 177, 251, *251*, 261, 264, *264*
    in Japan 265
    in the Netherlands 118
    in Scandinavia 121, 122, *185*, 186, *186*, 253, *253*
    in Vienna 53–4, *55*, 114, 138, 139
Fürstenberg factory 141
Futurama city, New York World's Fair 127
Futurism 24, 67, 82–5, 89, 90, 117, 146

GK Industrial Design Associates 283–4
G Mark scheme, Japan 192, 286
Gabo, Naum 88
Gaggia coffee-machines 176
Gaillard, Eugène *43*, 44, *44*
Galeries de l'Art Nouveau *43*, *43*
Galeries Lafayette 111
Gallaratese housing development, Milan (Rossi) 236
Gallé, Emile 45, 48–50, *48*, *51*
Galleria, Milan 240
Gambone, Guido 176, 178, *179*
Gardella, Ignazio 279
Garden City movement 15–17, *15, 17*, 24, 84
Garnier, Jean Louis Charles 10
Garnier, Tony 24–5, *24*, 96
Gaudí, Antonio 29, *29*, 31, 50, 60, 229
Gazette du Bon Ton 113
Geichler, Dr Fritz *195*
Genazzi, Eros and Luigi 178

General Assembly Building and
  Secretariat, Brasilia
  (Niemeyer) 159
General Motors *128*, 129–30,
  134, 200, 282
  Technical Institute (Saarinen)
  162
Geneva 167
geodesic dome (Fuller) 22, *166*,
  167
German Standards Commission
  74
German State Railways 142, *142*
Germany
  and architecture 29, 37, 82, *83*,
  85, 86, *86*, 88, 91–5, 105, 231–
  4, 236
  and decorative arts 56–8, 107,
  116, 118, 120, 253
  and industrial design 6, 9, 68,
  71, 72–4, 81, 137–45, 194–6,
  280, 288, 291
Gestaltetes Handwerk 142
Gestetner *131*
Giacobetti, Francis 270
Giacometti, Alberto 124
Giacosa, Dante 145, *145*, 189,
  199
Gibberd, Sir Frederick 104
Giedion, Sigfried 26
Gilardi, Piero 251, 264
Gilbert, Cass 28, *28*
Gill, Bob 254
Giugiaro, Giorgio 280–1, *281*,
  283
Givenchy, Hubert de 182
Glaser, Milton 251
Glasgow 31
  Four *41*
  School of Art (Mackintosh) 31,
  32, *32*, 60
glass
  in architecture 19, 82, *83*, *84*,
  86, *104*, 156, *157*, *158*, 214,
  219, 225, 240, *243*
  in decorative arts 45, 47, *48*,
  48–50, *51*, *54*, 59, *59*, 109,
  117, 122, 178, *178*, 185–7,
  186, 268, *269*
  in industrial design 141, *141*,
  210, *210*, 211, 294, *295*
Glasshouse, The 268
Gloag, John 148
Gočar, Josef 105
Goldmann & Salatasch store,
  Vienna (Loos) 35
'Good Design' exhibitions 173,
  191, *191*, 284, 286
Gorell Committee on Art and
  Industry 147
Gothic style 13, 14, 20, 28, *28*,
  216, *216*, *217*
Goudissart 112
Gowan, James 215, *215*
Graham, Bruce 223, *223*
Gramophone Company, Italian

national 147
Grand Central Station, New
  York 159
Grange, Kenneth 208, 276, *288*
  Industrial Design consultancy
  288
Granny Takes a Trip, London
  (English) 256
Grant, Duncan 67
graphic arts
  in America 59, 251, 256, 273
  in Britain 121, 251, 253–4,
  256–60
  in France 183, *183*
  in Germany 9, 120
  in Italy *250*, 251, *273*
  in Japan 267
  in the Netherlands 62
Graves, Michael 228, *228*, 234,
  235, 272, *272*
Gray, Eileen 65, 99–101, 106,
  111, 112, 113, *113*, 117, 118,
  118, 122, 276
Gray, Milner 205
Great Exhibition of 1851 19–20,
  179
Green Coca-Cola Bottles (Warhol)
  251
Greene, Charles and Henry 58,
  60
Greenwald, Herbert 154
greetings cards *267*, 273
Greiman, April 275
Gresley, Nigel 148, *149*
Gretsch, Hermann 141–2
Greyhound buses 133
Gropius, Walter
  in America 153, 156, 159, *159*
  and Bauhaus 91–4, 138–9
  and colleagues 96
  early work 82, *83*, 93
  in England 102
  influence 11
  influences on 36, 37, 68, 82, *82*
  principles 96, 215, 217
  pupils 173, 201, 223, 224
  quoted 14, *14*
Grosse Schauspielhaus, Berlin
  (Poelzig) 85, *85*
Groult, André 107, *111*, 112
Gruau, René 183, *183*
Guaranty building, Buffalo 25
Guerriero, Alessandro 272
Gufram chair
  (Gilardi) 251, *264*
  (Studio 65) *264*
Gugelot, Hans 196
Guggenheim Museum, New
  York (Wright) 166, *166*
Guild of Handicraft 39, *39*, 53
Guild House, Philadelphia
  (Venturi) 217
Guimard, Hector *30*, 31, 45,
  45
Gulbenkian, Calouste 48
Gulbenkian Foundation 48

Gunma Prefectural Museum,
  Takasaki (Isozaki) *243*, 245
Gustavsberg ceramic factory,
  Sweden 74–5, *74*, *75*, 76, 187,
  211, 268, 288

H55 exhibition, Hälsingborg 210
Habitat 287
Habitat project, Expo '67,
  Montreal (Safdie) 224–5, *224*
Habraken, John 218–19
Hadlands glassworks 211
Hälsingborg 210
Hamada, K. 192
Hamilton, Richard 181, *181*,
  248, 249
Hamnett, Katharine *276*, 277
Hampstead Garden Suburb,
  London (Unwin & Parker) 15,
  16
Hancock tower, Chicago
  (Graham) 223, 224
Hansen, Johannes *186*, 187
Hapshash and the Coloured Coat
  258, 259
Hard Edge Abstraction 249–51,
  264
Haring, Hans 86
Harlow, Jean 127
Harper's Bazaar 113, 175, 183,
  246, 256
Harrods 255
Harvard School of Architecture
  156, 158, 223, 224
Haslemere 230, *230*
hat, 'shoe' (Schiaparelli and Dali)
  125, *127*
Hat stand (Jones) 248
Haus Industrieform, Essen 191
Haus eines Kunstfreundes *41*
Havinden, Ashley 121
Havinden, John *120*, 121
Hawkins, L. Weldon 49
Heal, Ambrose 40
Hébrard 50
Heinkel, Wilhelm 142
Helensburgh 31, *31*
Helsinki
  National Pensions Institute
  (Aalto) 164
  railway station (Saarinen) 35,
  35
Hennebique, François 23, *23*
Henningsen, Poul 121
Hepworth, Barbara 169
Herbst, René 122, 276
Heritage, Robert 205
Herman, Sam 268, *269*
Herron, Ron 237
hi-fi 293
  unit (Castiglioni) *278*
Hiesinger, Kathryn B. 168–9
High Museum, Atlanta (Meier)
  236, *236*
High Tech 19, 239, 254
Highpoint flats, Highgate,

London (Lubetkin) *100*, 102
Hill House, Helensburgh
  (Mackintosh) 31, *31*
Hille 253
Hillingdon civic centre
  (Derbyshire) 226, *227*
hippie cult 259
historicism 6, 213, 228
Hitachi 284
Hitchcock, Henry-Russell 10,
  153
Hitler, Adolf 93, *105*, *105*, 141,
  142–5 *see also* Nazis
Hochschule für Gestaltung, Ulm
  6, 191, 195, 196, 253, 261, 280
Hockney, David 277
Hoepli 176
Hoffmann, Josef 6, 32, 33–4, *34*,
  53, 54, *56*, *57*, 82, 96, 114
Hogben, Carol 38–9
Hollywood 124
Home Life Insurance building,
  Chicago (Jenney) 25
Honda Motor Company 283, 284
  Accord 284
  Ballade 284
  C50 motorcycle *284*
  Civic 284
  S–360 284
  T–360 truck 284
Hong Kong and Shanghai Bank
  tower (Foster) 240, *240*, 244,
  244
Honolulu house (Ossipoff) *247*
Hood, Raymond 28, *28*
Hoppé, E. O. *142*
Horizons (Bel Geddes) *132*, 134
Horta, Victor 28–9, 29, *30*, 52,
  54, 55
Hot House, The (Branzi) 264
Hotel van Eetvelde *54*, 55
House Beautiful 247, *247*
House and Garden 247
Hoyningen-Huené, George 124
Howard, Ebenezer 15, 16
Howells, John Mead 28, *28*
Howson-Taylor, James 39
Hubbard, Gilbert 59, 60
Hudson steam locomotive
  (Dreyfuss) 133, *134*
Humana tower, Louisville
  (Graves) 228, *228*
Hunstanton 167
Hy–Mac excavator 288
Hyper-Realist school 249–51,
  267

IBM 199, *200*, 201
  building (Breuer) 159
INA–Casa housing initiatives
  196
'I can see for miles' (The Who)
  259
*I wonder what my heroes think of
  the space race* (Boshier) *248*
Iceland 186

Ideal Standard *198*, 199
Iittala glassworks *186*, 187, 210, 268
Ile de France 112
Illinois Institute of Technology 154
  buildings (Mies van der Rohe) *154*, 156
illustration 113, 124, *182*, 183, *183 see also* graphic arts
L'illustration 111, 112, *113*
Independent Group 249
India *26, 27*, 105, 159, 162, 164
industrial design 68–79, 128–49, 188–210, 278–96
Industrial Design 170, *192*
Industrial Design Competition, Japan 192, *192*
'Industrial Design as a New Profession' 191
Industrial Design Promotion Council, Japan 192
Industrial Style 254, *254, 255*
Industry, Department of 211
Institut de l'Esthetique Industrielle 191
Institut für Neue Technische Form, Darmstadt 191
Institute of Industrial Arts, Finland 186
Institute of Management, Ahmadabad (Kahn) 164
Interaction Centre, north London 237, *238*
International Congress of the Societies of Industrial Design (ICSID) 188
International Design Competition, Osaka 286
International Design Conference in Aspen 192
International Style 6, 93, 104, 151, 153, 156, 159, 163, 214, 223, 276
Ipswich 240, 243
Iribe, Paul 64, 65, 112, 113
iron 17, *19*, 20, 108, 109, *141*
Isokon 120
  flats, Hampstead, London (Coates) 104
Isozaki, Arata *243*, 244–5, *245*
Israel, Marvin *253*
ItalDesign 281–2, *281–2*
Italians, The (Barzini) 196
Italy 6,
  and architecture 24, 29, 82, 84–5, 105, 160, 162, 226, 228, 235–6
  and decorative arts 50, *52*, 117, 168, 175–8, 179, 181, *250*, 251, 253, 260–5, 272, 276, 277
  and industrial design 145–7, 188–9, 196–9, *196*, *198*, 199, 278–82, 288
'Italy—The New Domestic Landscape' exhibition 260,

261, 262, 265
Itten, Johannes 91

Jackson, Holbrook 38
Jacobs, Jane 214
Jacobsen, Arne 186
Jahn, Helmut 245
Jallot, Léon *106*
James, Charles 183, *183*
James, Mrs Charles *183*
James, Edward 125, *127*
Jameson, Conrad 220
Japan
  and architecture 159, 214, *243*, 244–5
  and decorative arts 40, 43, 180, *264, 265*–7, *266*, 268, 276
  and industrial design 188, 192–4, 196, 198, 282–6, 288, 291, 292–3, *294*
Japan Design Foundation 286
Japan Design House 192
Japan Industrial Design Promotion Organization (JIDPO) 286, *289*
Japan National Railways 283
Japan–USA Design Management Conference, Tokyo 285
Japanese Export Trade Association 193
Japanese Industrial Designers Association 192
Japanese Sewing Machine Co. 192
Java 62, *62*
Jena glass (Wagenfeld) *141*
Jencks, Charles 88, 225, 272–3
Jenkins Group 287
Jenney, William Le Baron 25
Jensen, Georg 187, *187*
jet propulsion engine 204
jewellery 47, 52, 56, 109, *109*, 268
'Jewish dancer' (Bakst) *64*
Jiricna, Eva *255*
Job cigarette-paper poster (Mucha) *47*
Johansson, Willy 211
Johns, Jasper 249
Johnson, Clarence L. 'Kelly' 134, 137, *137*, 295
Johnson, Philip 153, 155, 156, 226–8, *226*, 231, 286
Johnson Wax company buildings, Racine (Wright) 152, *152*
Johnston, Edward 39
Jones, Allen *248*, 249
Joseph shops 276
  Sloane Street shop (Norman Foster Associates) 254, *254*
Jouve, Paul 110
Jugend 56, 57
Jugendstil 56–8 *see also* Art Nouveau
Juhlin, Sven-Eric 286

Junghans 196
Just what is it that makes today's homes so different, so appealing? (Hamilton) 181, *181*, 249

KG dinner service (Kåge) 75, *75*
Kagawa Prefectural Centre (Tange) 244, *244*
Kåge, Wilhelm *74*, 75, *75*, 211
Kahn, Louis 164, *165*, 216, 241, 244
Kales, Josef 145
Kamali, Norma 277
Kampfbund für Deutsche Kultur 141–2
Kandinsky, Wassily 85, 92
Kandy-Kolored Tangerine Flake Streamline Baby, The (Wolfe) 174
Karlsruhe 174
Kartell 189, 261, 262, 278, 279, *279*
Katsuyama, M. 192
Kauffer, Edward McKnight 121, *121*
Kaufmann, Edgar, Jr. 173, 191
Kawasaki 194
Kelmscott Press 40, 60
Kennedy, John F. 257
Kensal Green flats, London (Fry) 102
Kensington Church Street house, London (Chermayeff and Mendelsohn) 102
Kenwood Chef food mixers (Grange) 288
kettles
  AEG (Behrens) *73*
  Braun HE1 (Weiss) *195*
Kew 19
Kieffer, René 110
King, Perry *279*
kitchen equipment 278–9
Kjaerholm, Poul 253, *253*
Klee, Paul 92
Klein, Calvin 272, 276–7
Klimt, Gustav 32, 56, *57*
Klint, Kaare 121, 185
Knoll, Florence 116, 171, *172*, 173, 174, *252*, 253, 276
Knoll Associates *252*, 253
Knoll Furniture Company 171, *171*, 172, *172*, 173
Knox, Archibald 40
Koch, Alexander *41*, 57
Kohn, J. & J. 54
Kok, Juriaan 62
Komenda, Erwin 145
Koppel, Henning 187, *187*
Körting & Matthiesen 141
Kosta glass factory 187, 268
Kramer, Ferdinand 140, *141*
Krier, Leon 234–6, *235*
Kroll, Lucien 219–20
Krom, Joan 254
Kruckenberg, Count 142

Kubitschek, Juscelino 159
Kubus modular containers (Wagenfeld) 141
Kunst und Handwerk 57
'Kunst und Technik' (Behrens) 72
Kuramata, Shiro *264*, 265
Kurokawa, Kisho 244, *244*, 245

La Maîtrise 111
Labino, Dominic 268, 277
labour exchange, Dessau (Gropius) 93
lacquer ware *107*, 109, 110, 112, 113, 117, *123*
'Lady's Bedroom' (Groult) 107
Lagerfeld, Karl 112
Laing, Gerald 249
Lake District houses (Voysey) 14
Lake Shore Drive, Chicago (Mies van der Rohe) 154, *155*
Lalique, René 47, *47*, 48, *48*, 109, *111*, 112
lamp(s)
  Akari (Noguchi) 265
  (Brandt) *138*
  Brazil (Shire) *275*
  MT (Mattioli) *261*
  Pileo (Aulenti) *276*
  Pillola (Casati and Ponzio) *262*, 264
  Treetops (Sottsass) *275*
Lancer Brothers 288
Lancia 280
Lang, Fritz 118, *119*
Lanvin, Jeanne 113
Laporte-Blairsy, Leo 47
Larche, Raoul 47, 48, *51*
Las Vegas 170, 174, *174*
Lasdun, Sir Denys 104, *221*, 222, 223, 240, 242
Larkin building, Buffalo (Wright) 82
lattice beam principle 22
Laurelton Hall (Tiffany) 60
Lausitzer Glasverein 141
Le Chevallier, Jacques 122
Le Corbusier (Charles-Edouard Jeanneret) 6, 96–9, *99*, *104*, 106, *122*, 151
  and colleagues 36, 101, 102, 122, *123*, 159
  designs reissued 276
  forerunners 85
  in Geneva 167
  influence 132, 214, 222, 224, 225, 236, *237*, 244, *244*
  in post-war period 160, *160*
  principles 24, 97, 125, 155, 214, 220, *222*, 225
  and purism 91, *96*
  quoted 12, 160
  Russian projects 90
  in Vichy France 152
Le Perthus 230
Leach, Bernard 180, 268

League of Nations building, Geneva (Le Corbusier) 101
LearFan aircraft 296, *296*
Learning from Las Vegas (Venturi) 217
Lefebvre, André *145*
Legrain, Pierre 65, 106, 110, *111*, 112
Leicester University engineering faculty building (Stirling and Gowan) 215, *215*
Leidman, Cheyco 272
Lenin, V. I. 88, 89
  tribune project (Lissitsky) *90*
Leningrad 90
Lepape, Georges 64, *65*, 113
Letchworth Garden City 15
Lever Brothers building, New York (Bunshaft) 156, *158*, 224
Levy, Julien 124
Lewis, D. B. Wyndham 67
Lexicon 80 typewriter, Olivetti (Nizzoli) *196*, 199, 280
Liberty, Arthur Lazenby 40
Liberty & Co. 40, *40*
'Liberty' style 40, 50 see also Art Nouveau
Lichtenstein, Roy 249
Liebknecht, Karl 94, *94*
lift doors, Chrysler building (Van Alen) *115*, 116
light bulbs 72, 77
light fittings 9, 177, 261, 262 see also lamp(s)
Lindberg, Peter 270
Lindberg, Stig 187, 211
Lindstrand, Vicke 187
Lindstrom, Hugo 209
Lingotto factory, Turin (Trucco) 24, *24*
Linke, François 62
Lippisch, Alexander 134
Lissitsky, El (Lazar) 89, 90, *90*, 91
Lillington Street flats, London (Darbourne & Darke) 220, *220*
Lisbon 48
Littleton, Harvey 268
Livemont, Privat 52
Ljungstrom, Gunnar 209
Lloyds building, London (Rogers) 240, *241*
Lockheed Aircraft Company 134, 137, 204, *296*
  P–38 (Johnson) 134, *137*
  P–80
  SR–71 Blackbird (Johnson) *295*
  Shooting Star (Johnson) 137
  Super Constellation *203*
  Vega monoplane (Northrop) 134
locomotives 133, *134*, 145, 148, *149*
Loewy, Raymond 129, *131*, *132*, 133, 192, *193*, 205

London
  and architecture 13, 14, 15, *15*, *16*, 19–20, *19*, 27, 102–4, 152, 156, 219, 220, *221*, 222, 226, 237, *237*, 240, *241*
  and decorative arts 60, 116, 248, 249, 254–6, 264
  and industrial design 70–1
  University of 222
London & North Eastern Railway *149*
London School of Economics 70
'Look Out', Los Angeles *275*
Loos, Adolf 32, 34–5, *35*, 101
Lopez, Antonio 277, *277*
Los Angeles 267, *273*, *275*
  Museum of Modern Art (Isozaki) 245, *245*
Louisville 228, *228*
Louvain, Catholic University of (Kroil) 219, *219*
Lovell house, California (Neutra) 99, 101
'Low-Cost Furniture Design' competition, MoMA 173
Luban chemical factory (Poelzig) 85, *85*
Lübeck farm complex (Haring) 86
Lubetkin, Berthold *100*, 102, 222
Lubs, Dietric 276
Lucas, Connell, Ward 104
Luckenwalde hat factory (Mendelsohn) 86
Lucky Strike cigarette packet (Loewy) *132*, 133
Lufthansa 142
Lui 246–7
Lunning, Frederick 186
Lunning prize 186
Lutyens, Sir Edwin 10–11, 15, *16*, 26, 27, 105
Lux Sport 277
Luxemburg, Rosa 94, *94*
Lynes, Russell 192
Lyons 25, 107
Lysell, Ralph 209

MARS Group 152
machine, cult of *116*, 117
McColl 287
McDonnell Douglas 'glass cockpit' 294, *295*
McFadden, David Revere 183
McHale, John 248, 249
McKim, Charles Follen 10
McKim, Mead & White 10, 28
Macdonald, Frances *41*
Mackintosh, Charles Rennie 6, 9, 14, *31*, 32, *32*, 39, 40, *41*, *43*, 53, 60, 64, 81, 113
Mackintosh, Margaret Macdonald *41*
Mackmurdo, Arthur H. 43
MacLaren, Denham 120–1
Mad 248

'Mae West' decor (Dali) *127*
Magasin du Printemps 110
magazine design 6, 253
magazines, colour 246–7
Magic Motorways (Bel Geddes) 132
Magistretti, Vico 262, *262*
Magnelli, Aldo and Alberto 196
Magnusson, Erik 276
mail-order marketing 76, 77, 128
Mainichi Press, Japan 192, *192*
Maison de l'Art Nouveau, Paris 32
Maison Moderne, La 44–5, *44*
Maison du Peuple, Brussels (Horta) 29, 52
Maison de Verre, Paris (Chareau and Bijvoet) 98, 99
Maison Swisse, Paris (Le Corbusier) *104*, 105
Majorelle, Louis 50
'Make and Mend' exhibition *168*
Makepeace, John 268, *269*
Maldonado, Tomás 195, 196
Malevich, Kasimir 117, 118
Mallet-Stevens, Robert 97, 99, 122, 276
Maltings, Snape, Suffolk (Arup Associates) 226, *226*
management science 76–9
Manchester 79
Mangiarotti, Angelo 262
Manhattan see New York
Manutius, Aldus 73
Marconi Mark IV television camera 288, *289*
Marcoussis, Louis 112
Mare, André 109
Marie Claire 246
Marin County Center (Wright) 166–7, *166*
Marinetti, Filippo Tommaso 82, 84, 117
Marinot, Maurice 109
Marne-la-Vallée flats (Bofill) 228, *229*, *231*
Martel, Jan and Joël 122
Martens, Dino 178
Marx, Karl 13, 76–7, 155, 194, 291
Massachusetts Institute of Technology 164
Matet, Maurice 111
Mathsson, Bruno 121
Matsushita, Konosuke 194
Matsushita Electric Industrial Company 194, 283, 285
Matta, Sylvano 277
Matthew, Robert, Johnson-Marshall & Partners 226, *227*
Mattioli, Giancarlo 261
Maugham, Syrie 124
Maxim's, Paris 45
Maybach, Wilhelm *72*
Mayne, Richard 194
Mead, William Rutherford 10
Meier, Richard 236, *237*

Meier-Graefe, Julius 40, 44, 45, 56, 57
Mellon Center for British Art, New Haven (Kahn) 164
Mellor, David 205, 208, *208*, 276
Melnikov, Konstantin 88, 89
Melotti, Fausto 178
Memphis studio 213, 272, *275*, 282
Mendelsohn, Erich 86, *86*, 101, 102, *102*, 132
Mendini, Alessandro 272
Mendl, Lady (Elsie de Wolfe) 124
Mercedes-Benz 191
Mérode, Cléo de 48
Messerschmitt, Willy 142
Messerschmitt 109, *142*, 148
Metabolists 244
metal clothing 256, *256*
metalwork 30, 31, 39–40, 53, 68, *84*, 109, 114, 117, 120, *273*
Métiers d'Art exhibitions 268
Métro, Paris (Guimard) *30*, 31, 45
Metropolis (Lang) 118, *119*
Meunier, Henri 52
Mewès, Charles 27, 60
Mewès & Davis 27, 60, *60*
Meyer, Adolf 82, 91, 93
Meyer, Hannes 90, 92, 156, 195
Michelin Company 145
Michelucchi, 145
Mies van der Rohe, Ludwig 94–6, *94*, 81, *81*
  in America 153–6, *154*, *155*
  and Bauhaus 81, 92–3, 116, 120
  and classicism 37, 94
  and colleagues 36, *36*
  designs reissued 253, 276
  and Expressionism 86, 94
  influence 162, 164, 173, 214, *217*
  influences on 94
  and Modernism 81, 95, 94–6, 146
  and Novembergruppe 94–5, 138
  principles 160, 167, 216
Milan
  and architecture *162*, *163*, 216, 236, 240
  and decorative arts 50, 175, 251, 272, *275*
  and industrial design 188, 189, 196, 279
  Polytechnic 196 see also Triennali
Miller, Arthur 200
Miller, Herman 171, 172, *172*, 174, *174*, 199, 204
Milton, John *41*
Minale Tattersfield 205
mingei movement 265
Mini (Issigonis) 188, *188*

minimalism 139, *140*, 214, *217*, 253, 254, 279
Ministry of Education building, Rio de Janeiro (Niemeyer) 159
Mir Iskusstva 62
Mirella sewing machines (Nizzoli) 198
Miyake, Issey 265–7, *267*
Model T Ford 77–9, *78*, *79*
Modern Architecture Research Group 104
'Modern Creed of Work, A' 71
Modernism 6,
  in architecture 10–37, 81, 82–105, 151, 152–67, 213, 214–45
  in decorative arts 81, 106, 107, *113*, 116–22, 175, 251–4, *252*, 260, *272*, 273–6
  in industrial design 70, 145, 146, 192, 196, 208
  Organic 169, 172–4, 176, *187*, *187*
Modigliani, Amedeo *111*
Moholy-Nagy, Laszlo 91, 116, 120
Mollino, Carlo 177–8, *177*
Mondrian, Piet 87, 88, 117
Mono, Rune 209
Monroe, Marilyn 249
Montagnac, Pierre-Paul 111
Montesquiou, Count Robert de 48
Montpellier housing scheme (Bofill) 228
Montreal *166*, 224, *224*
Monza 146
Moore, Henry 169
Moreau, Charles 108
Morris, May 39
Morris, William 71
  and architecture 12–14, 15, 17, 28, 82, 89
  and decorative arts 38, *39*, 40, 52, 53, 58, 60, 180
  and industrial design 68, 70–1, 290
Morris & Co. *70*
Morris shop, San Francisco (Wright) 166, *166*
Moscow 88, 91, 99
Moser, Koloman 32, 53–4, *55*, *56*, 113, 114
Moss, Richard 196
motor car industry 244, 293–4
  in America 77–9, 128–30, *128*, *170*, 200, 225
  in France *189*
  in Germany 72, 142–5
  in Italy 199, 280–2
  in Japan *192*, 284
  in Sweden 209–10
motor-scooter, Vespa 176, *196*
Motorama 200
motorcycles *192*, *284*
Mr Freedom 251

Mucha, Alphonse 45, *45*, 47, *47*
Muller, Gerd Alfred *195*
Munari, Bruno 286
Munich 40, 56, 57, 191, 234, *234*
mural, Plas Newydd (Whistler) *126*
Murano 178, *178*
Murray, Keith *146*
Musée des Arts Décoratifs, Paris 63, 268
Museum of Modern Art (MoMA), New York 133, *151*, 153, 154, 168, 173, *173*, 191, 192, 199, 201, 228, 265
Music Room for the House of an Art Lover (Mackintosh) *41*
Mussolini, Benito *105*, 145–6
Muthesius, Hermann 14–15, 74
Myklos, Gustav 106, 112, 122
Myrbach, Felician Freiherr von 53

NASA 134
N–1M aircraft (Northrop) 134
NSU 144
Nader, Ralph 200
Nagoya 194
Nancy 43, *43*, 48
Nast, Condé 175
Nathan, Fernand 111
National Board of Industry, Sweden 288, 290
National Design Organization, Norway 210–11
National Pensions Institute, Helsinki (Aalto) 164
National Recovery Act 128
'National' shops 285
National Theatre, London (Lasdun) *221*, 222
Navone, Paola 286
Nazis 92, 93, 94, 105, 141, 142, 156, 195
Necchi 199, 282, *283*
Nelson, George 129, 172, 201, 205
neo-classical style 27, *60*, 89, 108
Neo-Romantics 6, 124
Nervi, Pier Luigi 159, *159*, *163*
Netherlands 36, *36*, 62, 86–8, 91, 116–17
Neue Bauen 141
Neue Frankfurt, Das 141
Neue Gestaltung 141
Neue Sammlung Gallery, Munich 191
Neue Wohnen 141
Neue Zeit *140*
Neuilly *111*, 112
Neuman, Oscar 214
Neutra, Richard 99, 101
New Delhi (Lutyens) 26, 27, 105
New Haven 164, *165*
New Look 127, 182
New Orleans, square (Moore) 226

new technology 290–6
New Wave graphics 259, 273
New York
  and architecture 28, *28*, 156, 158, 159, *159*, 162, 166, *166*, 214, 216, *216*, 224, 226–8, *226*
  and decorative arts *115*, 116, *151*, 173, 270
  and industrial design 133
  University of 224
  World's Fair *127*, *127*
New York Central Railroad 133
New York Times 228
Newcastle 221, 223
News from Nowhere (Morris) 15
Newton, Helmut 270, *271*
Nicholson, William 39
Niemeyer, Oscar 105, 159
Nijinsky, Vaslav 62
Nikon cameras (ItalDesign) 282, *282*
'1919' chair (Rietveld) 116
Nissan Motor Company 284
Nizzoli, Marcello 189, 192, 196, *196*, *198*, 199, 280
Noguchi, Isamu 174, *174*, 265
Norman Foster Associates 254, *254* see also Foster, Norman
Normandie 111, 112
Northrop, John Knudsen 134
Northrop
  XB–35 aircraft 134, *137*
  YB–49 aircraft 134
Norwich 222, 240, *242*
Nothing Personal (Avedon and Baldwin) 253
Nova 270
Novembergruppe 94–5, 138
Norway 186, 187, 210–11
Noyes, Eliot, & Associates 199, *200*, 201
Nuove Tendenze 84–5
Nuremberg 194
Nyman, Gunnel 187

ONC (Olivetti Numerical Control Division) 280
Oak Park 82, 83
Obrist, Hermann 56
obsolescence, built-in (planned) 170, 200, *202*, 208, 246, 293
office, director's (Ponti) *175*
Ogle, David 208
Ohga, Norio 285
Ohnishi, Yosuke 267
Olbrich, Joseph 32–3, *32*, *33*, 57–8, *58*
Oldenburg, Claes 249, 251
Olivetti 196, 201, 262, 278
  Divisumma 24 calculator (Nizzoli) *196*, 198
  Lettera 22 typewriter (Nizzoli) 189, 192
  Lexicon 80 typewriter (Nizzoli) *196*, 199, 280
  MPI typewriter (Magnelli) 196

Programma 101 desk-top computer (Bellini) 280, *280*
Synthesis office chair (Sottsass) *280*
training centre, Haslemere (Stirling) 230, *230*
Valentine typewriter (Sottsass and King) 279
Olivetti, Adriano 196–9, 280
Olympic stadium, Munich (Otto) 234, *234*
Olympics, Tokyo 265
Olympics, Los Angeles, 1984 276
Omega Workshops 67, *67*
Op-Art fashions 256
Opera House, Paris (Garnier) 10
Orazzi, Manuel 48
Orchards, Chorleywood (Voysey) 14
Orfèvre et Verrier (Montesquiou) 49
'Organic Design in Home Furnishing' exhibition, MoMA 151, 173, *173*
Oriana 205
orientalism 113
Ornament and Crime (Loos) 34
Orrefors factory 122, 185, 187
Osaka 286
  World Fair 265
Osiris Visions Ltd 258
Ossipoff, Val 247
Otis lift 17
Otto, Frei 234
ottoman (Eames) *172*
Oud, Jacobus Johannes 87–8
Outline of European Architecture (Pevsner) 26
ovenware, Pyroceram 296
Oxford 215, *216*
Ozenfant, Amédée 97

PEL (Practical Equipment Ltd) 120, 148, *148*
Packard, Vance 200
Paimio sanatorium (Aalto) 121, 122
Palais Stoclet, Brussels (Hoffmann) 34, *34*, 54, *56*, *57*
Palazzo dello Sport, Rome (Nervi) *160*
Palladio 98, 239
Palmerston, Lord 13
Pampulha 159
Pan 56, 57
Pan Am tower, New York (Gropius) 159, *159*
Panasonic stereo radio *293*
panel, enamelled (Gambone) 176
Panton, Verner *256*
Paolozzi, Eduardo 248
paper bag (Hamnett) *276*
Paper Moon Graphics 267, 273
Paradise Lost (Milton) *41*
Paris
  and architecture 10, 21–4, 29,

34, 35, 96, 97, *98*, *104*, 105, 223, 230, 237, *238*, 240
and decorative arts 6, 43, 45, 50, 64, 81, 117, 118, 181–3, 248, 255, 276
Métro (Guimard) *30*, 31, 45
Park Avenue, New York 159, *159*
Park Güell, Barcelona (Gaudí) 29
Parker, Barry 16, *16*
Parker 25 pens 288
Parnham House 268–9
Parrish, Maxfield 59
Parti Ouvrier Belge 50–2
participation *219*, 220
Pasquier, Nathalie du 272
pasta, Voiello (ItalDesign) 280, *280*
Patout, Pierre 108, 112
Paulsson, Gregor 75, 116
Pavillon d'un Ambassadeur 107, 109, 111
Pavillon d'un Collectionneur (Ruhlmann) 108, *108*
Pavillon de l'Esprit Nouveau (Le Corbusier) 6, 106, 122
Pavoni, La 199, *199*
Paxton, Sir Joseph *18*, 19, *19*
Pazzi chapel, Florence (Brunelleschi) 228
Peche, Dagobert 54, 113–14
Pederson, Bent Gabriel 187
Pei, I. M. 224
Pelli, César 245, *245*
Penfield, Edward 59
Penn, Irving 174–5, *175*, 183, *183*, 270, *270*
Pennsylvania 164
Pentagram 286, *287*–8
Pentax calendar (Feurer) *271*
Pepsodent toothpaste 133
Perisphere *127*
Perret, Auguste 23–4, *23*, 96
Perriand, Charlotte 118, 122, *123*
Persson, Sigurd 210, 211
Pesce, Gaetano 263
Pessac 99
Pevsner, Antoine 89
Pevsner, Sir Nikolaus 6, *26*, 40, 68, 89
Philadelphia 217, 224, *272*
Museum of Art 168
Philips 286
Phillips, Peter 249
Photo-Realist school 249–51
photography *116*, 121, *124*, 174–5, *175*, 183, *183*, 265, 270–2, 270, *271*
Piaggio 196
Piano & Rogers 237, *238*, 239
Piel, Denis 270
Pileo lamp (Aulenti) *276*
Pillola lamp (Casati and Ponzio) *262*, 264
pilotis *98*, *99*, 160
Pininfarina 280, 282

Pioneers of Modern Design (Pevsner) 6, 26, 40, 68
Piranesi, Giovanni Battista *229*
Pirelli
poster (Fletcher, Forbes & Gill) *286*
tower, Milan (Ponti and Nervi) *162*, *163*
Piretti, Giancarlo 292
Piscator, Erwin *139*
pitcher (Gambone) *179*
plaque, bronze (Jallot) *106*
Plas Newydd *126*
plastics 134, 148, 151, 204, 250, 256, 279, *279*
Playboy 246–7, *246*, 248
Poe, Edgar Allan 128, 133
Poelzig, Hans 85, *85*, 137–8
Poiret, Paul 6, 64, *65*, 112–13, *183*
Poli, Flavio *178*
Poli, Paolo de *178*
Pollini 146
Pollock, Jackson 169, *171*
Ponteur *262*, 264
Ponti, Gio 146, 147, *162*, *163*, 175, *175*, 177, 196, *198*, 199, *199*
Ponzio, Emanuele *262*, 264
Pop Art and culture 181, *181*, 248–51, 255, 256, 264, *264*, 267, 273, 279
Porsche, Ferdinand 142–5, *145*
Porsche, Ferry 145
Porsgund porcelain factory 211
Port Murray interior (Womersley) *252*
Porte d'Honneur (Brandt) *106*
Portland 228
Portman, John 236, *236*
Portugal 21, *21*, 48
Post Office Savings Bank, Vienna 33, *33*, 60
Post-Impressionism 67
Post-Modernism 6, 11, 217, 225, 226, *226*, 254, 272–7, *272*
posters 9, *9*, *47*, 256, *258*, *286*
Postwar, Mayne 194
Potsdam 86
Powolny, Michael 114
Prague 35
Praktika dinner service (Kåge) *74*, *75*, 75
Pratt & Whitney Wasp Major engines 134
Pravda office, Leningrad (Vesnin) 90
Pre-Raphaelite Brotherhood 12
prefabrication *166*, 167, 230, 231, 232, *240*, 244, *244*
Presence of the Past, The (Krier) 234
Price, Cedric 237, *237*, *238*
Printz, Eugène 124
Problems of Design (Nelson) 201
Profeel component television system, Sony 286, *286*

Programma 101 desk-top computer, Olivetti (Bellini) 280, *280*
Prou, René 111
Proun projects (Lissitsky) 91
Prouvé, Jean 122
Pruitt-Igoe housing project, Saint Louis (Yamasaki) 226
Prutscher, Otto 114
Pryde, James 39
psychedelic style 256, *258*, 259
Pugin, A. W. N. 234, *235*
Puiforcat, Jean 110, 122
Pullman cars 130
Pulman Court, Streatham, London (Gibberd) 104
punk 259, *259*, *260*
purism
and Bauhaus 116, 185, 217
in Britain 146
in France 91
and Le Corbusier 97–8, *237*
in the Netherlands 91
in post-war design 168, 192, 223, 228, 251, *252*, 253–4
in Vienna 113
Purkersdorf sanatorium, Vienna (Hoffmann) 33
Pushpin Studios 251
Putman, Andrée 276
Pyro dinner service (Kåge) 75
Pyroceram ovenware, Corning 296

Quant, Mary 248
Quarti, Eugenio 50
Queen's College, Oxford 215, *216*
Queensberry, David 288

RCA television (Dreyfuss) 133
REM vacuum cleaner (Castiglioni) 189
Rabanne, Paco 256, *256*
Radical Design movement 6, 262–3, 272
radio(s)
Braun SK1 (Braun and Geichler) *195*
Ekco 147, *147*
Panasonic stereo 293
Sony TR-55 transistor 194, *194*
Sony ICF–111 *285*
Radio Show, Düsseldorf 196
railway system 21, 71, 133, *134*, 142, 145, 148, *149*
Rams, Dieter *195*, 196, 276
Rat für Formgebung 191
Rateau, Armand 113
Rathenau, Emil 72, 77, 196
Rathenau, Walter 77
Rationalism 146, 168, 276
rattan, lacquered 265, *267*
Rauch, John 216
Rauschenberg, Robert 249
Ray, Man *122*

razor, electric, Braun SM3 (Muller) *195*
Read, Herbert 205
Rebel without a Cause 247
Red House, Bexleyheath (Webb) 12, *13*, 14
Reformist tendency, Italy 261, 262–4
refrigerator (Loewy) *132*
Reich, Lilly 95, 118
Reichardt, Jasia 248
Reilly, Paul 288
Renault 4 *281*
Renault warehouse, Swindon *239*
Renouardt, Jane *110*
Reunion Hotel, Dallas (Becket) 236
Rhead, Louis 59
Rhodes, Zandra 239, *260*
Rhymney Engineering 288
Richards, Charles 115
Richards Medical Research building, University of Pennsylvania (Kahn) 164, *165*
Ricketts, Charles 40
Ricostruzione 6, 196
Rie, Lucie 180, 268
Riemerschmid, Richard 56
Riesener, Jean-Henri 108
Rietveld, Gerrit 87, 88, 116, *116*, 118
Rinascente, La, Milan 188, 189
Rio de Janeiro 159
Ritz Hotel, London (Mewès & Davis) 27, 60, *60*
Rivière, Théodore 48
Robert, Emile 109
Roberts, Tommy 251
Robes de Paul Poiret racontées par Paul Iribe, Les 64
robots 291
Robsjohn-Gibbings, J. H. 124
Roche, Kevin 224
Rock and Roll 247, 248
Rockefeller Center, New York 153
Rogers, Richard *239*, 240, *241*, *244*
Rolls-Royce Merlin engine 148
Romanesque style 36
Rome 24, 146, 160, 228
Ronan Point, London 214
Ronchamp 151, 160, *160*
Rondo-Cubists 105
Rosselli, Alberto 189
Rossi, Aldo 235–6
Roth, Emery 159
Rotterdam 87
Rousseau, Clément *111*, 112
Royal Academy of Arts, London 60
Royal Automobile Club, London (Mewès & Davis) 60
Royal College of Physicians, London (Lasdun) *221*, 222

Royal Institute of British Architects, London (Wornum) *103*, 104
Royal Society of Arts, London 205
Roycroft Press 60
Rozenburg factory 62, *62*
Ruand, Paul 113, *113*
Rubinstein, Helena 124, *125*
Rudolph, Paul 224
Rue Franklin, Paris (Perret) *23*, *23*, 24
rugs 121, 122
Ruhlmann, Jacques-Emile 6, 65, *66*, 107, *107*, 108–9, 112
Runcorn housing project (Stirling) 230–1, *232*
Rusakov workers' club, Moscow (Melnikov) *88*
Ruskin, John 13, 14, 24, 53, 58, 60, 82, 84, 89, 178, 180, 290
Ruskin pottery 39
Russell, Gordon 40, 178, 207
Russia 62, 87, 88–91, 99, 105, 117, *118*
rya (wall-hanging) 187

SAS 210, *210*, 211
SOM 156, 223–4, *223*
Saab 209–10, 288
    92 (Sason) 209, 210, *211*
Saarinen, Eero 116, *151*, 162, *162*, 163, 171, 172, *172*, 173, 176, 216, 224, *252*
Saarinen, Eliel 35–6, *35*, 116, *162*, 163, 171, 172
Saatchi & Saatchi 292
Sachsen-Weimar, Wilhelm, Grand Duke of 56
Safdie, Moshe 224, *224*
Sagrada Familia church, Barcelona (Gaudí) 29, *29*, 60
Sainsbury Centre, Norwich (Foster) 240, *242*
St James's Street, London 222
Saint Laurent, Yves 182
St Pancras station
    hotel (Scott) 20, *20*
    train-shed (Barlow & Ordish) 20, *20*
St Peter's, Rome 228
St Petersburg embassy (Behrens) 37
St Quentin-en-Yvelline *229*
Sakashita, Kyoshi 282
Salk Institute, La Jolla 164
Salon des Artists Décorateurs 65, 108
Salon des Refusés 32
'Salon de verre de Mme Suzanne Talbot, Le' (Ruand and Gray) 113, *113*
Salvation Army hostel (Le Corbusier) 105
Sambonet 278–9
Sambonet, Roberto 278
San Francisco 256

hotel (Portman) 236
Sanderson factory, London (Voysey) 14
Sanderson family *39*
Sandoz, Gérard 122
sanitary ware, Ideal Standard *198*, 199
Sant'Elia, Antonio 82, *83*, 84–5
Sapper, Richard 262, 276, 279
Sarfatti, Gino 177, 278
Sarpaneva, Timo 187, 210, 211
Sason, Sixten 209, *209*, 211
satellite, Echo 296
Sato, Pater 267, *267*, 277
Savoy Cocktail Book, The 114, 116
Säynätsalo town hall (Aalto) 164, *164*
scale, Toledo (Bel Geddes) *132*
Scandinavia 74, 116, 121–2, 162–4, 168, *168*, 183–7, 205, 208–11, *247*, 268, 288, 290
'Scandinavian Modern Design 1880–1980' exhibition, Cooper Hewitt Museum 183
Scandinavian Modern style 168, 181, 183–7
scanner, Toshiba 289
Scarpa, Carlo 178
Scarpa, Tobia 262
Scharoun, Hans 86, *86*
Scheeler, Charles *116*
Scheerbart, Paul 85
Schéhérazade 64, *65*, 118
Schellinck, J. 62, *62*
Schiaparelli, Elsa 125, *127*
Schick razors 133
Schinkel, Karl Friedrich 33, 94, 234
Schlemmer, Oskar 116
Schmied, François Louis 110
Scholl, Inge and Grete 195
School of Applied Art (Düsseldorf) 72
Schriver, Hermann 124
Schröder house, Utrecht (Rietveld) 87, 88
Schwintzler & Graff 141
Schwitters, Kurt 91, 92
Scotland 29, 31, *31*
Scotson-Clark, George Frederick 59
Scott, Douglas 286
Scott, Sir George Gilbert 13, 20, *20*
Scott, Mackay Hugh Baillie 39
Scott-Brown, Denise 216
screen, *Abacus* (Mills) 180, *180*
screen, lacquer
    (Dunand) *107*
    (Gray) 112
sculpture, neon ceiling (Fontana) *178*
Seagram Corporation 156
    tower, New York (Mies van der Rohe) 156, *157*, 224, 228

Sears, Richard 76
Sears Roebuck 76, 77, 128, *132*
Sears tower, Chicago (Graham) 224
Seattle World Fair 216, *216*
Second World War 6, 122, 146, 151, 168, 192, 196, 204, 288
Seguso, Archimede 178
Seidler, Harry 223
Seiko watches (ItalDesign) 280, *280*
'Selling Through Design' (Loewy) 205
'Sergeant Pepper's Lonely Hearts Club Band' (Beatles) 259
Sert, José Maria *44*
'served' and 'servant' space 164, *165*, 241, 244
Sèvres porcelain 45–7, 107, 110
sewing-machine(s)
    Japanese Sewing Machine Co. Ltd (Katsuyama and Hamada) 192
    Mirella (Nizzoli) 198, *198*
    Necchi (Giugiaro) 282, *283*
Sezession building, Vienna (Olbrich) 32, *32*, 33
Sezessionism 9, 32–4, 40, 52–8
    see also Art Nouveau
Sharp Corporation 194, 282, 283, 285
Shaw, Norman 15, *15*
Shire, Peter 272, *275*
Siemens 146
Siemens, Walter 72
Signe d'Or 191
silk, printed (Ruhlmann) *108*
Silver Studio 40
silverware 53, 110, 114, 180, *181*, 187, *187*
Sindbad armchair (Magistretti) 262
Siri glassware (Johansson) 211
Sirrah *261*
16 Points of a Plastic Architecture (van Doesburg) 87
Skellern, Victor *206*, 207
Skidmore, Owings & Merrill (SOM) 156, 223–4, *223*
Skylon 180
skyscrapers 25, 28, *28*, 86, 88, 90, 95, 116, 162, *163*, 224, *228*, *228*, 240, *243*
Slesin, Suzanne 254
Sloan, Alfred P. 76, 79, 130, 200
Smithson, Alison and Peter 167, 222, 248
Snail Room (Bugatti) 50, *52*
Snape Maltings, Suffolk 226, *226*
Société des Artistes Décorateurs 63, 111
Society of Industrial Artists 147, 206
Society of Industrial Designers 192

Sognot, Louis 111, 122
Soleri, Paolo 218, *218*
Sony Corporation 194, 283, 284–6
    compact disc player 286
    ICF–111 radio 285
    Profeel component television system 286, *286*
    SL–7300 Betamax video cassette recorder *285*
    TR–55 transistor radio 194, *194*
    tower, Osaka (Kurokawa) 244, *244*
    Walkman 265, *285* 286
Sorayama, Hajime 267
Sottsass, Ettore, Jr. 199, 263, 264, 272, *275*, 277, 279, 280, *280*
South America 159
South Bank 180
Southampton *286*
Soviet pavilion
    Paris exhibition *88*
    Berlin exhibition 91
Soviet Union *see* Russia
Sowden, George 272
Space-Age fashions 256
space frame 22
Space, Time and Architecture (Giedion) 26
Spain 29, 60, 94, 95, 120, 229, *229*
Spartacists, memorial to (Mies van der Rohe) 94, *94*
Speer, Albert 105, 152
Spitfire 148
    Supermarine VB *149*
stage design 62, 64
Stalin, Joseph 89
Stam, Mart 90, 91, 92, 118–20
State porcelain factory, Berlin 141
steel 23, 27, 82, 88
    tubular, furniture 118–20, *120*, 138, 146, 148, *148*
Stemp, Eric *182*
Stephenson, Robert 19
Stern, Bert 270
Stickley, Gustav 58, 59, *59*
Stile Industria 189
'stile Liberty' 40, 50 *see also* Art Nouveau
Stirling, James 88, 162, 215, *215*, 216, 228, 230–4, *230*, *232*, 235
Stock Exchange, Amsterdam (Berlage) 36, *36*
Stockholm 74
    City Library (Asplund) 26, 27
Stoclet family 32, 34
stone 228
Stone, Edward Durrell 153
stoves, cast-iron (Kramer) *141*
Strasburg 87, *88*
streamlining 134, *135*, *142*, 149, 175, 196, 209

Street, George Edmund 12, 13
Stromberg glass factory 187
Studebaker cars 133
Studio, The 59, 60, *123*
Studio 65, *264*
Studio Alchymia 272, 273, 282
Studio Yearbook, The 39
Studium-Louvre 111
Stuttgart 141, 144
　Staatsgalerie 231–2, *232*, 234
　Werkbund exhibition *86*, 95, *95*
Subes, Raymond 112
Süe, Louis 109, 124, *125*
Süe et Mare 109, *110*, 112, 124, *125*
suit
　(Dior) *182*
　with 'lip' pockets (Schiaparelli) *127*
Sullivan, Louis 10, 12, *24, 25*, 26, 29, 101
Sunar *272*
Sunday Times colour magazine 246
Superstudio 263
Supports: an alternative to mass housing (Habraken) 218
Suprematism 67, 117, *118*
Surrealism 6, 81, 124, *124, 125, 125, 127*, 168, 245, 256, *264*, 272
Sussex chairs (Morris & Co.) 70
Suzuki Diamond Free motorcycle *192*
Svenska Slöjdforningen 116, 211
Swannell, John *260*
Sweden 74, 116, 121–2, 168, *168*, 185–7, 209–11, 288, 290
Swedish Co-operative Union and Wholesale Society 211
Swindon 239
Swinging Sixties 248
Switzerland 167, 236, *236*
Sydney Opera House (Utzon) 162, 223, *223*
Sylphe, Edith la 48
Symbol place setting (Mellor) *208*
Symbolism *43*, 52
Synthesis office chair, Olivetti (Sottsass) *280*
Syracuse 59

TWA terminal, Kennedy Airport, New York (Saarinen) 162
table(s)
　(Kjaerholm) *253*
　(Knoll) *252*
　(Makepeace) *269*
　(Mollino) *177*
　(Noguchi) 174, *174*
tableware, plastic, BEA (Queensberry) *288*
Takasaki 245

Talachkino 62
Talbot, Suzanne 113, *113*
Tange, Kenzo 214, 244, *244*
Tanqueray, Paul *124*
tape-recorder, TTK 194
Tastemakers, The (Lynes) 192
Tatlin, Vladimir 88–9, *88*, 91
Taut, Bruno 82, *84*, 85
Taylor, Frederick Winslow 77, 78–9
Taylor, Richard 19
Taylorism 77, 78–9
Tchelitchev, Pavel 124
tea-rooms, Glasgow (Mackintosh) 31
tea-service (Dresser) 68
Teague, Walter Dorwin 129, 130–1, 192, *203*, 204
Team 4 *239*, 240
teapot
　Anchorage (Shire) *275*
　(Friedländer-Wildenhain) *138*
Technès 191
technology, new 290–6
Tecno 177, *177*, 261
Tecton group *100*, 102, 222
Teddy Boys 255
telephone (Dreyfuss) 132–3, *132*
television 293
　RCA (Dreyfuss) 133
　(Sapper and Zanuso) *279*
　Sony Profeel component system 286, *286*
　Sony TV -8-301 194
Templier, Raymond 122
Tenicheva, Princess Maria 62
Terragni, Giuseppe 105, *105*, 228
Terry, Quinlan 230
Texaco service station (Teague) 130, *130*
textiles *108*, 170, 268 *see also* fashion
Thatcher, Margaret 286
'Theatre Accident' (Penn) *175*
Third International monument (model by Tatlin) 88–9, *88*
Third Reich 141–5
'This is Tomorrow' exhibition 249
Thonet company 54, 138, *139*
'Throw-Away Aesthetic, A' (Banham) 170, 191
Tiffany, Louis Comfort 58, *59*, 60
Time 133
timber-frame system 225
Times, The 70, 205, 228
Tocqueville, Alexis de 128
Todt, Fritz 142
Toikka, Oiva 268
Tokyo 266, 285
　Olympics 265
Tokyo Tsushin Kogyo (TTK) 194
Toledo Museum of Art 268

Toledo Scale (Bel Geddes) *132*
Tolstoy, Leo 122
Tomorrow: A Peaceful Path to Reform (Howard) 15
Toorop, Jan 62
Torre Velasca (BBPR) 215
Toshiba 192, 283, *289*
Toulouse-Lautrec, Henri de 48
Toussaint, Fernand 52
Toyota SF *192*
Traction Avant 189
Trade, Board of 147, 178, 206, 207
Trade and Industry, Ministry of, Japan 192, 284, 286
traditionalism 26–8, 60, 102, 225
Trafford Park, Manchester 79
Train Bleu, Le 118, *119*
Trans-Atmospheric vehicles 296
Treetops lamp (Sottsass) *275*
Triennali, Milan 146, 147, *176*, 177–8, *185*, 186, 188, 196, *198*, 210, 278
Triumph Acclaim 284
trompe-l'œil 124, *125*, *126*
Trotsky, Leon 88–9
trouser suit, metal (Rabanne) *256*
Trucco, Matté 24, *24*
truck, fork-lift, Boss 288
Trylon *127*
Tugendhadt house, Brno (Mies van der Rohe) 95
Tsukasa, Tadashi 286
Turbeville, Deborah 270
Turin 175, 177, 196, 199, 280, 282
　International Exhibition 50, *52*
Turin, P. *106*
Twen 270
Two Paths, The (Ruskin) 290
2001 (Kubrick) 256
typewriters, Olivetti *see* Olivetti
'Typisierung' 74
typography 91, 120, 121, 253–4, *266*

UNESCO building, Paris (Breuer) 159
US Air Force 134, 296
US Defense Department 167
US Embassy, Tokyo (Pelli) 245
US Industrial Design 192
Ulm 195, 253, 280
Union des Artistes Modernes (U.A.M.) 122, 189, *189*
Unité d'Habitation, Marseilles (Le Corbusier) 160–2, *160*, 219
United States *see* America, United States of
Unity Temple, Oak Park (Wright) 82, *83*
Unsafe at Any Speed (Nader) 200
Unwin, Sir Raymond 16, *16*
Urban, Josef 114
Utility programme *146*, 168,

168, 179, 181, 206–7
Utrecht 87, *87*, 88
Utzon, Jørn 162, 223, *223*

Vackrare Vardagsvara (Paulsson) 75
vacuum cleaner
　(Castiglioni) 189
　Electrolux (Sason) *209*, 210, *290*
Vale Press 40
Valentine typewriter *see* Olivetti
Van Alen, William *152*
van de Velde, Henry 9, 34, 35, 42, 44–5, 52, 53, *53*, 56, 74, 82
van Doesburg, Theo 86–8, *88*, 91
van Doren, Harold 205
van't Hoff, Robert 87
vase, Wedgwood (Murray) *146*
Venice 178, *178*, 264
Venini, Carlo 178, *178*
Venturi, Robert 6, 216–18, *217*
Venturi & Rauch 216
Ver Sacrum 57
Vereinigung Bildender Künstler Österreichs 32
vernacular style 6, *11, 31*, 98, 101, 163, 181, 216, 218, 226
Vers une Architecture (Le Corbusier) 12, 97, 216
Versailles 229
Vertebra chair, Castelli (Ambasz and Piretti) 292, *292*
Vesnin, Alexander and Vladimir 90, *90*
Vespa motor-scooter 176, 196, *196*
Vever, Henri and Paul 47
viaduct, St Quentin-en-Yvelline (Bofill) 228, *229*
Vickers Ltd 69
Vickers Viscount (Edwards) 204, *204*
Victoria & Albert Museum 68, 259
Victory ware, Wedgwood (Skellern) *206*, 207
video cassette recorder SL-7300 Betamax (Sony) *285*
Vienna 9, 14, 32–3, 34, 35, *35*, 40, 43, 52–6, 56–8, 60, 63, 64, 67, 113–14
　School of Applied Arts 53
　Society of Visual Artists 32
Viennot, Jacques 191
Viganello House, Switzerland (Botta) *236*
Villa Hennebique, Sceaux *23*
Villa Savoye, Paris (Le Corbusier) 98, *99*
Villa Stein, Garches (Le Corbusier) *96*, 97
Ville Contemporaine (Le Corbusier) 97, *99*
Ville Radieuse (Le Corbusier) 160, 214, 225

Villeroy & Boch 141
Viollet-le-Duc, Eugène-
  Emmanuel 12, 17, 28, 52
Vionnet, Madeleine 113, *114*,
  127
Vitruvius 12
Vkhutemas school of design,
  Moscow 91
Vogel, Lucien 113
Vogue 113, 183, 246
  British *182*
  French *183*
Voiello 280, *280*
'Volksarchitektur' 144
'Volksauto' 144
Volkswagen 142–5, *145*, 191
  Golf (Giugiaro) 281, *281*, *283*
Volvo 288
  Amazon 210
Vorticism 67, 117
Voulkos, Peter 268
Voysey, Charles 10, 11, 14–15,
  31, 39, 40

Waals, Peter 39, *39*
Wagenfeld, Wilhelm 120, 141,
  141
Wagner, Otto 32–3, *33*, 60
Wakely & Wheeler *181*
Walden 7 apartment block,
  Barcelona (Bohll) 229, *229*
Wall Street Crash 122, 128, 141
Warff, Ann 268
Warhol, Andy *247*, *248*, 249, *251*
Warndorfer, Fritz 53
Warren, Michigan 162

Washington, DC 162, *162*
waste-bins (Kartell) *279*
Waste Makers, The (Packard) 200
watches, Seiko (ItalDesign) 280,
  280
Waterloo Station, London 180
Watson, Thomas 199
'Way-In', Harrods, London
  (Jiricna) 255
Weallans, Jon 251
Webb, Philip 12, *13*, 13, 14, 16
Weber, Bruce 272
Wedding Tower, Darmstadt
  (Olbrich) 33
Wedgwood *146*, *206*, *207*
Wegner, Hans 186, *186*
Weimar
  and Bauhaus 138
  memorial to war victims
    (Gropius) 91, *92*
  Republic 139
  school 56–7, 67, 91, 92 *see also*
    Bauhaus
Weiss, Reinhold *195*
Welch, Robert 205, 208
Welwyn Garden City 15, *17*
Wennerberg, Gunnar 74, 75
Werkbund Exhibition Theatre,
  Cologne (van de Velde) 35
Wesselman, Tom 249
Weymouth, Nigel 259
Whistler, Rex 124, *126*
White, Stanford 10
Whitechapel Art Gallery 249
Whittle, Frank 204
Who, The *258*

Wiener Werkstätte 32, 34, 53–6,
  56, 57, 63, 64
Wild Ones, The 248, *248*
Wilhelm, Grand Duke of
  Sachsen-Weimar 56
Wilkins, George Herbert 134
Wilkinson Sword razors 288
Willis Faber Dumas building,
  Ipswich (Foster) 240, *243*
Wilsgaard, Jan 210
Wilson, Wes 256
Wimmer, E. J. 114
Wines, James 245
Winslow house, Illinois (Wright)
  10, *10*
Wirkkala, Tapio 186, *186*, 187,
  211
Wirtschaftswunder 195
Wolfe, Tom 174
Wolfers, Philippe 52
Wolff Olins 206, 287
women 69, 117
Womersley, Peter 252
wood 120, 121, 122, 138, 151
wood carving, Art Deco 63
'Wood or Metal?' (Perriand) *123*
Woodfull, A. H. 204
Woolworth building, New York
  (Gilbert) 28, *28*
World Fair
  Osaka 265
  Seattle 216, *216*
World Trade Center, New York
  (Yamasaki) 88, 216, *217*
World's Fair, New York 127,
  127

Wornum, Grey *103*, 104
Worshipful Company of
  Goldsmiths 180
Worth, Charles Frederick 112
Wren, Sir Christopher 43
Wright, Frank Lloyd 10, *10*, 25,
  58, 60, *60*, *83*, 152, *152*, 164–
  7, *166*
  early work 36
  influence 36, 82, 87, 94, 164–
  7, 218, *218*
  and Modernism 101
Wright, Russel 192
Wright, Wilbur and Orville 71
wrist watch 68
Württembergische Metallfabrik
  141
Wyld, Evelyn 118

Yale University
  architecture faculty (Rudolph)
  224
  Art Gallery (Kahn) 164, 165
Yamaguchi, Harumi 267
Yamaha 284
Yamasaki, Minoru 216, *217*, 226
Yellow Submarine 259, *259*
Yokohama 194
young market 247–8

Zanuso, Marco 177, 199, 279,
  279
Zavanella, Renzo 178, *178*
Zeitgeist 97, 159
Zeppelin airship *142*
Zernell, Rune 209

ACKNOWLEDGMENTS

Akademie der Künste, Berlin: 84 above and below

Alchymia: 273

Emilio Ambasz: 292

Wayne Andrews: 10, 83 below, 153 above left & above right, 154, 155

Aram Designs Ltd: 265

Arcaid: title page, 30, 54 left & above right, 100, 101, 152, 161 below 165 below, 215 above & below, 216 above, 217 above, 220, 221 below, 222 below, 227, 230, 232 above & below, 233

Architectural Association: 17 (photo: F.R. Yerbury), 26 Yerbury, 28 left (photo: F.R. Yerbury), 28 right, 35 left (photo: F.R. Yerbury), 36 (photo: F.R. Yerbury), 87 below, 89 below (photo: F.R. Yerbury), 96 (photo: F.R. Yerbury), 98 above & below, 165 below, 166 below, 167 above, 217 above, 224, 236 above

Archivio: 263 (photo: Rodolfo Facchini)

Arcosanti: 218

Art Institute of Chicago: 127 above left

Artek: 164, 185

Arup: 226 right (photo: John Donat)

A T & T: 226 left

Audi Volkswagen: 144 above

Audience Planners: 27 below (photo: A.F. Kersting)

Austin Rover: 188

The Australian Information Service, London: 223 above

Roy Bacon: 193 above, 284

Bauhaus-Archiv: 80, 82 below, 83 above, 92, 93 below, 94 above & below, 95 below, 138 above left, above right & below, 139 below

BBC Hulton: 69 above & below, 127 below, 168

Beech: 296

Tim Benton: 29 left & right, 33 below right, 35 right, 37 below, 97 below

Bildarchiv Foto Marburg: 34, 53, 85 above & below

Hedrich Blessing: 223 below

Boilerhouse: 8, 74 left & right, 75 above & below, 131, 132 above, 209 above & below, 285 top right & below

Brionvega: 279 above

Canon: 218

Cassina: 261 right, 262 below

Martin Charles: 255

Chevrolet: 202 below

Christies, London: 110 below right

Christian Dior: 182

Citroën: 78 below, 189 below

Condé Nast Publications Limited, London: 183 right

Condé Nast, New York: 175 above, 183 left

Conway Library: 105

Daimler-Benz: 72

The Design Council: 71 below, 73 above & below, 130 below, 132 below, 133 above & below, 139 above, 147, 175 below, 176 below, 178 above, 190/191 (photo: Carl Ulrich Inc.), 192, 195, 197 above left & above right, 198 below left, 199, 200, 202 above, 203 above & below, 204, 206 below, 208, 280 above, 287 above, 288 below, 289 above

Charles Eames: 167 below, 201 above & below

Editions du Regard: 98

Electrolux: 290 left & right

E.T. Archive: 15, 18 above & below, 79, 82 above, 88 above, 135, 142 below

Fiat (UK): 281 top, 291

Fitch & Co.: 287 below

Fogg Art Museum: 14

Ford Motor Company Ltd: 78 above, 79, 293 below

Foster Associates: 242 above (photo: Morley von Sternberg) & below, 243 above (photo: Ken Kirkwood), 254 (photo: Ken Kirkwood)

Philippe Garner: 174 below, 266

Michael Graves, Architect: 228, 272 (photos: Paschall/Taylor)

The Grayling Company: 194, 285 top left, 286

Gustavsberg: 76

John Havinden: 121 left

Lucien Hervé: 97 above, 160, 161 above

Angelo Hornak: 25 below, 30 below left & right, 33 below left, 54 below right, 87 above, 88 below, 115, 153 below, 157, 158, 162 above & below, 163, 166 above, 238 above right

Hunterian Art Gallery, University of Glasgow: 41 above right

Ideal Standard: 189 below right (photo: Herbert Ballard)

Ideas for Living: 279 bottom right

Arata Isozaki: 243 below (photo: Yasuhiro Ishimoto), 245 above

ItalDesign: 282, 283 top, bottom left & bottom right

Kenwood: 283 above

A.F. Kersting: 11, 13, 16, 19, 27 above, 31, 32, 102

Knoll International: 219, 252 above

Leon Krier: 235

Lucien Kroll: 219

Kunstehalle Tübingen, Sammlung, Professor Dr. Georg Zundel: 181 below right

Kisho Kurakawa: 244 above

Denys Lasdun Redhouse & Softley: 221 above

Gerard Leyrus: 25 above

Lockheed Corporation: 137, 295

John Makepeace: 269 below (photo: Sam Sawdon)

Edward D. Mills: 180 below

Museum of Modern Art, New York: 150, 173

National Museum of Photography, Film and Television: 130 above

National Railway Museum: 149 below

National Trust: 126

Northrop Corporation: 136

Novosti Press Agency: 89 above, 90 left & right

Officiel de la Couture: 127 above right

Olivetti: 198 above

Pan Am: 159

Panasonic: 293 above

César Pelli: 245 below

Playboy, France: 246

John Portman: 236 below

Pressens Bild, Sweden: 169 below (photo: Tore Falk)

Cedric Price: 237 below, 238 above left

Private Collection: 40, 41 below, 44 above & below, 45 left & right, 46, 47 left & right, 48 above & below, 50, 52, 56 left & right, 57 above, 58 below left & below right, 63, 65, 106 above & below, 107 above & below, 108 above & below, 109 above, 110 left below, 111 above & below, 112, 113, 114 below, 118 above left, above right & below, 120, 121 left above, 122 above, 123 above & below, 124, 125, 170 above & below, 171 below, 172 above & below, 176 above, 177 below, 179 left & right, 180 above, 181 above & below left, 187, 247 left & right, 248, 249 left & right (courtesy: Allen Jones), 250 (courtesy: Fiorucci), 251, 253, 256 (courtesy: Paco Rabanne), 257, 258, 259, 261 below, 262 above, 264 above & below, 267 above (courtesy: Issey Miyake) & below, 269 above, 270 (courtesy: Clinique), 271 (courtesy: Pentax), 275, 276 left & right, 277 (courtesy: Lux Sport)

Private Collection, New York: 60

Quadrant Picture Library: 142 above, 149 above, 204, 294

Etienne Revault: 23 left, 23 right

RIBA: 103

Peter Roberts: 78 above, 128, 129, 144 below, 145 below, 281 below

Richard Rogers: 238 (photo: Martin Charles), 239 (photo: Morley von Sternberg), 241

Royal Commission on Historical Monuments (England): 20 above, 20 below

Saab: 211

Santi Caleca: 274

SAS: 210 below

Sotheby's, London: 38, 39 above left, above right, below, 41 above, 42, 43, 49, 51, 55, 57 below, 58 above, 59 above & below, 62, 64, 66, 109 below, 114 above left & above right, 117 above & below, 121 right, 122 below, 171 above, 174 above, 177 above, 178 below, 183 right, 184 (Cecil Beaton Archive), 186 left & right, 253, 268

Ettore Sottsass: 279 bottom left, 280 right

Ezra Stoller (© Esto): 237

Deyan Sudjic: 24 above & below

John Swannell: 260 (courtesy: Zandra Rhodes)

Taller de Arquitectura de Barcelona, S.A.: 229 above, centre & below, 231

Kenzo Tange Associates: 244 below (photo: Osamu Murai)

Times Newspapers Ltd: 119 above

Topham Picture Library: 104

Toshiba: 289 below

Toyota: 193 below

Ullstein Bilderdienst: 37 above, 86 above & below, 93 above, 95 above, 234

Victoria and Albert Museum: 67

Virginia Museum of Fine Arts, Richmond, VA., Sydney and Frances Lewis Collection: 110 above

Morley von Sternberg: 222 above

Wedgwood: 206 above

Whitney Museum: 251 below

William Morris Gallery: 70, 71 above

George Wimpey PLC: 240

Yale University Art Gallery: 165 above

Minoru Yamasaki & Associates: 216 below, 217 below (photo: Hedrich Blessing)

ZEFA: 21, 22